None Bolder

*The History of the 51st Highland Division
in the Second World War*

By the same author

Wall of Steel: The History of 9th (Londonderry) HAA Regiment, RA (SR)
North-West Books, Limavady, 1988
The Sons of Ulster: Ulstermen at war from the Somme to Korea
The Appletree Press, Belfast, 1992
Clear the Way! A History of the 38th (Irish) Brigade, 1941–47
Irish Academic Press, Dublin, 1993
Irish Generals: Irish Generals in the British Army in the Second World War
The Appletree Press, Belfast, 1993
Only the Enemy in Front: The Recce Corps at War, 1940–46
Spellmount Publishers, Staplehurst, 1994
Key to Victory: The Maiden City in the Second World War
Greystone Books, Antrim, 1995
The Williamite War in Ireland, 1688–1691
Four Courts Press, Dublin, 1998
A Noble Crusade: The History of Eighth Army, 1941–1945
Spellmount Publishers, Staplehurst, 1999
Irish Men and Women in the Second World War
Four Courts Press, Dublin, 1999
Irish Winners of the Victoria Cross (with David Truesdale)
Four Courts Press, Dublin, 2000
Irish Volunteers in the Second World War
Four Courts Press, Dublin, 2001
The Sound of History: El Alamein 1942
Spellmount Publishers, Staplehurst, 2002
The North Irish Horse: A Hundred Years of Service
Spellmount Publishers, Staplehurst, 2002
Normandy 1944: The Road to Victory
Spellmount Publishers, Staplehurst, 2004
Ireland's Generals in the Second World War
Four Courts Press, Dublin, 2004
The Thin Green Line: A History of The Royal Ulster Constabulary GC, 1922–2001
Pen & Sword Books, Barnsley, 2004

NONE BOLDER

THE HISTORY OF THE 51ST HIGHLAND DIVISION IN THE SECOND WORLD WAR

by

Richard Doherty

British Library Cataloguing in Publication Data:
A catalogue record for this book is available
from the British Library

Copyright © Richard Doherty 2006
Maps copyright © Spellmount Ltd 2006

ISBN 1-86227-317-0

First published in the UK in 2006 by
Spellmount Limited
The Mill, Brimscombe Port
Stroud, Gloucestershire GL5 2QG

Tel: 01453 883300
Fax: 01453 883233
Website: www.spellmount.com

1 3 5 7 9 8 6 4 2

Printed in Great Britain by
Oaklands Book Services
Stonehouse, Gloucestershire GL10 3RQ

Contents

There was a soldier, a Scottish soldier
Who wandered far away and soldiered far away
There was none bolder, with good broad shoulder
He fought in many a fray, he fought and won

To the memory of all who served in the 51st Highland Division in the Second World War, especially to those who gave their lives that others might live in peace.

Cuimhnich gaisg agus treuntas ar sinnsear
[remember our forefathers' valour and brave deeds]

List of Maps

Introduction

The history of the British Army is a history of its regiments, each of which has developed and sustained its unique ethos over as many as three centuries in spite of the efforts of bureaucrats and government to create a bland uniformity throughout the Army. There have been times, however, when the regimental ethos has been valued and nowhere was that more obvious than in the raising of Highland regiments from the clans and people who had opposed English rule in Scotland.

The Highland regiments have valued their customs, traditions and identities and these have sustained their soldiers in time of trial. But those regiments were also willing to accept a further identity – as elements of a Highland Division in the two world wars of the 20th century. In the British Army the division has a history as a fighting formation of just under two centuries, being created by Wellington in the course of the Peninsular War. Several divisions were created during that war and their heritage has been cherished by their successors to the present day.

With the birth of the Territorial Force in 1908 new TF divisions were created, including a Highland Division. However, this new formation could claim a heritage that went back to the Highland Brigade of the Crimean War, which eventually became the first Highland Division. During the Great War the Territorial Force's Highland Division was renumbered as 51st (Highland) Division and created a reputation second to none in the Allied armies. At the same time it became so totally identified with Scotland that it became a symbol of nationhood, a Scottish army that inherited all the history of the centuries since proud Edward's army was sent homeward 'to think again'. It was understandable that soldiers of the Black Watch, the Seaforth, Gordon, Cameron and Argyll and Sutherland Highlanders should also identify with the Highland Division and their pride in belonging to that Division was passed on to a new generation of soldiers in the Second World War.

The Second World War story of the Highland Division is one that begins with great sadness with the loss of much of 51st (Highland) Division at St Valéry in June 1940. To Scotland this was almost a mortal blow, a loss that was felt in every home in the Highlands and Islands and even farther south. Fortunately, part of the Division had been saved and there was a second-line Territorial Army division, 9th (Highland), created in 1939 as a duplicate of 51st, which was soon transformed into a new 51st (Highland) Division. Those who had been evacuated safely from France were included in its ranks as well as many who managed to escape from captivity, among whom was a future divisional commander, Tom Rennie, who would lose his life at the Rhine crossing in March 1945.

The reborn Highland Division went back to war in 1942 under Major-General Douglas Wimberley, surely one of the finest divisional commanders of the war, and fought from El Alamein through North Africa and Sicily and then from the fields of Normandy to the heart of Germany. Wherever it went no one was in any doubt that the Highland Division was present. The letters HD were often to be seen painted on walls or signs and the soubriquet 'Highway Decorators' was oft to be heard. But the true value of the Highland soldier was proved in battle and the reputation gained by their fathers in 1914–18 was maintained and increased by the men of the Second World War.

Not every soldier of the Division was a Highlander, or even a Scot. Their ranks included many Sassenachs, who were proud to serve alongside their Scottish cousins, and many fellow Celts from both Ireland and Wales. The Irish, especially, had no difficulty in identifying with Highland traditions and served as happily in the Division, and in the Highland regiments, as they would have done in an Irish formation.

For a short spell in early 1943 my father's regiment served with 51st (Highland) Division and that time left a lasting impression on this Irish Gunner unit. In later years I heard many of my father's old comrades talk with affection and respect of the Highlanders and of the many fellow Irishmen they met in the ranks of the Gordons and Seaforth especially. And the most outstanding Gunner officer of the Division, and its Commander Royal Artillery in Northwest Europe, was the redoubtable Jerry Shiel, an Irishman.

The Division's fame, its Celtic ethos and the Irish connections are among my reasons for writing this history of the Highland Division. But above all, I have done so because of the superb quality of the Division. There truly was none bolder and it has been a humbling experience to learn of just how proud Scotland is of its Highland Division and its soldiers. When I began my research for this book the threat to the identity of the Scottish regiments had not yet surfaced. Now that it has, and all that proud history may be subsumed in a single large regiment, it may also be appropriate to note that we will ne'er see your likes again.

Richard Doherty
Co. Londonderry
September 2005

Acknowledgements

It is only when he completes the task of researching and writing a book that the author can stand back a little and see how many people and organisations have helped in the process. So it is with this history of the most famous British infantry division of the Second World War. Having completed the task of writing the book I am now able to appreciate the amount of assistance I received along the way and to thank all those who helped me.

First of all I must acknowledge my debt to the National Archives, at Kew, Richmond, Surrey where, as always, the staff of the reading and search rooms have been exceptional in their endeavours. At the Imperial War Museum, the Department of Documents allowed access to the Memoirs of Major-General Douglas Wimberley, GOC of 51st (Highland) Division in the North African and Sicilian campaigns and I am grateful to Mr Rod Suddaby, Keeper of Documents at the IWM, for his assistance. Many of the images used in this book are from the Photographic Archive of the IWM and my thanks are also due to the staff at the Archive for their enthusiastic support and unfailing help.

The National Archives of Scotland also provided information for which I am most grateful as did the museums of the Highland regiments: The Black Watch; The Queen's Own Highlanders (Seaforth and Cameron); The Gordon Highlanders and The Argyll and Sutherland Highlanders. Each museum helped with bringing my research to the attention of their old comrades through newsletters and other media. I also appreciate very much the assistance of the museums in obtaining some of the photographs which appear in this book and I would like to thank their curators.

Major Donald Urquhart TD, second-in-command of The Highland Transport Regiment, Royal Logistic Corps, provided me with a history of his Regiment, which dates its antecedents back to the Supply and Transport Columns of the Highland Division of the Great War and which now bears the proud heritage of all those who served in the logistic support role in the Second World War. This helped to throw light on the support services who are often forgotten in accounts of the service of divisions, whether infantry or armoured.

Assistance in contacting wartime members of the Highland Division was also provided by a number of service magazines and I wish to record my gratitude to the editors of *Soldier*, *The Gunner*, the magazine of the Royal Artillery, *The Sapper*, the magazine of the Royal Engineers and *The Wire*, the magazine of the Royal Corps of Signals. Several Scottish national, regional and local newspapers also carried my request for information and these contacts proved most valuable. My thanks to all the papers that helped.

The Linenhall Library, Belfast was an invaluable ally in obtaining several long out-of-print works needed for my research and I am most grateful to the staff of the library. Likewise the Central Library, Foyle Street, Londonderry also assisted with inter-library loans of some books that, otherwise, were proving difficult to obtain.

A host of individuals came to my assistance as I researched the history of the Highland Division. My thanks are due to: Mrs V Billson, Dagenham, Essex; Nancy Binnie, Alnwick, Northumberland; Mr George Black, Sunderland; Mr John Borland, Glasgow; Mr Al Capleton, West Kirby, Wirral; Mrs Nancy Carroll, Bellshill, Lanarkshire; Mrs P M Cartes, Perth; Mr A Cochrane, Livingston, West Lothian; Mr John Conlon, Newcastle-upon-Tyne; Miss I Davidson, Pencaitland, East Lothian; Mr John C Dingwall, Aberdeen; Mr Malcolm Dobbing, Blyth, Northumberland; Mrs Elizabeth Docherty, Kirkintilloch; Mr William Duncan, Dundee; Mrs Betty France, Huddersfield; Mrs Sandra Gordon, Westfield, Thurso; Mrs Frances Gouldie, Kirkcaldy, Fife; Mr W H Grant, Edinburgh; Mr A W Hamilton; Mrs Cynthia Jardine, Nairn; Mrs Lorna E Johnston, South Shields; Mr E Kelly, Dover; Col. Oliver Lindsay CBE, FRHistS; Mrs A Lunny, Glenrothes, Fife; Mr Bob Lyall, Markinch, Fife; Mr Tony McAteer, Glasgow; Margaret McAteer, Denny, Stirlingshire; Mr John Macleod, Westhill, Inverness; Mr Archie McDonald, Ahoghill, Co. Antrim; Mrs Patricia McDonald, Erskine, Renfrewshire; Mr Peter McDonald, Broadstairs; Mr John Mackenzie, Midlothian; Mr Duncan M MacLennon, Auchtermuchty, Fife; Mr R T McLean, Glasgow; Mrs Anne Makin, Warrington; May C Malcolm, Glasgow; Mrs M Meek, Falkirk; Mrs Molly Mical, Edinburgh; Mr Bert Mitchell, Dingwall; Mr J W Mitchinson, Morpeth, Northumberland; Mr Alistair Muir, Cullen, Banffshire; Major J K Nairne, Winchester; Mr Alex S Napier, Kirkcaldy; Mr Peter Neville, Coatbridge, Lanarkshire; Mrs M Nic, Tain, Ross-shire; Mrs Joyce Nicholson, Carlisle; Mrs G Noble, Grantown-on-Spey; Mrs Helen J Philip, Aberdeen; Mr Malcolm A Potter, Dane End, Herts; Mr E P Puttick BA, Worthing; Mr D K Ritchie, Jnr, Glenrothes; Mr Douglas Robertson, Aberdeen; Jacqui Robson, Fortrose, Ross-shire; Mr Jim Russell, Glasgow; Dr Rhea Sheddon, Leven, Fife; Mr William Smith, Arbroath; Mr J Snaith, Middlesbrough, Mr William Stevenson, Stirling; Mr Darry Struthers, Lanark; Mrs Carole Taylor, Derbyshire; Mr Neil Turner, Alexandria, West Dunbartonshire; Major Neil Wimberley, Coupar; Mr F W

Whyte, Romford, Essex. Many of my correspondents were not themselves veterans of 51st (Highland) Division but were the widows or children of men who had served in the Division. Their pride was clear from their letters and I am most grateful to all of them for their help.

Quotations from documents in the National Archives appear by kind permission of the National Archives, Kew and those from documents in the Imperial War Museum by kind permission of the Trustees of the Museum and of Major Neil Wimberley. It has not proved possible to contact the family of Lieutenant George F Morrison, Black Watch, who was killed at El Alamein. Crown copyright material appears with the permission of the Comptroller of Her Majesty's Stationery Office. The photographs in the book are from a variety of sources and copyright ownership is indicated in the captions. I am grateful to the copyright owners for their permission to use these pictures.

As ever it has been a pleasure to work with Jamie Wilson and the team at Spellmount as this book has progressed from concept to reality. Their professionalism is of the highest order and provides an assurance that the finished work will be a quality production.

Finally, I must thank my wife, Carol, my children Joanne, James and Catríona and my grandson Ciarán for their patience and support.

Richard Doherty
Co. Londonderry
October 2005

CHAPTER I

The Highland Tradition

The Highland soldier has long been identified so closely with Britain's Army that it is difficult to conceive of that Army without its kilted Highlanders, who have become almost as much a trademark as the Guards regiments. However, the early relationship between Highlander and red-coated soldier was one of enmity as the Scots resisted the spread of English power and influence into the Highlands and supported the claims of the Stuart dynasty to the thrones of England, Scotland and Ireland. In time, however, these enemies became friends with the service of Scottish soldiers from the Highlands an accepted part of British military life.

The first Highland soldiers to serve the Crown did so as a form of police force. These were the men of the independent companies that patrolled, or watched, the Perthshire hills from 1725. From their dark attire they were known as the Black Watch and were absorbed into the Army in 1739 as the Highland Regiment of Foot, becoming the 42nd Foot in 1751, the 'gallant forty-twa', when numerical designations were assigned.[1] It was not long – 1758 – before the regiment's title changed to the 42nd (The Royal Highland) Foot but it took another 103 years to have the title Black Watch included officially and then only as a subtitle. In 1881, with the Childers Reforms, the regiment became The Black Watch (Royal Highlanders) which was modified to The Black Watch (Royal Highland Regiment) in 1934. The Childers Reforms also brought about an amalgamation with the 73rd (Perthshire) Foot, which had begun its existence in 1758 as the 2nd Battalion, 42nd (The Royal Highland) Foot. Thus the Black Watch is the senior Highland regiment of the Army.[2] (The Highland Light Infantry (HLI), although bearing a Highland title, was a Glasgow regiment. In 1959 it was transferred from the Highland Brigade to the Lowland Brigade and amalgamated with a Lowland regiment, The Royal Scots Fusiliers, to form a new Lowland regiment, The Royal Highland Fusiliers (Princess Margaret's Own Glasgow and Ayrshire Regiment).)

Further Highland regiments followed the 42nd, although some, such as the Atholl Highlanders, Fraser's Highlanders and the Queen's Own Royal Regiment of Highlanders – were short-lived.[3] Others survived and, after

Childers, left the Highlands with five regiments: The Black Watch, Seaforth Highlanders, Gordon Highlanders, Queen's Own Cameron Highlanders and Argyll and Sutherland Highlanders. And the most junior of these – the Argylls – had created one of the Army's legends at Balaclava when the 93rd Highlanders stood in line to hold off a Russian cavalry charge. This feat was reported by *The Times* whose correspondent, W H Russell, described the battalion's stand as a 'thin red streak tipped with a line of steel'. This soon became 'the thin red line' of popular legend.

The 93rd's stand at Balaclava occurred during the Crimean War, a conflict that also witnessed the formation of the first Highland Division under Sir Colin Campbell, who did much to further the reputation of the Scottish soldier but, especially, the Highlander. Campbell's division was built on the foundation of a Highland Brigade that included 42nd Black Watch, 79th Camerons and 93rd Highlanders.[4] In the forty years that followed the Crimean War a Highland brigade or division was re-formed and disbanded on a number of occasions. With the South African, or Boer, War another Highland Brigade took the field.[5] (Appendix I shows the antecedents of the five Highland regiments that would form 51st (Highland) Division.)

By the end of the 19th century the reputation of Highland regiments was such that they were regarded as the Army's élite. They had served in almost every campaign and war fought by Britain during that century and earned many decorations for gallantry, including the Victoria Cross, instituted in 1856. It should be noted, however, that not all who served in Highland regiments were Scots; the ranks included Sassenachs from south of the border and even more of their fellow Gaels, Irishmen from across the Irish Sea whose numbers made up the single largest proportion of the Army throughout much of the century.[6] Some regiments even lost their Highland identity through a lack of Highlanders in their ranks.[7] But the achievements of those regiments that became the five Highland units made an indelible stamp on the British psyche. Their fighting prowess and colourful uniforms – especially their kilts, which were really an 18th-century English invention – combined to make the image of the Highland soldier synonymous with the Army.

In addition to 'the thin red line' already mentioned, Highlanders had been present at the relief of Lucknow during the Indian Mutiny, where the pipes of the 78th Highlanders were said to have played 'the sweetest of all music',[8] and in many of the small wars that kept the Army almost constantly engaged during the century. An indication of the level of that engagement in small wars is shown by the record of the 92nd (Gordon) Highlanders who were on active service in Afghanistan in 1880 before moving to southern Africa and active service in Natal in 1881 followed by a move to Egypt in northern Africa and yet more active service the next year.[9] Such was the lot of the 19th-century soldier, not least the Highlander. Such was the mettle of the forebears of 51st (Highland) Division.

A reform of the reserve forces in 1908 – the Haldane Reforms – brought about the birth of the Territorial Force, within which were fourteen infantry divisions, each composed of battalions of part-time soldiers, often known as 'Saturday night soldiers'.[10] One of these was 1st (Highland) Territorial Division. Recruited from the Highlands and Islands north of the Clyde and Forth valleys, the Division included twelve battalions of the five Highland regiments formed in three brigades, initially known as 1, 2 and 3 Highland Brigades.[11] In 1914 the Division mobilised for war and concentrated at Bedford for training before moving to France in late-April/early-May 1915. Some of its original units, sent to France between November 1914 and March 1915 to reinforce other formations and battalions from west Lancashire, were now included. These were 1/4th Royal Lancaster Regiment, 1/4th Loyal North Lancaster Regiment, 1/8th Liverpool (Irish) Regiment and 2/5th Lancashire Fusiliers; 6th Scottish Rifles, a Lowland unit, relieved the Lancashire Fusiliers at the end of May.[12]

At this time the Highlanders' numerical designation was changed to 51st Highland Division, a decision that caused some upset.[13] (Brigades were also re-designated as 152, 153 and 154.) Nor were the soldiers entirely happy to learn that they were known as 'Harper's Duds', a soubriquet derived from the name of their GOC (General Officer Commanding) – Major-General Harper – and the divisional sign HD that appeared on their vehicles and any buildings they occupied. However, by the end of the war, soldiers of 51st Highland Division were proud of their revised designation and bore the soubriquet of Harper's Duds as if it were a badge of honour. Rather than being thought 'duds' the Highlanders were considered one of the finest fighting formations in the British armies.[14]

The Division's first major battle was at Festubert in May 1915. As noted, the original composition of the Division had changed considerably by the time it arrived in France. Its original brigades had been the Argyll and Sutherland Brigade (6th, 7th, 8th and 9th Argylls), the Gordons Brigade (4th, 5th, 6th and 7th Gordons), and the Seaforth and Camerons Brigade (4th, 5th and 6th Seaforth and 4th Camerons).[15] However, 4th Seaforth, 6th Gordons and 7th Argylls had gone to France in October and November 1914 and their places had been taken by 2/4th Seaforth, 2/4th Gordons and 2/9th Argylls. In France in May 1915 the brigades deployed as follows: 152 Brigade – 5th and 6th Seaforth, 6th and 8th Argylls; 153 Brigade – 6th and 7th Black Watch, 5th and 7th Gordons; 154 Brigade included the English TA battalions; 6th Scottish Rifles remained with the brigade when 2/5th Lancashire Fusiliers returned.[16] By the end of the year the English battalions had departed to 55th Division and 6th Scottish Rifles had been reduced to cadre and posted to the base while 4th and 5th Black Watch, 4th Seaforth and 4th Camerons had joined.[17] This new line-up was short-lived; by February 1916 the brigade disposed 9th (Highland) Royal Scots (a battalion raised from Highlanders living in Edinburgh), 4th Seaforth, 4th Gordons and 7th Argylls. Of course, 9th Royal Scots were not the sole Royal Scots battalion in 51st (Highland) Division, which also included 8th Royal Scots as divisional pioneer battalion.

Festubert proved a bloody introduction to battle for the 51st. The Division, part of Douglas Haig's First Army, sustained heavy casualties in a battle that pushed the Germans out of a well-fortified position along a front of four miles to a depth of some 600 yards. Haig considered that the Highlanders had been committed to action while 'practically untrained and very green in all field duties' although the BEF commander, French, was pleased with the overall performance of Territorial soldiers.[18] Following Festubert, 51st Highland Division remained in the line near Laventie before, on 26 July, beginning a move that would take them to Méricourt on the Somme. In September Lieutenant-General Bannatine-Allason, who had brought the Division to France, relinquished command and was succeeded as GOC by Lieutenant-General Harper.

The Division's soldiers made many friends in the Picardy region where the Highlanders were billeted in local villages and farms and many soldiers spent their spare time helping their hosts in the fields. Familiarity with the music of the Highlanders also grew in the area, and especially with the pipes; each morning pipers greeted the dawn with the strains of 'Johnny Cope' and each evening French villages and farms echoed to the sounds of traditional Scottish airs. A kinship developed between 'paysan' and Highlander that was to leave an indelible mark in the memories of both and which some saw, romantically perhaps, as a folk memory of the 'auld alliance'.[19] More than that, it was to form part of the foundation of the legend of 51st Highland Division which, by 1918, was considered one of the best fighting formations in the British armies in France and was certainly the best known.

Since the purpose of this book is to tell the story of the Highland Division in the Second World War it is impossible to do other than summarise its service in the Great War. But even a summary tells a remarkable tale. Highlanders fought in most of the battles on the Western Front including the Somme offensive of 1916, during which the Division took part in the attacks on High Wood, capturing Beaumont Hamel, where the memory of the Jocks is immortalised in the Highland Division Memorial. Later the Highlanders were engaged in the First and Second Battles of the Scarpe and the capture of Roeux, all part of the Arras offensive while, in the Third Battle of Ypres, they fought at Pilckem and on the Menin Road. Cambrai, the first major tank offensive, also saw the Highland Division play its part and during 1918 the great battles of St Quentin, Bapaume and Estaires found it heavily engaged; the Division lost many casualties at Estaires. Later in 1918 the Highlanders were part of the Allied armies pursuing the broken German armies in the 'Hundred Days Offensive'. The Highland Division was at Cambrai when the armistice came into effect on

11 November 1918. Three battalions moved to Germany in February 1919 as part of the Army of Occupation but by March 1919 all other battalions had been reduced to cadre strength.[20]

The reputation of the Highland soldier had been enhanced by the achievements of 51st Highland Division in the Great War. When the Territorial Army, as the TF was renamed in tribute to the Territorial soldiers of that war, was created in the post-war Army, it was natural that the title of 51st (Highland) Division should be included in the TA. Across the Highlands and Islands, men flocked to become 'Saturday night soldiers' in the Gunner, Sapper, Infantry and other units of the new Division. When the call came to march to war again they would write another illustrious page in the history of the Scottish soldier.

Notes

1. Mileham, *The Scottish Regiments,* p. 178
2. Ascoli, *The British Army,* p. 115
3. Frederick, *Lineage Book of British Land Forces,* Vol. I, pp. 379–88
4. www.army.mod.uk/2div/organisation/51_Scottish_Brigade.htm
    See also Salmond, *The History of the 51st Highland Division,* pp. 2–3 for a different background picture which suggests that the first Highland Division may have been the army that faced Agricola's Romans at Mons Graupius in the first century AD. Salmond also argues that Wade's Highland Companies began the tradition of the Highland soldier in the Army.
5. Ibid
6. Doherty, *Clear The Way!,* p. 3
7. National Army Museum, London, *Road to Waterloo* Exhibition. This includes a diagrammatic representation of the home addresses of the personnel of a Highland regiment which lost its Highland identity.
8. From the poem written by John Greenleaf Whittier celebrating the relief of Lucknow. Paradoxically, this very patriotic Scottish ballad was written by an American.
9. Mileham, op cit, pp. 248–9
10. www.army.mod.uk/2div/organisation/51_Scottish_Brigade.htm
11. www.1914-1918.net/51div.htm *The Long, Long Trail*
12. Ibid
13. www.army.mod.uk/2div/organisation/51_Scottish_Brigade.htm
14. www.1914-1918.net/51div.htm op cit
15. Ibid
16. Ibid
17. Ibid
18. Ibid
19. Ibid
20. Brewsher, *The History of the Fifty First (Highland) Division 1914–1918,* pp. 403–8; www.1914-1918.net/51div.htm op cit

CHAPTER II

Ready for War

The routine of training for the TA battalions and other units of 51st (Highland) Division continued through the late 1930s. Each volunteer soldier spent an annual camp with his unit as well as several weekends and, usually, one night a week as part of the training programme, attending drill halls throughout the Highlands and Islands. Change came to the artillery units on 1 November 1938 but it was a change of nomenclature rather than of routine; the Royal Artillery redesignated its field brigades as regiments and from this date 75th, 76th and 77th (Highland) Field Brigades became Field Regiments. (These units had been re-formed in February 1920 as 1st, 2nd and 3rd Highland Brigades of the Royal Field Artillery and had been redesignated as 75th, 76th and 77th in 1921. Three years later they became Field Brigades of the Royal Artillery with the ending of the demarcation between Field and Garrison artillery.[1])

The Munich crisis in the autumn of 1938 and Neville Chamberlain's famous piece of paper that guaranteed 'peace for our time' brought a temporary breathing space for Britain's forces but with an accompanying sense of urgency. When Hitler reneged on the Munich agreement in March 1939, the Secretary of State for War, Leslie Hore-Belisha, announced a doubling of the Territorial Army, to be achieved by asking every TA unit to create a duplicate.[2] Such expansion was not restricted to the infantry: in the artillery of Highland Division, each regiment transferred two of its four batteries to form the nucleus of three new field regiments. Of course, expansion also meant that each major formation would duplicate itself and in the case of 51st (Highland) that duplicate was 9th (Highland) Division, a revival of another Great War formation, first raised in 1914 as 9th (Scottish) Division and part of Kitchener's New Armies, to which the duplicate formations and units of 51st (Highland) were assigned.[3]

Although the danger of war with Germany had been appreciated for some years, the Cabinet did not agree to the creation of a British Expeditionary Force for deployment on the European mainland until February 1939.[4] As with the BEF of the Great War, this new force was to support France in the event of hostilities with Germany; it would consist, initially, of four regular infantry divisions and a mobile division with TA divisions reinforcing it as they became available.[5] However, the time between creation and deployment meant the new BEF could not be as professional a body as its predecessor. With the peacetime Army starved of funds and equipment, training had suffered. In addition, much of the Army had been employed on garrison duties across the empire and its training had reflected, to a large extent, that task. There were insufficient tanks, artillery and infantry anti-tank weapons. Veterans of the period recall exercises in which coloured flags indicated anti-tank guns, machine guns or vehicles, including tanks or carriers.[6] In all, the Cabinet's authorisation of a new BEF was almost a triumph of optimism over reality as was the doubling of the TA and the introduction of conscription for the first time in peacetime Britain. The shortages that already existed were exacerbated by the resultant rapid manpower expansion.

The first formations assigned to the BEF and, therefore, the first to leave Britain for France in 1939, were those from the Regular Army. These included the senior formations of the Army, among them 1st Division, the 'Spearhead' from its formation sign, 2nd Division, later to gain fame at Kohima, 3rd Division, commanded by Bernard Montgomery, 4th Division, which would see much service in Tunisia and Italy, and 5th Division, commanded by Harold Franklyn. First to move were the four senior regular divisions, which went to France soon after the outbreak of war, followed by 5th Division in October.[7] The first TA division – 48th (South Midland) – arrived in January 1940.[8] At this point the BEF, commanded by Lord Gort of Limerick VC, was split into two corps – I and II – each of three divisions, but it was intended to increase its strength considerably with further TA divisions forming part of that expansion.[9] (Gort was both a commander-in-chief – of British forces in France – and an army commander – of the field army constituted by the BEF's two corps and this dual role would later create problems for him and his forces. The plan to increase the BEF to the strength of two field armies would have necessitated two army commanders and left Gort as CinC but this was never achieved.) Among the TA divisions chosen to join the BEF was 51st (Highland) Division which would form III Corps alongside 42nd (East Lancashire) and 46th (West Riding) Divisions.[10] The Division's GOC was 56-year-old Major-General Victor Fortune who had assumed command in 1937.[11] Although a Lowlander, from the Borders, Fortune was a commander respected by the Highland soldiers; he had seen service in the Great War in which he had commanded 1st Black Watch and earned the DSO. In everything but birth he was regarded as a Highlander.[12] Bernard Fergusson described him as:

a famous Black Watch character: he was the only officer of the Regiment who, coming to France with the 1st Battalion in 1914, went straight through to the end of the war fighting hard, without ever a scratch. Nobody doubted in January, 1940, but that he would distinguish himself in this new war; but equally nobody guessed, and least of all himself, in what unexpected role that distinction would be won.[13]

On 25 August 1939 key parties of the Division's units were called out.[14] Seven days later the Regular Army was ordered to mobilise for war and the Territorial Army was embodied. Across the towns and villages of its recruiting area, the soldiers of 51st (Highland) Division reported for duty on 2 September.[15] Gunners of 76th and 127th (Highland) Field Regiments reported to their regimental and battery headquarters. Both regiments had their HQs at Dundee, although the RHQ personnel of the latter were at Leven, with 303 and 304 Batteries of 76th Field at Dundee while the batteries of 127th Field were at Arbroath – 301 Battery – and Leven – 302 Battery. On embodiment the orders of battle were modified to give 302 and 303 Batteries to 76th Field and 301 and 304 Batteries to 127th Field which was then transferred to 9th (Scottish) Division. Similar patterns were followed in 75th and 77th (Highland) Field Regiments producing 126th and 128th (Highland) Field Regiments.[16]

Before long the Division had moved to Aldershot, the home of the Army, where the final touches were to be put to its preparation for deployment to France. Exercises were carried out and the routine of training took on a more immediate air as the soldiers made ready for active service. Christmas was spent in Britain and there was an opportunity for some leave but it was obvious that the new year would not be very old before the Division joined the BEF.[17] A visit by the King and Queen was confirmation, if such were needed, of an imminent overseas move. On 18 January 1940 Their Majesties King George VI and Queen Elizabeth inspected 154 Brigade at Bordon with Queen Elizabeth inspecting 6th Black Watch; she was Colonel-in-Chief of the Black Watch, in which her brother had served and died in the Great War, and took a keen personal interest in the regiment. Following the inspection, King George walked through the units of the brigade, which was assembled by companies on either side of the road.[18] Next day the Colonel of the Gordon Highlanders, Sir James Burnett of Leys Bt CB CMG DSO, visited 5th and 6th Gordons at Aldershot. Both battalions, accompanied by two Canadian Scottish units – 48th Highlanders of Canada and 75th Toronto Scottish – marched past Sir James, who had commanded 51st (Highland) Division from 1931 until 1935, on Corunna parade ground.[19] The parade was commanded by Brigadier G T Burney, who had assumed command of 153 Brigade on 5 January, and massed drummers and pipers played as the brigade marched past in columns of three.[20] The war diarist of 6th Gordons noted that this was the 'Last occasion on which the battalion paraded in kilts' as these garments were to be handed into store before embarkation. Although he might have believed this to be the case it was not so; the Gordons would parade again in kilts in the years ahead. In 5th Gordons, chagrin at the loss of the kilt was expressed more strongly: the CO ordered that a kilt be burned on the barrack square at Bordon to symbolise the fact that the English had now taken the kilt from the Highlanders, something they had been trying to do, unsuccessfully, for two centuries. Not content with this symbolic ceremony, the battalion also erected a stone memorial to the loss of the kilt, the inscription on which ended with the words: 'We hope not for long'. [21]

By the end of January elements of the Division were moving to France via Southampton. HQ 153 Brigade crossed to le Havre on board the troop-ship *Ulster Monarch*, a Belfast–Liverpool ferry that had been impressed into Admiralty service and which would achieve considerable fame in its own right during the war. On 30 January 6th Gordons arrived in le Havre to find that billeting arrangements left the battalion's platoons spread over about seven miles. While that dispersal created inconvenience in itself, both the local telephone system and electrical supply were out of order as a result of frost damage. Furthermore, the local countryside was water-logged as a thaw had set in. It was hardly an auspicious beginning to the Division's time in France.[22]

During February the Division moved to new stations with 152 Brigade at Wingles, 153 at Béthune and then Lillers and 154 at Lillebonne from which it moved to the Don area and thence to Merville at the end of the month.[23] The latter brigade had not arrived in France until February, its move from England having been delayed by heavy snow.[24] Whenever weather permitted training continued; 75th (Highland) Field Regiment noted that it was unable to move 'for at least two days' due to 'thaw precautions' enforced by the French authorities to preserve their roads. However, the regiment was able to move to the divisional concentration area near St Pol by 12 February.[25]

By the end of February, General Gort's headquarters had decided to 'stiffen' 51st (Highland) Division with a regular battalion replacing a TA battalion in each brigade. Through his corps commander, General Fortune suggested that this might be accomplished in either one of two ways: by removing from each brigade the junior battalion of the regiment with two battalions in that brigade and substituting its regular counterpart or by creating regimental brigades.[26] Neither suggestion was implemented: there was no regular Argyll battalion in the BEF to permit the former while the latter would have left the Camerons unrepresented in the Division.[27] So it was that 6th Black Watch, 6th Seaforth and 6th Camerons were replaced by 1st Black Watch in 154 Brigade, 2nd Seaforth in 152 Brigade and 1st

Gordons in 153 Brigade.[28] Handovers were accomplished with some ceremony but also with some sadness and although Fortune had hoped that the revised order of battle might be temporary this was not so. However, the infantry remained Highland and thus the integrity of the Division was not threatened. Both artillery and engineers lost Highland units in this 'stiffening' with 76th and 77th (Highland) Field Regiments replaced by the regular 17th and 23rd Field Regiments while 238 (Highland) Field Company was replaced by 26 Field Company.[29]

Each infantry division included a cavalry regiment charged with reconnaissance, but which could also perform other tasks, including flank protection. In 51st (Highland) Division this role fell to a Lowland yeomanry regiment, 1st Fife and Forfar Yeomanry under Lieutenant-Colonel R G Sharp, which crossed to France with the Division.[30] However, the regiment did not impress in training and, before the Highland Division was committed to the front line, it was transferred to 1 Armoured Reconnaissance Brigade (two armoured reconnaissance brigades were formed in early 1940 by re-organising the divisional cavalry regiments of the BEF. Initially assigned to 1 Armoured Recce Brigade, 1st Fife and Forfar Yeomanry was later transferred to 2 Armoured Recce Brigade[31]) and replaced by another Scottish yeomanry regiment, 1st Lothians and Border Horse, commanded by the, then, youngest CO in the Army, Lieutenant-Colonel Mike Ansell of the Inniskilling Dragoon Guards.[32] At first Ansell's appointment, one of many in which TA officers were relieved by Regulars as COs, was unpopular but he soon proved an effective and efficient CO and his approach to discipline and training later paid dividends. (Ansell relieved Lieutenant-Colonel H J Younger on St Patrick's Day. Younger remained with the Regiment, reverting to the rank of major and assuming the duties of second-in-command.[33]) At this time a light cavalry regiment disposed twenty-eight Mark VIB light tanks and forty-four Bren-gun carriers.[34] Neither the light tank nor the carrier was well-armoured, nor did either carry much in the way of armament. The Vickers light tank had 14mm of armour plate, just over a half-inch, and carried only machine guns but could travel at speeds up to 40mph while the Bren-gun carrier was similarly thin-skinned but, as a tracked vehicle, also had respectable cross-country performance.[35]

As already noted, the BEF was neither as well equipped nor trained as its predecessor of 1914 and one area in which the new force was lacking was in anti-tank weapons. The anti-tank gun establishment of an infantry division, excluding field guns temporarily employed as anti-tank weapons, included forty-eight 2-pounder guns in the divisional anti-tank regiment and nine 25mm guns in each of the brigade anti-tank companies;[36] the latter were French Hotchkiss guns, purchased as an interim solution to the shortage of anti-tank weapons; Swedish Bofors 37mm anti-tank guns had also been bought.[37] In the Highland Division's anti-tank companies there were only nine 25mm guns in all, a situation mirrored in 48th Division while three other TA divisions – 42nd, 44th and 50th – had none of these weapons at all.[38] Plans to improve the BEF's equipment existed but, as a temporary measure, it was decided that the deployment of reinforcing divisions to France could be accelerated if a lower establishment in manpower and weaponry was accepted. Such divisions were to be known as defensive divisions and might form up to 40 per cent of the strength of the BEF, which, by the summer of 1940, was scheduled to include two field armies, First and Second, with at least two corps in each army.[39]

The BEF was preparing for war in a variety of ways but the emphasis in the French army, which the BEF was reinforcing, was on defensive warfare and it was natural that this should be reflected in the British formation. As Bernard Fergusson noted:

> The reputation of the French Army stood high in those days. Between the wars it was supposed to have almost a monopoly of professional soldiering; there were few to whisper that all might not be well with it.[40]

In the years since the 1918 Armistice the French army had developed a 'fortress mentality', illustrated by the investment of much of the nation's military budget into building the Maginot Line. This fortifications system stretched from the Swiss frontier to the Franco-Belgian-Luxembourg border but was not a continuous line; a series of camouflaged, underground fortresses with artillery pieces that lifted hydraulically to their emplacements constituted its main strength, together with intermediate blockhouses, or strongpoints, an anti-tank ditch, barbed wire and a mass of embedded steel tank obstacles.[41] Although the BEF was to hold the line north of the French armies along the border with Belgium, British troops, including the men of 51st (Highland) Division, were to have direct experience of the Maginot Line.

Such was the strength of the belief that the Maginot Line, and its German counterpart, the Siegfried Line, would prevent a war of movement that a Trench Warfare Training and Experimental Establishment was created in Britain to which personnel from the BEF, and from units due to deploy to France, were sent for instruction.[42] On the ground in France, soldiers had little doubt that senior officers believed that the present war would be a repeat of the Great War as they were assigned to digging trenches and creating defensive positions for static warfare. This work was part of a northward extension of the Maginot Line, known as the little Maginot, or Gort, Line,[43] but, in spite of the effort expended, the BEF would never attempt to defend it, moving forward into Belgium when the Germans invaded that country.

As the BEF made its preparations, some British troops were deploying to the Maginot Line to serve alongside their French allies. In December 1939 the practice of posting an infantry brigade from the BEF to the Saar area in Lorraine was begun to give those brigades some combat experience against German troops.[44] Gort felt that the practice could be extended to allow the deployment of a division rather than a brigade, thereby providing battle training and inoculation for greater numbers of the BEF. By the end of March the French High Command had accepted Gort's suggestion that the British element in the Saar area should be at divisional strength and the BEF was invited to deploy a division there under French command.[45]

The BEF's first choice was Harold Franklyn's 5th Division but this formation was diverted to other tasks on 9 April when the Germans invaded Denmark and Norway; Franklyn's men were to make ready for a move to Norway.[46] In their place, Gort's staff chose 51st (Highland) Division as the first British division to move to the Saar.[47] However, the formation that would move would be much-reinforced; in addition to its own units the Division would include two pioneer battalions – 7th Royal Norfolks and 6th Royal Scots Fusiliers – as well as two machine-gun battalions – 7th Royal Northumberland Fusiliers and 1st Princess Louise's Kensington Regiment – while the Gunner and Sapper elements would also be increased.[48] With this strengthening, 51st Divisional Group, or Saar Force as it was to be dubbed, would muster some 21,000 personnel. The Division's first operational order, dated 18 April, caused some annoyance in the Lothians who took exception to the abbreviation L & B Horse being used to describe the regiment as well as the use of Lothian rather than Lothians in the full title.[49]

D-Day for 51st Division's move to the Saar was 16 April when 154 Brigade began moving by rail.[50] This brigade was to take over the sector already manned by British troops with the sector expanding as the remainder of the Division arrived. By 19 April the main body of the Division began its move, codenamed 'Poets', and the final elements arrived in Lorraine on 29 April.[51] At 3.00am on 22 April HQ 152 Brigade received a telephone message from Divisional HQ warning of rumours that German paratroopers were landing in the Arras area but this was 'yet another false alarm' and the Brigade returned to preparations for its move.[52] On 1 May the reinforced division officially became Saar Force, relieving the French 7th Infantry Division of Third Army in the Hombourg-Budange sector with an advanced HQ at the hamlet of Hombourg-Budange which sits across a *carrefour* between the Saar and Moselle rivers, about eighteen miles north-east of Metz.[53] The Highlanders' new area of operations was a considerable contrast to the bleak area they had left and was a rich green countryside of undulating hills, well watered by many streams, patched heavily with forest, sprinkled with orchards and numerous villages. The fields were wet, the ground soft, when the Highlanders arrived, but the weather was improving, and before long the midday sun was hot enough. ... there was something like enchantment in the warmth and beauty of Lorraine. The woods were beech, and the huge pale trees were dressed in the brilliance of new leaves. The forest-floor was patched with lilies of the valley, and all the orchards were in bloom.[54]

The takeover was not always straightforward and there were difficulties in fitting British weapons and equipment into French strongpoints. This reflected an earlier problem at Dranoutre fort where 4th Camerons' war diarist noted that the Gunners had to fit 18-pounders into emplacements intended for French guns.[55]

The Highlanders found that the Maginot Line was based on a series of lines, a development initiated by the Germans in the latter phase of the Great War. In 154 Brigade's sector there was a front line – *ligne de contact* – behind which was a support line – *ligne de soutien* – a retreat, or recoil, line – *ligne de recueil* – and a stop line – *ligne d'arrêt*.[56] Those sectors taken over by the other two brigades were similar, save for the absence of support lines. The tactical concept was that the first two lines would break up an attack, as well as preventing enemy reconnaissance of the main Maginot Line, while, in the case of a major attack, the defenders could withdraw to the retreat line; these forward lines were known as *la Couverture*.[57] The stop line was seen as the line of final defence, not to be given up under any circumstances. To cover withdrawal from the forward lines, and assist in breaking up enemy attacks, there was a series of *brisants*, V-shaped defensive works harking back to a much earlier era, situated in front of the forts.[58] However, as when Fifth British Army took over part of the front line from the French in early-1918, the Highlanders found that much work had still to be done on these defences.[59]

Many of the *brisants* had not been finished and the stop line was in a similar state with no effective trench system. The pioneer officer of 4th Camerons, having inspected the line, calculated that securing the defences would require a minimum of 600 coils of barbed wire, 1,200 pickets for wire, 2,000 sheets of revetting material, 2,000 A-frames and 80,000 sand-bags.[60] Worse still was the fact that many forward platoon-posts were no more than log cabins 'with a dense perimeter of barbed-wire'.[61] Since the ground that fringed the woods was so wet the French had decided to build up rather than dig down but they had chosen to use wood, which was certainly not bulletproof. The pioneer battalions – Norfolks and Royal Scots Fusiliers – were soon busy demolishing the cabins and replacing them with more effective positions.

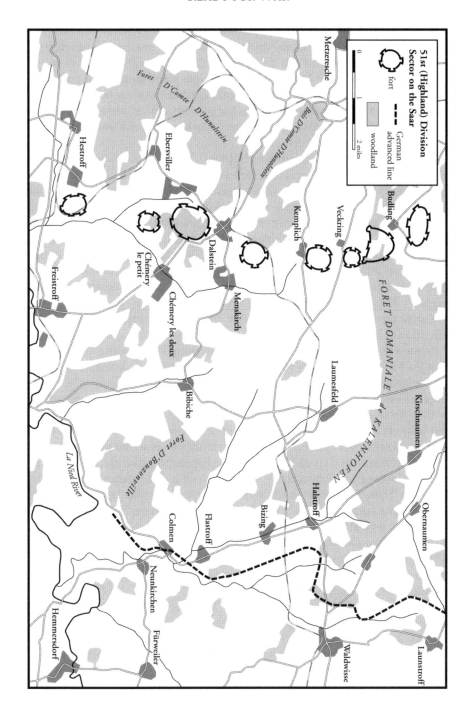

51st (Highland) Division
Sector on the Saar

fort

German
advanced line

woodland

0   1   2 miles

In terms of depth of defence the front line was anywhere between five and nine miles forward of the forts. The support line, where it existed, was about a mile behind the front line with the retreat line a few miles farther back. East of the Maginot Line the French authorities had created a 'killing zone' by evacuating villages and farms in the area, thus removing concern about civilian casualties. On the other hand, an eerie atmosphere prevailed with only birdsong or artillery fire breaking the unnatural spell that seemed to envelop the land.[62]

Until its move to Lorraine the Highland Division had seen very little warlike activity. In this it was similar to most formations of the BEF whose GHQ situation reports (SitReps) between December 1939 and March 1940 added to the impression that little was happening. Most SitReps read 'situation normal' or 'nothing to report, quiet night'.[63] Some included basic details of patrols or of sounds heard from enemy lines, including transport movement and even, at one stage, a cement mixer. Occasionally there were reports of shelling, bombing or small-arms fire. One report noted 'one dog shot by right platoon of centre company, otherwise quiet night'.[64] This was the time dubbed the 'Phoney War' by the press, or the *drôle de guerre* by the French. With the move into the Saar area, 51st (Highland) Division expected to see much more activity.

Some Highlanders were surprised, on moving into the line, to discover that the French soldiers there had come to an unofficial arrangement with their opponents to reduce the amount of warlike behaviour on either side. This was especially true in the area of the French 102nd Regiment, which was to be relieved by 152 Brigade. As part of the *modus vivendi* worked out by both French and Germans in that sector, small parties of fewer than six men were never fired at while ration trucks were allowed unmolested passage twice each day, at 10.00am and 4.00pm. Nor did 102nd Regiment seem to believe in night activity and were not pleased when their neighbours, a Foreign Legion unit, who did not share the regiment's lack of offensive spirit, patrolled aggressively.[65] Elsewhere, however, French battle patrols stalked the area between the lines under cover of darkness while German patrols were doing likewise. HQ of 154 Brigade reported a 'very disturbed night' on 1 May with much shooting and artillery fire.[66] Part of this was probably due to German awareness of fresh troops in the positions facing them.

The German troops who held the advanced positions of the Siegfried Line had the great advantage of knowing the country. Many were local men who had poached the woods they now patrolled, and were familiar with every yard of the ground. Their patrols were aggressive, and dominated the area. On a front so thinly held it was impossible to keep them out, and sometimes they penetrated as far as Waldweistroff. They made much use of trained dogs, and of tricks to unnerve the defence: such as removing from the wire of a platoon-perimeter the empty tins strung upon it to give warning of trespassers.[67]

That increased hostile activity by the Germans was due to their having identified their new foe is also possible since the Great War reputation of the Highland Division would have been known to the enemy's officers. Certainly the Highlanders were determined that there should be no easy life for their neighbours across no man's land and a patrolling routine intended to dominate the ground between Maginot and Siegfried Lines was established quickly. Each battalion had a well-trained battle patrol whose task was to ensure that the enemy could not relax at night; the patrols were also intended to deter German reconnaissance of the Divisional sector while gaining as much intelligence on German units and dispositions as possible. A chronicler of the Division's time in France described the purpose of these patrols, which went out

> to hamper and observe the enemy, to provoke him to fight. It was the Divisional policy that the routine patrol should be carried out in so enterprising a fashion as to make deliberate raiding unnecessary, and the nightly stalking of the enemy – with grenade and tommy-gun, the patrol with their faces blackened – was done with persistent energy and a high spirit.[68]

On 3 May 4th Camerons moved to Ising Camp for training and then took up positions at Dampont Farm on 8/9 May. Thus this battalion had only established itself in new positions when the order '*mise en garde*' was received on 10 May as the Germans invaded the Low Countries. That morning the Camerons came under fire but there was no immediate attack in their sector.[69] That '*mise en garde*' order was received throughout the Division, leading to battalions dispersing to battle positions. There had been few indications that an attack would come on 10 May although 1st Gordons had noted 'a great increase in artillery activity' during the 6th, which was attributed to re-ranging by a new German unit.[70] In the early hours the Gordons had experienced a raid with leaflets, written in French, suggesting that the Germans had either not positively identified the Highlanders or had no English leaflets, fired from shells.[71]

The German attack on the Low Countries was, of course, an attack on France. It was clear that the Germans intended to avoid assaulting the Maginot Line and would instead make a flanking movement – a sickle sweep or *Sichelschnitt* – on their foes. With the offensive underway, General Gamelin, CinC of the Land Forces of Britain and France, issued a special order of the day.

This morning was launched the attack which we have foreseen since last October. A struggle to the death has begun between ourselves and Germany. For all the Allies the watchword must be: Coolness, Vigour and Faith. As Marshal Pétain said 24 years ago:- 'Nous les aurons' (We'll get them in the end.)[72]

In the contemporary phrase 'the balloon had gone up'. The Allied armies now made ready for full-scale combat with the enemy. The BEF was ordered to abandon its carefully prepared positions and advance into Belgium to support the Belgian forces and protect that country. Alone of the major frontline formations of the BEF, 51st (Highland) Division remained in position but was prepared to take the fight to the foe. Fighting patrols at night were stepped up and on the night of 11/12 May a 'special patrol' of 1st Black Watch moved out from Winkelmerter under Second Lieutenant D Campbell whose report of the patrol has survived.

We left Winkelmerter at 2105 hours and proceeded in [an Easterly] direction. [The original document reads 'in a Westerly direction' but there is a handwritten query above the word 'Westerly' which suggests that this should read 'Easterly'. Had Campbell led his patrol in a Westerly direction he would have been taking them away from the enemy.]

Owing to the moon and lack of cover our progress was very slow.

At 0050 hours when we were within 100 yards of the Railway embankment, we heard men talking and the sound of groans, but could take no immediate action as the sounds came from a hollow under the embankment and we could not approach without showing ourselves.

By 0110 hours we were moving in extended order across the hollow and we saw a dim figure disappearing over the Railway embankment. We found two shell craters at pt 41152886, and there were tracks where figures had lain and tracks as if a body had been dragged away. We searched this area but found nothing further.

Movement was heard in the culvert at 41142885 and also down the Hermesbach at pt 41152884. Grenades were thrown on both occasions. We then searched the whole of this area and found some Small Arms Ammunition and numerous signs of where men had lain up, and the marks, where bodies had been dragged away, were again clearly visible. It was now 0315 hours and after driving the East bank of the Hermesbach the patrol reported back at 0435 hours.

N.B. A red light was seen waving at pt 41052896, when the patrol left the Winkelmerter.[73]

At HQ 154 Brigade the war diary noted a quiet night for the night of 9/10 May 'but much aircraft activity noted at 0500'. From 4.00am the Luftwaffe was reported to have bombed Metz, 'entered Holland, Belgium and Luxembourg [and] bombed Switzerland'. The *'mise en garde'* order was received at 6.30am and the brigade plan was put into operation with 6th Royal Scots Fusiliers laying mines before being ordered to hold the *ligne de recueil* until the withdrawal of the contact battalion.[74]

When the 'balloon went up' the frontline Highland battalions were 4th Camerons, which had relieved 2nd Seaforth on the 8th, 1st Black Watch, which had relieved 8th Argylls on the 9th, and 4th Black Watch, which had relieved 1st Gordons on the 7th. Elements of the Lothians were also in the line; a troop of three light tanks supported each brigade while the carrier personnel of each squadron in rotation carried out infantry duty in the line. However, any thoughts that the Division would hold the Maginot Line were to disappear as the progress of the German advance made redundant the very concept of that line.

Notes

1. Frederick, *Lineage Book of British Land Forces*, Vol. II, p. 520
2. www.army.mod.uk/2div/organisation/51_Scottish_Brigade.htm
3. Ibid
4. Fraser, *And We Shall Shock Them*, pp. 19–21
5. Ibid; NA Kew, WO197/34, BEF, organizations & establishments; WO197/39, Composition of the BEF
6. A number of pre-war veterans have described this practice to the author, who first learned of it from his late father who served in The Royal Irish Fusiliers during this period.
7. NA Kew, WO197/34, BEF, organizations & establishments
8. Ibid
9. NA Kew, WO197/39, Composition of the BEF
10. Ibid
11. Salmond, *The History of the 51st Highland Division*, p. 4
12. Ibid
13. Fergusson, *The Black Watch and the King's Enemies*, pp. 20–1
14. NA Kew, WO167/496, war diary, 76 (H) Fd Regt, 1939
15 Ibid
16. Ibid
17. NA Kew, WO167/406, war diary, 152 Bde, 1939–40; WO167/407, war diary, 153 Bde, 1940; WO167/409, war diary, 154 Bde, 1940
18. NA Kew, WO167/409, war diary, 154 Bde, 1940
19. NA Kew, WO167/747, war diary, 6 Gordons, 1939–40
20. Ibid
21. Ibid; David, *Churchill's Sacrifice of the Highland Division*, p. 11

22. NA Kew, WO167/495, war diary, 75 (H) Fd Regt, 1939–40; WO167/747, war diary, 6 Gordons, 1939–40
23. NA Kew, WO176/406, war diary, 152 Bde, 1940; WO167/407, war diary, 153 Bde, 1940; WO167/409, war diary, 154 Bde, 1940
24. NA Kew, WO167/409, war diary, 154 Bde, 1940
25. NA Kew, WO167/495, war diary, 75 (H) Fd Regt, 1939–40
26. David, op cit, p. 10
27. Salmond, op cit, p. 4; NA Kew, WO167/456, war diary, 1 F&F Yeo, 1940
28. Joslen, *Orders of Battle*, p. 146 & p. 150
29. David, op cit, pp. 20–1; NA Kew, WO167/455, war diary, 1 L&B Yeo, 1940
30. David, op cit, p. 22
31. Ibid
32. NA Kew, WO167/34, BEF organizations & establishments
33. NA Kew, WO167/455, war diary, 1 L&B Yeo, 1940
34. Fergusson, op cit, p. 22
35. David, op cit, p. 13
36. NA Kew, WO167/34, BEF organizations & establishments; Hogg, *Allied Artillery of World War Two*, p. 145
37. NA Kew, WO167/34, BEF organizations & establishments
38. Ibid; WO197/39, composition of the BEF; WO167/314, war diary (GS) 51 (H) Div, Jan–Jun 1940
39. NA Kew, WO197/39, composition of the BEF
40. Fergusson, op cit, p. 22
41. Salmond, op cit, p. 6; David, op cit, pp. 8–9
42. Doherty, *Clear The Way!*, p. 290
43. David, op cit, pp. 8–9
44. Ibid, p. 12
45. Ibid
46. Ibid
47. Ibid; NA Kew, WO197/124, move to Saar
48. David, op cit, p. 12; Salmond, op cit, pp. 7–8; NA Kew, WO197/124, move to Saar
49. NA Kew, WO167/455, war diary, 1 L&B Yeo, 1940
50. NA Kew, WO167/409, war diary, HQ 154 Bde
51. NA Kew, WO197/68, move to Saar
52. NA Kew, WO167/406, war diary, 152 Bde, 1940
53. Salmond, op cit, pp. 8–9; NA Kew, WO197/124, move to Saar; Linklater, *The Highland Division*, p. 12
54. Linklater, op cit, p. 12
55. NA Kew, WO167/720, war diary, 4 Camerons, 1939–40
56. David, op cit, pp. 12–13
57. Linklater, op cit, p. 14
58. David, op cit, p. 13
59. Ibid; Salmond, op cit, pp. 8–9
60. NA Kew, WO167/720, war diary, 4 Camerons, 1939–40
61. Ibid
62. Linklater, op cit, p. 12
63. NA Kew, WO197/36, SitReps, GHQ BEF, Dec '39–May '40

64. Ibid
65. David, op cit, pp. 16–17
66. NA Kew, WO167/409, war diary, 154 Bde, 1940
67. Linklater, op cit, p. 12
68. Ibid, p. 15
69. NA Kew, WO167/720, war diary, 4 Camerons, 1939–40
70. NA Kew, WO167/744, war diary, 1 Gordons, Mar–Jun 1940
71. Ibid
72. NA Kew, WO167/710, war diary 1 BW, Aug 1939–Jun 1940
73. Ibid
74. NA Kew, WO167/409, war diary, 154 Bde, 1940

CHAPTER III

Disaster Strikes

On 11 May General Fortune issued a directive to Saar Force telling his soldiers that Winston Churchill had succeeded Neville Chamberlain as Prime Minister on the 10th, that the German advance had been stalled in Luxembourg and that the Germans were finding Dutch resistance much tougher than expected.[1] Only the news about the new occupant of 10 Downing Street was accurate.

Fortune also underlined the importance of holding firmly the *ligne de contact* and of 'obtaining an identity'. Active patrolling was encouraged while any enemy attack was to be exploited immediately by the Tank Troop as soon as information was received, or even before that if enemy artillery and mortar fire suggested an imminent attack.[2] Although Fortune was determined that his Highland soldiers, and their Lowland armoured comrades, should provide an aggressive defence against the enemy, conditions were unsuited to employing light tanks in a counter-attack role. Before long hard evidence that this was so was provided.

B Company of 4th Black Watch were holding positions at Betting when they came under attack.[3] These positions included a post at Betting itself, held in platoon strength, which created a salient into no man's land. When he learned that this platoon was being surrounded, Lieutenant-Colonel Macpherson, CO of 4th Black Watch, ordered the Lothians' troop at his HQ, under Second-Lieutenant A S Chambers, to advance to Betting.[4] There followed an incident that was both tragic and comic. One tank was knocked out before reaching Betting by enemy shellfire although the crew escaped unharmed. Chambers returned to search for this tank and suffered the ignominy of having his own machine bog in marshy ground. The third tank tried to tow him out but without success, and it also bogged. Although both tanks were extricated, Lieutenant Chambers' vehicle 'got hopelessly bogged' in a ditch. When two passing carriers offered assistance, Chambers ordered No. 2 Tank to return to Remeling, and the Crews of No. 1 & 2 Tanks to remove the feed blocks of guns, etc, and board the Carriers. We eventually took shelter in a barn near Betting for the night as we could not get back along the road. Very heavy shelling took place in the early part of the night. The following morning at 0500 hrs we proceeded to the edge of the wood, and camouflaged the Carriers. I then reported back with my Crews to Remeling.[5]

The entire episode had been an object lesson in how not to employ tanks. When a second armoured intervention some days later had a similar costly result, the concept of using the Lothians in a counter-attack role was abandoned.[6]

When Colonel Ansell learned of the fate of the tank troop at Betting he decided to lead an expedition to rescue the stricken No. 1 tank but this failed because the vehicle's steel-wire tow rope had ensnared in a track during the previous attempt. Only the radio could be salvaged and two men were wounded when enemy shellfire fell on the rescue party.[7] Ansell's action may have been courageous but it was also foolhardy and not the type of incident in which a commanding officer should have been involving himself.

By midnight 4th Black Watch, save for a company still in difficulties, had been relieved by 5th Gordons. The latter battalion's CO was

very much struck by the seriousness in [the soldiers'] faces, and how they put their confidence in their officers. I wondered how many would ever again possess those boyish faces.[8]

During 11 and 12 May enemy activity against the Highland Division had been restricted to small-scale attacks against forward platoon, company or, at most, battalion fronts. That was to change on the 13th when the Germans launched a major assault against two Highland brigades and flanking French troops. At first this appeared to be no more than an engagement between two fighting patrols. When a patrol of 2nd Seaforth, led by Second-Lieutenant Blair was returning to its own lines, at about 2.00pm, it was ambushed by a concealed German patrol. In the ensuing skirmish one Seaforth was killed and two wounded.[9] Two hours later, however, heavy shelling of the front line began with especially intense fire in the sectors held by 153 and 154 Brigades.[10] At battalion HQ of 1st Black Watch, signal flares indicating an enemy attack were spotted from the forward positions of both flank companies, A Company in the Hartbusch wood and D Company on the edge of the Grossenwald. D Company called for defensive fire from the divisional artillery which helped stop the German advance; accurate rifle and Bren-gun fire ensured that the enemy was pinned down. When ammunition supplies were running low, tanks of

No. 1 Troop of the Lothians arrived and one of the vehicles was carrying fresh ammunition. D Company's commander decided to deploy the tanks in a counter-attack role which was unsuccessful: one tank ditched and the others were knocked out by anti-tank guns.[11]

In the meantime the ammunition delivered by the Lothians had been issued, with some difficulty, to the forward posts and the Black Watch soldiers were able to continue effective harassing fire on their foe. Such was the tenacity of this defence that the Germans had to admit defeat and called off their attack, having lost some forty dead; the defenders had lost only five dead, including two from the Lothians, and eight wounded, two of whom were also Lothians.[12] Following this clash, Ansell was again to be seen leading a party to recover maps, radios and firing blocks from his damaged tanks. On this occasion he was escorted by a fighting patrol of Black Watch under Second-Lieutenant David Campbell who, for his work on this occasion, and the previous day, was awarded the Military Cross, one of the first two officers of 51st (Highland) Division to be so decorated.[13]

Elsewhere the Germans had achieved more success. The battalions holding those flank sectors taken over from the French had not yet completed improving their defences; it had been the defences established by the previous British occupants of the centre sector that had played such an important role in 1st Black Watch's defence.[14] Fourth Black Watch had been preparing to hand over to 5th Gordons and 134 members of the latter had been in the battalion's forward positions when the Germans struck. Once again the attack was preceded by a heavy bombardment that wreaked considerable damage and inflicted serious casualties, especially on the battalion's right flank. In the subsequent desperate fighting Sergeant Sidney Newman earned the Distinguished Conduct Medal for his gallant conduct and leadership. His was 'a fine example of bravery under heavy fire during repeated enemy attacks' which encouraged those around him as they saw Newman carrying a Bren to several different positions 'firing on the enemy, and so repelling the main force of the attack on his post'. Finally, however, the post was evacuated on orders from battalion HQ.[15]

In A Company's sector, Sergeant William Clark showed courage and leadership of a quality similar to that of Sidney Newman but his gallantry was not officially recognised. Clark had been killed by German machine-gun fire and Lieutenant-Colonel Macpherson recommended him for the DCM but this medal could not then be awarded posthumously.[16] Only the Victoria Cross or the Mention in Despatches could be posthumous awards and neither was gazetted. Later in the war, a blind eye was turned on many occasions to this rule and posthumous awards were made. (In such cases, the *London Gazette* would usually indicate that the recipient had 'since died' or been 'killed in action' but it would not acknowledge the fact that, in many cases, the recipient was already dead when the paperwork for the award was initiated.) On the battalion's left flank, B Company was holding the Betting salient but was forced to withdraw under the pressure of the assault.[17]

C Company, holding the Grand and Petit Woschler woods, came in for probably the fiercest attention from the Germans for this sector was one of their two objectives in 4th Black Watch's area; the other was the Grossenwald. Once again the pattern of intense bombardment then an infantry attack, by at least 150 men, was followed and once again the defence was stubborn with Bren and rifle fire taking a heavy toll of the attackers. This caused the Germans to break off the attack for the time being but they left one skilled sniper behind who became a serious nuisance to the defenders. Company HQ, sited towards the back end of the Grand Woschler, had also fought off a major infantry attack. This had looked set to succeed until a second German bombardment fell short of the Scottish positions and caused so many casualties among their own infantry that the latter were forced to pull back.[18]

Elsewhere along the line 4th Seaforth had relieved 4th Camerons who had lost section posts in the Tiergarten and had generally had a rough time. However, they had scored a moral victory over the Germans who had been tapping the Highland Division's forward telephone cables but found that they could not understand the Camerons. This was not a difficulty in deciphering the accents of the Camerons but in recognising the very language that they spoke: the Cameron men chose to use Gaelic when talking over the telephone. Before handing over to the Seaforth, the battalion regained some of its lost ground from the Germans.[19]

Pressure was exerted on all the front line battalions, each of which inflicted considerable suffering on its attackers. The Gunner regiments, called upon to support the infantry on many occasions, did good work, disrupting attacks and causing many casualties among the Germans. One soldier of 1st Black Watch, Private J McCready wrote home to tell his family that his friends

> Price and Fisher had an excellent time with a Bren gun and a rifle, their bag of the enemy was put down as 44 in an afternoon. It was all stormtroopers in that action, but the Black Watch was more than a match for them, they proved nothing better than good target practice as some of the boys said.[20]

Early on 14 May 5th Gordons were subjected to an artillery bombardment that saw some 3,600 shells drop on one company front in ninety minutes, cutting telephone lines and flattening barbed wire. Following the bombardment came the infantry but, if they expected to find the Gordons shocked into submission, they were mistaken and suffered heavy losses as the Gordons fought them off.[21] Seventh Argylls, who relieved 1st Black

Watch in the line, also fought off a determined attack and in front of one platoon's positions they counted the bodies of thirteen Germans.[22] Next morning D Company, 5th Gordons was hit hard and contact was lost with two forward posts. Patrols sent out to re-establish contact were forced back by intense machine-gun fire. At 5.00am three of D Company's posts were cut off when German artillery concentrated fire on them. An hour later came an infantry attack, which was fought off. Then followed a bombardment that lasted three hours during which no contact was made with the posts while attempts to reconnoitre were driven back by heavy machine-gun fire. D Company later reported that it was holding on in its last position but with only twenty-eight men. Although the company commander wanted to fight forward to rescue his lost platoons this was impossible; their posts had been overrun, the soldiers were dead or captured, and the company survivors were withdrawn under covering fire provided by a fighting patrol.[23] Within hours the entire Division would be beginning its withdrawal from the Maginot positions.

While 51st (Highland) Division had been thus engaged with the enemy the BEF had been fighting its own campaign. With the German invasion of Belgium, the Gort Line, on which so much time and sweat had been expended, was abandoned and the BEF, following the Allied strategic plan, advanced into Belgium to meet the invaders.[24] In the Great War the BEF had maintained a hold in a small corner of Belgium throughout the war but this was not to be repeated. Highly mobile German ground forces, including tanks and infantry with artillery support, struck into Belgium with the Luftwaffe providing an aerial umbrella, as well as tactical support and interdiction of the defenders' lines of communication, and managed quickly to knock their opponents off balance. In the overall attack against France, Belgium, The Netherlands and Luxembourg, the Germans deployed some 200,000 soldiers and about 3,700 aircraft.[25] One of Belgium's most vaunted defences, the fortress at Eben Emael on the Albert Canal, fell to a German airborne attack with seventy-eight glider-borne infantry landing on top of the fortifications in ten gliders, thereby achieving complete surprise and driving the garrison of over 1,000 men into the fortress's underground passages.[26] Before long the Belgians were withdrawing in the face of the attacking forces. On the day of the invasion, Allied specialist demolition teams landed in The Netherlands to destroy facilities, including oil storage depots, that might be of value to the invaders.[27] This action brought a strong protest from the Dutch monarchy but before long the Dutch royal family was being evacuated by the Royal Navy to exile in Britain.[28]

On 11 May Luxembourg fell and Belgian forces continued falling back. Belgian troops demolished the bridges over the Meuse river on the 12th to delay the advance of German ground forces. Next day, German armour crossed the Meuse at Sedan to punch into the French defences.[29] One of the panzer generals was to become a legend: Erwin Rommel. He would also take the surrender of the Highland Division in June. Seven German armoured divisions, led by General Heinz Guderian, one of the fathers of armoured warfare, struck through the Ardennes, hitherto believed to have been impassable to tanks, and established bridgeheads across the Meuse on 14 May.[30] Guderian's forces were supported by aircraft, including Junkers Ju87 Stuka divebombers. (Although the name Stuka was a generic title for any divebomber it became associated most closely with the gull-winged Ju87 so that that aircraft was known as 'the Stuka'.) In operations against these bridgeheads the Royal Air Force and the *Armée de l'Air* lost heavily. It took only one more day for the Dutch army to capitulate and, by the 17th, German troops had occupied Brussels, Louvain, Malines and Namur, going on to seize Antwerp the following day as well as Cambrai and St Quentin in France.[31]

On 20 May German troops took Amiens, reached the Channel coast and surrounded Arras. By the 23rd, General Gerd von Rundstedt's forces had smashed through the French defences at Sedan while the Allies had begun evacuating Boulogne on the Channel coast as enemy forces closed on that port.[32] All looked lost for the Allies, especially when Hitler's war directive 13, issued on 24 May, ordered the destruction of all Allied forces in Artois and Flanders as well as an aerial assault on Britain.[33] However, on 25 May, when Boulogne fell to the Germans and with much of the BEF's fighting strength as well as French and Belgian troops trapped around Dunkirk, the Führer ordered his armoured forces in France and Belgium to stop.[34] This order, apparently designed to allow the infantry to close up while the Luftwaffe dealt with the concentration of Allied troops in the Dunkirk perimeter, was to prove critical in giving Britain sufficient breathing space to evacuate the BEF, and many French and Belgian troops, across the Channel. It would not, however, save 51st (Highland) Division from its fate; only a portion of the Division would be evacuated from France.

By 15 May it had become clear that the forward positions of the Division could not be held against the increasing German pressure and General Fortune, following consultation with General Condé, ordered withdrawal to the *ligne de recueil* to match the French withdrawal on either flank. This was a difficult manoeuvre to execute, as is always the case when in contact with an enemy, but the forward battalions made their way back to a line the defences of which had yet to be completed.

It lay about three miles in front of the Maginot Line, on a forward slope. The field of fire was good, but the wire was thin, communication trenches were poor, and an anti-tank ditch had been only half-dug. The Germans, however, did not press their advance. Extensive demolitions had been prepared along the Divisional front, and beside every charge two Sappers had waited patiently for the blessed order to blow. It came – and roads went skyward, bridges collapsed, trees tumbled. The German advance was usefully impeded: they came no further than the Obsterwald.[35]

Although the Division remained in the Maginot Line for the next few days, with battalions prepared to hold the rear lines, and the Lothians acting as infantry, 'this was mere temporising'; orders to move were awaited but there was no feeling of despondency. The Highlanders knew that they had done well in their first battles, which was acknowledged by General Condé of Third Army when he commented that the 'Highlanders of 1940 have renewed the tradition of Beaumont-Hamel'.[36]

On 20 May the Division passed into army group reserve and was ordered to the vicinity of Etain, about twenty miles north-west of Metz; this move was complete by the 22nd and, next day, 154 Brigade was en route to Varennes, north-west of Verdun, to be followed by the Lothians. The Germans were believed to have broken through west of Montmédy and 51st (Highland) Division was deploying to meet them. As the sun rose on 25 May as much of the Division as could be moved by motor transport was concentrated in the Grandpré-Varennes area; the remainder were already in transit by train.[37]

There was considerable indecision in the French high command at this time while the French government was suffering a crisis of conscience in which it was split between those who saw no chance of holding back the Germans and who, therefore, believed that France should sue for an armistice and those who wanted to continue the fight to save France from the humiliation of defeat. The prime minister, Paul Reynaud, was one of the fighters but his deputy, Marshal Philippe Pétain, appointed only on 17 May, was among the defeatists while senior French soldiers had lost or were losing their faith in Gamelin.[38] The battle for France had become two discrete elements with German armoured and motorised divisions flowing through an increasing gap between Arras and the Somme towards the Channel coast and ports. Boulogne had fallen, with a Guards Brigade evacuated, while Calais was holding out against two panzer divisions; but the Green Jacket Brigade holding Calais was already doomed. The main body of the BEF and the Belgian Army were in retreat and the principal area of operations was decreasing all the while towards the coast. In the triangle formed by Cambrai, Arras and Valenciennes, desperate and confused battle raged.

Although the initial French intention had been to deploy the Highlanders in the defence of Paris, this had been overtaken by the Montmédy scare and the subsequent move to Varennes. But the Division was not to dig in there, being ordered to move to le Mans, prompting one CO to note that they had moved to Verdun only to be told to move to le Mans.[39] Thus began the move to Normandy. Although the story of the retreat to Normandy is one of sadness and loss there were moments that could inspire laughter amongst veterans many years later. One such moment involved Driver Andy Young and 'The Dundee Weaver'. The latter was a tipper lorry that was carrying the G1098 equipment of 525 (Ammunition) Company, RASC. This equipment included

> cookers, pots and pans, food and all the normal 'junk' found in these institutions. Not being the world's best driver, Young went to change down going uphill but instead of putting his hand on the gear lever, he activated the tipper lift control mechanism. The scene behind him as the equipment tumbled about the road with vehicles following can be imagined, as can the language of those who had to sort it all out.[40]

As the Highlanders were on the roundabout journey to Normandy the Royal Navy had already begun Operation DYNAMO, the evacuation of the BEF and its French and Belgian allies from the beaches around Dunkirk. On 19 May Reynaud had relieved Gamelin as CinC and replaced him with General Maxime Weygand, another septuagenarian Great War veteran. Weygand had proposed a counter-attack towards the north to regain contact with the Allied armies in Belgium and northern France but his plan was doomed to failure and, by the 23rd, Gort, realising that there would no counter-attack to restore the integrity of the Allied armies, ordered the two British divisions at Arras to withdraw to the Haute Deule canal.[41] This withdrawal was the beginning of the move that would take the bulk of the BEF back to the Channel ports and evacuation to Britain.

On 28 May 152 Brigade arrived in the Haute Forêt d'Eu, on the Bresle river, and by the next day the entire Division was moving into positions from Senarpont to Eu, a line of about eighteen miles, with Divisional HQ at St Léger-au-Bois.[42] The contemporary received wisdom was that a division should hold a front of no more than four miles of properly prepared positions and should have a reserve; the Highlanders had neither properly prepared positions nor a reserve. On 51st Division's left was IX French Corps while, on its right, were supposed to be French marines. Along the Bresle the Camerons of 152 Brigade had found the remnants of a Basque regiment that had suffered heavily in The Netherlands; they had recently been withdrawn from Breda. Between these Cameron Highlanders and Pyrenean highlanders there was a shared spirit and the Camerons provided the Basques with some anti-tank weapons to bolster their defences. But the news from elsewhere was not good: Belgium had surrendered and German troops had crossed the Somme near Abbeville, establishing bridgeheads at Abbeville and at St Valéry-sur-Somme. The Abbeville

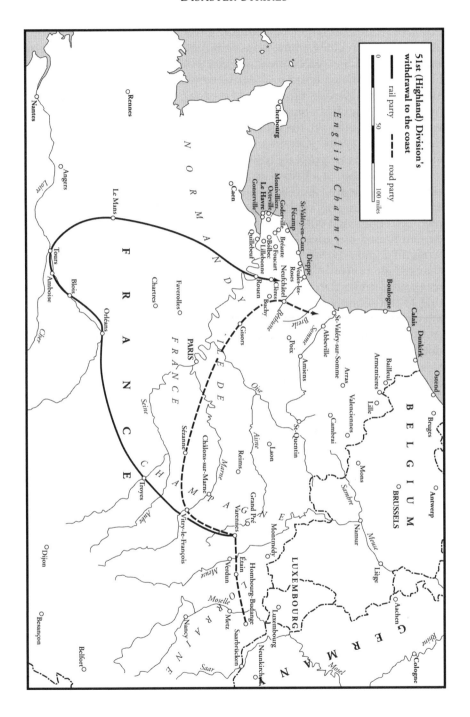

51st (Highland) Division's
withdrawal to the coast

rail party

road party

bridgehead was the larger, constituting a triangle with its apex at Huppy and its base along the Somme from Petit Port to Pont Rémy. On the morning of 29 May Allied forces, including elements of the British 1st Armoured Division and French armour under General Charles de Gaulle, counterattacked the Abbeville bridgehead, pushing the apex back to between Moyenneville and Miannay. The villages of Bienfay and Moyenneville were retaken. However, the British armour had been repulsed with heavy losses and the partial success gained was achieved by the French.[43] The attack had not been properly co-ordinated.

The appearance of a British armoured division requires some explanation. First Armoured Division, under Major-General Roger Evans, had arrived in France only on 14 May, and had been rushed out without completing training and without its full equipment or manpower. It included two armoured brigades – 2 and 3 Armoured Brigades (formerly 2 Light Armoured and 1 Heavy Armoured Brigades. The designations had been changed on 14 April.[44]) – and a support group – 1 Support Group – and was placed under command of Seventh French Army on 25 May, transferring to the recently created Tenth Army on the 29th.[45] In the Abbeville attack 1st Armoured Division had suffered considerable losses and Evans, its GOC, considered that it was no longer fit to fight and would not be so until it had been re-equipped and re-organised.[46] Since 1st Armoured was to come under Fortune's control, Evans arrived at the Highlanders' HQ to apprise Fortune of his situation. The pair agreed on a compromise: while those vehicles of 1st Armoured that required repair and overhaul would be withdrawn to base workshops, the remaining serviceable tanks and the division's personnel would remain with the Highland Division. From the remnants of his two armoured brigades (the regiments of the brigades were: The Bays, 10th Hussars and 9th Lancers in 2 Armoured Brigade and 2nd, 3rd and 5th Royal Tanks in 3 Armoured Brigade.), Evans was able to create a composite regiment of tanks. Support Group was virtually intact and included a battalion of infantry, a Sapper company and two Gunner regiments, one of light anti-aircraft and one of anti-tank artillery.[47]

At this stage a further British formation entered the equation. This was an ad-hoc division created from units along the BEF's lines of communication (LoC). To reduce the risk of German air attack on base units and ports the BEF had arrived in France through the westernmost ports and had established its base areas to the west also. Since these were now cut off from the main body of the BEF, logistic support troops, although inadequately equipped and not fully trained, were being formed into three infantry brigades under command of Brigadier A B Beauman DSO, who had been Commander, Northern District LoC. Known as Beauforce, and soon to be renamed Beauman Division, these brigades would also play a part in the story of the Highland Division. In fact, Beauman arrived at Fortune's HQ on the same day as Evans, bringing him the grim news that le Havre had been all but evacuated and that Rouen would now be the supply centre for Fortune's Division. Furthermore, Beauman's men were holding a line along the Béthune river from Dieppe to Rouen and were the only troops covering the rear of 51st Division's positions.[48]

Although the French renewed the attack at Abbeville, using armour, infantry and aircraft, they had no further success. The aircraft were met by a thick concentration of light anti-aircraft fire and the ground troops made no impression on the German bridgehead. Included in this attack was B Company 1st Black Watch, which was assigned the task of capturing the Grand Bois of Cambron. Against heavy machine-gun fire the Jocks advanced, wiped out the machine guns and took their objective in the woods. However, a French attack on Cambron was repulsed, leaving the Black Watch with an unprotected flank and forcing B Company to withdraw to conform with their neighbours.[49]

When General de Gaulle expressed concern that his troops might not be able to hold Bienfay and Moyenneville, Brigadier Stewart of 152 Brigade deployed 2nd Seaforth to reinforce the French in both villages. Within hours, and by 6.00am on 31 May, two companies of the Seaforth were in Bienfay with another two in Moyenneville.[50] Stewart's other battalions, 4th Seaforth and 4th Camerons, were at Béhen and Limeux. However, this redeployment only increased the pressure on the Division. Later that day General Altmayer, commanding IX French Corps, ordered Fortune to hold the line along the Somme from Erondelle to the sea. This included taking over Bienfay and Moyenneville in which 152 Brigade now relieved the French troops that the Seaforth had been reinforcing. The French had agreed to eliminate the German bridgehead at Abbeville before handing over to 51st but had failed to do so thus making Fortune's situation much more difficult than expected. On 1 June the Division assumed its new positions along the south bank of the Somme with the Seaforth and Cameron Brigade on the right, 153 in the centre and 154 on the left.[51] Although a divisional reserve of the Lothians and a brigade composed of elements of 1st Armoured's Support Group was created this was quickly reduced when the Lothians had to relieve French troops on the extreme right of the divisional line, from Erondelle to Tourbières.[52]

Although de Gaulle's troops had been redeployed, plans were made for a renewal of the attack on the Abbeville bridgehead. The French 31st Division had arrived with armour and artillery support as well as infantry and it was planned to use this formation in an attack to push the Germans back before they could bring up sufficient reinforcements to allow them to renew their offensive. A fireplan involving some 250 guns and lasting over three hours was drawn up.[53] Due to language difficulties – no French officers spoke much English and few of their British counterparts had more than a smattering of schoolboy French – it was agreed that French artillery would support French troops and British artillery the Highlanders. At 3.00am on 4 June, the day on which the last British troops left Dunkirk and Churchill promised that Britain would fight 'on the beaches, … on the landing grounds, … in the fields, … and in the streets', the artillery opened its bombardment. Thirty minutes later, tanks and infantry, both Scots and French, advanced on their first objective, the six miles of ground 'overlooking the water-meadows from Caubert on the right to the Cambron woods on their left'.[54]

On the right, 4th Camerons were to attack Caubert and a wooded ridge dubbed the 'Hedgehog' while in the centre French tanks, supported by 4th Seaforth, advanced against the Mont de Caubert on which stood Caesar's Camp, a Roman fort, with the aim of clearing the ground between the two main roads to Abbeville. For 1st Gordons, advancing from Cahon on the left, the objective was the Cambron woods and the spur overlooking the village of Cambron.[55] As these attacks were going in, 154 Brigade was to prevent any German attempts to reinforce the bridgehead. However, in one of those twists of happenstance that seem to occur so often in war, the Germans had also planned an attack for this morning and their leading infantry had moved out on the Highlanders' right only minutes before the Allied artillery opened fire. Thus these troops were not caught in the bombardment and as B Company of 4th Camerons advanced towards the 'Hedgehog' they ran into German troops concealed in a field of rye. German machine guns caused many casualties amongst the Camerons and fierce fighting developed. From this bloody encounter only one officer of B Company survived: Second-Lieutenant Robertson led the forty survivors of the company into a wood north-west of Mereuil-Caubert to link up with A Company. Having re-organised what remained of his company, Robertson made his way back to battalion HQ to ask for more ammunition so that he might resume the attack on the 'Hedgehog'. He was refused permission to do so when he revealed the losses that B Company had suffered.[56]

D Company, advancing on the battalion left, also met German troops but fought their way through to reach their objective. However, only fifty men of the two right-hand platoons, under Second-Lieutenant David Ross, made it on to the objective while the other platoons had been raked by enemy machine-gun fire along the Route Nationale and from Mont de Caubert where Caesar's Camp remained in German hands. The centre attack, on Mont de Caubert, had been made by a battalion of French heavy tanks and a battalion of *Chasseurs portés*, motorised infantry, but the tanks had suffered heavily from an undetected minefield and from anti-tank guns that had not been spotted until they opened fire. Those few tanks that made it to the Mont were forced to retire, either to refuel or because the Germans drove them off. German artillery was dug in to the chalky ground of Caesar's Camp and only a long and concentrated bombardment would have knocked them out. Some *Chasseurs portés* advanced as far as Yonval, west of the Caubert ridge, but were forced to retire.[57]

The second wave of the attack saw 4th Seaforth advance, supported by a French light tank battalion, which approached Mont de Caubert from Bienfay but, once again, the tanks were knocked out by mines or anti-tank gunfire. The survivors showed great courage and determination, pressing on in spite of their losses.

> They saw their leaders hit and disabled, but without doubt or hesitation followed, steering their vehicles into the deadly fire of the German anti-tank guns, till they too were killed. Their tanks lay inert and useless, or burst into flame. They were all put out of action.[58]

The Seaforth continued without the armour and ran into intense machine-gun fire that cut the Highlanders down like corn. But the Scots could equal the French tank crews in courage and the survivors pressed on with their advance with some reaching the first objective, some 600 yards up the slope. Here Sergeant Donald MacLeod, the only survivor of his platoon, earned the DCM. With his platoon commander killed, MacLeod took command and led the remnants forward until, in the face of machine-gun fire, all but he had fallen. Although badly wounded, MacLeod went on alone to reach his objective. MacLeod ought to have been captured but he evaded the Germans for the next two days and nights and made his way through enemy lines to rejoin his battalion.[59]

B Company of 4th Seaforth was all but wiped out and its commander, Major Simon Fraser, who had foreseen his own death, was killed while leading the handful of survivors of his company towards the objective.[60] The battalion's CO, Lieutenant-Colonel Houldsworth was awarded the DSO to mark both his own leadership and the sacrifice made by his soldiers. Another Seaforth, Private James Morgan, received the DCM. Although wounded himself in both arms, and having spent the day lying in the open, Morgan carried in another soldier who had been wounded severely and did so under cover of darkness and over almost two miles.[61] By the end of the day the battalion had been reduced to about half its fighting strength.[62]

For 2nd Seaforth there was some success. The battalion captured one of the Bienfay woods and, on their left, C Company of 1st Gordons, moving up from Cahon, reached the edge of the Grand Bois west of Cambron by 9.00am in spite of heavy machine-gun fire from concealed German posts that reduced the company to forty men. Two platoons of the Gordons' D Company also made their objective and, by 11.00am, were in position for the next phase of the attack while the remnant of C Company held the northern end of the wood. The Gordons believed that the enemy had no great strength in the area, although his machine-gun posts were well sited, and were eager to continue but the overall situation demanded that they be withdrawn as even their current location was untenable;[63] French losses in armour and infantry were such that the attack could only be described as a failure.

Although 154 Brigade had been assigned the role of preventing enemy reinforcement, the CO of 8th Argylls, Lieutenant-Colonel Grant, thought that this might be achieved in an aggressive manner and suggested a local attack at St Valéry-sur-Somme. Permission was refused but Grant, undaunted, planned and staged a diversion. With Major Towers, commanding a battery of 17th Field Regiment at St Blimont, Grant arranged the bombardment of German machine-gun posts in the marshes near St Valéry and of the area at le Crotoy, across the Somme, where enemy forces were, apparently, concentrating. While this bombardment had no immediate effect on the battle it inflicted considerable casualties on the Germans.[64]

Losses in 152 Brigade had been severe with twenty officers and 543 soldiers killed, wounded or missing.[65] Among the latter was Second-Lieutenant David Ross, he who had led the survivors of D Company 4th Camerons on to their objective, but, on 6 June Ross arrived at Martainville with a fellow officer and sixty Camerons whom 'he had led through ten or a dozen miles of country infested by the enemy's mobile forces'.[66] As with Sergeant MacLeod and Private Morgan, he had shown a determination not to be beaten in spite of all that the enemy had thrown at him.

With the Allied assault beaten off it could only be a short time before a fresh German attack was launched. Now reinforced, the enemy attacked at daybreak on 5 June, making the strongest effort against 154 Brigade's thin eight-mile front from Quesnoy to le Hourdel and the coast. The brigade's predicament was made worse by having no reserve, 1st Black Watch being detached to 153 Brigade. Enemy forces fell heavily on the brigade's two battalions of Argyll and Sutherland Highlanders. Seventh Argylls held Saigneville, Mons and Catigny and faced motorised infantry, with mobile machine guns and some armoured vehicles. B Company, supported by a machine-gun section of Northumberland Fusiliers, drove off an attack on Saigneville and called down artillery fire on Germans forming up in a nearby ravine. Although their telephone line to battalion HQ was cut at 8.00am, 'they had sufficient peace and appetite to eat a quiet breakfast half an hour later'.[67] At Mons, C Company was surrounded by an estimated 1,000 enemy infantry while D Company, at Catigny, repelled an attack by light tanks before withdrawing to Blimont, which was held by an 8th Argylls company. Second-Lieutenant Green of C Company, who had only joined the battalion, was left at Mons with his platoon to hold the Arrest crossroads. He was not heard from again and touch was lost with both advanced companies while battalion HQ at Franleu was also surrounded. It was proving a grim day for the Argylls.[68]

As the German advance continued it swept around the beleaguered Argylls and as the enemy by-passed the forward companies of 7th Argylls their neighbours to the right, 1st Gordons, were left holding a salient between Saigneville and Gouy while German troops thrust past them towards Quesnoy where A Company was surrounded and a reinforcing company came under fire from mortars and small arms while crossing a ridge. However, after some fierce fighting, some control was regained in the Gordons' sector and the battalion was ordered to face left and occupy the high ground overlooking the Cahon-Hymmeville railway.[69]

To the right of 1st Gordons, 1st Black Watch held a two-and-a-half-mile front between Lambercourt and Toeuffles but the battalion positions were good with plenty of natural cover that, in many places, overlooked some 1,000 yards of open country. Their action was described by Private McCready.

> Cpl Spalding was killed in this position, which was the best the Battalion had, he was killed by a sniper who was spotted by one of the A/T Detachment. Cpl Spalding was soon avenged. We held these positions for two days, and hand-to-hand fighting took place in D Company area. The enemy had to cross a river and advance up hill over open ground, they evidently had no idea of our position. C Co[mpan]y held their fire until they were 200 yards away, then let them have it. I was reinforcing one of the A/T guns at that time, as Martin was badly shell-shocked and another A/T man was killed. D Co[mpan]y fire was terrific, the enemy had no chance at all. Nutting was badly wounded then in 5 different places, but he was very cheerful although he must have been suffering terribly. That same day Bn. HQ was shelled, the CO's batman was killed, and the RSM wounded in the hand …[70]

As well as the defiance of 1st Black Watch, French machine guns and artillery also wreaked considerable execution among the Germans. Nonetheless, the latter held the advantage in both numbers and firepower and the Black Watch company at Lambercourt was driven back. The battalion line swung back on Toeuffles and this new position was held until nightfall.

The Lothians, it will be recalled, were deployed as infantry with A Squadron on the right of the front, occupying high ground to the right of Mereuil-Caubert. They had taken advantage of the breakdown of a French tank by pressing the machine into service as a strongpoint, using its 2-pounder gun and machine gun. When C Squadron at Bray was hit by a German attack the carrier troop from A Squadron was sent to its aid and helped repel the attackers. Then it was A Squadron's turn to come under attack when German infantry made a sudden appearance in their sector.

Two German scouts rounded a corner to find themselves confronted by the French tank whereupon the leading scout raised his hands in surrender. His companion shot him in the back before he, too, was despatched by someone in A Squadron. Then came the main thrust of the attack with mortars and machine guns supporting the infantry. The tank's main gun proved very effective against the machine guns, putting many out of action. A Squadron held its position until noon when shells for the tank ran out. German artillery was becoming more accurate as their gunners registered the Lothians' positions and some outposts were evacuated. In the late afternoon orders to withdraw 'if possible' were received. The squadron leader, Major Dallmeyer, was able to extricate his command, although it was a very difficult task, and, following a hazardous march, rejoined the regiment before midnight with the twenty-five survivors of his squadron; he had lost forty men that day. Regimental HQ had been hit hard during the day, suffering attack by divebombers that prompted a move from the Bois de Bailleul to Doudelainville. C Squadron also returned to the regimental fold that evening.[71]

Now began the Division's rearguard action with orders being issued for a withdrawal to positions on a line from Limeux via Limercourt, Moyenneville, Valines and Escarbotin to Hautebot, which was to be held 'if possible' until thirty minutes before midnight of 5 June. At the same time, preparations were to be made for a defence on the line of the Bresle river. In the ensuing withdrawal A and B Companies of 8th Argylls could not be extricated from their positions and were left behind.

By 6.00pm HQ of 154 Brigade had been withdrawn to Dargnies and the brigade's artillery had been pulled back, save for two troops of 17th Field trapped at Ochancourt. As dusk fell the brigade's situation was that 8th Argylls were believed to be holding a line from Ault to Escarbotin through Tully, 7th Northumberland Fusiliers were holding between Escarbotin and Fressenville whence 4th Black Watch held the line to Feuquières. However, the overall situation was confused and contact had been lost with 153 Brigade on the right. It was known that forward German elements were already between Dargnies and the Bresle; some of the Bresle bridges had already been demolished.[72]

Meanwhile 152 Brigade had withdrawn to the line of the railway from Oisemont to the main Blangy-Abbeville road but had suffered heavy losses in the bridgehead battle, had fought a day-long rearguard action and the soldiers were now too tired to stop any determined assault. During the afternoon some 200 men of 4th Camerons had been attacked three times in succession by flights of three Ju87s. As the Camerons were retiring across open fields there was no cover and the men could only lie down and hope for the best. But there were no casualties, and the only recorded damage was a water bottle through which three bullets passed.[73] Lying down to avoid injury from the Stukas also allowed the Camerons to practise that adage of old soldiers: rest when you can; many men fell asleep even while the sirens of the bombers howled above them.

This story of exhausted men pulling back was repeated throughout the Division that day. The Aberdeen Gunners of 75th (Highland) Field Regiment engaged the enemy over open ground and survived several narrow escapes. Two guns of B Troop each fired over 850 shells and, by the end of the day, some Gunners were unconscious from exhaustion.[74]

Some of the most desperate fighting of the day took place around the village of Franleu where 7th Argylls came under attack soon after daybreak. Brigadier Stanley-Clarke, of 154 Brigade, despatched 4th Black Watch and ten French tanks from divisional reserve to the relief of the Argylls but even this reinforcement could make little impression on the advancing foe and, in spite of the efforts of the Black Watch and the French tankmen, it was impossible to reach Franleu.[75] However, the Argylls held on stubbornly, although their only heavy weapons were a single mortar and a machine-gun section of Northumberlands. These had done great damage and had assisted in driving back two determined attacks on the village. But heavy casualties had been caused by German fire and in the afternoon the machine-gun section was knocked out, followed, a little later, by the mortar. As the afternoon wore on German reinforcements, including three tanks and an estimated 400 infantry, arrived and the relentless pressure increased. At about 5.00pm the Argylls' last ammunition truck was hit by a mortar bomb and exploded, demolishing battalion HQ. With no reserve of ammunition and no hope of reinforcement, the Argylls' CO, Lieutenant-Colonel Buchanan, decided that his men should try to break out of Franleu to rejoin the Division.[76]

Although it was impossible to contact the outlying sections, the other Argylls were told to use what vehicles they could find and attempt to break through the German positions. Some, led by Buchanan himself, were able to reach the battalion transport parked at farm buildings some hundred yards away, and several trucks and two carriers raced for freedom. Many had to be left behind, including the badly wounded but three volunteers chose to stay with them, including the battalion chaplain, the Reverend Duncan McInnes, who had already done sterling service tending to wounded throughout the day; Padre McInnes had even braved enemy sniper fire to fetch water for the wounded in the aid post in the basement of the local school. By the end of the day 7th Argylls had ceased to exist as a fighting unit; some 523 personnel were dead, wounded or missing.[77]

Dawn on 6 June found the Highland Division holding an attenuated line from Oisemont to Friaucourt, through Vismes and Fressenville. But this was a line that could not be maintained and, already, German units had penetrated it in places, especially near Dargnies. Elements of the Division had already been withdrawn across the Bresle and the French 31st Division was leaving the area for east of the Somme. Although the Division had orders to delay the Germans on the present line for a limited period, it was to withdraw across the Bresle to take up a line from Blangy to the sea. But delaying the Germans along what was already a porous line was an impossible task.

> The pretence of holding, even for a day, an intermediate line between the Somme and the Bresle had to be abandoned. We had neither enough troops nor sufficient fire-power to meet the enemy's attack, the main stream of which was now flowing against our coastal flank. The Germans could no more be contained than water in a basket; our line, torn open on the left, was as full of holes as wattle, and there were no adequate reserves with which to close them. It had become perfectly clear that General Fortune could hope for nothing better than a rearguard action, by which he might punish and delay the German advance, maintain the cohesion of the Division, and keep touch with the French formations that were falling back on his right.[78]

Withdrawal from engagement with an advancing enemy is the most difficult of all manoeuvres and is much more difficult when those trying to withdraw are exhausted. So it was with the men of 51st (Highland) Division in those June days. There was no time to sleep, nor to recuperate or re-organise. Soldiers of 1st Black Watch, during a spell when they were 'remote from the enemy's ground forces' managed to sleep for a few hours in spite of being under attack by German aircraft.[79] Such was the state of exhaustion amongst the Highlanders.

The guns of 51st (Midland) Medium Regiment had been assigned to Saar Force and remained to support the Highland Division. On 6 June the regiment was positioned west of Blangy in the Haute Forêt d'Eu and was in action against the left of the German line when orders were received to engage Ponts-et-Marais. To do so, the guns of a troop of 215 Battery

> had to be manhandled and swung round 120 degrees. Maps were scarce. The troop had one only, which was very crumpled and showed no contours. But line and range were measured on it, the angle of sight was guessed, a hundred yards was added for the meteorological factor – or for luck – and the new line transferred to the gun from a director seventy-five yards away. ... An OP reported that the shelling was most effective.[80]

As the shells dropped on Ponts-et-Marais, the overall impression of the battle was one of confusion. Near Gamaches, 1st Gordons were preparing to cross the river but their CO was concerned that enemy troops might have broken though on his left and might cut his battalion off. He contacted 75th (Highland) Field Regiment, which was withdrawing owing to a shortage of ammunition, some of whose guns were retiring through Gamaches. These guns were then deployed to cover the Gordons as they crossed the river by bridge. Darkness was falling as 4th Black Watch crossed at Beauchamps, where they had endured heavy bombardment, to take up new positions near Incheville forest. However, the Germans had already penetrated to there and presented an immediate danger to the Black Watch.[81]

Following a day of intensive fighting along an eight-mile front, 154 Brigade could now muster less than half its fighting strength. Fortunately, some help was at hand in the form of A Brigade of Beauforce, which was deployed in support of 154 Brigade south of the Bresle river, facing the Forêt d'Incheville. As we have seen, Beauforce was an improvised formation, composed of units that had been serving on the BEF's lines of communication and A Brigade reflected that improvisation. Its constituent battalions were 4th Buffs, 4th Border Regiment and 5th Sherwood Foresters, all TA battalions which had never served together as a brigade and which were lacking in both training and equipment. Nonetheless, they would give a good account of themselves and their arrival was a blessed relief for the Highlanders.[82]

Fighting continued throughout the 6th and on the following morning the defences comprised five sectors. From Blangy to Monchaux, on the right, was 152 Brigade with 153 holding to Gamaches on their left. Left of 153 Brigade, holding to Beauchamps, was 154 Brigade and from Beauchamps to Eu was A Brigade while 6th Royal Scots Fusiliers held from Eu to the coast. However, it was hardly a solid line, which was demonstrated when the battered remnants of 152 Brigade were withdrawn into reserve in the Haute Forêt, their place in the line being taken by French troops. A Brigade had also taken over positions that ought to have been held by 154 Brigade in the area where enemy troops had already crossed the river from Beauchamps. The tactical priority was to eliminate the German pocket in the Incheville forest which was to be achieved by sealing the exits from the forest and then seeking out the enemy.

A Brigade was assigned this task and launched a counter-attack that was, at first, reported to have secured the line of the Bresle. But German troops remained in the forest and were proving difficult to winkle out. Fourth Borders advanced into the forest to push out the enemy and were led with considerable vigour and courage by their CO, Lieutenant-Colonel Tomlinson. With a company of Sherwood Foresters under his command, Tomlinson sought out the enemy over the next two days, ensuring that if the Germans could not be eliminated, neither could they filter to the south. Although the battalion was not fully trained, it was able to bottle up the enemy in a corner of the forest; this ensured that they provided no danger to the Division. When Tomlinson's battalion was told to withdraw one of his companies had been surrounded near the riverbank and could not be extricated. Undaunted, these men, mostly part-time soldiers only months before, continued to give battle and, although there was no possibility of relief, went on doing so for five days.

The Luftwaffe continued to be a menace with divebombing attacks and strafing by fighters. There was little in the way of air defence. Those few RAF fighters operating from airfields in Normandy – they flew in from England each morning and returned each evening – were heavily engaged in supporting the French, who were in even more dire circumstances than the Highlanders and thus the latter saw but little of British fighters. German artillery was also very active and although the Division's own Gunners, the field regiments and 51st Medium, continued harassing German columns and positions, they could not stop the enemy's inexorable advance. Although a further reinforcement, of 900 men, arrived from Rouen on the morning of the 7th, there was further bad news later that day: the French line had been broken at Amiens and German armoured columns were advancing on Rouen. IX Corps was being split from Tenth Army by this advance and 51st (Highland) Division was about to be cut off from its supply base at Rouen.

Before the panzers reached Rouen a train was loaded with shells and anti-tank mines for the Highland Division and set off for a temporary ammunition dump at Foucart. However, it never arrived and it seems that it must have been intercepted and captured by German forces en route. The alternative supply centre could only provide fuel and ammunition for rifles and machine guns and thus the loss of the train from Rouen worsened the predicament faced by the Highlanders.

The morning of 8 June brought a little good news with the return of the two companies of 8th Argylls who had earlier been cut off and, it had been assumed, captured. Prominent in the return of A and B Companies was Major Lorne Campbell – who would later earn the Victoria Cross in North Africa – who went forward from Brutelles on the afternoon of the 5th. Campbell's company was forced to go to ground by German armour but he was able to lead his men to Woignarue which he considered attacking before deciding that he could be more usefully employed occupying the villages of Ault and Friaucourt, which would allow him to prevent any further enemy penetration to the south. However, this plan was thwarted when it was learned that the Germans had already passed through Friaucourt, thereby cutting off Campbell and his men. Even so, Campbell opted to occupy an area around the lighthouse at Ault which commanded the nearby countryside. When he reached there he found some French marines with a 75mm gun and a platoon of 6th Royal Scots Fusiliers already in occupation. The 75mm proved defective, breaking down at the first attempt to use it but Campbell set about establishing a defence at Ault in anticipation of an Allied counter-attack which, he believed, his small force would be able to assist.

When it became clear that there would be no counter-attack, Campbell and his two company commanders agreed to try to make their way back to their own lines and moved out shortly before midnight. They were without the French marines who had surrendered to an attacking German force with tanks. Marching on a compass bearing, and having to make several diversions to avoid enemy troop concentrations, the Argylls made steady progress in spite of some engagements with the enemy and, as noted, rejoined their brigade on the morning of the 8th. Lorne Campbell was later awarded the DSO.

By now two German divisions, 5th and 7th Panzer, the latter commanded by Major-General Erwin Rommel, were at Buchy, fifteen miles north-east of Rouen and, with German tanks some thirty miles behind it, the Bresle line became redundant. For IX Corps and 51st (Highland) Division, the only feasible retirement route now lay west of Rouen over the Seine. The French command issued orders for redeployment along the line of the Béthune, for which the Highland Division would need to use all its transport to carry out a double lift since there were only sufficient vehicles to carry half the personnel. Fortunately the forward infantry were able to withdraw from their positions under cover of darkness – the Germans had demonstrated a general reluctance for night operations – and the move to the new positions was almost complete by daylight, although there was much work to be done in preparing defensive locations. Once again the Germans co-operated, this time by not immediately following up the withdrawal. The sole element of the Division in contact with the enemy during the 9th was The Lothians and Border Yeomanry who were covering the left flank of the withdrawal.

With so much of the BEF now back in Britain – although other elements remained in France and there were plans in London for further troops to land in Brittany – many must have wondered when they might be evacuated from France. At Divisional HQ some might even have felt that that moment was approaching when Royal Navy officers arrived at the Château de la Chaussée to discuss the possibility of evacuation from le Havre. Plans had already been made for this at Portsmouth and it was estimated that some 23,000 men would need to be lifted; a flotilla of transports escorted by nine destroyers was assembling off le Havre that night to execute the operation. If the Germans exploited their penetration towards Rouen it was believed that they might move westward along the Seine's north bank to cut off the retreat of IX Corps and trap that formation against the Channel coast. Further German advances also raised the possibility that evacuation might be possible only through Dieppe. However, it was believed, wrongly, that the entrance to that port had been blocked. That left a small fishing harbour twenty miles west of Dieppe as a possible evacuation port should le Havre become unusable. The fishing harbour was St Valéry-en-Caux; but this had a difficult entrance, overlooked on both sides by high ground. The Royal Navy's view, therefore, was that le Havre was the only practicable port through which to evacuate.

As a result of this decision, Brigadier Stanley-Clarke of 154 Brigade was ordered to take an ad-hoc force to defend le Havre. Stanley-Clarke's formation included HQ 154 Brigade with the remnants of his Argyll battalions, 4th Black Watch, 6th Royal Scots Fusiliers, A Brigade of Beauman Division and appropriate Gunner, Sapper and other specialist and support troops. Normally this might have been dubbed Clarkeforce but instead it was christened Ark Force. The explanation for this title is that the force was created in the village of Arques-la-Bataille and thus an Anglicised corruption of the village name was adopted. Others believe that, while this played a part, the title 'Ark' was a reference to Noah's ark and that this force had two of everything, as had Noah.

General Fortune made a personal appeal to Prime Minister Winston Churchill for 'all the air support that England could spare' and informed his senior officers of the dangers they faced. Although the Royal Navy stood ready to lift the Division and its Allies from le Havre there was no guarantee that this could be accomplished; the Germans might prevent the Division even reaching le Havre, if they made a swift strike north to interpose a strong armoured force between the Highlanders and the port. From General Weygand came the cryptic message 'Nous sommes au dernier quart d'heure. Tenez bon'.

Stanley-Clarke was ordered to deploy Ark Force on a line stretching from Fécamp to Lillebonne from which he could cover the withdrawal of IX Corps, including the Highland Division, to le Havre. General Altmayer, commanding IX Corps, estimated that the withdrawal would take three nights, as it was not advisable to move by day, and would not commence until 13 June. This seemed a very slow withdrawal but, although Fortune urged a faster move, the French forces were unable to move faster than marching pace since most of their troops were infantry and much of their transport was horse-drawn. While 51st (Highland) Division had transport sufficient to move all its own men and Fortune could, therefore, ensure the safety of his command by a rapid move to le Havre, this was out of the question for a professional soldier since it would endanger greatly the left flank of his French allies.

Ark Force moved to its new positions on the night of 9 June in conditions that almost defied belief. The darkness was intensified by burning oil refineries at le Havre and along the Seine, the black, greasy smoke from the blazing tanks making the drivers' tasks all the more difficult; and they had also to cope with crowds of refugees straggling along the roads as well as French artillery batteries that were on the move. Not surprisingly, therefore, several units of Ark Force had not reached Fécamp by 10.00am on the 10th. By then, French intelligence reports suggested that the Germans were already nearby. A little after midday an officer arrived at Ark Force HQ with the news that the Highland Division now appeared to be cut off from le Havre and that General Fortune instructed that Brigadier Stanley-Clarke should use his own initiative in selecting a defensive line. It seemed that circumstances had made Ark Force redundant in its intended role.

Time had not permitted adequate reconnaissance of the proposed Fécamp-Lillebonne line but a shorter line from Octeville to Montivilliers had been reconnoitred by the garrison of le Havre and it was now decided that the units of 154 Brigade, with 75th (Highland) Field Regiment and a machine-gun company, should hold this shorter line while A Brigade, supported by 17th Field Regiment and a second machine-gun company, should deploy from Lillebonne to Goderville, using some French fixed positions between Fécamp and Lillebonne. The inner line was occupied without incident but the outer line was a different story with the Buffs finding German troops at Fécamp and suffering heavily in the ensuing engagement while 17th Field Regiment deployed between Lillebonne and Bréauté without infantry support; the regiment deployed its guns in an anti-tank role, covering approaches from the east.

As Ark Force was deploying into its positions the rest of the Highland Division was in action. Early in the morning of 10 June, the day on which Italy declared war on France and Britain, 1st Black Watch occupied a position along the Varenne with their left flank at Martigny. The soldiers were exhausted and even slept on their feet as they marched. They had been fighting or marching since 30 May with no opportunity for rest. Indeed, there had been little opportunity for any rest since the German offensive had been launched a month before. Nor were they to have any chance to rest in this new position for the Germans were soon attacking, with the first wave of infantry advancing behind a crowd of refugees. This was but the first of many assaults, accompanied by shelling and mortaring. Although an artillery battery was on call, the Gunners were running low on ammunition but their forward OP was useful as a means of communication since the forward companies were otherwise cut off from battalion HQ. A determined German attack at about 5.00pm brought a report of a breakthrough on the left but the Black Watch, with orders to hold the line until 9.00pm, held on defiantly. Then came fresh orders to hold on until 10 o'clock. Once again the Black Watch did so, to receive yet more orders to hold on until 11 o'clock. With this final order, and it was the final order to hold the line, came instructions to dump everything but the clothes they wore and their weapons, to allow more room for personnel in the vehicles that would carry them. The battalion held on as ordered and then broke contact with the enemy, marched several miles to find their transport, boarded the vehicles and were driven to Ouville.

But still there could be no rest. First Black Watch was deployed to hold the line of the railway through St Pierre-le-Viger. They had demonstrated the quality of their training as regular soldiers in their defence along the Varenne and they were ready to do so again. But time was running out, both for the battalion and for the Highland Division.

In the early morning of 10 June news that German tanks were approaching Dieppe reached HQ of 51st (Highland) Division. One hour later, at 6.30am, came news that tanks were only six miles away from the HQ at la Chaussée while yet more tanks had been seen west of the Durdent river, thereby eliminating any hope of using le Havre for embarkation. Fortune called his brigade commanders to a conference: if the Division were to be evacuated the sole choice was now St Valéry-en-Caux, which was scarcely the most suitable port but the Royal Navy was prepared to do its level best to evacuate the Allied forces through it; but it was now imperative that those forces should move quickly to St Valéry and there draw a defensive perimeter around the town. Plans were made for the perimeter and dispositions of units.

The Royal Navy was already investigating St Valéry and its reconnaissance of the coast brought unpleasant news. German guns were now deployed on the cliffs and HM Ships *Ambuscade* and *Boadicea* were both hit by shellfire, the former while reconnoitring off St Valéry and the latter four miles to the west as she was taking off a group of soldiers. Although ships were off St Valéry on the night of the 10th and their boats entered the harbour they found no waiting soldiers, although a rescue tug, *Stalwart*, did embark wounded men. On the 11th, HMCS *Restigouche* took off some soldiers from Veules, about four miles along the coast to the east. But French consent had yet to be given for an evacuation; this was not received until 5.00pm on the 11th.

For the perimeter around St Valéry the three battalions at the rear of the Béthune line – 2nd Seaforth, 1st Gordons and 4th Gordons – were now ordered to form the western edge of a box along the Durdent while the forward battalions on the Béthune would withdraw to a line running southward to the area of Fontaine-le-Don from Veules-les-Roses. The left flank at Veules would be formed by a battalion of The Duke of Wellington's Regiment, from Beauman Division, with 4th Seaforth and 5th Gordons south of them and 1st Black Watch on the right. These deployments would form three sides of the box and French troops would complete the final side. While the French were en route, the Lothians would reconnoitre the gap while the Norfolks would be ready to move out of divisional reserve to cover it if necessary. Once again the Lothians were proving their worth and Colonel Ansell seemed to appear anywhere he was needed.

The move was made at night, and despite all efforts by the hard-working Divisional Provost Company to control traffic, the road from Ouville was, in some places, as crowded as the road to Epsom on Derby Day. The French were in retreat, many in total disorder. Not all, indeed, had cast away discipline with hope – before the day was done the Black Watch were to see Frenchmen of a different mettle – but great numbers were in open flight. By good fortune, however, neither Luftwaffe or German tanks were active in the early hours of the 11th, and by nine o'clock, or earlier, the sides of the box about St Valéry were occupied, and the Highland battalions had begun to dig themselves in.[83]

With no opportunity for full reconnaissance, the perimeter around St Valéry could not be a complete defensive line but was established as a series of defended localities. Once again the Germans were using one of their favourite tactics, a left hook; this time it was a short hook north-wards to Dieppe and then to Fécamp, from where it moved east towards St Valéry. The Lothians, ordered to reconnoitre the Durdent river rather than their original objective, found German troops at Cany bridge and in Veulettes; bridges between Cany and Veulettes had been destroyed. An attack at Cany by the Lothians pushed the Germans back for the loss of two tanks and a reconnaissance to Bosville, to the south-east, established that the latter village was still in French hands. However, the situation at Veulettes was markedly different; although a reinforced C Squadron was ordered to hold the Germans there 'at all costs' the Squadron was forced to withdraw towards St Valéry that evening while the other squadrons fell back on Cailleville.

The Germans had made their mark elsewhere on the perimeter with both 4th Seaforth and 5th Gordons taking casualties in stiff fighting. At St Pierre-le-Viger, 1st Black Watch were told to reconnoitre a line from Gueutteville to Cailleville to which they would withdraw during the afternoon and be ready to embark that night. However, the forward companies of the Black Watch at St Pierre-le-Viger were under constant and increasing pressure which, by 6.00pm, had left some fifty men dead or wounded. When the CO went back to brigade HQ he was unable to return to his battalion HQ because of machine-gun fire but did find his way to his other companies. These were attacked by infantry and tanks that were fought off in the early evening but the attack was renewed at dawn and the Black Watch companies were overrun.

The forward Black Watch companies were reinforced by a French cavalry squadron, all regular soldiers who were determined to fight on. Even when their commandant was wounded mortally the troopers continued to obey his orders: to hold the line until darkness fell. Along the eastern perimeter the pressure was intense: Stukas wailed down to bomb the defenders while tanks probed forward with infantry supporting them and when the tanks drew back mortar bombs and shells continued to fall in the defenders' lines. And communication was becoming increasingly difficult: despatch riders were falling victim to ambushes by German machine gunners. But while the eastern perimeter continued to hold the same could not be said for the western approach, which had already been penetrated. The three battalions assigned to the Durdent line had not been able to reach the river in time and were trying to hold an alternative line that ran south from le Tot. In two woods that straddled the road through le Tot were the men of 2nd Seaforth while a company of Norfolks filled the gap between the Seaforth and the Camerons. But the Seaforth were without anti-tank weapons, save for Boys anti-tank rifles, as their anti-tank platoon had been left with the Duke of Wellington's, who were on the other side of St Valéry. Thus when German tanks appeared from the direction of Veulettes there was little that 2nd Seaforth could do to stop them.

Although the Highlanders were able to cripple some tanks, and artillery behind them knocked out more, the panzers crashed their way through the line and made for their objective, the high ground sheltering the harbour at St Valéry from the Channel. This had been held by French troops who succumbed to the German advance. Before long there was also fighting in the south-western outskirts of the town, which had already suffered considerable damage from shelling and bombing. There were few troops in St Valéry itself. These included Divisional HQ, 51st Anti-Tank Regiment, most of 7th Norfolks, a company of 1st Kensingtons and some RASC personnel; the Norfolks, Kensingtons and anti-tank gunners were to hold a line around the outskirts of the town and cover the final withdrawal of the units in the perimeter.

With German troops and armour now in the outskirts of St Valéry the prospects of an evacuation through the harbour were looking less and less likely. When Major Rennie, the GSO II at Divisional HQ, and a Royal Navy officer began a reconnaissance of the beaches they were fired on by German machine gunners from the west hill; they were similarly harassed in the town. Nor was there any signal from the relieving ships, which the naval officer had been expecting.

Meanwhile 1st Black Watch had sent their wounded back to the town, in an office truck and a carrier, while the diminished companies held on until almost 10 o'clock when, with their French comrades, they pulled back to Gueutteville where they found no one with any information on 153 Brigade. Other units were also falling back, although the orders to withdraw into the town, having first destroyed all except personal arms and ammunition, never reached 2nd Seaforth, who continued to hold out.

But the Royal Navy had had its own problems. Ships had entered St Valéry harbour on the night of 10 June but left next morning to take up station off the coast, where they received unwelcome attention from the Luftwaffe and from German guns on the coast which led to a move farther off the coast. When the evacuation of le Havre began on the 11th, the Admiralty also issued orders for the evacuation of St Valéry, but it was now too late. Fog had descended, obscuring the view of the coast and delaying the ships' return and when vessels finally closed the beach, at about 12.30pm on the 12th, it was to find German troops ensconced firmly on the cliffs and in the town. Four boats carrying landing parties were sunk. An alternative plan had to be made but it was now too late to save most of the Highland Division. Some troops were evacuated from the beaches at Veules but the sloop *Hebe II* was sunk and her captain lost.

A new and smaller perimeter was established in St Valéry as it became clear that there would be no evacuation that night. During the night the Germans approached 2nd Seaforth in the woods at le Tot and claimed that there had been a general surrender of the Highland Division and French troops and requested the Seaforth to comply. The battalion's officers, uncertain whether to believe this, asked for time to reflect on the demand and then called for volunteers among the wounded to go over to the Germans. When these men, both walking wounded and stretcher-borne, arrived in their lines, the Germans believed that the Seaforth had surrendered. In fact, the survivors lay hidden in the woods until darkness the next night and then split into small parties to try to make their way through the German lines. Few, however, succeeded.

Another surrender demand to 1st Gordons had been rejected flatly as the battalion continued fighting. The other regular battalion of the Division, 1st Black Watch, had resumed the march into St Valéry where the survivors, about 140 men, deployed on high ground close to a cemetery about a mile and a half north-east of the town. This was the ground that Fortune had chosen for his last stand and the Black Watch were able to retrieve Brens, anti-tank rifles, food and ammunition from deserted trucks. Before long they were again in action, with mortar bombs falling from front and rear and tanks approaching on the left flank. Likewise, on the eastern outskirts, Seaforth, Gordons and Camerons

> with discipline and native resolution to combat mortal weariness, had ... organised their last resistance. But confusion by now was more typical of the scene than order, and discipline prevailed as islands in a fearful chaos. ... during the night of the 11th a French artillery regiment told the Kensingtons that the war was over, and at eight o'clock on the morning of the 12th our Allies capitulated.[84]

Victor Fortune was now faced with the worst decision of his military career: to fight on to the last man or to surrender his Division to the Germans. There was no doubt that the Division, if ordered, would fight to the very end in the streets and houses of St Valéry, would take all that the Germans could throw at them, as the Black Watch were doing at the cemetery, and would do so not to hold St Valéry but for the reputation of their Division and the pride of Scotland. Against that, Fortune had to weigh the prevailing situation. His Gunners had no shells left; their guns had been abandoned after the breech blocks had been removed; his Sappers had no stores left and were fighting as infantry; food and small-arms ammunition were limited. To ask his men to fight on would be to ask them to commit suicide. The only alternative was surrender. And that was the choice that General Fortune made. At 10.00am, Major Thomas Rennie went to the cemetery to order the survivors of the Black Watch to cease fire and surrender. Men stood and wept, hardly believing the order they had received. Some time later,

> the last fragment of the Gordons, unarmed, were allowed to march
> past their General. Marching in the rain, they gave him Eyes Right!
> And the Fifty-First Division went into eclipse.[85]

The official surrender of the Highland Division was made to Major General Erwin Rommel of 7th Panzer Division by General Fortune. Rommel later recorded his pleasure at taking the surrender of this particular British division.[86]

But not all of the Division was captured. Major J Y Dallmeyer of the Lothians led a party of soldiers to Veules where they were rescued by the Royal Navy whose ships also lifted over 2,300 British and French troops along the coast.[87] The largest element to get away, however, was Ark Force, which had been intended to hold the perimeter at le Havre while the Division was evacuated through that port. In the changed circumstances, much of Ark Force was able to get away from le Havre. A Brigade embarked under cover of darkness and rain during the night of 11–12 June. On the 12th most of 154 Brigade made it into le Havre and were embarked in the early hours of 13 June to sail to Cherbourg whence they made the final voyage to England. One subaltern of 17th Field Regiment even managed to have seventeen of his regiment's 25-pounder guns embarked and taken to safety.[88]

Others were later to join those who had been evacuated. As the men of 51st (Highland) Division began their long march to prisoner-of-war camps, many escaped from the column of march and made their way home to Britain. Among the latter, Major Thomas Rennie, who had been Fortune's GSO II, was one of two officers who slipped away from a column of prisoners near Lille just over a week later. After a series of adventures the two men – the second was Major Ronnie Mackintosh-Walker MC, commanding 4th Camerons – reached Spain, crossed the border to

Portugal and flew home from Lisbon.[89] Neither would survive the war, being killed in action: Rennie died as GOC of 51st (Highland) Division at the Rhine crossing in March 1945.

Notes

1. NA Kew, WO167/315 HQ 51 (H) Div (GS), 1940
2. Ibid
3. NA Kew, WO167/711, war diary, 4 BW, 1940
4. Ibid
5. NA Kew, WO167/455, war diary, 1 L&B Yeo, 1940, account by 2/Lt Chambers
6. Ibid; David, *Churchill's Sacrifice of the Highland Division*, pp. 24–5
7. Ibid, p. 25
8. Quoted in Linklater, *The Highland Division*, p. 18
9. NA Kew, WO167/819, war diary, 2 Seaforth, 1940
10. NA Kew, WO167/315 HQ 51 (H) Div (GS), 1940
11. NA Kew, WO167/710, war diary, 1 BW, 1940; WO167/455, war diary, 1 L&B Yeo, 1940
12. David, op cit, p. 26–30; NA Kew, WO167/710, war diary, 1 BW, 1940; WO167/455, war diary, 1 L&B Yeo, 1940
13. NA Kew, WO167/710, war diary, 1 BW, 1940; WO167/455, war diary, 1 L&B Yeo, 1940, account by Lt J R Johnston
14. NA Kew, WO167/711, war diary, 4 BW, 1940
15. Ibid
16. Ibid; David, op cit, p. 32
17. NA Kew, WO167/711, war diary, 4 BW, 1940
18. Ibid
19. NA Kew, WO167/720, war diary, 4 Camerons, 1940; WO167/813, war diary, 4 Seaforth, 1940
20. Quoted in Linklater, p. 18
21. NA Kew, WO167/746, war diary, 5 Gordons, 1940; David, op cit, p. 38
22. NA Kew, WO167/704, war diary, 7 A&SH, 1940
23. NA Kew, WO167/746, war diary, 5 Gordons, 1940
24. Ellis, *The War in France and Flanders*, pp. 35–6
25. Ibid, p. 44; Hook, *World War II Day by Day*, p. 27. Ellis quantifies the total German strength as eighty-nine divisions, ten of which were armoured, in three army groups, and two Luftflotten. Hook quotes figures of 200,000 troops and 3,000 aircraft; his figure for troops represents the front-line strength of an army group.
26. Hook, op cit, p. 27; Shepperd, *France 1940*, pp. 34–6
27. Hook, op cit, p. 27
28. Ellis, op cit, p. 51
29. Ibid, pp. 43–4
30. Ibid, p. 44
31. Hook, op cit, p. 28
32. Ibid, p. 29
33. Trevor-Roper, *Hitler's War Directives*, p. 67

34. Hook, op cit, p. 29
35. Linklater, p. 21
36. Quoted in Linklater, pp. 21–2
37. NA Kew, WO167/315, HQ 51 (H) Div (GS), 1940
38. David, op cit, p. 47
39. Linklater, op cit, p. 23
40. Young, *The Highland Division Transport and Supply Column*
41. Ellis, op cit, pp. 131–2; Fraser, *And We Shall Shock Them*, p. 66. Fraser comments: 'By this decision Gort saved the BEF.'
42. NA Kew, WO167/315, war diary, HQ 51 (H) Div (GS), 1940. The 152 Bde war diary for May 1940 has not survived.
43. David, op cit, p. 62
44. Joslen, *Orders of Battle*, pp. 148 & 151
45. Ibid, p. 14
46. Ibid, pp. 148 & 151
47. Ibid
48. David, op cit, p. 56
49. NA Kew, WO167/1412, war diary, HQ Beauman Div, 1940; David, op cit, pp. 56–8
50. NA Kew, WO167/710, war diary, 1 BW, 1940
51. NA Kew, WO167/819, war diary, 2 Seaforth, 1940; David, op cit, p. 62
52. NA Kew, WO167/315, war diary, HQ 51 (H) Div (GS), 1940; WO167409, war diary, 154 Bde, 1940. The 153 Bde war diary for May 1940 has not survived.
53. David, op cit, p. 62; WO167/455, war diary, 1 L&B Yeo, 1940
54. David, op cit, pp. 61–2; Salmond, op cit, pp. 10–12; NA Kew, WO167/315, war diary, HQ 51 (H) Div (GS), 1940
55. Linklater, op cit, p. 33; David, op cit, pp. 68–70
56. Linklater, op cit. David, op cit, pp. 86–9. No war diary for 1 Gordons has survived for June 1940.
57. David, op cit, pp. 77–84
58. Ibid
59. Linklater, p. 35
60. David, op cit, pp. 76–7
61. Ibid, pp. 70–1
62. Ibid, p. 76
63. Ibid, pp. 76–7
64. Ibid, p. 84
65. Ibid, pp. 86–9
66. Ellis, op cit, p. 267
67. David, op cit, p. 84
68. Linklater, p. 37
69. Ibid, p. 38
70. David, op cit, p. 99
71. Ibid, p. 101
72. Quoted in Linklater, pp. 39–42
73. David, op cit, pp. 133–6
74. Ibid, p. 136
75. Linklater, op cit, p. 43

76. Ibid; WO167/495, war diary, 75 (H) Fd Regt, 1940
77. Ellis, op cit, p. 271; David, op cit, pp. 103–9
78. David, op cit, pp. 103–9
79. Ibid
80. Linklater, op cit, p. 53
81. Ibid
82. Ibid, p. 55
83. David, p.127; Salmond, *The History of the 51st Highland Division*, p. 12 Much of the subsequent material relating to the withdrawal to St Valéry is drawn from Linklater (pp. 54–75), and from David, who describes the retreat in excellent detail. Other material is extracted from several war diaries, although not all diaries for the period have survived.
84. Linklater, pp. 86–7
85. Ibid, p. 89
86. *The Rommel Papers*, p. 65
87. Ellis, op cit, p. 293
88. Ibid; David, op cit, p. 242
89. David, op cit, p. 244

CHAPTER IV

The Division Reborn

Eric Linklater wrote of the tragedy of St Valéry that

> To Scotland the news came like another Flodden. Scotland is a small
> country, and in its northern half there was hardly a household that
> had not at least a cousin in one of the Highland regiments. The disas-
> ter, for a little while, seemed overwhelming, because, to begin with,
> nothing was known of the Division except the apparent shame of its
> surrender, and the undeniable capture of nearly six thousand men.[1]

In the wake of the disaster at St Valéry it seemed as if the proud title of
51st (Highland) Division might be lost to the Army and to Scotland for
the remainder of the war. However, such was the reputation gained by the
Division in the Great War and its importance to Scotland that it was decided
to form a new Highland Division. And it was then that the doubling of the
TA just over a year earlier proved a godsend. It will be remembered that a
duplicate of 51st had been formed in the shape of 9th (Highland) Division.
The latter was commanded by Major-General Alan Cunningham, himself
a Scot, who had become GOC on 26 June and, although 9th Division had
a fine reputation from the Great War, Cunningham believed that 51st was
more important to the people of Scotland and had no hesitation in offering
his command to become the reborn 51st (Highland) Division.[2]

On 7 August 1940 the brigades of 9th (Highland) Division – 26, 27
and 28 Brigades – became 152, 153 and 154 Brigades (In the case of 154
Brigade, elements of which had escaped from France, the brigade was
used to consolidate the remaining units of 51st (Highland) Division and
it was officially returned to full strength by the absorption of 28 Brigade.)
while the division itself became 51st (Highland) Division.[3] As before,
152 Brigade was the Seaforth and Cameron Brigade, but now including
4th/5th Seaforth, 7th Seaforth and 5th Camerons. Less than a month
later the regular 2nd Seaforth, now re-formed, replaced the regiment's
7th Battalion in the brigade while, in April 1941, the combined 4th/5th

Seaforth would be amalgamated as the 5th Battalion. Battalions of Black Watch and Gordons had constituted both the original 153 Brigade and 27 Brigade and, therefore, the new 153 Brigade had a similar order of battle with 5th Black Watch, 1st Gordons and 5th/7th Gordons, the latter joining in October 1940 to replace 9th Gordons. The reconstituted 154 Brigade included Black Watch, Seaforth and Argyll battalions at first but the order of battle was later adjusted to include 1st and 7th Black Watch and 7th Argylls; this was the line up of the brigade that would fight from El Alamein to Germany.[4]

In September 1940 the Seaforth and Cameron Brigade welcomed a new commander: Brigadier Douglas Neil Wimberley.[5] A Cameron Highlander – he had been commissioned into that regiment in 1915 – Douglas Wimberley was a Highlander to the core. Born in Inverness, he had served in 51st (Highland) Division in the Great War, earning the MC and becoming a major at the age of 21, a double majority. His grandfather had served with the 79th Highlanders during the Indian Mutiny. Wimberley had commanded 1st Camerons in the BEF and when the battalion was being re-formed after Dunkirk did his utmost, to the frustration of many in the War Office, to retain the Highland identity of the Camerons, refusing to accept drafts that included soldiers from other parts of the United Kingdom. To his soldiers, Wimberley was 'Tartan Tam' on account of his enthusiasm for all things Scottish.[6]

When Douglas Wimberley took over command of 152 Brigade the Division was still commanded by Alan Cunningham. The latter moved on in October 1940 and, for two weeks, 51st (Highland) Division was commanded by Brigadier A C L Stanley-Clarke, who had commanded 154 Brigade and Ark Force in France, who held the reins until the arrival of a new GOC: Major-General Neil Ritchie, a Black Watch officer, who was an enthusiastic proponent of the ethos of the Highland Division.[7] Ritchie, however, had never commanded anything larger than a battalion; commissioned into the Black Watch in 1914 he had a distinguished record with the regiment, being wounded at Loos in 1915 and earning the DSO in 1917 and the MC the following year. Both awards were earned in the Middle East where Ritchie spent much of the war. He had also served two generals – Brooke and Wavell – as a staff officer, in which capacity he was considered 'able and cool-headed';[8] he would later serve a third: Auchinleck. Ritchie was not to take the Division to war, however, as he was posted to the Middle East in June 1941 to another staff appointment. Brigadier C B Wainwright acted as caretaker GOC for a week until the new divisional commander arrived. This was Wimberley, who assumed command on 11 June 1941.[9]

'Tartan Tam' had left 152 Brigade on promotion to major-general in May 1941 when he became GOC of 46th Division.[10] When Ritchie was appointed to his new Middle East staff post he lobbied, successfully, to have Wimberley succeed him as GOC of the Highland Division. The latter was recalled from 46th Division to his spiritual home with the Jocks of 51st and would lead them for over two years, finally relinquishing command in August 1943, following two highly successful campaigns.

In the months after Dunkirk the Army's main priority was defending the United Kingdom against invasion and those formations rescued from France were now deployed, largely, on coastal defence tasks. Equipment was still scarce and the priority for what was available went to those most likely to face an invader. That did not include the Highlanders, who were stretched thinly along the north-east coast of their native Scotland but, gradually, matters improved and new equipment began arriving.[11] It was also difficult for a formation so thinly spread to carry out training at brigade and divisional levels, although efforts were made to do so, and there was, naturally, the question of morale. Soldiers whose lives seemed to be devoted to watching the grey waters of the North Sea, suffering the cold winds from that sea and wondering what the future held for them were almost certain to have problems with morale. Much of their time was spent in ensuring that their weapons were fit for use, that their positions were protected as well as possible and in learning how to combat seaborne or airborne invaders. Commanders at all levels did their best to ensure that morale was maintained and their efforts included reconstituting the Divisional Concert Party, the 'Balmorals', which had a tradition going back to 1915. The original 'Balmorals' of this war had been captured at St Valéry and so Major-General Neil Ritchie decided that the concert party should be reborn.[12] The first rehearsal took place in the town hall in Dufftown in October 1940 and the following month the 'Balmorals' gave their first performance to an appreciative audience in His Majesty's Theatre in Aberdeen.[13]

When Wimberley became GOC, he continued to encourage the 'Balmorals' whom he saw as a unifying force within the Division. In June 1941 he told the NCO in charge of the party, Sergeant Barker of the Gordons, a drama critic in civilian life, that there was not really a Highland Division,

> just a series of battalions – the Black Watch, the Seaforth, the Argylls, the Camerons and all the rest. You can be a unifying force. Travelling as you do from one to the other it is up to you to convey the general tone and spirit of the Division as a whole. I want to build up an esprit de corps – the tradition of the old Highland Brigade. I want you to help me get over the idea.[14]

With Divisional HQ at Aberlour House, Banffshire and brigade HQs at Dingwall, Elgin and Banchory it will be seen just how spread out the battalions were and why Wimberley was concerned that they should

see themselves as part of a greater body rather than being isolated enti-
ties.[15] To help create that feeling of belonging, Wimberley encouraged the
soldiers to feel proud of their units, their brigades and, above all, their
Division. They should have, he said, 'a guid conceit o' themsel's' at all
times to achieve which he encouraged wearing regimental tartan whenever possible and the use of unit signposts indicating clearly the presence
of a Highland Division unit.[16] The Divisional cypher, the letters HD in red
within a red circle, was to become one of the best known in the Army, not
only because of the Highlanders' achievements in battle but also because
of their practice of painting the sign wherever they went. This practice
led to the soubriquet 'The Highway Decorators'. With pride in one's unit
goes pride in appearance and Wimberley believed that a soldier should
always look smart and that 'spit-and-polish' would achieve that objective, which also boosted morale. Nor did he think that responsibility for
looking smart lay entirely with the individual soldier. He ensured that his
soldiers would always look as smart as circumstances allowed through
the ready availability of new uniforms to replace worn suits. One of the
first occasions that he put this into practice was when 7th Black Watch
came back from duty in the Shetlands in September 1941. The battalion
paraded before Wimberley at Fochabers Castle but their battledress had
seen much better days and Wimberley's reaction was to have the entire
battalion re-clothed.[17] This fostering of a Highland Division esprit de
corps was intended to make men feel that they belonged to the Division as
if to a family and to be reluctant to leave the divisional family; Wimberley
noted that 'one difficulty in 1941/2 was to prevent the drain of too many
first class young officers and men leaving the Division before we could
get overseas'.[18]

While the Division was still engaged on its coastal defence duties in north-
east Scotland, a new unit was added to its order of battle: 51st (Highland)
Reconnaissance Battalion, which came into being on 8 January 1941 at
Blervie House near Forres in Morayshire. Next day Lieutenant-Colonel E
H Grant, an Argyll who had also served in the Royal Flying Corps in the
Great War, arrived to take command.[19] There was a change of nomencla-
ture on 22 January when the battalion was ordered to assume the title 51st
Battalion The Reconnaissance Corps.[20] This was a new corps, created in
January 1941 following one of the recommendations of the Bartholomew
Report into the performance of the BEF in France.[21] With the cavalry regiments that had traditionally carried out the reconnaissance role for field
formations now needed in the RAC, it was decided to create a specialist
corps to reconnoitre for infantry divisions with each such formation that
took to the field having its own reconnaissance battalion. In the case of
the Highland Division its Reconnaissance Battalion was formed from
the brigade anti-tank companies which had reflected the order of battle

of each brigade: 152 Brigade Company included Seaforth and Cameron Highlanders; 153 was made up of Black Watch and Gordons and 154 of Black Watch and Argylls.[22] These became, respectively, A, B, and C Companies, later Squadrons.

Needless to say, each recce unit quickly began asserting its own identity and thus the order that 51 Recce should adopt the title 51st Battalion The Reconnaissance Corps, omitting the 'Highland' descriptor. However, it was not long before the battalion asserted its specific identity when permission was received from HM King George VI to adopt a Hunting Stuart flash.[23] This was used first on uniform sleeves and was later painted on the left side of steel helmets; it was also added as a backing to the cap badge on the Balmoral bonnet adopted by the battalion.[24] In June 1942 all reconnaissance battalions were officially renamed regiments and that for the Highland Division bore the title 51st (Highland) Reconnaissance Regiment; cavalry nomenclature – squadrons and troops – was adopted within the regiments.[25]

Later in the year came another addition to the Division's strength. This was a machine-gun battalion, 1/7th Middlesex Regiment.[26] Although the Middlesex – the 'Diehards' – were Sassenachs they soon became a valued element of the Highland Division and honorary Highlanders. Wimberley had been keen to have as many units as possible from the Highlands or, failing that, Lowland Scotland but no Scottish regiment had been converted to the machine-gun role and thus he had to be content with the Middlesex. He had more success with 40th Light Anti-Aircraft Regiment, a Highland TA regiment formed at Inverness in September 1939, while 61st Anti-Tank Regiment was also a Highland TA unit. Initially the War Office had proposed an English unit as the Divisional LAA regiment but Wimberley had argued that this would dilute the Scottish character of his Division, to be told that the Royal Artillery did not recognise 'tribal' loyalties. Eventually, he was told that the final word lay with the CinC of Anti-Aircraft Command, General Tim Pile, and Wimberley drove to AA Command HQ at Stanmore to put his request to General Pile. 'Mercifully he was an Irishman' and understood Wimberley's argument perfectly; it was Pile (whose father had been Lord Mayor of Dublin and was a Home Rule supporter[27]) who assigned 40th LAA Regiment to the Highland Division.[28]

Throughout this period battalions had been welcoming new recruits. Although many came through the training depots, some trained with their battalions. Bert Mitchell, from Aberdeen, enlisted in the Gordon Highlanders in January 1942 and was told to report to Gordonstoun School where the regiment's 5th/7th Battalion was stationed.

About 80 of us appeared there on our training. We were formed into an 'R' Company and were trained by the battalion sergeants. In the meantime my fiancée was also called up and had to report to the Cameron Barracks in Inverness so we did see quite a lot of each other then, until we were told we would be moving to England.[29]

That move was made in April 1942 and the Highland Division's place in north-east Scotland was taken by 52nd (Lowland) Division.[30] The Aldershot area was the new home for the Highlanders with battalions dispersed throughout the area.

At Aldershot the Division undertook intense training to prepare the soldiers for active service. Although accommodation left much to be desired the weather proved favourable and the pace of training left little time to grumble about the billets. As well as the inevitable fitness training, or PT, and route-marching, there were exercises in co-operation with tanks and in fighting tanks, which included experiencing tanks driving over slit trenches in which soldiers sheltered. And there was also training with the Division's machine-gun battalion, 1/7th Middlesex, to familiarise the infantry with the effects of live machine-gun fire. This involved the Middlesex firing their Vickers MMGs over the heads of the Highlanders at night.[31] This was a terrifying experience intended as 'battle inoculation' and some preparation for encountering the German MG34 and MG42 machine guns, although the chatter of the Vickers could not match the savage screech of the German weapons, commonly known as Spandaus.

New uniforms and equipment were issued that made it clear that the Division was destined for tropical climes but whether this would be the Middle East or the Far East was not yet known; the pith helmets received by the soldiers could mean either. Unfit soldiers were transferred to other units and those who would be going overseas had to undergo inoculations by the medical officers. This was far from a pleasant experience; in those days, long before disposable needles, the same needle would be used until it became too blunt to penetrate skin.[32] Although the needle was sterilised between each use this was not always successful and many men had adverse reactions to the injections. (One of the author's uncles, serving in the Royal Signals, was left almost paralysed by such an injection. Although he made a partial recovery he never recovered even an average degree of fitness and was awarded a 100 per cent war disability pension, which he continued to receive until his death in 2000.) Others suffered the pain of being injected with a blunt needle.

Not all the needles were wielded by RAMC personnel as the Highlanders had to sew new Divisional and unit insignia on their uniforms.[33] This was to be done before 1 June when Their Majesties King George VI and Queen Elizabeth were due to inspect the Division. As Colonel-in-Chief of the Cameron Highlanders, the King wore the regimental kilt while the Queen wore her Black Watch brooch.[34] After the inspection came an instruction from the War Office that all insignia that might identify a division or unit was to be removed, apparently for security reasons. The instruction was not well received in the Army, especially in the Highland Division where Wimberley's 'guid conceit' was already quite strong.

Following the royal inspection, Wimberley received a letter from Buckingham Palace telling him how much Their Majesties had enjoyed their inspection of the Division and commenting on

the outstanding success of the visit of the King and Queen to your Division. It is impossible to imagine a better-run show and I hope, if you have not already done so, you will let the troops know how delighted their Majesties were with everything they saw. You must indeed feel proud of your splendid Command.[35]

Less than three weeks later the Division quit Aldershot with some elements travelling to Liverpool, others to Bristol and yet others to Clydeside[36]. On the Mersey, Severn and Clyde, they boarded transports that would take them to the seat of war. They were bound for

active service for a destination and a fate unknown. [The Division] was to travel far, to earn great renown, and to suffer almost 16,000 casualties before its task was done. On 21st June, in dense fog, one contingent sailed down the Clyde, foghorns, not pipes, playing them out and not until Islay lay astern did the sun shine on the armada of transport vessels with the escort of destroyers and corvettes. Six days out the defence was strengthened by the battleship Malaya.[37]

It was routine for convoys travelling to the Middle East or Far East to go far into the Atlantic before changing course for the west coast of Africa (some convoys almost made a complete Atlantic crossing before heading for Africa) and thus it was a long voyage to their first landfall, the port of Freetown in Sierra Leone. Any thoughts of shore leave were dispelled, however, when it was announced that, because of the danger of malaria, no one would be allowed ashore. Instead the men were dosed with quinine and issues of mepacrine tablets and mosquito-repellent cream were made. Wimberley took the opportunity to visit each ship that carried elements of his Division.[38]

Although no one was allowed ashore, local traders in their little boats travelled out to the ships to try to sell their produce. In spite of warnings about the dangers of eating fruit purchased in this manner, many yielded to the temptation of succulent looking fruits and succumbed thereafter to the punishment inflicted on their digestive systems and bowels. Refuelling complete, the ships departed Freetown and, a few days later, crossed the Equator where the traditional ceremony of 'crossing the line' was observed on almost every vessel.[39] This proved a pleasant interlude in a voyage that had the potential to be very boring and damaging to morale. So that this would not happen a wide range of activities was organised on every ship. These included the inevitable PT, but there were also schools in various aspects of military knowledge as well as recreational pursuits; among the latter was Highland dancing.[40] Some time was left to study the stars at night or to watch the various escorts provided by the aquatic natives of the south Atlantic while entertainment was provided by the Pipes and Drums.[41]

The next landfall was made in South Africa when the convoy dropped anchor at Cape Town. Personnel were allowed ashore and it was a rare experience to spend time in a city with no blackout. Many gifts were showered on the troops when they were ashore, including fruit, cakes, confectionery and cigarettes.[42] 'There we were in port for 4 days, and were allowed ashore twice during that time, then off again, still no word where to. As we had been issued with tropical kit we thought it would be India!'[43] After Cape Town, the convoy anchored off Durban where only those troops aboard one ship, HMT *Stratheden*, were allowed ashore to be accommodated overnight at Greynell racecourse. While in Durban the Pipes and Drums of 7th Black Watch beat 'Retreat' in the city square to the delight of the inhabitants.[44] As the convoy lay off Durban, General Wimberley, who had sailed on *Stratheden*, and two of his senior staff, Colonel Roy Urquhart, the GSO I, who was later to command 1st Airborne Division at Arnhem, and Colonel J A Colam, the AQMG, left the Division to fly to Cairo. They did so as 'civilians' since the flight took them through neutral Portuguese territory; Wimberley was, allegedly, a traveller for a distillery and Urquhart a piano tuner.[45]

On 26 July the Division's main body sailed from Durban. By now some, mainly officers, had heard the news from North Africa. Rommel had taken Tobruk and reached the Egyptian frontier where he had been stopped by Eighth Army, under command of the CinC, Middle East, General Sir Claude Auchinleck. A complete South African division had been captured at Tobruk where the Camerons' 2nd Battalion had also gone 'in the bag'. The great naval base at Alexandria, HMS *Nile*, eastern home of the Mediterranean Fleet, had been abandoned and British civilians evacuated from both that city and Cairo. However, it seemed that not only had the Axis been stopped – at a place called El Alamein – but Eighth Army had also attempted to push them back. And so it appeared all was not lost in North Africa as the convoy sailed up the east coast of Africa towards Aden. This meant that the Division might still be bound for Egypt rather than India; this was finally confirmed at Aden where the convoy split in two. Needless to say, the arrival at Aden on 6 August was heralded by the various corps of pipes and drums playing 'The Barren Rocks of Aden'.[46]

From Aden some ships sailed for India and others for Basra in Iraq while those eight vessels carrying 51st (Highland) Division made for the Red

Sea. As the convoy entered the Gulf of Aden on 4 August the war diarist of 153 Brigade HQ noted that the temperature increased greatly. The ships left Aden on 8 August and from the following day until the 12th were in the Red Sea where it was 'extremely hot but [a] head wind, although hot and full of sand does cool the ship slightly'.[47] That heat exacerbated conditions below deck where men were accommodated in cramped conditions, with hammocks slung wherever space could be found; some even slept on mess tables.[48]

On 11, 12 and 13 August the Division disembarked at Port Tewfik and travelled overland to the great concentration of camps at Qassassin,[49] not far from Tel el Kebir, where some of the Highland regiments had fought in 1882 and earned the eponymous battle honour. (These included The Black Watch, The Seaforth and The Cameron Highlanders). There were some fifty camps at Qassassin, each numbered and each sharing the same basic dimensions – 1,000 by 500 yards – and amenities.[50] These were no holiday camps and although there were some amenities and entertainment such as film shows and concert parties most of those who spent any time at all there recall most vividly the flies and the heat. Qassassin was a place best left behind. But this was where the Highlanders would begin accustomising themselves to desert conditions. By coincidence they had arrived at almost the same time as Eighth Army's new commander, Bernard Law Montgomery, an idiosyncratic Irishman who would leave an indelible mark on that army and also on 51st (Highland) Division, which he would later describe as the finest British infantry formation under his command.

Initially training concentrated on restoring personal fitness which had deteriorated during the nine-week voyage. And so there was PT and route-marching. The latter was carried out by day and by night so that soldiers might learn how to follow the sun in daylight in a terrain without noteworthy features and to use the stars to guide them by night. Drivers also spent time learning and practising the skills they would need for travelling in the desert.[51] The peculiar conditions of desert warfare also led to the introduction of company navigating officers whose role was to ensure that attacking troops would not drift off course. Navigating officers were to achieve this by advancing along the line of the company axis holding a compass and keeping the men of the company on the correct bearing. Lieutenant George Morrison, from Crieff in Perthshire, was one of 7th Black Watch's navigating officers and he wrote home to his mother on 29 August explaining his new role.

[I use] sun compass, oil compass, astro and azimuth tables, protractors and all the rest. The desert is like the sea and needs deadly accurate navigations, as there is not a single landmark to help you at all, it's as flat and desolate as the moon must be. It's a big responsibility, but I'm pretty good at the sun compass now; I've been studying it since we landed. It's an eerie job going out into the unknown and very often the unmapped as well. It means that every man of these hundred men depends on me, the navigator, to guide them perhaps a hundred miles over the desert, and it's my job to keep watching and checking all the way. Still, for a Morrison, nae bother at all!![52]

The forthcoming offensive at El Alamein would take a heavy toll of navigating officers and George Morrison would be among those who paid with their young lives.

That the Highlanders were still getting used to conditions was indicated by the numbers afflicted by dysentery, known as 'gyppy tummy', a condition described by one officer as 'the worst' of all the plagues of Egypt. He went on to comment:

In the politer histories, gyppy is written off in a sentence. This is wrong. It filled our minds, in some cases to the exclusion of anything else, throughout our early weeks ashore, and to anyone who fought with the Eighth Army it is a memory which will remain when much else has faded. Gyppy tummy was dysentery in any of its forms, but was most commonly used to describe the mild type which was a mortification of the flesh and spirit but was not positively crippling. It was spread by the multitudinous flies, and could develop within a few hours. One might eat a good tea, feel a little off colour at dinner, and be anything from uncomfortable to raving two hours later. The normal attack lasted three or four days, during which the victim had acute diarrhoea, no appetite and a constant feeling of nausea. ... Few of us escaped. Hundreds went to hospital, and life for the gallant few who remained was one long trek across the desert to the latrines.[53]

No one was immune to the condition, the effects of which lessened over time but it was always in the background although most were able to continue working. The training routine helped to divert minds and raise morale and a visit by Prime Minister Winston Churchill, accompanied by General Sir Alan Brooke, Chief of the Imperial General Staff, was a tremendous morale booster.[54] The premier addressed the officers of each battalion but noted that the Division was not yet 'desert worthy'.[55]

One of the myths created by Montgomery is that his arrival in the desert meant an end to any plans that Eighth Army might withdraw into the Nile Delta. In fact, plans to defend the Delta, and Cairo, continued to be refined after he assumed command of Eighth Army but these were the responsibility of the new CinC, Middle East, General Sir Harold Alexander, another Irishman, and thus Montgomery was able to make his misleading statements. But those plans for defending the Delta were to affect directly the Highland Division since the first operational task to which it was assigned was that of holding the Delta against a possible attack by Rommel. As a result the Highlanders became part of Delta Force.

Delta Force was a strong command and Wimberley was appointed as GOC. The force numbered some 60,000 personnel and was basically a corps.[56] GHQ in Cairo was aware, through Ultra, that Rommel was preparing for another attack on the El Alamein line and Delta Force was the long stop for Eighth Army, designed to bring Rommel's forces to a standstill should they outflank Eighth Army. The Division's dispositions were to be on the south-western and western approaches to Cairo with Divisional HQ at Gezira Island, 152 Brigade on the Delta Barrage, 153 Brigade, with HQ at Mena Camp, along the El Giza-Mena canal, 154 Brigade providing the garrison at the crossing at the Delta Barrage; 51 Recce, with 239 Field Park Company RE under command, covering Gezira and the bridges across the Nile; 1/7th Middlesex covering crossings along the El Mulut canal, with a platoon of MMGs amongst the pyramids; and the divisional artillery deployed along the Nile valley from Mena to Cairo.[57]

Nobody regretted bidding farewell to Qassassin in the last week of August as the Division moved to Mena via El Khatatba and prepared for the possible appearance of Panzer Armee Afrika. It was also possible to increase the tempo of desert training and Generals Morshead and Freyberg, GOCs of the Australian and New Zealand Divisions respectively, provided personnel to assist in this training.[58] The Highland Division was to learn much from their antipodean cousins, especially the Australians with whom they established a particular rapport.

When Rommel launched his offensive on 30–31 August, Eighth Army was more than ready for him and Delta Force was not called into action. Nonetheless, the Force was ready; 51 Recce spent the first five days of September patrolling from Beni Yusuf to the Nile while a mobile squadron was created under Major Hutchison as a divisional reserve. This squadron patrolled until 5 September when danger had obviously passed and it was disbanded.[59] At 5.30am on the 5th the LAA gunners attached to 154 Brigade shot down a Ju88 which crashed in the minefield area at Alum Shaltut. Two airmen were subsequently collected from No. 601 Squadron, RAF, and sent to the prisoner-of-war cage at El Agami.[60]

Montgomery had defeated Rommel in what became known as the Battle of Alam el Halfa and the opposing forces now began preparations for the next phase of the campaign, with Eighth Army enjoying a considerable logistical advantage over its foe. In 51st (Highland) Division attention could now focus on training for desert warfare and, especially, for the Division's part in Eighth Army's forthcoming offensive. As well as training in moving in the desert, there were various exercises at battalion, brigade and divisional level; Exercise CRAIGELLACHIE was intended 'to practise making gaps through enemy minefields'[61] and each brigade undertook this scheme. There were also signals exercises and training in co-operation with tanks of 23 Armoured Brigade. Camouflage was vital in the desert and lessons in camouflaging vehicles, positions and personnel were included in the training schedule. On 25 September Divisional HQ issued an instruction on camouflaging steel helmets which on no account were to be 'painted in one colour, e.g. light sand, as this has been proved to be quite ineffective'.[62] Instead, a disruptive pattern was to be applied or camouflage netting that was similarly patterned, with 60 per cent being light coloured, was to be used. Face veils were to be treated similarly; where neither was available hessian from ordnance was to be painted with black or dark brown camouflage colour in a disruptive pattern.[63]

The liaison that had already developed between Australians and Highlanders extended to an affiliation with 9th Australian Division that saw each brigade in turn move into the Australian sector for a week during which they learned much from their mentors. Lessons were absorbed on patrolling, creating and camouflaging defensive positions and the need for silence at night, as well as a complete blackout. By 18 September, Wimberley could write that he had now seen

> a good deal one way and another of the Australians whom we are affiliated to. They seem to me a most competent lot of officers and a magnificent lot of men. The relations between both is excellent. The troops are self-reliant, and full of initiative. I wish all our men were as good. Their kindness and helpfulness to us is unbounded and they have had much battle experience and the confidence that engenders. I am certain,
> a. That we will get on well together,
> b. They can teach us a tremendous lot.

> There is one respect, however, in which we differ very greatly – that is in our standards of battle discipline. No doubt their standards suit their type of officer and men, suit their past environment, and suit their national temperament. It will not, however, suit ours, of that I am certain, at all events until we are as battle hardened as they are, and have a full team of real proved fighting leaders for our regimental officers and NCOs, and have weeded out the rest.[64]

It was obvious to all that a 'big push' was being prepared. The Highland Division had relieved 44th (Home Counties) Division at El Hammam, not far from El Alamein, in early September where its task was to hold reserve defensive boxes protecting Eighth Army's left flank and rear areas. Wimberley was spending much time in the line and, from maps and personal observations, had a training area constructed for his Division. This lay some ten miles south of their boxes and was a full-scale replica of that sector of the enemy front that the Highlanders would assault in the offensive. It included minefields and barbed wire as these would be found on the real thing and over this area the battalions trained.[65] The Gunners of the three field regiments played their part as the brigades practised advancing by night behind an intense artillery bombardment with the MMGs of the Middlesex adding their contribution. Attacks to a depth of 8,000 yards were made, at the end of which the attackers would seize their objectives, re-organise to meet the inevitable counter-attack, a trademark of German tactics, dig new slit trenches – the enemy's would be registered accurately by his artillery and mortars – and lay new minefields. Such training was not only realistic but also dangerous and, inevitably, lives were lost; these included Major Sir Arthur Wilmot, second-in-command of 1st Black Watch who, with five other members of the battalion, perished when rounds from a 25-pounder fell short during an exercise on 2 October.[66]

In spite of such incidents morale was high amongst the Highlanders, one reason for this being that Wimberley had persuaded Montgomery to allow his soldiers to wear their distinctive flashes. Contrary to War Office wisdom, Wimberley considered that the morale effect of the HD signs far outweighed the implications of identifying the Division to the enemy; in fact, he considered it important that the enemy should know their foe. As a result, the Division's stores had included thousands of cloth badges.[67] The needles came out again to stitch HD and other cloth badges on to uniforms while similar flashes were applied to steel helmets. Montgomery also gave permission for other formations to wear such distinctions.

At El Hammam the men of 153 Brigade were living in dug-in bivouacs and the brigade's office and wireless trucks were also dug in for protection while all other transport was dispersed widely to reduce its vulnerability to attack from the air.[68] The value of such dispersion was demonstrated at 154 Brigade's HQ on 2 October when two Messerschmitt Bf109s dropped four small high-explosive bombs but caused neither casualties nor damage.[69] On 1 October 152 Brigade moved into the front line under operational command of 9th Australian Division with Brigade HQ 'occupying excellent concreted dugouts built by the New Zealanders as part of the original Alamein defences'.[70] A week later the brigade was relieved by 153 Brigade and moved to occupy the El Halfa area. On 9 October 152 Brigade began special training in its role for the offensive. This continued until the 17th: laying the start-line for the Division would be the task of 5th Seaforth while 5th Camerons would assist the Sappers in making gaps through both British and enemy minefields and 2nd Seaforth 'practised extensively in co-operation with Army tanks, taking part in exercises with 23 Armoured Brigade'.[71] Meanwhile, 51 Recce was re-organised into two discrete elements, a composite squadron and an infantry squadron in which form the regiment would fight in LIGHTFOOT.[72]

The pace of life was increasing as D-Day neared. Montgomery and Alexander had been under pressure from Churchill to mount an offensive in late September, at the time of the full moon, but Monty had responded that this was premature, that he would attack at the October full moon and could guarantee success if he did so, which he could not do in September. He also said that if Churchill was adamant about September then he, Montgomery, would not be Eighth Army's commander. With Alexander's full support, Montgomery had his way and D-Day was to be 23 October when Eighth Army would assault the enemy lines in Operation LIGHTFOOT.[73]

Montgomery had planned a set-piece battle, having concluded that this was what Eighth Army was best suited to. He possessed superiority in tanks and artillery but his advantage in infantry was not as good as he would have wished. The Desert Air Force had established supremacy over the battle area and thus the Luftwaffe and Regia Aeronautica were denied the opportunity to observe the preparations underway in Eighth Army's rear areas; in any case these were camouflaged skilfully with tanks disguised to appear as lorries and artillery likewise concealed. A deception plan to convince the enemy that the attack would come in the southern sector was also in operation; the presence of 7th Armoured Division, the Desert Rats, in that sector added to this deception.[74]

The LIGHTFOOT plan allowed for a preliminary bombardment by aircraft and artillery followed by an infantry advance through the minefields, in which gaps were to be made by Royal Engineers and specially formed minefield clearance teams to allow Eighth Army's armour to follow the infantry and break into the enemy lines. Montgomery expected that this breakthrough would be made on the first night of the offensive, 23–24 October, and that Eighth Army could then exploit those initial gains to crumble the enemy's defences along the entire line. He believed that the entire operation would take about twelve days. LIGHTFOOT had a major flaw: the infantry who would advance first – including 51st (Highland) Division – belonged to XXX Corps while the following armoured formations belonged to X Corps. Thus Montgomery had superimposed one corps on another in the same strip of battleground; this was not a recipe for success. Furthermore, Montgomery had little appreciation of the limitations of armour and was simply asking too much of them on that first night. And he had probably been persuaded that the lack of trust between infantry and armour meant that the armoured commanders were not enthusiastic about getting to grips with the enemy.

The Highland Division's plan of attack was complete by 19 October. Montgomery placed the Highlanders between the desert veterans of 9th Australian and 2nd New Zealand Divisions on their right and left flanks respectively. Thus Wimberley could be confident that his flanks would be secure. His final plan for the assault required 5th Seaforth to lay some nine miles of white tape to mark the Divisional start-line and the approaches for

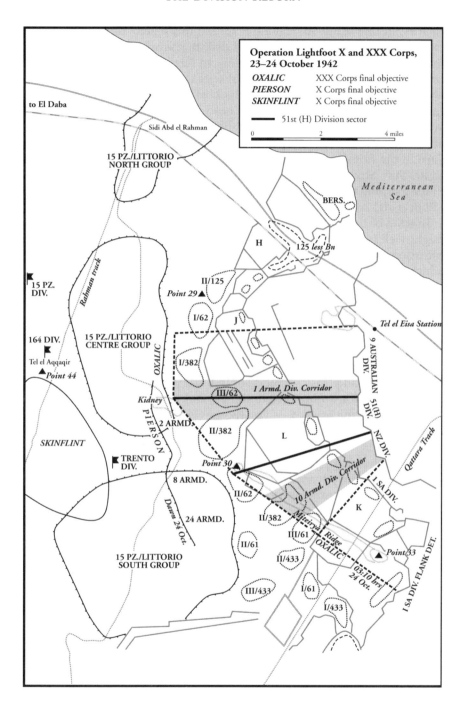

Operation Lightfoot X and XXX Corps, 23–24 October 1942

OXALIC	XXX Corps final objective
PIERSON	X Corps final objective
SKINFLINT	X Corps final objective

51st (H) Division sector

0   2   4 miles

to El Daba

Sidi Abd el Rahman

15 PZ./LITTORIO
NORTH GROUP

*Mediterranean
Sea*

BERS.

H

125 *less Bn*

II/125

15 PZ.
DIV.

Point 29

I/62

J

Tel el Eisa Station

164 DIV.

15 PZ./LITTORIO
CENTRE GROUP

I/382

9 AUSTRALIAN DIV.

51(H) DIV.

Tel el Aqqaqir

Point 44

III/62

1 Armd. Div. Corridor

Kidney

NZ DIV.

Qattara Track

SKINFLINT

2 ARMD.

II/382

L

TRENTO
DIV.

Point 30

1 SA DIV.

8 ARMD.

II/62

10 Armd. Div. Corridor

Dawn 24 Oct.

24 ARMD.

II/382

Miteiriya Ridge

K

Point 33

II/61

III/61

OXALIC

15 PZ./LITTORIO
SOUTH GROUP

II/433

I/61

03:10 hrs
24 Oct.

1 SA DIV. FLANK DET.

III/433

I/433

each assaulting battalion. Having practised this several times in the training area, the Seaforth had evolved a drill that worked well and allowed them to discharge their task effectively. In fact, they laid the lines twice; on the first occasion they used signal wire that would not be obvious to enemy eyes and then, after dusk on the 23rd, white tape was secured to the cables. Great care had to be taken to ensure that approach lines were laid accurately so that the attacking battalions would not go off course.[75] The attacking troops were to reach their assembly positions through eleven gaps in the British minefields of which three, codenamed, from north to south, Sun, Moon and Star, had already been made. Assisting the Sappers in the gapping task were the men of 5th Camerons. The third battalion of 152 Brigade, 2nd Seaforth, was to act as divisional reserve.[76]

In spite of the pressure of preparation some found time to write what might well be a last letter home. This was certainly the case for George Morrison of 7th Black Watch who wrote a 'wee letter' on 16 October in which he told his mother that

> I feel excessively cheery and optimistic right now and this death business doesn't bother me in the least. So if I do get one – don't be too sad – it's too late to be sad and I wouldn't like it. If you would just get the organist to play Handel's Largo in my memory in the kirk one Sunday morning – then that's as far as you should grieve for me. ... So don't be sad please – remember this war is being fought to protect people like you from horrible things, and it's only right that some should have the privilege – yes, the privilege, to give themselves for the cause of the good and the right.[77]

During the training period the Highlanders had come to know their tasks well. They were to advance through the gaps following a rolling bombardment that would take them on to three intermediate lines, codenamed Green, Red and Black Lines, before the final objective, Blue Line. Enemy strongpoints, all of which were given Scottish place names as codenames, would be met at and before these lines. (These were: on Green Line – Arbroath, Forfar, Creedan, Dollar, Mons Meg, Paisley, Drummuir and Inverness; on Red Line – Turriff, Insch and Killin; on Black Line – Dufftown, Braemar, Strichen, Perth, Greenock, Boath and Dundee; on Blue Line – Aberdeen, Stirling, Nairn and Kirkcaldy.) The advance would be on a two-brigade front, with each front broadening as the brigade moved forward. On the right was 153 Brigade with two attacking lines while 154 Brigade, on the left, had four lines. This apparent imbalance was due to enemy defences being thicker on the right than on the left; each battalion would operate on a front of about 600 yards. However, 154 Brigade was strengthened for the assault by the addition of elements of 51 Recce and 50th Royal Tanks. A Middlesex machine-gun company supported each brigade.[78]

On the night of 22–23 October the soldiers of the Highland Division moved up to slit trenches dug just behind the jumping-off line. There they spent the following day, restricted to their two-man trenches, as they waited for darkness. With darkness came hot food, visits from senior officers and last-minute orders. As the hours and minutes ticked down to H-Hour, the Jocks stretched their legs, checked their weapons and made ready for the Highland Division's return to action.

Notes

1. Linklater, *The Highland Division*, pp. 7–10
2. Joslen, *Orders of Battle*, pp. 55 & 83; Salmond, *The History of the 51st Highland Division*, p. 19
3. Joslen, op cit, pp. 273–5 & pp. 337–41
4. Ibid
5. Salmond, op cit, p. 19
6. Ibid, pp. 19–21
7. Ibid
8. Keegan, *Churchill's Generals*, p. 208
9. Joslen, op cit, p. 83
10. Ibid, p. 75
11. Salmond, op cit, p. 25
12. Ibid, p. 24
13. Ibid
14. Quoted in Salmond, op cit, p. 24
15. Salmond, op cit, pp. 24–5
16. Ibid, p. 23
17. Ibid
18. Wimberley, *Memoirs, Vol II*, p. 23
19. NA Kew, WO166/634, war diary, 51 (H) Recce, 1941
20. Ibid
21. NA Kew, WO106/1741, Bartholomew Cttee Report
22. Meek, *A Brief History of the 51st (H) Reconnaissance Regiment*, p. 2
23. NA Kew, WO166/634, war diary, 51 (H) Recce, 1941
24. Ibid
25. Doherty, *Only The Enemy in Front*, p. 5
26. Delaforce, *Monty's Highlanders*, p. 26
27. Doherty, *Ireland's Generals in the Second World War*, p.89
28. Wimberley, op cit, p. 24
29. Mitchell to author
30. Salmond, op cit, p. 25
31. Delaforce, op cit, p. 27
32. Salmond, op cit, p. 25
33. Ibid
34. Wimberley, op cit, p. 26
35. Quoted in Salmond, op cit, p. 25

36. Salmond, pp. 25–6
37. Ibid, p. 26; Wimberley, op cit, p. 27
38. Salmond, op cit, p. 26
39. Ibid
40. Delaforce, op cit, p. 29
41. Salmond, op cit, pp. 26–7
42. Mitchell to author
43. Salmond, op cit, p. 26–7; Delaforce, op cit, p. 30
44. Wimberley, op cit, p. 29
45. Salmond, op cit, p. 27
46. NA Kew, WO169/4295, war diary, 153 Bde, 1942
47. Ibid
48. NA Kew, WO169/4163, war diary, HQ 51 (H) Div (GS), 1942
49. Salmond, op cit, pp. 27–9; Delaforce, op cit, p. 32; Borthwick, *Battalion*, p. 17
50. Salmond, op cit, p. 29; Delaforce, op cit, p. 32
51. IWM DS/MISC/63, Lt George F Morrison
52. Borthwick, op cit, p. 18
53. Salmond, op cit, p. 29; NA Kew, WO169/5017, war diary, 1 Gordons, 1942
54. Salmond, op cit, p. 29
55. Salmond, op cit, p.29
56. NA Kew, WO169/4163, war diary, HQ 51 (H) Div (GS), 1942; WO169/4171, war diary, 51(H) Recce, 1942; WO169/4295, war diary, 153 Bde, 1942; Doherty, *Only The Enemy*, p. 27
57. NA Kew, WO169/4164, war diary, HQ 51 (H) Div (GS), 1942
58. NA Kew, WO169/4171, war diary, 51 (H) Recce, 1942
59. NA Kew, WO169/4298, war diary, 154 Bde, 1942
60. NA Kew, WO169/4292, war diary, 152 Bde, 1942
61. WO169/4164, war diary, HQ 51 (H) Div (GS), 1942
62. Ibid
63. Ibid
64. Ibid
65. Wimberley, op cit, p. 37
66. Ibid, p. 33
67. NA Kew, WO169/4295, war diary, 153 Bde, 1942
68. NA Kew, WO169/4298, war diary, 154 Bde, 1942
69. NA Kew, WO169/4292, war diary, 152 Bde, 1942
70. Ibid; WO169/5058, war diary, 2 Seaforth, 1942
71. NA Kew, WO169/4171, war diary, 51 (H) Recce, 1942
72. Doherty, *The Sound of History*, **p.**
73. Montgomery, *Memoirs*, **p.**
74. NA Kew, WO169/5059, war diary, 5 Seaforth, 1942
75. NA Kew, Wo169/4292, war diary, 152 Bde, 1942
76. Wimberley, op cit, p. 39
77. IWM, Morrison, op cit
78. NA Kew, WO169/4298, war diary, 154 Bde, 1942

CHAPTER V

El Alamein

At 9.40pm on 23 October the order FIRE was given to Eighth Army's artil-lery and some 800 guns crashed out the first salvo of the greatest artillery bombardment of the war to date, the heaviest such since the Great War. The initial aim of the bombardment was to destroy the Axis artillery and this counter-battery fire continued for fifteen minutes. It was supported by RAF Wellington bombers dropping their deadly cargoes on the enemy rear areas and by Hurricane fighters that strafed the Axis lines. In 153 Brigade the war diarist noted that the bombardment had been very effec-tive 'as there was no reply from the enemy batteries either during the C.B. programme or for some time thereafter'.[1] Along the XXX Corps front of some seven miles, almost 500 guns – field and medium – engaged about 200 Axis artillery positions, firing 1,800 shells in the first fifteen-minute programme. Then the guns fell silent all along the front. (Along the Corps' front were disposed, from right to left, 9th Australian, 51st (Highland), 2nd New Zealand, 1st South African and 4th Indian Divisions. The last formation was to remain in reserve, although it was to carry out some operations in support of the overall plan.)

The Gunners were now preparing to move on to the second phase of their fireplan. Five minutes later, they opened fire again, this time targeting Axis forward infantry positions. Now was the time for the infantry of XXX Corps to move forward. In 51st (Highland) Division's positions the battalions made their final preparations, soldiers rechecked their weapons for the last time and pipers tuned up ready to pipe their companies into action.

Montgomery's plan called for XXX Corps to advance on that first night as far as

> the MITEIRIYA ridge ... believed to be the limit of the depth of the enemy position, some 6,000 yards from our front line. NZ Div was then to be prepared to exploit SW and the AUSTRALIAN Div Northwards so as to widen that gap. 4 Ind Div was to carry out raids along RUWEISAT ridge.[2]

The line that XXX Corps was to reach was codenamed *Oxalic*. With *Oxalic* taken the armour was to pass through two corridors, Northern and Southern, to reach the line codenamed *Pierson*. The Northern corridor for the armour of 1st Armoured Division lay astride the Australian/ Highlander boundary. Within 51st (Highland) Division, *Oxalic* was known as Blue line and there were three intermediate lines on which the attackers would pause for re-organisation: Green, Red and Black lines. Across the divisional front were five attacking infantry battalions, plus the divisional reconnaissance regiment, making six separate attacks; 50th Royal Tanks supported the Division. From right to left the first phase was carried out by 5th Black Watch, 5/7th Gordon Highlanders, 1st Black Watch, 7th Argyll and Sutherland Highlanders, 51 Recce and 5th Cameron Highlanders. In four areas, the plan was for attacking battalions to go all the way to the final objective but the flanking battalions, 5th Black Watch and 5th Camerons, would be relieved on Red line by 1st Gordons and 7th Black Watch respectively. Along Blue line lay four of the enemy's strongest defensive points, Aberdeen, Stirling, Nairn and Kirkcaldy, the first at the feature known as the Kidney, from its shape on the map. The last was at the north-west end of the Miteiriya Ridge.

As the infantrymen stepped off, the skirl of great Highland pipes sounded even above the roar of the guns. Wimberley's men had no difficulty hearing their kilted pipers as they played them into battle with regimental and company marches. The strains of *Heilan' Laddie* accompanied 5th Black Watch on the right flank, those of the Argylls *Monymusk* while 5th Camerons on the left advanced to *The Inverness Gathering*. For Scottish and Irish soldiers the pipes are more than musical instruments; they are also psychological weapons and their value to morale is immeasurable. On the flanks of 51st (Highland) Division, the strains of pipe music could be heard by both Australian and New Zealand troops as they began advancing and the morale effect of the pipes transmitted itself to those men.[3]

But the pipers march in a place of great danger and often pay the highest price for their efforts. Such was the case with Piper Duncan McIntyre, a 19-year-old with 5th Black Watch. McIntyre led A Company towards their first objective Montrose. He must have known that he was facing death but he could not have expected his name to achieve posthumous legendary status in both his regiment and the Highland Division. As A Company moved forward, Duncan McIntyre played as men fell 'all around him in the intense concentration of enemy artillery, mortar and small-arms fire'.[4] McIntyre was wounded but continued playing. Although he was struck a second time, still his pipes could be heard. Then, as the assault went in on Montrose, Piper McIntyre broke into *Heilan' Laddie* and his complete disregard for his own safety was an inspiration to his comrades as they completed the deadly advance on the enemy strongpoint. Montrose was taken by A and B Companies but young McIntyre had been hit a third time, by a mortar bomb that knocked him to the ground. And yet he continued to play as the life ebbed from his body.

> In the morning they found him with his beloved pipes under his arm, his fingers rigid on the chanter, true to the last to his Clan motto, 'Per Ardua'.[5]

Duncan McIntyre had shown the type of courage that merits the award of the Victoria Cross and it was felt in his battalion that he deserved such distinction. Both the brigade commander and General Wimberley agreed that this was so and a recommendation was submitted for the Cross. Unfortunately this was unsuccessful and McIntyre's sacrifice went unmarked save in the minds of all who served in the Highland Division.[6]

The capture of Montrose was followed by that of Arbroath, taken by C Company and Forfar by D. Then A Company passed through en route to its next objective, which was on Red line, the limit of the battalion's advance. By midnight, 5th Black Watch had achieved its objectives and it was time for 1st Gordons to pass through towards Black line and Blue line. The leading companies of 5th Black Watch had suffered heavily and even as the survivors of A Company were assembled by Lieutenant Davey an RE officer, Lieutenant Denton, was killed at Lieutenant-Colonel Rennie's side. As the Black Watch soldiers dug in they were joined by their heavy weapons, the anti-tank guns and mortars, while the second-in-command, Major Thornson, arrived with a very welcome hot meal.[7]

For 1st Gordons Kintyre was the first objective but the battalion lost its CO, Lieutenant-Colonel 'Nap' Murray, who was wounded soon after its advance began. Major Hay took over as CO, although he, too, was wounded later. Nonetheless, the battalion moved forward, its pipers playing lustily as they had at Longueval in an earlier war. Soon Red line was reached whence Captain Keogh went forward to Black line with a tape-laying party. Casualties had been light to that point but the battalion now began to suffer heavily: C Company met strong resistance and many fell, including Captain Thomson and Lieutenant Williamson, both of whom later succumbed to their wounds. D Company came up on Valentines of 50th Royal Tanks to join B Company but the tanks ran into an uncharted minefield and five were blown up. With one company reduced to an officer with eighteen men, the Gordons dug in and waited for daylight when they became spectators to a long-range tank battle between British and Axis tanks. This engagement was fought out over a four-hour period and, on the British side, involved the tanks of The Queen's Bays, which fired on their foe at some 3,000-yards range.[8]

At 10.00am it was learned that Braemar had been taken by A and C Companies although Captain Skivington of C Company had been killed

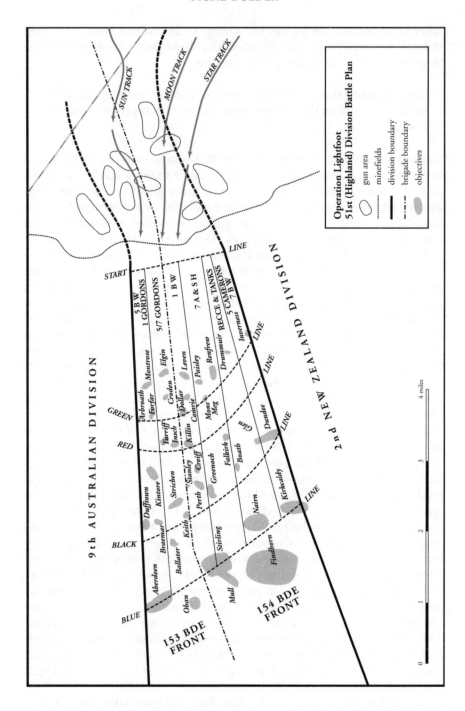

Operation Lightfoot
51st (Highland) Division Battle Plan

gun area
minefields
division boundary
brigade boundary
objectives

9th AUSTRALIAN DIVISION

2nd NEW ZEALAND DIVISION

153 BDE FRONT

154 BDE FRONT

SUN TRACK

MOON TRACK

STAR TRACK

START LINE

GREEN LINE

RED LINE

BLACK LINE

BLUE LINE

5 B W
1 GORDONS
5/7 GORDONS
1 B W
7 A & S H
RECCE & TANKS
5 CAMERONS
7 B W

Arbroath
Montrose
Forfar
Croden
Elgin
Dollar
Leven
Killin
Comrie
Paisley
Renfrew
Drummuir
Inverness

Turriff
Insch
Stanley
Creiff
Greenoch
Mons Meg
Glen
Dundee

Dufftown
Kintore
Scrichen
Keith
Perth
Falkirk
Boath
Nairn
Kirkcaldy

Aberdeen
Braemar
Ballater
Stirling
Findhorn

Oban
Mull

0 1 2 3 4 miles

as he led his men in a final bayonet charge on the enemy positions. Sixty-one of the company fell but Skivington had remained cool as he took his men forward.

> His magnificent example inspired the remnants to maintain a steady and ordered advance until the objective was reached. It was when leading a bayonet charge against the last enemy strong-point that he fell, mortally wounded. He never wavered from his first resolution, as his last order to the twenty-two that remained was: 'C Company – advance!'[9]

On the left of 5th Black Watch and 1st Gordons the other element of 153 Brigade's advance was carried out by 5th/7th Gordons whose task was to carry through to Blue line. Led by A and B Companies, the Gordons moved forward quickly. In fact they were so fast that the leading soldiers were poised to assault their first objective before the artillery bombardment had moved on from it. To avoid running into British shelling the Gordons lay down until the bombardment lifted and then passed through the first minefield to take their objective. This was achieved quickly and without major loss although Lieutenant Stuart was killed at the head of a mopping-up party trying to clear some enemy machine guns. Most losses, however, came from enemy artillery or mortar fire. Green line was soon occupied and Sappers cut the wire in front of the Gordons, with the loss of several men, allowing the Gordons to move against Red line. As they advanced a body of soldiers was spotted in front but, fortunately, these men were recognised as Black Watch before any harm had been done; they were from 5th Black Watch and had moved too far to their left.[10]

At Red line, some 4,500 yards from their start-line, the Gordons spent an hour re-organising; A and B Companies dug in while the advance to Black line, some 2,500 yards ahead, was taken up by C and D Companies. These latter had to retire a short distance to avoid British shells that were falling short but the advance was then resumed. However, D Company met sustained machine-gun fire from enemy positions and many men were lost, including the company commander, Captain Sharp. C Company were forced to dig in but were fortunate that mortars and machine guns had joined them. The intense machine-gun fire that had all but wiped out the company came from the enemy post codenamed Strichen. And so the situation remained until dawn when tanks of 2 Armoured Brigade passed between the two Gordon battalions into the minefields ahead to begin an armoured clash that would last for days. This was the limit of the battalion's advance, although they took Strichen next day.[11]

Thus 153 Brigade was short of its objective at *Oxalic*, a situation it shared with the Australians on the right flank.[12] It will be remembered that 154 Brigade was to hold a broader front along *Oxalic*, or Blue line, and we will now consider how its units fared. The brigade advance was broken into four sectors with 1st Black Watch on the right flank. This battalion, the senior Highland battalion, reached Black line swiftly, overcoming all opposition on the way; they too almost ran into their own artillery, such was the speed of their advance.[13] On the left flank of the Black Watch were 7th Argyll and Sutherland Highlanders, commanded by Lieutenant-Colonel Lorne Campbell, who had earned distinction in France and would do so again in Africa. Campbell's Argylls were to advance to take the Stirling strongpoint on Blue line and had been allocated a squadron of Valentine tanks from 50th Royal Tanks, allowing some of the infantry to ride into battle on the tanks. C and D Companies led the advance, their pipers playing *Monymusk*, and, by 11.00pm, the first objective had fallen. After re-organising they set off for Red line at 11.30pm and were successfully ensconced at midnight. However, opposition began stiffening and Axis gunners were finding the Argylls' range while some British shells were falling short. The Argylls dug in but, at 1 o'clock, they advanced on Greenock. This point was held by Italians who initially put up their arms in a gesture of surrender but then attacked the Argylls; a bloody skirmish, with bayonets being used, ensued. The Highlanders emerged victorious but both C and D Companies had suffered heavily. D Company had lost all its officers and an entire platoon was wiped out by an explosion; their machine gunners, the Sassenachs of the Middlesex, had also suffered grievously. Nonetheless, Black line was secure although Campbell's battalion was too weak to advance to Stirling. As with the Australians, their supporting tanks had also been delayed by mines and Campbell decided to dig in.[14]

The remainder of 50th Royal Tanks, under their CO, John Cairns, was with 51st Reconnaissance Regiment for the assault on Nairn. There had been much debate about the role of 51 Recce in the desert with suggestions that it be re-organised as a divisional cavalry regiment or as a carrier regiment. However, these were turned down and, eventually, 51 Recce reformed with two squadrons: a composite squadron and an infantry squadron.[15] In this guise the regiment fought at Alamein. Composite Squadron suffered its first casualties almost as soon as it moved off, when one man was killed. Two assault troops covering Sappers making gaps in the minefields had a particularly active night. Although assault troops reached the lying-up positions from which the attack on Nairn was to be launched, the final objective was not achieved. Tanks of 50th Royal Tanks were to 'attack, capture and annihilate' Nairn but German anti-tank gunners thought otherwise. At 3.00am, as the tanks began their advance, the leading Valentines were struck by anti-tank fire; as one withdrew it laid smoke to obscure the gunners' view. The German gunners also turned their attention to 51 Recce's carriers, knocking out four in seconds. When the smoke cleared, the tanks had withdrawn, save for three crippled and abandoned Valentines. One scout troop of 51 Recce had but a single carrier left. The attack on Nairn had come to a stop.[16]

On the right flank 5th Camerons had advanced with their pipers playing *The Inverness Gathering*. Objectives secured, the advance on that flank was passed over to 7th Black Watch. In spite of all the difficulties facing them, the battalion made it through to the final objective, Kirkcaldy, a piece of ground some thirty feet high that dominated the surrounding terrain. Many casualties were suffered from enemy shelling, especially in A and D Companies. This was the battalion in which served George Morrison, the 21-year-old subaltern from Perthshire, he who, on 16 October, had written his 'wee letter' to his mother lest he became a casualty in the battle. As 7th Black Watch moved out on their advance the company navigating officers, compasses in hand, led their companies, marking the route to be followed. Not surprisingly, navigating officers suffered a high casualty rate. Within an hour, six of the battalion's navigating officers had been killed or wounded. Among the dead was George Morrison, who had told his mother that 'this death business doesn't worry me in the least'. The young officer had kept faith with his men to the end and had done without question a job that he knew carried a very high risk of costing him his life; but he had been prepared to take that risk and to give his life 'for the good and the right'.[17]

George Morrison's battalion suffered heavily. By the time Black line was reached the leading companies were reduced to little more than platoon strength. However the battalion had one advantage; Kirkcaldy lay on the end of Miteiriya Ridge and was easily identifiable, especially with enemy fire coming from it – in other areas there had been confusion over the exact location of objective lines. Captain Charles Cathcart, of Pitcairlie, was given command of the two composite companies that the Black Watch could muster for the final assault. A cautious advance soon became a charge worthy of Highlanders of yore, taking Cathcart's men in among the defenders of Kirkcaldy. Fighting with bayonets and hand-to-hand, 7th Black Watch secured the objective by 4.00am. This was the sole part of *Oxalic* that the Division captured that night. At the end only fifty men of Cathcart's little force were still standing.[18]

At daybreak on the 24th Eighth Army had not made the progress that Montgomery had planned. The infantry of XXX Corps had reached *Oxalic* only along part of its length. Freyberg's New Zealanders had not only taken *Oxalic* in their sector but, in places, had gone beyond to the bottom of the ridge's forward slope. In the Australian sector, the line had been reached in the northern half but Morshead's battalions were about a mile short in the southern sector. The same applied in the right half of the South African sector and along three-quarters of the Highlanders' front. However, the armour had achieved less success.[19]

Montgomery's plan for X Corps had relied on the progress made by both infantry and Sappers but many, including Freyberg, had considered that the plan had not allowed enough time for the Sappers to complete their task. Dawn on 24 October proved Freyberg to have been right.[20] Furthermore, Montgomery's insistence on pushing the armour through the infantry of XXX Corps had led to massive traffic congestion as the leading units of the armoured brigades tried to use the same tracks as the tails of XXX Corps' formations. Tanks of 2 Armoured Brigade (which included The Queen's Bays, 10th Royal Hussars and 9th Royal Lancers.[21]) were to pass through the northern corridor, which lay astride the Australian/Highlander boundary, to *Oxalic* and then to the objective line for the armour, *Pierson*. However, Montgomery had also declared that, where the infantry had not reached *Oxalic*, the tanks would have to fight their way forward. This had proved impossible; the tanks met determined enemy opposition and well-sited anti-tank guns took a heavy toll of the British tanks and the next element of the plan could not be executed. Montgomery had intended that 2 Armoured Brigade would be joined by 8 and 24 Armoured Brigades, which were to pass though the southern corridor in Freyberg's sector and the armour would then form a new line, anchored at either end by their infantry brigades, 7 Motored and 133 Lorried, to protect XXX Corps against Axis armoured attacks. But, as dawn broke, some of these brigades were still making their way through the corridors; both 24 Armoured and 133 Lorried Infantry Brigades were still behind Eighth Army's infantry.[22]

Tank battles continued to rage and, in the afternoon of the 24th, Lieutenant-Colonel MacKessack's 2nd Seaforth, which had been held in corps reserve, was returned to Wimberley's command and we shall shortly look at how he deployed this battalion. Other elements of the Division had also fought well. The field artillery regiments had played a full part in the fire plan and their exhausted Gunners continued to serve their guns in providing support to infantry and armour. Such was the intensity of the shooting that the guns had to be rested for ten minutes every hour and their barrels cooled. The Division's light AA and anti-tank regiments – 40th LAA and 61st A/T – were also engaged and in the course of the battle both regiments lost their COs; Lieutenant-Colonels Richard A L Fraser-Mackenzie, a Scot, and John H W Evatt, from Essex, were killed.[23] We have already seen that the machine gunners of 1/7th Middlesex had also been committed to battle – Wimberley had included a special exhortation for his Sassenachs in his pre-battle order of the day – with companies attached to each attacking brigade and a third supporting 9th Australian Division. The Diehards fought with total professionalism, lending the best possible machine-gun support to their infantry comrades; they, too, suffered many casualties.

Throughout the 24th the emphasis of operations lay in the air with ground operations limited to those of 1st Armoured and 51st (Highland) Divisions in the northern corridor.[24] Following Montgomery's order for intense air support on the XXX Corps front, light bombers and fighter-bombers harassed enemy positions. Battlegroups of the German 15th Panzer and Italian Littorio Divisions were attacked; eight bombers were lost and twenty-seven damaged. British and American aircraft were involved in these operations and the Desert Air Force flew almost a thousand sorties, most supporting ground forces. RAF aircraft intercepted a group of Junkers Ju52 transports, escorted by Messerschmitt Bf110s, destroying five transports and damaging severely six others. In XIII Corps' sector cannon-armed tankbuster Hurricanes strafed a German armoured unit operating captured British Stuart tanks, destroying seven Stuarts and damaging five. Other Allied aircraft attacked enemy landing grounds at El Daba and Qotafiya. However, in the early afternoon dust put two fighter strips out of action and fighter patrols over Axis forward landing strips and the battle area were cancelled so that escorts could be provided for the many bombers in the air.[25]

Air reconnaissance showed little change in enemy dispositions at first light while, during the day, Intelligence staff reported no signs of 15th Panzer, 21st Panzer or 90th Light Divisions on the move.[26] Leese, commanding XXX Corps, who had visited Miteiriya Ridge with Freyberg, was satisfied that his infantry were well placed to meet any counter-attack. Although signs of counter-attacks were reported, none developed but Axis artillery became active everywhere. This was no surprise to the men of 7th Armoured Division in the south who had already experienced considerable harassment from those guns.

In the meantime operations by 1st Armoured and the Highland Divisions were taking place to try to improve the northern corridor. There had, however, been some confusion in communications, due to the presence of elements of two corps in the same area. When Freyberg had asked for 8 Armoured Brigade to support his own 9 Armoured Brigade to restore the momentum of the battle his request was routed from his tactical headquarters to XXX Corps HQ and thence via X Corps to 10th Armoured Division, returning by the same circuitous route. This bureaucracy was exacerbated by the fact that Lumsden, commanding X Corps, and Gatehouse, of 10th Armoured Division, were temporarily out of contact. The former was in the northern corridor and Gatehouse was on Miteiriya Ridge where he saw the losses suffered by Freyberg's armour in their move down the forward slope. Observing indications of possible counter-attacks, Gatehouse considered that his armour should give all possible defensive support to the New Zealanders. From Freyberg he learned of a clear gap that would allow tanks to move to the New Zealanders' right flank. Although this was contrary to what Lumsden had said, Gatehouse ordered 24 Armoured

Brigade to cross behind 8 Armoured and on to the ridge on their right, a move begun eventually by 47th Royal Tanks.[27]

Then came a contrary order from Lumsden. Unable to contact Gatehouse, the corps commander sent his order directly to 24 Armoured's headquarters. Lumsden's order was for a move behind 8 Armoured and then into and across the Highlanders' sector to help 1st Armoured Division in the northern gap; the brigade was not to move to the right of the New Zealanders.[28] Confusion resulted and momentum was lost. This was probably fortunate for 51st (Highland) Division since, had 24 Armoured carried out Lumsden's order, there might have been even more – and disastrous – confusion in the Division's sector.

The Highlanders had almost lost their commander that morning. Setting out to visit 1st Black Watch at the front, Wimberley's jeep was blown up; his driver and another soldier were killed and another officer very seriously wounded. Wimberley was hurled from the jeep, knocked unconscious and he even thought for a time that he was dead.[29] He was out of action for the rest of the morning which left the Division without overall control. However, he returned to the front in the afternoon to find disagreements between his own brigade commanders and battalion COs and 2 Armoured Brigade about the positions each had reached.

> … great difficulty was experienced in locating the position of units in terms of map reference … largely due to the complete absence of any natural features which could be recognised as unmistakable landmarks. The difference in map locations of the same unit as given by 51 Division and 1 Armoured Division was as great as 1000 or 1200 yards, and even the two Divisional Artilleries could not agree on this matter.
>
> Shortly after 1000 hours 24 October, Corps Royal Artillery contacted 51 Division and offered the assistance of Royal Artillery observation posts in overcoming this difficulty, but at 1135 hours the offer was declined. At 1920 hours the Commander, Corps Royal Artillery again suggested that leading units which were uncertain of their location should, after giving half an hour's warning, fire five green Verey lights at an agreed time, and that the Flash spotting posts would then plot their positions accurately.[30]

Such disagreements would influence some phases of the developing battle. Not only was there disagreement over the location of features but there was even confusion about one of the best-known features of the battleground; Kidney 'Ridge' was really a depression but, due to a misreading of map symbols, was referred to in the manner that has since become familiar.[31]

At this point it is worth looking at what was happening on 'the other side of the hill'. Initially, all that Axis commanders could be certain of was that an artillery bombardment of Great War proportions was taking place along the front, smashing their communications network. As a result General Georg Stumme, commanding the Panzer Armee in Rommel's absence on sick leave, was all but blind. Concerned about low stocks of ammunition, he ordered the Axis artillery not to retaliate immediately, although their capacity for an effective response following the punishment they had taken must be doubted. One Italian unit, 62nd Infantry Regiment of Trento Division, suffered so badly that many soldiers fled. Most Axis infantry heavy weapons were destroyed by shellfire and Stumme's HQ thought that British tanks were assaulting their positions, having destroyed 62nd Infantry Regiment and two battalions of 164th Division. However, it was also believed that Axis artillery had stopped a British breakthrough in the north and that 7th Armoured Division in the south had broken through the outposts before being stopped by the main defence line.[32]

Stumme decided on a personal reconnaissance, Rommel fashion, to clarify the situation. Refusing an escort or a wireless vehicle since, he said, he was travelling only as far as 90th Light Division, he set out with Colonel Büchting and his driver, Corporal Wolf. The trio overshot 90th Light's positions and, driving right to the front, were engaged by Allied troops, probably Australians. Büchting received a fatal head wound and Wolf turned the car about and accelerated away. He did not realise that Stumme had been preparing to jump out but, apparently, hung on to the side of the vehicle, suffered a heart attack and fell; he had been suffering from high blood pressure. Only when Wolf slowed his pace did he realise that he had lost Stumme whose body was not found until the next day.[33] This loss had an adverse effect on Panzer Armee's HQ. General Ritter von Thoma, Afrika Korps' commander, took over and decided that any British penetrations could be sealed off by local counter-attacks. He also chose to keep 21st Panzer and Ariete Divisions in the south and maintain 90th Light in reserve rather than mounting a decisive counter-action.[34]

By early afternoon, Montgomery's chief of staff, Major-General de Guingand, could report that there were no signs of movement by either 21st Panzer or 90th Light Division and that some 1,000 prisoners, about two-thirds of them Italian, had been captured. Eighth Army casualties were uncertain but did not exceed 3,000, mostly in XXX Corps; Highland Division losses were about 1,000, the New Zealanders had lost about 800 men and the Australians and South Africans some 700 in total, almost evenly divided between the two divisions.[35] Wimberley was now bringing forward 2nd Seaforth who, supported by 50th Royal Tanks and the divisional artillery, were to clear the northern lane by attacking the enemy strongpoints of Strichen and Keith, short of Black line.[36]

Three companies of 2nd Seaforth passed through 1st Black Watch and advanced to form a bridgehead through the minefield holding up 2 Armoured Brigade. Lieutenant-Colonel MacKessack had had very little time to prepare his battalion for this operation, which was intended to permit Sappers to clear the way for 2 Armoured Brigade's tanks. Nonetheless, the Seaforth advanced and, despite heavy casualties, achieved their objective. Eighty-five men were lost with B Company losing every officer and the company sergeant-major; it was rallied for a successful charge on its objective by the company clerk. Soon after this, B Company was reinforced by a platoon of A Company which also brought up the battalion medical officer, food, water and reserve ammunition. Both Strichen and Keith were taken. The casualties included men hit by British artillery fire, 'almost certainly due to the uncertainty as to the real location of the troops'.[37] Although 9th Lancers and 10th Hussars had followed the Seaforth, the Bays took a wrong turning to end up in the Australian sector.[38]

However, 9th Lancers then lost contact with the Seaforth and veered towards the Australian sector where they met the Bays, returning after driving into minefields and meeting anti-tank guns, which claimed six Shermans. Both regiments then advanced through the minefields, their Sappers leading them along the Australian/Highlander boundary. Eventually 9th Lancers and 10th Hussars were ordered to 'advance in support of 51 Div and not to wait for MTF'.[39] At 3.50pm 9th Lancers reported that they were through the first minefield and engaged with enemy tanks. From 15th Panzer and Littorio Divisions, these had the advantage of the sun behind them. With 10th Hussars having also encountered Axis tanks, a fierce tank battle developed with 2 Armoured Brigade supported by the Priests of 11th (HAC) RHA. As night fell the enemy withdrew, leaving twenty-one burning tanks behind.[40] Although British losses were similar the Stirling strongpoint had been overrun, aided by a diversionary attack by 50th Royal Tanks which drew fire from 88s in Stirling; the regiment lost nine tanks to mines. The Divisional artillery had also played a crucial role with Lieutenant-Colonel William Anthony Sheil, of 128th Field Regiment, earning the DSO for his part. With the Highland infantry close to the target and enemy tanks in the area, Sheil, who had been ordered to engage Stirling with concentrated fire from all his guns,

> considered the task so important and so difficult that he undertook it himself [as a FOO]. He worked his way forward to an observation post within 500 yards of the locality, identified our own troops, and then ranged his regiment on the actual enemy defences while our own and enemy tanks fired at each other over his head. Our own tanks then advanced, and he saw the enemy anti-tank gunners man their guns. He brought down a regimental concentration on them and saw them run back to their dug-outs.[41]

When the British tanks were engaged by 88s firing from the flank, Sheil ordered his regiment to pound the Stirling area, which they continued to do throughout the day. This destructive fire played its part in forcing the Germans to abandon the position. During that period, also, two Seaforth companies, under Major A M Gilmour, performed especially sterling service by holding an isolated position against considerable enemy pressure.[42]

The confusion over locations now became more significant. Believing his brigade start line to be some 3,000 yards, or more, farther west than it was, Brigadier Fisher now considered that two of his regiments were on the northern hinge of *Pierson*, while the other was just short of the objective. Still believing this, 2 Armoured Brigade withdrew about 500 yards that night, having lost twenty Shermans in all.[43] But they were far short of *Pierson*. Fisher's report to 1st Armoured Division HQ led Briggs to order 7 Motor Brigade's battalions to advance; by midnight those battalions were close behind the forward positions.[44] Reports reaching Montgomery that evening suggested satisfactory progress in the northern corridor.

Montgomery described the events of that night as the time 'when the real crisis in the battle occurred'.[45] Plans for the night 24–25 October, the night of the full moon, included a breakout by 10th Armoured Division in the southern corridor; 9 Armoured Brigade would withdraw to allow 24 Armoured to attack south-westwards, its axis on the northern boundary of the original divisional break-through sector. South of 24 Brigade, 8 Armoured Brigade would also attack; both were to punch through to *Pierson* to join 2 Armoured. In the course of the day this plan was altered to bring 9 Armoured Brigade and the New Zealand Divisional Cavalry in on the left while 133 Lorried Infantry Brigade took over the positions hitherto held by 8 and 9 Armoured Brigades and 5 New Zealand Brigade. The latter would then follow 9 Armoured Brigade in an exploitation role. Likewise, 133 Lorried Infantry would follow their armour towards *Pierson*. For this operation divisional engineers were to clear as many sixteen-yard gaps as possible in the minefield on the ridge. In their sectors, 9th Australian and 51st (Highland) Divisions were to undertake less ambitious operations.[46]

Freyberg was not convinced that 10th Armoured Division 'was being properly set up for its attack' and reported his misgivings to Leese.[47] This was the night when de Guingand, learning from Leese of Freyberg's concerns, felt compelled to disturb Montgomery's sleep and convene a conference of the Army commander and the commanders of X and XXX Corps.[48] Leese and Lumsden were summoned to Montgomery's caravan at 3.30am 'to galvanise the whole show into action'. Having established the locations of the various formations, Montgomery

> told both corps commanders that my orders were unchanged; there
> would be no departure from my plan. I kept Lumsden behind when

the others had left and spoke very plainly to him. I said I was determined that the armoured divisions would get out of the minefield area and into the open where they could manoeuvre; any wavering or lack of firmness now would be fatal. If he himself, or the Commander 10th Armoured Division, was not 'for it,' then I would appoint others who were.[49]

In his *Memoirs*, Montgomery claims that all the armour had debouched into the open by 8.00am with Eighth Army now in the position he had intended to have achieved a full twenty-four hours earlier.[50] This was far from being true.

There had been forward movement by some of the armour and Freyberg seems to have inspired this but it was not as much as Montgomery later claimed. Although two armoured brigades had linked up, they were not on *Pierson* as they, and their HQs, believed. More success had greeted the Australian effort of that night in which 20 Brigade had advanced to its final objective.[51]

In the Highland Division sector there had also been progress with 1st Gordons, whose two forward companies had been cut off, reunited on the night of the 24th on Black line from which, under Major James Hay, they advanced to secure Aberdeen, on the north-eastern rim of the Kidney feature. This advance was led by D Company supported by a platoon of 1/7th Middlesex. Negotiating some barbed wire they were spotted by a German patrol which, receiving no response to a challenge, turned about and made off. Shortly after this, flares went up and they were greeted with mortar and small-arms fire. Then, to their surprise, they met soldiers of 7th Rifle Brigade, one of 1st Armoured Division's motor battalions, who had advanced through the Australian sector and were to deploy in support of 2 Armoured Brigade. However, their vehicles had been blown up by mines and fire from Aberdeen had them pinned down. The Gordons and Middlesex were obliged to dig in alongside the riflemen but the ground was almost solid rock, making it impossible to dig down more than a foot. There they were on virtually open ground when dawn broke on the 25th. The Middlesex gun crews and Rifle Brigade anti-tank gunners were on open ground and suffered heavily from enemy fire that day. Although attacked by German and Italian tanks the Green Jacket anti-tank gunners with their 6-pounders proved more than a match for the enemy and, supported by field artillery, fought off the attacks; at least fourteen enemy tanks were disabled.

This was the first infantry versus armour action of Alamein and the first of several manifestations that were to follow (exemplified on both sides) of the helplessness of tanks in the face of stoutly-manned anti-tank guns. It was a fine and highly significant little action that has hitherto remained in obscurity to nearly all but those who took part in it.[52]

An attempt that night by 1st Gordons to relieve the men before Aberdeen was unsuccessful although a small party managed to get water to the beleaguered Gordons, Diehards and Green Jackets.[53]

During the 24th, 5th/7th Gordons had consolidated their hold on Insch and Turrif and seized Strichen which had eluded them the previous night.[54] That day also, 7th Argylls endured heavy shelling in their positions with their Pipe Major, Ian Maclachlan, lost to sniper fire. That night the battalion advanced again, seizing Nairn on Blue line in a silent attack. Opposition had been heavy from the moment the Argylls assembled on the start-line and there were many losses; A and D Companies lost all their officers and sergeants led the companies in the final bayonet charge that drove the enemy from Nairn. Once again the Divisional artillery had played a vital part with 126th (Highland) Field Regiment silencing a single 88 close to Nairn.[55]

By the night of 26 October, the Highland Division had advanced six miles, taken all its objectives and suffered over 2,000 casualties. The infantry had done all that Montgomery had asked but the armour remained stalled and Eighth Army was losing its momentum. It was time for a rethink and Montgomery now began to review the situation and seek an alternative strategy to succeed LIGHTFOOT.

To his revised plan Montgomery gave the codename SUPERCHARGE. He intended to re-organise his forces and strike anew at the Axis line, this time along the axis of the coast road. However, Rommel, who had returned quickly to Africa, had foreseen this and moved the bulk of his German forces into the northern sector ready to meet Eighth Army's assault. Then, on 29 October at 11.00am, Montgomery decided to change the focus of his attack, sending it against the junction of the Italian and German troops. He had been persuaded to change his mind following a visit by Alexander and his chief of staff, Major-General Dick McCreery. The latter had identified the inherent flaw in Montgomery's plan and de Guingand was persuaded to convince Montgomery that the revision was his own idea.[56] With the plans for SUPERCHARGE taking shape, formations were withdrawn from the line to prepare for the renewed offensive. The armour was to regroup and the principal infantry formations involved in SUPERCHARGE were to be the Australian and New Zealand Divisions.

By 30 October Freyberg's Division had suffered over 1,500 casualties.[57] Moreover, following its losses earlier in the year, the division deployed only two infantry brigades – 9 Armoured Brigade was an integral, if temporary, element of the division – and he was concerned about further heavy losses. Because of this Freyberg told Montgomery that he was unwilling to accept the risks involved in leading another major operation with his New Zealanders. Aware that Freyberg, as a Commonwealth commander, had the right of appeal to the New Zealand government and keen to have him in command of the assault, Montgomery proposed a compromise. The assault would be commanded by HQ 2nd New Zealand Division but with brigades detached for the operation from other divisions: the Royal Sussex Brigade from 44th (Home Counties), the Durham Brigade from 50th (Northumbrian) and the Seaforth and Cameron Brigade from 51st (Highland); the Greek Brigade would also be available if required. Freyberg accepted this compromise, although the Royal Sussex Brigade was placed under Wimberley's command and the New Zealand Division's order of battle for SUPERCHARGE became 5 New Zealand Brigade, 151 (Durham) Brigade, 152 (Seaforth and Cameron) Brigade and 9 Armoured Brigade. Additional support was provided by 24 Armoured Brigade while 6 New Zealand Brigade, temporarily under Wimberley's command, was to revert to Freyberg when the operation began.[58]

Freyberg also persuaded Montgomery to delay D-Day for SUPERCHARGE by twenty-four hours to allow time for proper preparation. Thus the assault was to be launched on the night of 1–2 November with the attack beginning at 1.30am on the 2nd.[59] This allowed the infantry the maximum of moonlight but only four and half hours in which to achieve their objectives. Once again, strong artillery support was provided; Eighth Army's guns would fire 50,000 rounds in those four and a half hours. Leading the attack would be the Durham and Seaforth and Cameron Brigades, the latter on the left flank; left flank protection was to be provided by 133 (Royal Sussex) Brigade. Valentine tanks from 8th and 50th Royal Tanks were to support the two brigades whose objectives were codenamed Neat for the Highlanders and Brandy for the Durhams. With those objectives taken, the tanks of 9 Armoured Brigade would pass through to attack the enemy anti-tank guns dug in along the Rahman track and then seize Aqqaqir Ridge, creating a breach for 1st Armoured Division to burst through. Brigadier C E Lucas Phillips, an El Alamein veteran, summarised the respective roles of infantry and armour:

> The infantry ... were only a means to an end. Theirs was the task to storm the approaches to the citadel. It was for the armour to break in the gates and to destroy the enemy within. The most critical of all tasks was that designed for 9th Armoured Brigade, who were to break open the gate so long locked by the enemy's anti-tank guns, now ranged in strength along and before the Rahman Track.[60]

Freyberg planned that the infantry would move forward from their tapes at 12.55am, the guns opening fire ten minutes later, H-Hour. Neat and Brandy were to be taken at 3.45am allowing the tanks of 9 Armoured Brigade to begin advancing at 5.45am. An hour later, X Corps would take over to pass 1st Armoured Division through 9 Armoured Brigade. As well as the artillery support, RAF and Fleet Air Arm squadrons were to bomb the enemy positions and minefield task forces had been formed, as for LIGHTFOOT.[61]

On the evening of 1 November Rommel's forces were still counter-attacking in the Australian sector. In spite of hard fighting, Morshead's men had the situation well under control. Nothing suggested that Rommel expected a major attack south of the Australians; from his dispositions it seemed he still expected any further attack to be along the main road in the north with 21st Panzer Division apparently positioned to counter any such attack. Eighth Army believed that there had been no significant change in Axis dispositions. The intelligence available to Montgomery suggested that German forces were concentrated in the northern sector with Italian troops on the front that the New Zealand Division was to attack. Rommel, who had not used the opportunity for counter-attack presented by Eighth Army's re-organisation, seemed focused on the operations against the Australians to relieve Thompson's Post; it appeared that he had no idea of the strength or direction of the attack about to fall on Panzer Armee Afrika.[62]

The attack began on time under cover of a heavy bombardment and the assaulting brigades moved forward through dust and smoke, each on a 2,000 yards frontage. From the ranks of 5th Seaforth and 5th Camerons came once again the savage but inspiring strains of Highland pipes. A hunting horn sounded from the ranks of 9th Durhams, answering the call of the pipes. As in LIGHTFOOT the advancing Jocks had fashioned St Andrew's crosses from rifle-cleaning flannel, affixing strips of the fabric to the braces of their webbing as identification marks.[63]

Freyberg later commented that the Highlanders' advance went 'like a drill'.[64] On the right were 5th Seaforth, with 5th Camerons to their left and 2nd Seaforth following to 'mop up' while the brigade commander, George Murray, was in constant wireless contact with all three battalions and with Freyberg. Neat was reached by 4.17am and there the two leading battalions went into action against enemy tanks.[65] D Company, 5th Camerons, however, had lost all their officers, except the company commander. At this point Company Sergeant-Major James Ahern took command of one platoon and company HQ and

led them in a most aggressive manner against seven enemy tanks which he found on the company's objective. He then proceeded to organize these platoons in a defensive position and got them dug in.

An Irishman, born in Queenstown, now Cobh, County Cork, Ahern was awarded the Military Medal for his inspiring leadership and example.[66]

Artillery support was now coming down and, by 5.25am, the enemy tanks were retreating and the Camerons' heavy weapons and supporting anti-tank guns were arriving. Re-organisation was soon complete; casualties for 152 Brigade were not more than forty per battalion.[67] The contrast with D-Day for LIGHTFOOT could not have been greater: although carried out in the full heat of battle the operation had been completed with more smoothness than many battle exercises. The New Zealanders had achieved their objectives although Rommel believed that he had halted the British advance. 'After some heavy fighting we succeeded in halting this advance by throwing in the 90th Light Division's reserves. The enemy steadily strengthened his forces in the wedge he had driven into our line.'[68] However, Rommel's 'wedge' was the planned limit of the infantry penetration; the battle was now to pass to X Corps' armour.

Although the enemy counter-attacked 152 Brigade's positions during the afternoon of 2 November, their efforts were repulsed and that evening the Brigade, now returned to Wimberley's command, made a fresh attack, supported by 50th Royal Tanks, advancing almost a mile in little more than twenty minutes.[69] No casualties were suffered but some 100 Italians were taken prisoner. Next day it was the turn of 7th Argylls of 154 Brigade to take up the baton; the battalion was ordered to attack the enemy strongpoint at Tel el Aqqaqir on the morning of the 4th. With artillery support from seven regiments, the Argylls advanced on their objective but their greatest danger came from shells falling short since the enemy had abandoned the position and the Argylls were able to walk in. There they found a considerable amount of the impedimenta of a divisional HQ, including Afrika Korps badges and Iron Crosses. Needless to say, many of these were liberated as souvenirs and the battalion even staged a mock investiture to present the Iron Cross to their CO; many Jocks were spotted with the German decoration pinned to their chests.[70]

By now, the enemy defences had been broken and the Panzer Armee had begun a withdrawal, leaving several Italian formations, which had no transport, to fight a rearguard. It was time for Montgomery to organise a pursuit of the fleeing Axis forces in order to bring about their complete destruction. But the general who had planned the set-piece battle so well had not made adequate arrangements for the pursuit and Rommel's depleted forces were able to get away. Although 51st (Highland) Reconnaissance Regiment was committed to the initial pursuit to Fuka, and captured 500 prisoners, the entire Division was withdrawn to re-organise, concentrating at El Daba and Sidi Haneish.[71]

In the wake of the battle, Oliver Leese, XXX Corps' commander, sent a message of congratulations to the men of the Division to which Douglas Wimberley added his own special footnote:

In the last 14 days, we of the 1942 Edition, have, I am sure, reminded Scotland that we too were chipped off just the same block of Northern Granite that provided the best British fighting Division of the last great War.[72]

There could be no doubt that the Division had settled the score for St Valéry and would go on to bring even more credit to its name in the years ahead.

Notes

1. NA Kew, WO169/4295, war diary, 153 Bde, 1942
2. NA Kew, WO201/605, Battle of Egypt, narrative by Lt-Col Oswald
3. Kippenberger, *Infantry Brigadier*, p. 229
4. Salmond, *The History of the 51st Highland Division*, p. 39
5. McGregor, *Spirit of Angus*, p. 39
6. Wimberley, *Memoirs, Vol II*, p. 45
7. McGregor, op cit, p. 39
8. NA Kew, WO169/5017, war diary, 1 Gordons, 1942
9. Salmond, op cit. p. 44
10. NA Kew, WO169/5018, war diary, 5/7 Gordons, 1942; Salmond, op cit, p. 45
11. Salmond, op cit, pp. 45–6
12. Doherty, *The Sound of History*, p. 123
13. Salmond, op cit, pp. 42–3
14. Ibid, p. 40; NA Kew, WO169/4986, war diary, 7 A&SH, 1942
15. NA Kew, WO169/4171, war diary, 51 (H) Recce, 1942
16. Doherty, *Only The Enemy*, p. 123
17. IWM DS/MISC/63, Lt George F Morrison
18. Doherty, *The Sound of History*, p. 123
19. Ibid, pp. 128–9
20. Ibid, p. 131
21. Joslen, *Orders of Battle*, p. 148
22. Doherty, *The Sound of History*, p. 131
23. Salmond, op cit, p. 38n; CWGC website, www.cwgc.org
24. Doherty, *The Sound of History*, p.145
25. Playfair, *The Mediterranean and the Middle East*, Vol IV, pp. 43–4
26. Ibid, p. 43
27. Doherty, *The Sound of History*, pp. 145–6
28. Ibid, p. 146
29. Wimberley, op cit, p. 42
30. NA Kew, CAB44/102, p. 299
31. Doherty, *The Sound of History*, p. 147
32. Ibid, pp. 147–8
33. Ibid
34. Ibid, p. 148
35. Quoted in ibid, p. 148

36. Doherty, *The Sound of History*, p. 148
37. NA Kew, CAB44/102, p. 301
38. Ibid
39. NA Kew, WO169/4219, war diary 2 Armd Bde, 1942
40. Ibid
41. *Volunteers from Éire who have won distinction serving with the British Forces,* p. 12
42. Ibid; Salmond, op cit, p. 47
43. NA Kew, WO169/4219, war diary, 2 Armd Bde, 1942; Doherty, *The Sound of History*, p. 49
44. Doherty, *The Sound of History*, p. 149
45. Montgomery, *Memoirs*, p. 219
46. Doherty, *The Sound of History*, p. 150
47. Freyberg, *Freyberg*, p. 401
48. Ibid
49. Montgomery, op cit, p. 130
50. Ibid
51. Doherty, *The Sound of History*, p. 153
52. Lucas Phillips, *Alamein*, p. 214
53. Ibid
54. NA Kew, WO169/5018, war diary, 5/7 Gordons, 1942
55. NA Kew, WO169/4986, 7 A&SH, 1942; CWGC website, www.cwgc.org
56. Doherty, *Ireland's Generals in the Second World War*, pp. 155–6
57. Doherty, *The Sound of History*, p. 202n
58. Ibid, pp. 202–3
59. Ibid, p. 200
60. Lucas Phillips, op cit, p. 331
61. Ibid
62. Doherty, *The Sound of History*, p. 207
63. Ibid, p. 209
64. Wimberley, op cit, p. 52
65. NA Kew, WO169/4292, war diary, 152 Bde, 1942
66. Doherty, *Irish Men and Women*, p. 233; NA Kew, WO169/5059, war diary, 5 Seaforth, 1942
67. NA Kew, WO169/4292, war diary, 152 Bde, 1942
68. *Rommel Papers*, p. 317
69. NA Kew, WO169/4292, war diary, 152 Bde, 1942
70. NA Kew, WO169/4986, war diary, 7 A&SH, 1942
71. NA Kew, WO169/4171, war diary, 51 (H) Recce, 1942; WO169/4164, war diary, HQ 51 (H) Div (GS), 1942
72. Wimberley, op cit, p. 51

CHAPTER VI

Victory in North Africa

Re-organisation meant an opportunity to smarten up and return to the now well-known excellent turnout of the Division's soldiers. There was much 'spit and polish' while the Divisional sign appeared on track signs and many other locations. By now the Highlanders were becoming known as the 'Highway Decorators' from their habit of painting HD on almost any available surface in the Division's area. Wimberley considered the ability to smarten up after a battle to be the first test of a first class fighting formation and his Highlanders did not disappoint him.[1]

Re-organisation also meant absorbing reinforcements to replace those lost in battle. Each unit had its newcomers while those who had survived wondered at how they had done so. Bert Mitchell described the days of the battle as the worst of his life. After it was over he was promoted to lance-corporal, commenting that there was probably no one else who wanted the chevron.[2] Tom Rennie, CO of 5th Black Watch, was one of those decorated for his part in the battle, being awarded the DSO. However, Rennie did not forget those of his battalion who had been killed; at a memorial service on 8 November the names of the sixty-eight dead were read out by him and the pipers played the 'Flowers of the Forest'. In 153 Brigade Armistice Day – 11 November – was observed 'in the field' and, once again, the strains of 'Flowers of the Forest' could be heard 'in memory of those of their regiments who fell in the last war and who have fallen in this'.[3]

On 19 November 153 Brigade left for Tobruk to be followed by the remainder of the Division between the 21st and 24th. The war diary of 153 Brigade notes that General Montgomery joined the officers of the Brigade HQ for lunch on St Andrew's Day[4] but that of 152 Brigade reported a disaster shortly after this in 2nd Seaforth when three men 'walked into a field of S mines and were wounded'.[5] During a rescue bid, several more became casualties with ten men being killed and another thirteen wounded. Captain Donald Mackenzie of the Seaforth was among the dead, who also included two Sappers and an orderly from the RAMC who had come to help; the wounded included the CO, Colonel MacKessack, and the RSM.[6]

On the 20th 152 Brigade held a Brigade MT Show with classes for every type of vehicle, including captured enemy vehicles that units had impressed into service. This latter class was won by 5th Camerons with a Chevrolet 3-tonner, a vehicle that had changed hands twice. As well as the MT Show, there were platoon drill and infantry anti-tank gun drill competitions and the day was rounded off by the Massed Bands playing 'Retreat'. Although the day began with a heavy sandstorm, making for miserable conditions in the morning, the wind dropped and the afternoon turned out very well. 'Tea was taken at Bde HQ in a very large and splendidly equipped Italian tent, two of which had been found, one being used as the Officers' Mess and the other as a men's rec tent'.[7]

As they advanced the Highlanders were able to see the awful country over which the desert campaign had been fought since June 1940, including Knightsbridge and the Halfaya Pass, known to soldiers as the Hellfire Pass. From Acroma to Bir Hacheim, which 152 Brigade reached on the 28th, 'the ground was full of old minefields and defensive works'.[8] The lessons in navigation using the sun proved invaluable as convoys rolled forward over some of the most inhospitable land in Africa. Water was short and there was no local produce to be bought to supplement the rations. It was during this period that the Division learned that it would lose its Reconnaissance Regiment. Colonel Grant had been called back to Cairo where, at GHQ, he was told that 51 Recce was to return to the Delta to re-organise as a motorised infantry battalion. On 14 January 1943 the Regiment became 14th Highland Light Infantry, a title that was received with dismay. In spite of its name the HLI was a Lowland regiment and conversion to a Lowland title was probably the worst fate that could befall any Highland unit. The Jocks gave voice to their disapproval at a vesting day parade when, in the presence of senior HLI officers and members of the General Staff from Cairo, their response to a call for three cheers was 'three hearty boos'.[9]

In early December it seemed that the Division might have to fight another set-piece battle. The enemy was reported to be holding positions at Mersa el Brega, known to British desert veterans as El Agheila, the farthest point reached by British troops in previous offensives, and Wimberley's staff drew up plans for an assault, scheduled for 13 December. However, the Axis stand at Mersa el Brega was a feint and when 152 Brigade attacked the village it found no enemy. But there were signs of his recent presence, not least many dead bodies. There were also numerous mines and the Division's casualties came from these. Two Black Watch battalions, 1st and 7th, spearheaded the attack with the former suffering many casualties from mines. They were joined by 7th Argylls and when parties of the latter went to move corpses for burial they found that many had been booby-trapped and some twenty men became casualties. Lying about the former enemy positions were a lot of attractive souvenirs but the temptation to take some of these, which included rations, bottles of wine and items of uniform, had to be resisted due to the danger of booby-traps.[10]

The Division was now withdrawn into corps reserve and concentrated around El Agheila as 7th Armoured Division passed through to take up the pursuit. This temporary withdrawal from action provided an opportunity for training and exercises, including night exercises with armour to practise attacks through minefields. Of course, there was also time for sport and recreation, to celebrate Christmas and to welcome in 1943. The 'Balmorals' were called into action while the Black Watch presented a pantomime called 'The Agheila Angels' that featured an orchestra of accordion, bugle, drums, trumpet and violin.[11] Church services and a menu that included turkey, plum pudding and beer marked Christmas Day, while 7th Black Watch took delivery of a consignment of whisky.[12] During this period the Division also bade farewell to Brigadier Houldsworth of 154 Brigade who, on Montgomery's recommendation, was posted home as the first commander of the new School of Infantry at Barnard Castle. He was succeeded as brigade commander by Tom Rennie, who had commanded 5th Black Watch and had recovered from being wounded.[13]

At the beginning of January the Division was joined by a new regiment, and a strange addition to an infantry division: 9th (Londonderry) Heavy AA Regiment was placed under command of the Division for the advance to Tripoli. Initially, one battery – 25 HAA Battery – joined on 11 January near Nufilia, coming under command of the CRA 'and deployed on a mobile basis to protect the advance' of the infantry.[14] Another battery deployed to protect troop concentrations and mineclearing Sappers. Mines were, once more, proving a considerable menace. Only the main road and a track, known as Highland Division Track, had been cleared of mines and advancing units had to exercise great care. In spite of this there were still casualties. One veteran of the Londonderry Regiment recalled that, when a gun and its Matador tractor got into difficulties, another Gunner jumped over the tapes that Sappers had laid to mark the dangerous areas to assist in the rescue operation. That Gunner returned in the same fashion but moments after the lorry and gun moved off a mine exploded just where they had been stopped.[15] By 20 January all three batteries of 9th (Londonderry) HAA Regiment were under command of the Highland Division to provide air defence as the infantry closed on Tripoli; the regiment also had 138 LAA Battery under command.[16]

The 3.7-inch heavy anti-aircraft guns of the Londonderry Regiment had been assigned to the Division for the final element of Eighth Army's advance on Tripoli, the last remaining city of Italy's empire in Africa. As the New Zealand and 7th Armoured Divisions moved inland towards Tripoli, 51st (Highland) Division was to advance by the coast in four phases dubbed SILK, SATIN, COTTON and RAGS. In SILK, 154 Brigade was to make contact with the enemy before capturing and consolidating positions at Buerat in SATIN. COTTON would follow as the Division advanced on Tripoli while, in RAGS, Sappers would clear the coast road for wheeled transport. On the night of 14 January, 154 Brigade launched SILK to be followed by 153 Brigade launching the attack – SATIN – twenty-four hours later. In SATIN, 1st Gordons, supported by Scorpions and 40th Royal Tanks and with Middlesex companies covering the flanks, led the way. Shelling and mines caused some casualties while seven Scorpions were knocked out but the Gordons had broken the enemy line and Axis troops were withdrawing. Now 5th/7th Gordons passed through their regular comrades and moved south-westwards with 5th Black Watch also passing through to move north-westwards. Tanks, anti-tank Gunners, Sappers and Diehards advanced in support.[17]

The successful completion of the first two phases allowed 152 Brigade to initiate COTTON on the 16th. There was a brief delay due to the late arrival of a supply of fuel while the gap through the minefields was still narrow, although the Sappers were working hard to improve it. The Brigade moved forward by lorry, knowing that the enemy had established a line across the road some forty miles ahead at Churgia, about a third of the way to Misurata, the objective. Leading the advance were 5th Camerons who ran into Axis artillery fire at long range. The CO was wounded, a number of lorries were hit, and many personnel were killed or wounded. Nonetheless the advance continued and the Camerons and 5th Seaforth were on high ground overlooking Misurata on the 19th. By-passing the town they continued to the south of Zliten.[18]

In the meantime, Brigadier Murray, commander of 152 Brigade, entered Misurata, around which a cordon had been placed, with C Company 2nd Seaforth on the 18th. Under his command, Murray also had a Sudan Defence Force detachment, which was to assume a police role when Misurata was reached. However, the Sudanese had moved on to the village of Crispe, to the east, where they encountered a rearguard party of Germans from 90th Light Division. In this encounter the Sudanese suffered several casualties. Fortunately, the Germans had no intention of remaining in their positions.[19]

Wimberley now ordered 154 Brigade to make for Homs, by-passing Misurata. This proved a difficult advance as retreating Axis troops had carried out many demolitions and planted many mines. At Leptis Magna, birthplace of the Roman Emperor Septimus Severus, the worst conditions were met, forcing 1st Black Watch, who had been leading the advance on the south flank, to quit the open country and fall in behind the 7th Battalion who had been advancing along the road. The latter battalion, helped by local Senussi labour, had been constructing a diversion around the demolitions as well as clearing mines. By nightfall the Black Watch battalions were on the western edge of Homs and engaged with the Axis rearguard across the road. The area was dominated by a fort, some four miles west of the village, known as Homs castle but dubbed Edinburgh Castle by the Highlanders, and the enemy line was anchored on the fort. Axis defences stretched from the sea in the north on their left flank to the deep Wadi Zenadi in the south on their right flank. Tenaciously held, the line was a major obstacle and 1st Black Watch's forward troops were pinned to the ground by accurate shell and small-arms fire; among the battalion's casualties was General Fortune's son, Lieutenant Bruce Fortune, who was wounded while leading a patrol; he was later awarded the MC.[20]

Since Homs Castle was not an objective that could be taken by frontal assault without significant loss, General Wimberley ordered Brigadier Stirling, now commanding 154 Brigade as Rennie had been wounded again, to mount a flanking attack on the coastal side. To this attack were committed three battalions led by 7th Argylls, followed by 7th Black Watch and then 2nd Seaforth, with support from tanks of 40th Royal Tanks and a battery of 25-pounders from 126th Field Regiment. Stirling's objective was to get his command astride the road near Corradini, some fourteen miles away, and cut off the enemy. However, it was not a simple operation as Axis engineers had excavated a deep and wide anti-tank ditch across the road in front of Homs Castle, an obstruction that continued to the sea.[21]

A Company 7th Black Watch crossed the ditch, followed by the other companies of the battalion. All then set off on foot, without their heavy weapons, to cut the main coastal road beyond Wadi Genima, some sixteen miles away. However, the Black Watch misidentified a wadi some half a mile short of Genima as their objective and, having crossed it and crested the far side, spotted a convoy of vehicles moving along the road. Fire was opened on the vehicles before it was realised that they were British and an order was given to cease fire. However, although the vehicles were British they had been captured by the enemy and were in Axis use. The enemy troops now returned fire against the Black Watch whose A Company was on an exposed forward slope. When the enemy were reinforced by some anti-tank guns and a tank the situation became perilous and A Company's forward elements were overrun. It was at this stage that some of the Diehards, who had portered their heavy Vickers guns forward, got into position to open fire on the attackers from the left flank and forced their withdrawal.[22]

The Black Watch had not been the first troops to mistake the wadi for Genima. Before them the same error had been made by 2nd Seaforth who then attacked the enemy post at El Nab, as did their 5th Battalion. However, 5th Seaforth were attacking from the front, having come at El Nab from a bad angle. Thus they had to traverse hilly, broken country and their attack splintered into small group attacks rather than a cohesive battalion effort. Some soldiers even fought alone at times. After

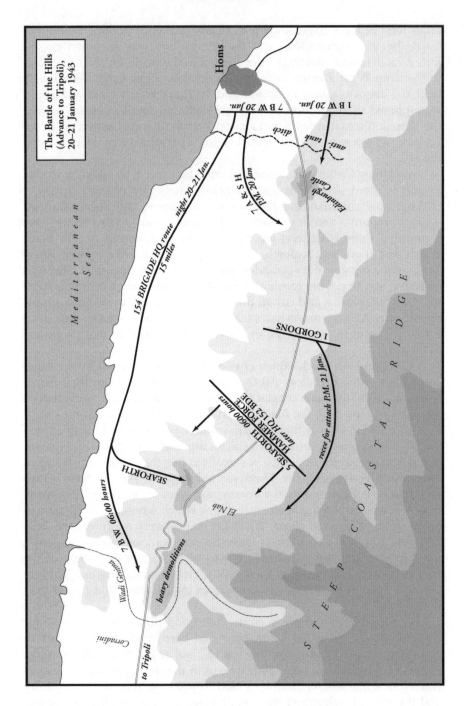

twenty-two hours' fighting, 2nd Seaforth took their objective while the 5th Battalion

> had made a great show in their frontal attack, despite snipers, hand-grenades and dug-in machine-guns. They had to fight very hard, especially with the bayonet. The Germans made several vicious counter-attacks, and B Company had a particularly hefty time.[23]

When the Germans put down a smoke-screen, a further counter-attack was expected and the Seaforth made ready to meet it but the smoke had been released to cover a German withdrawal. The battle for El Nab, which became known as the Battle of the Hills, was over.[24]

It was probably the effects of this flanking attack that caused the Germans at Homs Castle to evacuate their positions also. No one felt sorry that they had gone since the prospect of a frontal attack on the fort was not pleasant. Sadly, Montgomery chose to send for Wimberley on the 20th 'and gave him an imperial "rocket".' Monty thought that the Highlanders 'seemed to be getting weary, and generally displayed a lack of ginger'.[25] His assessment could hardly have been more divorced from reality.

Now came the turn of Hammerforce to advance. This battlegroup was commanded by Brigadier Richards of 23 Armoured Brigade, which had become almost a part of the Division. Under his command, Richards now had a tank squadron, a field battery, two troops of 61st Anti-Tank Regiment, some Sappers and RAMC personnel, in addition to a company of 2nd Seaforth and A Company of the Diehards; a company from 1st Gordons was later included. Hammerforce's task was to mount a rapid pursuit of the retreating enemy and on 21 January it passed through 5th Seaforth to race for Castelverde.[26]

However, making speed was difficult as demolitions had left the road cratered in so many places. Not until the morning of the 22nd did Hammerforce reach Castelverde to find it abandoned. Hammerforce then began filling in craters while 22 Armoured Brigade passed through. The latter met further demolitions which led to Hammerforce deploying its shovels again. Eventually, 22 Armoured found a passable route to the left while Hammerforce moved straight ahead. In the meantime, Wimberley was re-organising the Division for its forward move. Shortages of vehicles and fuel meant that some elements had to be left behind, including a Gunner battery, 1st and 7th Black Watch, 2nd Seaforth, 5th/7th Gordons, 5th Camerons and some of 1/7th Middlesex.[27]

Tripoli fell to Eighth Army on 23 January.[28] The city had not been defended, Rommel deciding to withdraw into Tunisia where the terrain was more suitable for defensive warfare. Tripoli's fall marked the end of the Italian empire in Africa and brought humiliation to Benito Mussolini who had hoped to create a modern Roman empire in the Mediterranean.

As British troops drove into Tripoli that January morning, Italy's part in the war as an Axis partner was entering its final phase.

The Highlanders were the first major element of Eighth Army to enter Tripoli with men of 1st Gordons riding on tanks of 40th Royal Tanks accompanied by a company of 2nd Seaforth in lorries; it was 5.30am on the 23rd. General Wimberley followed closely with his Tactical HQ while the main divisional HQ was established in Tripoli Stadium before noon.[29] The entire Division was quartered in and around Tripoli with 153 Brigade assigned as the local garrison. Almost all accounts of the campaign note that 11th Hussars, the Cherrypickers, were the first British troops into Tripoli. However, that story is disputed by veterans of 9th (Londonderry) HAA Regiment, recce parties of which entered Tripoli before the Hussars and watched the cavalrymen come into the city.[30] Since 9th Regiment was still under command of the Highland Division it seems that the Division can claim the distinction of being the first into Tripoli.

From El Alamein to Tripoli is a distance of some 1,400 miles, which Eighth Army had covered in three months, an achievement that Montgomery described as 'probably without parallel in history' and one that would not have been possible 'unless every soldier in the army had pulled his weight all the time'.[31] The soldiers of 51st (Highland) Division had certainly pulled their weight and this applied not only to the infantrymen but also to the Gunners, Sappers, RASC and RAMC personnel as well as the men of 23 Armoured Brigade. From El Alamein to Tripoli they had left many dead comrades and saw many others injured. Some had fallen to mines and booby traps, some to direct enemy action but they had all contributed to the success that Eighth Army had now achieved.

But the overwhelming feeling among the Highlanders was not of jubilation but rather of exhaustion. Bernard Fergusson wrote that

> The Jocks were now somnambulists to a man, but they worked their way forward, on vehicles when they could, on foot when they must, until they found a crater with nobody working on it. When at last the armour entered Tripoli, at every filled-in crater it passed little groups of Jocks sleeping beside their completed navvy-work. …
>
> Anyway, Tripoli was won; and the Jocks had every right to – and many of them did – sleep for forty-eight hours clear. They had come a goodish way.[32]

Fergusson might have been writing about the Black Watch but his comments were true for the entire Division which was to remain in Tripoli for almost a month as Eighth Army built up its logistical tail for further action. It was not, however, a rest, save in the sense that the Highlanders were not on active operations. Instead, there was the sometimes tedious task of providing guards for vital installations and unloading ships in Tripoli harbour, which was soon back in operation. But there was also the opportunity to remember those who had lost their lives and to celebrate what had been achieved since October. And 'The Balmorals' were in action, playing to some 1,800 men in the Miramare Theatre, which had been re-named HD Theatre with the letters HD glistening in red above the door, as they did on many other buildings in and around Tripoli.[33] General Wimberley had produced tins of red paint from his jeep for the first HD sign to be painted in the town, the paint having been obtained from a local hospital which the GOC had noticed 'had a freshly-painted Red Cross sign'.[34] The padre of 1/7th Middlesex opened a regimental institute on the 28th, 'complete with reading room, writing room and rest room, and even a bath with hot water!'.[35]

General Montgomery visited the Division, congratulating the soldiers on all that they had done since joining Eighth Army. Another visitor was General Sir Harold Alexander, CinC, Middle East, who took the salute at a march past of the Division on 3 February.[36] Among those who witnessed the parade was Brigadier Howard Kippenberger of 2nd New Zealand Division. Of the Highlanders he wrote

> They had brought their kilts with them – where they found room in the transport I cannot imagine. The battalions moved along the Corniche and passed the saluting base in the little square under the Citadel. As they turned into the square they caught the skirl of the pipes, every man braced himself up, put on a swagger, and they went past superbly. I had climbed on to a tank to watch and for an hour was almost intoxicated by the spectacle.[37]

This spectacle was repeated the following day, this time for the benefit of the Prime Minister who was visiting Eighth Army. Churchill and Sir Alan Brooke, the CIGS, were present for a Victory Parade in Tripoli in which 51st (Highland) Division, led by General Wimberley, was prominent. A hundred pipers, all kilted, followed their GOC with representatives of the Divisional Gunners, Sappers and Signals, a representative Highland brigade, including soldiers from each of the Highland regiments, Black Watch, Seaforth, Gordons, Camerons and Argylls, under Brigadier George Murray, as well as a party from 1/7th Middlesex.[38] Not to be outdone by their Gaelic comrades, the Diehards had also applied much spit and polish and in the drive past 'our trucks and turnout looked exceptionally fine – amply borne out by a photograph by the APFU'.[39] The Highlanders' turnout would have impressed even a Guards' sergeant major; webbing had been blanco-ed, boots polished to a mirror-like shine, uniforms immaculate and, of course, the kilts adding the final touch of panache and colour.

Leading the Division, Douglas Wimberley travelled in a Bren-gun carrier flying a Divisional flag emblazoned with the setts of the Highland regiments.[40] His carrier was named 'Beaumont Hamel', after the Division's first major battle in 1916. Other carriers bore either battle honours, such as Assaye, Waterloo and Balaclava, or the names of districts from which the Division drew its soldiers. The GOC wrote that

> I have never felt prouder in all my life. As the Pipes and Drums played our famous Highland Regiments past in turn to the strains of 'Highland Laddie', Pibroch O'Dhomnuill Dubh', the 'Cock of the North' and 'The Campbells are Coming' my heart was very full and there were tears in my eyes. However, I was certainly in good company that day. I noticed the same in Alan Brooke's and as for Winston, the tears were running down his cheeks.[41]

Brooke confirmed Wimberley's observations, writing

> It was quite one of the most impressive sights I have ever seen. The whole division was most beautifully turned out, and might have been in barracks for the last 3 months instead of having marched some 1200 miles and fought many battles during the same period. ... As I stood alongside of Winston watching the Division march past, with the wild music of the pipes in my ears, I felt a lump rise in my throat and a tear run down my face. I looked round at Winston and saw several tears on his face... For the first time I was beginning to live through the thrill of those first successes that were now rendering ultimate victory possible. The depth of those feelings can only be gauged in relation to the utter darkness of those early days of calamities when no single ray of hope could pierce the depth of gloom.[42]

Next day the Highlanders lent their Pipers and Drummers to the New Zealanders for their Divisional parade outside Tripoli. Churchill was later to tell the House of Commons that he had never seen troops march with the style or air of the Desert Army and that the Highland and New Zealand Divisions paraded as if they had just marched out of London's Wellington Barracks. And, of course, it was at Tripoli that Churchill uttered his famous praise of the men of Eighth Army: 'After the war when a man is asked what he did, it will be sufficient to say "I marched and fought with the Desert Army".'[43] Speaking to some of those who were working as stevedores at Tripoli docks, Churchill commented that they were 'unloading history'. The author's father, serving with 25 HAA Battery of 9th (Londonderry) HAA Regiment, was present when Churchill made this comment.

There was more history to be made in a much more bloody fashion and to this form of history-making the Division returned when its first elements quit Tripoli on 12 February. By now Eighth Army had moved into Tunisia where another Allied force, First Army, was also engaged. First Army had landed in French north-west Africa in Operation TORCH as Montgomery's command began its advance out of Egypt. Both armies now came under overall command of General Sir Harold Alexander as CinC, 18 Army Group. The Allied strategy was to trap the Axis forces between the armies and destroy them. To fulfil that strategy, Eighth Army was advancing on the defensive line constructed by the French to protect Tunisia from the expansionist attentions of the Italians in Libya: the Mareth line. Sometimes described as the Maginot line of Tunisia, the Mareth line presented a formidable barrier to anyone seeking to invade Tunisia from the east.[44]

First to leave Tripoli were the men of 153 Brigade but lack of vehicles meant that the infantry had to march most of the way to Ben Gardane. On St Valentine's Day, 5/7th Gordons became the first battalion of the Division to enter Tunisia, where they came under command of 7th Armoured Division.[45] As the other elements of the Division moved forward Wimberley noted that 7th Armoured and 51st (Highland) Divisions were the 'only Eighth Army formations forward at Medenine'[46]; the prospect of an offensive would have to await the arrival of further formations. Moving up to the new front line carried its own risks and lives were lost, but not always from enemy action. On 23 February the BBC's Godfrey Talbot witnessed the deaths of three members of 239 Field Park Company, Royal Engineers as they drove in convoy towards the front. Talbot broadcast a description of the scene in which a lorry suddenly burst into flames and a young officer jumped from another to run towards the burning vehicle with its load of high explosives while a soldier from the burning truck clambered over the back to get at the flames. Their efforts were in vain for, as the officer reached the truck, there was 'a tremendous explosion'. The soldier who left the lorry's cab also died, as did a third man.

> We stood, rather helpless, at the roadside, beside a flaming mass. Not speaking much ... This wasn't enemy action; not the heat of battle. But we had seen again an example, one of a thousand, of the selfless courage and sacrifice of the British Soldier ... We felt very humble.[47]

One of the dead, and probably the man Talbot had seen clambering over the lorry, was Driver William Watt, from Murtle in Aberdeenshire, aged 27. Driver Watt had been a member of a musical group, the 'Harmonisers', who had often entertained their comrades in France, Britain and North Africa.[48]

On 26 February came the news that Rommel had broken off his attack on the Americans in Tunisia. Ultra intelligence confirmed that an Axis attack on Eighth Army was imminent. Montgomery thought such an attack might 'upset the preparations for our own attack on the Mareth Line',[49] scheduled for 19 March. He ordered the New Zealanders forward

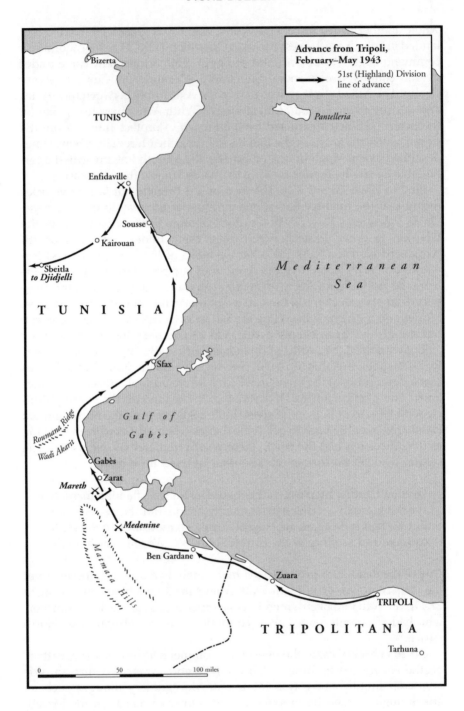

Advance from Tripoli,
February–May 1943

→ 51st (Highland) Division
line of advance

Bizerta

TUNIS

Pantelleria

Enfidaville

Sousse

Kairouan

Sbeitla
to Djidjelli

T U N I S I A

M e d i t e r r a n e a n
S e a

Sfax

Roumana Ridge

Wadi Akarit

G u l f   o f
G a b è s

Gabès

Zarat

Mareth

Medenine

Ben Gardane

Matmata Hills

Zuara

TRIPOLI

T R I P O L I T A N I A

Tarhuna

0   50   100 miles

from Tripoli to strengthen the front-line force and ordered Eighth Army to ensure that its positions were ready to meet and break Rommel's attack.

The Highland Division front was very long and Wimberley was concerned about the threat from enemy armour against which he had insufficient anti-tank guns. He expressed his concern to Montgomery who arranged for an additional anti-tank battery to come under Divisional command.[50] Thus strengthened, Wimberley set about adjusting his dispositions to meet the expected attack. He deployed his troops in strongpoints that covered the intervening ground with machine guns and anti-tank guns while a forward light screen of carriers would give the enemy the impression that the main defences were much farther forward than was the case. A typical Highland Division defensive outpost was that on Wadi Melah where Melaforce included the D Companies of the Seaforth and Cameron Brigade: 2nd Seaforth, 5th Seaforth and 5th Camerons. Less 154 Brigade

> the Division had been ordered to take up positions on the line of Wadi Zessar with 22 Armoured Brigade on the right flank and 7th Armoured Division holding the section South of the Medenine–Mareth road. 152nd Infantry Brigade were to occupy the Southern sector of the Divisional front. 5 Seaforth were to be the centre battalion of the Brigade.[51]

On 2 March 128th (Highland) Field Regiment moved into locations behind Wadi Zessar and the guns engaged enemy attackers next day. On the 4th the Regiment deployed in the wadi itself and continued to fire defensive tasks, engaging and beating off enemy infantry attacks.[52] The real attack from Panzer Armee Afrika, now restyled First Italian Army (this change occurred on 20 February when Axis forces in Tunisia had been re-organised as Army Group Afrika, under Rommel's overall command. The Army Group included Fifth Panzer Armee, under General Jürgen von Arnim, and the former Panzer Armee Afrika, now commanded by the Italian General Messe. Afrika Korps was included in Messe's First Italian Army), came on the morning of 6 March when, under cover of fog, General Messe launched three panzer divisions, with 160 tanks, and four two-battalion battlegroups, supported by 200 guns, at Eighth Army's positions. However, the terrain forced the Axis infantry to bunch up, presenting the artillery and the Middlesex machine gunners with good targets, which they engaged with devastating effect. As the fog burned away the attackers became ever more exposed. There was some air support from the Luftwaffe and Regia Aeronautica, with 'a certain amount of dive-bombing'[53] but, although Axis troops made some progress into Eighth Army's positions, and even moved forward again three times, the enemy was driven back by spirited counter-attacks.

Possibly the hardest hit battalion of the Division was 1st Black Watch. Posted on the left flank of the Division, the Black Watch had a Queen's battalion, from 7th Armoured Division's 131 Lorried Infantry Brigade, on the left. The Queen's were forced back, allowing enemy troops to penetrate the gap and threaten the exposed flank of the Highland Division. However, a company of Black Watch turned left immediately and counter-attacked while the Queen's did likewise, the gap was filled and the position restored. In 7th Argylls' sector the enemy also threatened to break through but the Argylls launched a counter-attack that soon had them retreating. To the south, 201 Guards Brigade, perched on high ground dubbed the Wellington Hills, stood up to all assaults and rebuffed the enemy with heavy losses; this had been the main element of the enemy attack.[54]

Messe, 'a competent, conscientious, realistically pessimistic [commander], and not exactly a fighting general'[55] was forced to call off the attack with the loss of some fifty tanks, all but seven of which had fallen to the anti-tank gunners of the infantry and Royal Artillery, the latter deploying some of the new and highly-effective 17-pounder guns. There was even a troop of captured 88s in use against the Axis tanks. In Highland Division's area the defensive plan had worked well and the outpost screen had helped to knock the enemy off balance; having accepted this screen as the main line he had made his main effort against it, only to find that he was hitting thin air and had to regroup for a fresh assault. Both Eighth Army and 51st (Highland) Division had demonstrated the ability to fight a successful defensive battle.

The Axis forces now retreated behind an outpost line along Wadi Zigzaou and Montgomery chose not to launch a pursuit, preferring to continue with his plans for the assault on the Mareth Line, Operation PUGILIST. Rommel had quit Africa on 9 March to try to persuade both Mussolini and Hitler that a tactical withdrawal some forty miles to Wadi Akarit would shorten the Axis line and ease the burden of defence. Hitler agreed to a partial withdrawal to Wadi Akarit with mobile troops remaining on the Mareth Line but this was countermanded by the Italians on the orders of the Comando Supremo; this was still an Italian theatre. Rommel was ordered to take sick leave and would not return to Tunisia where his place was taken by von Arnim. Along the Mareth Line four Italian and two German divisions were deployed. These were Young Fascist, Trieste, 90th Light, Spezia, Pistoia and 164th Light Divisions.[56] Three panzer divisions were behind the line: in immediate reserve was the much-weakened 15th Panzer; 21st Panzer covered the Gabes Gap; and 10th Panzer was in deep reserve behind Wadi Akarit.[57]

As already noted the Mareth Line had been described as the Maginot Line of Africa, an appropriate analogy since its genesis was similar. However, the Mareth Line was much shorter, stretching from the Mediterranean coast to the Matmata Hills beyond which conventional wisdom had held that an impassable sand sea made a left-flanking movement impossible. The Germans had increased the defences of the line which now included concrete blockhouses, steel gun cupolas and a huge crop of mines. In all, there was a front of about twenty miles and the task facing Eighth Army was the greatest since El Alamein. Later, as Eighth Army moved forward to Wadi Akarit, Wimberley had an opportunity to study the line in detail and recorded being

> most struck by the strength of the Mareth Defences. Not only was there plenty of concrete to be seen, but there were complete communication trenches, and forward saps, such as reminded me of the 1914–18 War.[58]

A frontal attack would be extremely costly, especially as Wadi Zigzaou provided a natural anti-tank obstacle. An Intelligence Summary issued by Divisional HQ noted that the wadi was

> tidal as far as MR [map reference] 623103, where the water level varies from 3 to 12 feet. The ground on either bank from here to the sea is alleged to be so boggy as to be quite unsuitable for any movement, even infantry. From 623103 to 610097 the cliffs are sheer, the drop is not less than 10 to 12 feet, and the surface is extremely boggy and after rain may have as much as 2 to 3 feet of standing water.[59]

Additional work had been carried out on the banks of the wadi to make it even more of an obstacle for tanks. Although frontal assault would be costly the option of flanking left seemed to be ruled out. Or was it? Montgomery considered that a flanking movement was essential and, having learned that two French officers had studied the area in 1938 and reported that the area south of the Matmatas should not be considered impassable, he ordered the Long Range Desert Group to reconnoitre a suitable route for an attacking force. With the increased use of four-wheel-drive vehicles the outflanking of the Mareth Line by skirting the Matmatas to the Tebaga Gap and thence to El Hamma was now feasible. Montgomery cast his plans accordingly. The enemy was also aware of the 1938 French reconnaissance and its outcome.[60]

The final plan was for XXX Corps – 4th (Indian), 50th (Northumbrian) and 51st (Highland) Divisions with 201 Guards Brigade – to break into the line at the northern end, close to the coast, roll it up and then thrust for Gabes. Freyberg's New Zealand Corps – 2nd New Zealand Division, reinforced by 8 Armoured Brigade and General Leclerc's Free French L Force – would flank the Matmatas to establish themselves on the Gabes–Matmata road, thereby cutting off the enemy. When XXX Corps reported success, X Corps – 1st and 7th Armoured Divisions – would exploit that success to strike for the port of Sfax. The latter operation would comply with 18 Army Group's strategic objective of taking Tunis by, first, pushing Eighth Army through the Gabes Gap and, second, seizing enough airstrips to strangle Army Group Afrika.[61]

Operation PUGILIST was to begin on 20 March with 50th (Northumbrian) Division, in action for the first time since El Alamein, making the main attack in the coastal sector. Before D-Day, Major-General Nicholls, the divisional commander, ordered the seizure of an Axis outpost line along Wadi Zeuss, some three miles in front of Wadi Zigzaou and, on the night of 16–17 March, 69 (Yorkshire) Brigade attacked the line; 5th East Yorks and 6th Green Howards were joined by 5th/7th Gordons, on loan from the Highland Division. By daylight the three attacking battalions had taken their objectives and were established a mile beyond Wadi Zeuss. In this assault, Major Napier of 5th/7th Gordons distinguished himself by showing

> great determination in a night attack on a Mareth Line outpost, when he took 'C' Company through two very large minefields and completed an excellent night's work by capturing the enemy position.[62]

In war it is rare that an operation goes according to plan and the Battle of Mareth was no exception. The first grit to enter the work of Montgomery's plan was brought down by heavy rain that transformed the floor of Wadi Zigzaou into a morass, impassable by armour. This created major problems for 50th Division whose infantry crossed the wadi – the CO of 7th Green Howards, 'Bunny' Seagrim, earned the Victoria Cross for his leadership and courage in the attack but was killed at Wadi Akarit before the award was announced – but found their supporting armour halted by the difficult conditions.[63] In spite of the best efforts of infantry, armour and engineers, the attack was stalled. During the night of the 23rd, Montgomery decided that the flanking move should be reinforced and that 50th and 51st Divisions, with 7th Armoured, would remain near the coast in a containment role. Horrocks' X Corps, less the Desert Rats, would join Freyberg's New Zealand Corps as it struck south of the Matmatas.[64] At Montgomery's request, II (US) Corps would strike south-east towards Wadi Akarit to assist Eighth Army.

Thus the Highland Division's role became subsidiary to the breaking of the Mareth Line. Nonetheless, the Division was involved in the fighting in XXX Corps' sector with 5th Seaforth and 5th Camerons of 152 Brigade deploying to support the Northumbrians by holding a section of the Wadi Zigzaou anti-tank ditch. Initially the Camerons were to place a company under command of the Seaforth but this was increased to two companies and then the entire battalion. The Seaforth had relieved 7th Green Howards on the night of the 21st and the Camerons were now to fill in on their right but the enemy fired star shells as B and C Companies of the Camerons moved up, pinning down the infantry. At much the same time, rounds from the Divisional artillery fell short and hit the Camerons. The battalion had lost every radio set by dawn and eventually endured some twenty hours of shelling. In all, 121 men became casualties and no gains had been made. Both battalions suffered heavily – the Seaforth had almost 100 casualties – and were ordered to retire under cover of smoke early on 24 March. Later, as he inspected the anti-tank ditch, Douglas Wimberley saw not only all 'the debris of war' but also 'the still unburied dead of my Seaforth and Camerons, many of whom still lay where they had fallen'.[65] Not for nothing did a Seaforth officer comment that 'the anti-tank ditch will never be forgotten so long as there is a man left alive who lay in it'.[66]

In the coastal sector the Highlanders were ordered to maintain pressure on the enemy by mounting subsidiary attacks and by aggressive patrolling. On the night of 24 March, 5th Black Watch was ordered

to advance to secure a dominating feature called 'Carrier Hill' and it was decided to put in a two-Company attack with a supporting [bombardment] from Corps Artillery. 'A' Company was on the Start Line ready to move at 2100 hours ...; 'B' Company on the Left moved off ten minutes ahead of H-hour and made towards the Wadi to secure the Left flank.[67]

Tragically, some of the artillery pieces had not been adjusted to take account of the lower night temperature and many rounds fell short, right in the midst of A Company as they waited on their start-line. Many were killed but the Company moved off towards the objective only to be shelled there again by their own artillery.[68] Sergeant Thomas Jennings found himself on the objective with a small group of soldiers and much confusion. He organised the defence of the position and held on against heavy mortar fire – from the enemy this time – and several determined counter-attacks. Eventually the CO ordered the survivors of A Company to withdraw and they came back with twenty-seven Italian prisoners. B Company had two platoons in the wadi and were shelled by both sides, but without loss. Major Blair Imrie, the second-in-command, went forward to B Company to order a withdrawal; three Italians were made prisoner.[69]

The unfortunate Black Watch were relieved by 1st Gordons while 5th/7th Gordons, who had also taken part in the night's operations, had taken all their objectives. In a subsequent message, Leese wrote of 5th Black Watch

It speaks worlds for their discipline and esprit de corps that the Battalion reached their objectives and captured 30 prisoners of war, after being shelled heavily by our own guns on the Start Line.[70]

while Wimberley added that the 'Battalion did everything expected of the Royal Highlanders and the Highland Division'.[71]

The left hook by Freyberg's and Horrocks' corps achieved complete success and First Italian Army withdrew to the line of Wadi Akarit, which flows 'into the sea some 15/20 miles north of Gabes'.[72] Eighth Army followed up and prepared to attack 'the last natural barrier against access to the coastal plain of Tunisia from the south'.[73] Since Comando Supremo had accorded priority to the Mareth Line, Messe had done little to the Akarit position before 27 March. However, the position was naturally formidable although part of its strength was disappearing as warmer weather dried out the salt marshes at the Chott el Fedjadj on which rested the western flank of the Axis line. Montgomery, it seems, was unaware of this, although Messe appreciated that the marshes were no longer impassable. Behind the wadi and to the left rose the dominating bare Roumana ridge, over a mile long and 1,600 feet at its highest (Point 198), while a minefield and an anti-tank ditch lay between Eighth Army and Wadi Akarit. 'That ... ditch was practically on the edge of the Wadi, at some points actually cutting into it'.[74] Breaking through at Wadi Akarit to make for Sfax was not going to be a straightforward task for Eighth Army.

Montgomery planned a direct attack with XXX Corps making the initial assault and X Corps exploiting the breakthrough. Leese's corps included the same three divisions as at Mareth – 4th Indian, 50th (Northumbrian) and Wimberley's Highlanders – with 201 Guards Brigade. 'Gertie' Tuker, GOC of 4th Indian Division, considered that his troops would be in their element on the high ground and so argued for a modification of the initial plan, which Montgomery conceded. This made little difference to the Highland Division which was to assault Roumana ridge and the defences at the south-western end of the ridge, making some crossings of the anti-tank ditch. To the right of the Highlanders, and under Wimberley's command, 201 Guards Brigade would maintain pressure on the enemy defenders. Montgomery was anxious that the assault should be made as soon as possible, rather than waiting for the full moon and so decided on a daylight attack on 6 April, although the Indians would have begun moving into the hills the night before so that the Fatnassa feature (described by Wimberley as 'a tangled mass of higher ground ... which rose up to a height of 300 metres above the plain'[75]) would be in their hands by 8.30am on the 6th. H-Hour for the Highlanders was 3.30am on 6 April, but the first part of their advance was to be silent; the Divisional artillery would not open fire until 4.15.[76]

While Tuker's men made their way through the mountains, the Highlanders made their final preparations, including once again fashioning St Andrew's crosses from rifle-cleaning cloth as identification. The Division was to attack on a two-brigade front, with 154 Brigade on the right and 152 on the left, while 153 Brigade held the base line. On the right, 7th Argylls were to attack across the minefield, cross the anti-tank ditch and the wadi to form a bridgehead through which 7th Black Watch would pass before making a left (westward) turn in the wadi to mop up enemy resistance as far as Roumana. Meanwhile, in 152 Brigade's sector, the attacking battalions, 5th Seaforth on the right and 5th Camerons on the left, were to take the left end of Roumana ridge after which 2nd Seaforth would pass through, make a right turn and mop up from south to north; this would bring 2nd Seaforth into contact with 7th Black Watch on the lower ground. To the left of 152 Brigade, 69 Brigade, the sole attacking brigade of the Northumbrian Division, would also be attacking on to the ridge while 201 Guards Brigade was to the right of 154 Brigade.[77]

The first elements of 154 Brigade's attack were mine-clearing Scorpions followed by tanks of 40th Royal Tanks, which towed anti-tank guns of 241 Anti-Tank Battery. Sappers also advanced to bridge the ditch. The latter performed superbly. In spite of intense machine-gunning and shellfire, they had not only gapped the minefield but bridged the ditch by midday. At 5.15 the Argylls went forward, crossed the minefield and the ten-foot-deep ditch to seize their first objectives. Throughout they had tremendous support from the machine guns of the Middlesex. The full pressure of enemy reaction was now turned on the Argylls with Axis artillery pounding them from the Roumana heights. However, the Highland field guns broke up the first enemy counter-attacks on the Argylls.[78] The CO of the Argylls, Lieutenant-Colonel Lorne Campbell DSO, realised quickly that the gap created in the ditch by the Sappers did not align with the lane cleared through the minefield for vehicles. Since it was vital to bring anti-tank guns up to the most forward positions, Campbell

took personal charge of the operation.

It was now broad daylight, and under very heavy machine-gun fire and shell-fire he succeeded in making a personal reconnaissance and in conducting operations which led to the establishing of a vehicle gap.

Throughout the day Lt-Col Campbell held his position with his Battalion in the face of extremely heavy and constant shell-fire, which the enemy was able to bring to bear by direct observation.

At about 1630 hours determined enemy counter-attacks began to develop, accompanied by tanks. In this phase of the fighting Lt-Col Campbell's personality dominated the battlefield by a display of valour and utter disregard for personal safety which could not have been excelled.

Realising that it was imperative for the future success of the army plan to hold the bridgehead his Battalion had captured, he inspired his men by his presence in the forefront of the battle, cheering them

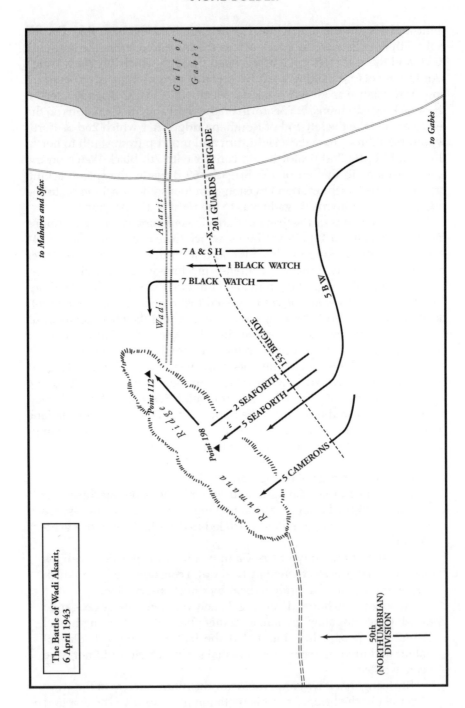

Gulf of Gabès

to Gabès

to Mahares and Sfax

Akarit

X 201 GUARDS BRIGADE

7 A & S H

1 BLACK WATCH

7 BLACK WATCH

Wadi

5 B W

153 BRIGADE

2 SEAFORTH

5 SEAFORTH

5 CAMERONS

Point 112

Point 198

Ridge

Roumana

The Battle of Wadi Akarit,
6 April 1943

50th
(NORTHUMBRIAN)
DIVISION

1. The commanders: A disconsolate Major-General Victor Fortune at St Valéry with the victorious Major-General Erwin Rommel of 7th Panzer Division. The photograph was taken with Rommel's personal camera. Rommel wrote of the capture of Fortune as being 'a particular joy for us'. (IWM: RML342)

2. The commanders: Major-General Douglas Wimberley pictured in North Africa. Wimberley took over the reformed Highland Division and turned it into one of the best fighting formations in the Army. He was regarded as the father of the Highland Division and all ranks were sorry when he left them after the Sicilian campaign. (Major Neil Wimberley)

3. The commanders: Major-General Tom Rennie looking both determined and thoughtful as he lights up his pipe 'somewhere in north-west Europe'. Rennie had excelled at all levels of command and believed in leading from the front. He had received a number of wounds during his time with the Division. Although he commanded 3rd Division on D-Day he returned to the Highland Division as its GOC soon after. He was killed while inspecting his troops during Operation PLUNDER, the Rhine crossing. (IWM: BU1518)

4. *Above left:* The commanders: Major-General J H MacMillan. Known as 'Babe', he was the last wartime GOC of the Highland Division and commanded from the Rhine to the final German surrender. (Museum, The Argyll and Sutherland Hldrs)

5. *Above centre:* The commanders: Brigadier 'Nap' Murray who commanded 1st Gordons at El Alamein and went on to be an outstanding commander of 152 Brigade. Promoted to major-general, he commanded 6th Armoured Division in the final phase of the campaign in Italy. (Author's collection)

6. *Above right:* Staff-Sergeant D K Ritchie, RASC, 1939. Sgt Ritchie had served in the Black Watch in 1917–18. He rejoined the regiment's 4th/5th Battalion at Dundee in 1933 as a signals sergeant but was transferred to 526 Company RASC in 1937 and promoted to staff sergeant. His son, also D K Ritchie, also joined 526 Company but was too young to serve with the Highland Division in France. (Mr D K Ritchie)

7. *Above:* Two happy highlanders: Privates Hendry Fitzsimmons (L) and John Gunn of 5th Seaforth Highlanders, pictured at an annual camp before the war. Neither survived the war. Fitzsimmons was killed in Tunisia in April 1943 and Gunn in Normandy in June 1944. (Mrs Sandra Gordon)

8. TA soldiers of 4th Black Watch, 153 Brigade, leave their barracks en route to southern England with the Highland Division as part of the British Expeditionary Force. (J K Ritchie)

9. *Far left:*Piper George MacLeod who had served in 4th Camerons. In 1939 he piped Island TA soldiers on to the ferry that would take them to the mainland to join the Division. (Anne Makin)

10. *Left:*Angus Gunn, brother of John Gunn, at annual camp at Balblair in August 1939. (Mrs Sandra Gordon)

11. The Harmonisers. A musical ensemble formed from personnel of the Highland Division. This photograph was taken in France in 1940; the men are all wearing battledress. Seated on the left with his accordion is Dvr William Watt, of 239 Field Park Company RE, who was killed in the advance from Tripoli on 23 February 1943 when the lorry he was driving caught fire and then exploded. (Mrs H J Philip)

12. *Right:* Not everyone captured at St Valéry remained in captivity. Many escaped and made their way home to Britain. HMS *Kelvin* picks up former prisoners off the French coast in December 1940. Thirteen men of the Highland Division were among those rescued by *Kelvin*. (IWM: A2428)

13. *Far right:* Private Bernard Charles Bailey, RAOC. A Brummie, known inevitably as 'Bill', he was captured at St Valéry, after he had helped destroy many of the Division's vehicles. He spent five years in a PoW camp and was forced to mine coal. After service with the Highlanders, he said he never wanted to hear bagpipes again as long as he lived. (Mrs Jacqui Robson)

14. *Right:* Private Bert Mitchell, Gordon Highlanders, and his wife, Jessie, who were married at Camberley on 9 June 1942 before the Highland Division was posted to North Africa. (Bert Mitchell)

15. *Far right:* Getting his knees brown in Egypt, Private Joe Ritchie, Argyll and Sutherland Highlanders. General Wimberley was keen that his soldiers should wear as much of their traditional Highland dress as possible, thereby proclaiming the Scottishness of the Division. Pte Ritchie wears a Balmoral bonnet or Tam o'Shanter. (Robert Lyall)

16. Also in Egypt, a group from 5th Seaforth, with Sergeant Angus Gunn standing on the left. (Mrs Sandra Gordon)

17. Adapting to desert life, this group of Highlanders leave no doubt about their nationality. A mixture of uniforms is evident with two men wearing pullovers on top of their shirts and two others appear to be wearing battledress blouses. Only one man has camouflaged his helmet with hessian, or scrim, although this should have been the case with all. (IWM: E18649)

18. The unit is unknown but these are Gunners of the Highland Division in Egypt. Some have already got their knees quite brown. On the left, standing, is Gunner William Henry Nicholson. Many of the men in the photograph are English but were proud to be Highland Gunners. (Mrs Joyce Nicholson)

19. El Alamein. A medical orderly attends to two casualties of the Highland Division, soldiers of the Black Watch, during the battle. (IWM: E18630)

20. El Alamein. One of the greatest dangers was mines, the Germans having laid almost 500,000 in minefields dubbed the 'Devil's Gardens'. Royal Engineers of the Highland Division carry out the laborious and dangerous task of clearing mines. Note the divisional sign on the shoulder strap of the Sapper nearer the camera. (IWM: E18937)

21. *Above:* El Alamein. A group of 258 German prisoners taken by the Black Watch being marched into the British lines. Note the cairn at the left which marks one of the El Alamein tracks with the track symbol on the pole. (IWM: 18691)

22. *Left:* Marble Arch. This triumphal arch, built by Benito Mussolini, marked the border between Cyrenaica and Tripolitania. It was a landmark on the march to victory in North Africa for Eighth Army soldiers, including those of the Highland Division. (Author's collection)

23. *Opposite above:* Soldiers seem to attract animals. 'Wee Willie' was adopted by 152 (Seaforth and Camerons) Brigade at Mersa el Brega and is seen, complete with bonnet, with Captains Donald McKillop, John Mitchell and William Milne, all from Inverness. Note the kilts which were supposed to have been left in Britain. (IWM: 2271)

24. The kilts appeared in strength for this occasion, Eighth Army's victory parade in Tripoli in February 1943. The Highlanders were described as looking as smart as if they had just left Wellington Barracks in London. (IWM: HU87552)

25. There were some who thought that HD stood for Highway Decorators. Soldiers of the Division wasted no opportunity to emblazon the divisional symbol anywhere on their route. On one occasion, General Wimberley even found the red paint necessary and handed it over to some enthusiastic signwriters. These Highlanders are painting the wall of a house in Sfax. (IWM: NA1918)

26. Toothache is no respecter of soldiers at war. An Army dentist examines an officer of the Highland Division at his open air surgery in Tunisia in March 1943. (IWM: NA1508)

27. Good co-operation existed between the Highlanders and their armoured support. Soldiers of the Division move forward on the Valentine tanks of an armoured regiment. (IWM: NA1673)

28. In the Mareth Line. Gordon Highlanders in action at the Wadi Zessar. Battledress is still in use in March 1943 as the weather has not yet reached the high temperatures of summer. (IWM: NA1052)

29. *Above left:* In the Battle of Wadi Akarit, on 6 April, Lance-Corporal Hendry Fitzsimmons of 5th Seaforth (see photo 7) was killed in action. He was 23 years old. This is his original grave with its cross made by his comrades. He is now buried in Grave III B.13 in Sfax war cemetery. (Mrs Sandra Gordon)

30. *Above right:* It was also at Wadi Akarit that the Division earned its first VC, a posthumous nomination for Piper McIntyre at El Alamein having been rejected. The Victoria Cross was awarded to Lieutenant-Colonel Lorne Campbell DSO of 7th Argylls for his outstanding courage and inspiring leadership in the break-in battle. Although wounded and in pain, Lorne Campbell refused to be evacuated until the battle had been won. (Museum, The Argyll and Sutherland Hldrs)

31. Planning for Operation HUSKY, the invasion of Sicily. Officers of 1st Black Watch discuss their part in the operation. Lieutenant-Colonel C N Blair, the commanding officer, is in the centre. (IWM: NA4177)

32. Operation HUSKY, 10 July 1943. Infantrymen of the Division wade ashore from their landing craft. (Private photo)

33. Soldiers of 5th Seaforth in Sicily. Note the presence of at least one kilt and the inevitable small boy drawn to the soldiers. The heat has encouraged the wearing of shorts by almost everyone in the photo. (Mrs Sandra Gordon)

34. Bert Mitchell of the Gordons poses beside the wreck of a German tank in Sicily. (Bert Mitchell)

35. Sergeant Alexander Innes, Seaforth, who was awarded the Military Medal in Sicily. From Forres, Innes, who was known as Sam, was later transferred to another Seaforth battalion and served in the Italian campaign. (Mrs Cynthia Jardine)

36. Back in Britain, January 1944, Bert Mitchell wears the ribbon of the Africa Star on his battledress blouse. (Bert Mitchell)

37. They could never resist emblazoning the divisional sign wherever they went. An NCO of another formation looks at a morale-boosting sign erected by the Highland Division in Normandy in July 1944. (IWM: B7493)

38. Off again! Soldiers of the Gordons at the East India docks boarding the ship that will take them to Normandy. While the first soldier is smiling, his comrades look much more pensive as they contemplate what lies ahead. (IWM: B5216)

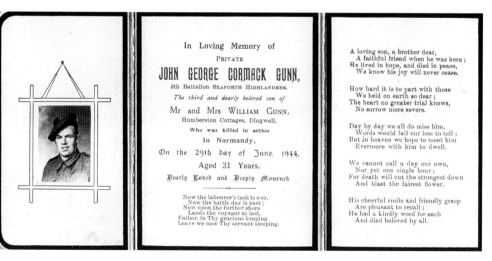

39. Private John Gunn (see photo 7) was killed during the fighting for Normandy on 29 June. This is the official notification of his burial in Ranville cemetery which was sent to his parents in February 1946. (Mrs Sandra Gordon)

Mayfair 9400. Extn 647.

Form E.2.

Tel. No.: *Victoria 1444. Est. 644.*
Any further correspondence on this subject should be addressed to:—

THE DIRECTOR,
Graves Registration and
Enquiries,
as opposite.

and the following number quoted:—

PLP/2995/AG13.

THE WAR OFFICE, (A.G.13),
32, Grosvenor Gardens,
Curzon Street House
Curzon Street,
London, S.W.1.

London, W.1.

14TH February, 1946.

Dear Sir,

I have to inform you that your son, 2820092,

Private J.G.C.Gunn, 5th Battalion, Seaforth

Highlanders

is buried in Ranville British Cemetery, France,

(5 miles East North East Caen).

PLOT III. ROW. B. GRAVE No. 20.

Yours faithfully,

For DIRECTOR
GRAVES REGISTRATION AND ENQUIRIES.

Mr. Gunn.

Wt.43427/5845. 100,000. 11/44. W. & J. J. Gp.20-51-2.
Wt.46627/5845. 100,000. 1/45. W. & J. J. Gp.20-51-2.

J.5882.

In Loving Memory of

PRIVATE

JOHN GEORGE CORMACK GUNN,

5th Battalion SEAFORTH HIGHLANDERS,

The third and dearly beloved son of

Mr and Mrs WILLIAM GUNN,

Humberston Cottages, Dingwall,

Who was killed in action

In Normandy,

On the 29th day of June, 1944,

Aged 31 Years.

Dearly Loved and Deeply Mourned

Now the labourer's task is o'er,
Now the battle day is past;
Now upon the further shore
Lands the voyager at last.
Father, in Thy gracious keeping
Leave we now Thy servant sleeping.

A loving son, a brother dear,
A faithful friend when he was here;
He lived in hope, and died in peace,
We know his joy will never cease.

How hard it is to part with those
We held on earth so dear;
The heart no greater trial knows,
No sorrow more severe.

Day by day we all do miss him,
Words would fail our loss to tell;
But in heaven we hope to meet him
Evermore with him to dwell.

We cannot call a day our own,
Nor yet one single hour;
For death will cut the strongest down
And blast the fairest flower.

His cheerful smile and friendly grasp
Are pleasant to recall;
He had a kindly word for each
And died beloved by all.

40. John Gunn's family produced this memorial card for their son. It symbolises the pain and pride of a family who had lost a loved one in the service of his country. (Mrs Sandra Gordon)

41. At the beginning of September 1944 the Highland Division liberated St Valéry, repaying a debt to the men of 1940. Pipers from 152 Brigade play Scottish airs for the people of the town in the main square of St Valéry with soldiers of their brigade in the background. (IWM: BU1509)

42. November 1944 and patrols of 5th/7th Gordons check out buildings in the village of Kaatsheuvel, north of Tilburg in The Netherlands. The division's soldiers had a preference for wearing the Balmoral as often as possible rather than the steel helmet. (IWM: B11584)

43. Between operations there was often much time to be filled for the infantrymen. Here a group of soldiers from the Seaforth read newspapers, read and write letters and drink tea while waiting for Operation PLUNDER, the Rhine crossing. (Author's collection)

on and rallying them as he moved to those points where the fighting was heaviest.

When his left forward Company was forced to give ground, he went forward alone into a hail of fire and personally reorganised their position, remaining with the Company until the attack at this point was held.

As reinforcements arrived he was seen standing in the open directing the fight under close-range fire of enemy infantry, and he continued to do so although already painfully wounded in the neck by shell-fire. It was not until the battle died down that he allowed his wound to be dressed.[79]

Even then, Lorne Campbell refused to be evacuated and stayed with the Argylls as darkness fell, the fighting died down and the position was secure. He was later awarded the Victoria Cross for his 'gallantry and magnificent leadership'.[80]

Lieutenant-Colonel James Oliver led 7th Black Watch into the fray at 6.25am. The battalion suffered very heavy shelling in the minefield, the enemy artillery having registered the gap, but passed through that obstacle and the anti-tank ditch. Although heavy machine-gun fire was directed on the battalion from the right, 7th Black Watch had taken its objectives by 9.30am.[81] However, 2nd Seaforth had run into difficulties in the second phase of the attack on Roumana and this impinged on Oliver's battalion, who were unable to perform their mopping-up role in the wadi since they were under direct observation from enemy artillery on the northern point of Roumana. Later in the day an attack by German infantry, supported by tanks, overran some of the battalion's forward positions and infiltrated between the Black Watch and the Argylls.[82] Reinforcements came forward from 1st Black Watch but, that night, 7th Black Watch were ordered to pull back 1,000 yards to conform with the Argylls; this manoeuvre was completed successfully.[83]

On 152 Brigade's front, 5th Seaforth and 5th Camerons had begun their attack on the ridge at 3.30am, advancing 'through a wilderness of rocks' on which the British guns 'roared and blazed'.[84] Following behind 5th Seaforth was the regiment's 2nd Battalion, who were to move to the right to seize the extreme east end of the ridge and Point 112, which was a 'slight eminence above the general ridge'.[85] For 5th Seaforth the 'first encounter with the enemy was with half-dressed Italians, rubbing the sleep out of their eyes and very anxious to know their way to the prisoner-of-war cage'.[86] By 5.45 the battalion had secured its objective and, shortly thereafter, 2nd Seaforth, who had made their right turn along the ridge crest, were on Point 112, although the two leading company commanders had become casualties; the final attack was directed by the adjutant, Captain McHardy. However, these were not positions where men could dig in; the rocks prevented that. Enemy mortars were soon dropping their bombs on the Jocks and, at about 6.45, the first counter-attacks were made. Many casualties were caused by the mortars and the problems of the Seaforth battalions increased when German machine guns were brought up to fire on them. Under such effective fire and with no possibility of digging in, the Seaforth suffered on until a strong counter-attack forced withdrawal from Point 112. The flanks of both 5th Seaforth and 7th Black Watch were thereby exposed and the latter, especially, suffered from the enemy enjoying direct observation of their positions.[87]

However, Lieutenant-Colonel R D Horne, CO of 2nd Seaforth, now led three counter-attacks on the ridge. Although the battalion did not recapture Point 112, Horne established a defensive line farther down the slope. The Seaforth held this new line for the rest of the day in spite of being mortared and machine-gunned by a determined foe. Many examples of courage were shown by the two Seaforth battalions, not least that of Private D M Bridges of the 5th.

> For six hours this man was practically responsible for the security of the right flank of his Battalion. By the skilful use of his Bren gun he time and again prevented parties of the enemy from infiltrating to the rear of his Company's position, and, as the citation for his Military Medal reads, 'thereby preventing the position from being overrun'.[88]

General Wimberley was observing the battle 'with German field glasses'[89] and could see the Seaforth's difficulty. He, therefore, ordered 5th Black Watch to reinforce 152 Brigade on Roumana. Advancing in broad daylight, the two leading companies of Lieutenant-Colonel 'Chick' Thomson's battalion entered the battle for Point 198, the highest part of the ridge. Although the battalion suffered some fifty casualties, the position was secured but the Germans still held the key to Point 112. Wimberley also asked the commander of 201 Guards Brigade to stage a feint to draw some of the enemy pressure from 154 Brigade.

On the extreme left of the Highland Division attack, 5th Camerons began their advance at 3.30am and traversed the lower slopes of Roumana 'into the wadis running from its left-hand side'[90] where the battalion began consolidating on the first objective. At 6.30 tea and sandwiches were issued to all men except those of Battalion HQ; the truck carrying their food had broken down and never reached the rendezvous point.[91] To their left 69 Brigade had been held up by enemy opposition and so the Camerons not only had to face the counter-attack that the German 90th Light Division was making on 5th Seaforth but also had to guard an open left flank. But the Camerons held their positions throughout the day and were able to support 5th Black Watch's advance to the aid of 5th

Seaforth. Once again there were many tales of courage, not least of which was Company Sergeant-Major Ian MacRae of D Company, 5th Camerons. On three occasions CSM MacRae led bayonet charges against the enemy during which he killed nine enemy soldiers. 'He simply had no concern at all for his own safety, and in the end was shot dead.'[92]

The battle raged throughout the day and the Divisional artillery and Middlesex machine gunners played vital roles. It was the nature of their role that the Diehards fought in sub-units, attached to the attacking battalions to whom their MMGs were a welcome addition to battalion fire-power. The machine gunners shared the dangers of the Highland infantry as they advanced on their objectives and while holding their positions against counter-attack. One platoon was forced to withdraw from its position on Roumana when it came under fire from the crest while a section of No. 13 Platoon, with 5th Seaforth, lost half its men before reaching the summit.[93]

A correspondent for *The Times* commented that the Highlanders, by breaking the German hold on Roumana, had accomplished 'one of the greatest heroic achievements of the war'[94], marked by the award of the Division's first Victoria Cross of the war. (Two other men were also awarded the Victoria Cross: Subadar Lalbahadur Thapa of 1/2nd Gurkhas, 4th Indian Division, and Private Eric Anderson, 5th East Yorkshires of 50th Division. Anderson, a stretcher-bearer, was killed in the battle.) But, although the fighting died down by nightfall, it was far from certain that the battle was over, although Brigadier Douglas Graham of 153 Brigade was confident that the enemy would withdraw. Wimberley called a conference with his brigade commanders at 153 Brigade HQ where he learned of the extent of the losses of the battalions of the two attacking brigades. Furthermore, 153's two battalions of Gordons were holding long fronts while 5th Black Watch, the divisional reserve, had been committed. Should the enemy counter-attack next day the situation for the Division could be very serious.

But Douglas Graham's optimism was proved to be well founded when patrols along the front reported that the enemy had gone at dawn. The Battle of Wadi Akarit was over and the Highland Division had played a major part in Eighth Army's success. A Divisional Intelligence Summary commented that the day had 'marked the fiercest fighting that the Division had experienced in this campaign'.[95] However, the enemy had suffered heavily and some 3,000 prisoners were taken, in addition to the dead and wounded. Early on the morning of 7 April, Eighth Army's armour set out in pursuit of the enemy.

Leese ordered a rapid advance on Sfax and 23 Armoured Brigade led off on 9 April with 5th/7th Gordons. The Division re-organised and Spear Force, including 1st Gordons in place of 5th Black Watch 'who had been forced to debus', with Gunners and Sappers, was the next element to set off on the road to Sfax, followed in turn by the balance of 153 Brigade. (Plans for the creation of Spear Force had been in place since 1 April. Spear Force, including 23 Armoured and 153 Brigades 'was to be retained in readiness to move forward once a bridgehead had been made over the Wadi Akarit'.[96]) Along the road to Sfax, Spear Force met a strong German rearguard on the Wadi Cheffar. Difficult terrain and intense artillery fire precluded the tanks making much progress but Lieutenant-Colonel Fausset-Farquhar's 1st Gordons deployed in an attack that had the enemy quitting his positions before nightfall. So rapid was this withdrawal that the Gordons took many prisoners and a number of guns. There was now no obstruction on the road to Sfax and A Company 1st Gordons were the first Eighth Army troops into the town at 9.00am on the 10th; Spear Force B followed at noon. When Montgomery visited Sfax next day a guard of honour was provided by 7th Black Watch; the guard wore kilts for the occasion.[97] The Highland Division now moved into reserve in the Sfax area as Eighth Army continued its advance on Enfidaville.[98]

On the night of 21–22 April the Division relieved the New Zealanders and 4th Indian Division in the Enfidaville area. Eighth Army's advance had come almost to a stop and the emphasis in the race for Tunis now switched to First Army; the Highlanders were to hold their new positions but would not be advancing. In the area of the Garci mountain, Takrouna and the Snout there was to be no rest for the Division as it held positions, carried out patrolling and endured considerable enemy shelling. The artillery was kept busy with a programme of counter-battery fire. On 5 May the war diary of 126th (Highland) Field Regiment noted that shoots were also conducted by AOPs (Air Observation Posts).[99] Such was the ground that mules had to be used to supply the forward positions. At last General Leclerc's Free French troops arrived to relieve the Division which moved into a rest area near Monaster during the first week of May.[100] The war in Africa was almost over but plans were already in hand for the next phase of operations in the Mediterranean and General Wimberley flew to Cairo on 7 May to learn that his Division would be playing a major part in the opening phase of Operation HUSKY, the invasion of Sicily.[101]

In Wimberley's absence, Douglas Graham assumed temporary command but, only a few days later, was promoted to command 56th (London) Division. His soldiers were sorry to see him go for he had been a popular and very capable commander. The only non-Highlander to command a Highland Brigade during the war, Graham was a Cameronian who learned and appreciated the ways of the Highland men.

Before his trip to Cairo, the GOC had sought Montgomery's permission to seek out Scots from reinforcement holding units and from the various lines of communication units. This helped bring some Scottish reinforcements to the Division which had lost many men in the recent battles.

Even when he was in Cairo, Wimberley continued to seek out Scottish reinforcements.[102] He learned that his former Reconnaissance Regiment, now 14th HLI, was to be used as a 'beach brick' in HUSKY and argued that the battalion should be returned to 51st (Highland) Division. 'Sandy' Monro, CO of 14th HLI, a Cameron, supported his argument and eventually it was agreed that the battalion should return as reinforcements; it was disbanded in June but most of its men found their way into battalions of the Highland Division. Some had already joined 1st Black Watch and 5th Seaforth on 31 May. (A draft of 100 personnel, including four officers, went to the Black Watch and 120, including six officers, to the Seaforth.)[103]

The North African campaign came to an end on 12 May when von Arnim surrendered all Axis forces in the theatre to the Allies. Strangely the event merits little mention in war diaries of the Division, although the Highlanders were present at the subsequent Victory Parade in Tunis where, once again, they acquitted themselves well with a turnout that evoked many favourable comments.[104] Although the fighting was over, there was now much preparation to be done but there was also an opportunity for some rest as well as training. For the first phase of the latter, however, the Division, which had travelled some 1,850 miles from Egypt, was to move to yet another country, crossing the border into Algeria and concentrating around the coastal towns of Djidjelli and Bougie. The Division was to live under canvas 'to keep hard' and the camps were more cramped than those in the desert but there was a water supply.[105]

Training followed the recognised pattern but with an unfamiliar addition: boarding and disembarking from assault vessels. For the infantry this meant becoming familiar with LCAs (landing craft, assault), LCIs (landing craft, infantry) and LSIs (landing ships, infantry). There were also LCMs (landing craft, motor), LCTs (landing craft, tanks) and LSTs (landing ships, tank). An LCA could carry a full platoon of infantry, an LCI some 200 men, plus stores and an LSI about 1,500 men; LSIs also carried LCAs and LCMs, which carried two or three vehicles, slung from davits.[106] Boarding these, especially with vehicles such as carriers and light trucks, was practised and there were also sessions on waterproofing the vehicles so that the troops could wade ashore.

In this period after the campaign there was an opportunity for recreation. Football, as ever, proved popular, in spite of the heat, as did various other sports while concert parties, including ENSA troupes, were welcome diversions and, of course, there were films to be watched. Competitions for the pipers were held and at Divisional level the winner was Lance-Corporal W Macdonald of the Seaforth whose tune was named 'Wadi Akarit'.[107] There were also visitors to welcome, including Sir John Dill, who visited 152 Brigade on 2 June, Montgomery, Alexander and the Secretaries of State for War and Air. A detachment of 250 members of the Division travelled to Algiers to be inspected by the King on 23 June and

General Wimberley was the sole guest at a private lunch for His Majesty.[108] In early-July, as final preparations were underway, the Scottish comedian Will Fyffe paid a visit to the Division.[109]

HQ 152 Brigade noted that 'NAAFI/EFI [Navy, Army and Air Forces Institute/Expeditionary Forces Institute] stores are much improved as far as cigarettes and chocolate are concerned but only the local wine is available for the wet canteen and beer is rationed to one bottle per head per week'.[110] However, good quantities of fresh food were included in the rations. The Brigade training programme began at dawn and there was a long break in the middle of the day. A team from the Combined Training Centre provided experts 'in the use of landing craft, mountain warfare, village fighting, rock climbing and the use of pack mules'.[111] Practically all troops were able to bathe in the sea every day and each unit had a day off every week but entertainments in the area were limited and tickets for events were rationed.[112] On 17 June, Brigadier Murray, who had been awarded a Bar to his DSO on the 8th, was admitted to hospital and Brigadier MacMillan MC arrived in his place on 25 June. Murray, at 50 probably the oldest combatant officer in the Division, was evacuated to the UK.

Brigade exercises were held, followed by a Divisional scale exercise and the units got to know how to operate with the Royal Navy. Earlier, in Cairo, Wimberley had been pleased to meet the 'Sailor' who would be 'responsible for landing my Division on the beaches of Europe'.[113] This was Admiral Rhoderick McGrigor, a Scot, who would later become First Sea Lord.[114] Following the major exercises came a move to Sousse in Tunisia, an unpleasant area with the prospect of malaria.[115] Anti-malarial precautions were increased and there was also concern about sandfly fever but this was only a staging post in the Division's travels to a new seat of war.

There was training in street fighting in Sousse where the Division put the final polish on its preparations for Operation HUSKY. The initial landing was to be made by 154 Brigade Group, under Tom Rennie, now recovered from his most recent wound. Rennie's Group was to include the battalions of 154 Brigade – 1st and 7th Black Watch and 7th Argylls – with 11th Royal Horse Artillery (RHA), 50th Royal Tanks, less two squadrons, two companies of 1/7th Middlesex, 244 Field Company RE, 176 Field Ambulance RAMC and some smaller elements as well as a battalion group based on 1st Gordons which included, in addition to that battalion, 456 Battery RA, a squadron from 50th Royal Tanks, a company of 1/7th Middlesex, 275 Field Company RE, 174 Field Ambulance and other details. XXX Corps' maintenance area was to be Portolapo Bay but, since this was thought to be well defended, landing beaches, codenamed Red and Green, were selected on either side of it. The Gordon Group was to land on the northern, or Green, beach and 154 Brigade Group on Red beach.

Then, but a few days before our expedition set sail, the GSOIII, Intelligence, MacMillan, came to me … in high glee. In his hand were some newly-taken photos of landing beaches.[116]

The reason for MacMillan's exuberance was soon obvious. In the photographs could be seen a number of women in bathing suits and caps. Since they were enjoying the beaches it meant that there were no mines to be dealt with.[117] This was good news indeed.

Those units on LCIs and LCTs were to travel first to Malta whence they would make the second journey to Sicily. The remaining vessels would sail directly from Africa to Sicily, rendezvousing with the Malta craft some seven miles off the Sicilian coast. With D-Day set for 10 July the crossing to Malta began on the 5th and, next day, troops were disembarking in Valetta before moving into camps on the town's outskirts. Some units were inspected by Lord Gort VC, who was now Governor of Malta GC, and on the 7th Montgomery came to visit. With his usual panache the little general gathered troops about him. He told the Gordons Group, dubbed Green Force, that 'I have never seen fitter men'.[118] He was received enthusiastically by several units and his visits boosted their already high morale.

As the vessels of the invading force set sail from Valetta harbour, pipers played them out to sea, Pipe Major Anderson, 1st Gordons, performing the honours for his craft.[119] Ahead lay Sicily and a campaign that would last thirty-nine days with the Highland Division playing a major part in the fighting.

Notes

1. Wimberley, *Memoirs, Vol II*, p. 52
2. Mitchell to author
3. NA Kew, WO169/4295, war diary, 153 Brigade, 1942
4. Ibid
5. NA Kew, WO169/4292, war diary, 152 Brigade, 1942
6. NA Kew, WO169/, war diary, 2 Seaforth, 1942
7. NA Kew, WO169/4292, war diary, 152 Brigade, 1942
8. Ibid
9. Doherty, *Only The Enemy in Front*, p. 31
10. NA Kew, WO169/4292, war diary, 152 Bde, 1942; WO169/4986, war diary, 7 A&SH, 1942
11. McGregor, *The Spirit of Angus*, p. 56
12. NA Kew, WO169/10181, war diary, 7 BW, 1943
13. NA Kew, WO169/ 4298, war diary, 154 Bde, 1942
14. Doherty, *Wall of Steel*, p. 105; NA Kew, WO169/9872, war diary, 25 HAA Bty
15. Doherty, *Wall of Steel*, p. 105

16. Ibid, p. 107
17. Salmond, *The History of the 51st Highland Division*, p. 62
18. Ibid, p. 63; NA Kew, WO169/8955, war diary, 152 Bde, 1943
19. Salmond, op cit, p. 63; NA Kew, WO169/8955, war diary, 152 Bde, 1943
20. Wimberley, op cit, p. 71; Fergusson, *The Black Watch and the King's Enemies*, p. 146; Salmond, op cit, p. 64; WO169/10178, war diary, 1 BW, 1943
21. NA Kew, WO169/8791, war diary, HQ 51 (H) Div (GS), 1943; WO169/8963, war diary, 154 Bde, 1943
22. NA Kew, WO169/8963, war diary, 154 Bde, 1943; WO169/10181, war diary, 7 BW, 1943; WO169/10260, war diary, 1/7 Mx, 1943
23. Salmond, op cit, p. 66
24. Ibid; WO169/10292, war diary, 5 Seaforth, 1943
25. Montgomery, *Memoirs*, p. 154
26. Salmond, op cit, pp. 66–7
27. Ibid, p. 67; Wimberley, op cit, p. 72; NA Kew, WO169/8791, war diary, HQ 51 (H) Div (GS), 1943
28. Playfair, *The Mediterranean and the Middle East, Vol IV*, p. 239
29. Salmond, op cit, p. 67; Wimberley, op cit, p. 81
30. Doherty, *Wall of Steel*, p. 107. Following the publication of this book, the author was given information from veterans of 9th (Londonderry) Regt that indicated that they, as members of recce parties, were already in Tripoli when 11th Hussars arrived. One veteran, Gnr Tommy McCready, recalled shouting at the Cherrypickers to ask what had kept them, a question that was not well received.
31. NA Kew, WO169/8791, HQ 51 (H) Div (GS), 1943
32. Fergusson, op cit, p. 153
33. Salmond, op cit, p. 72
34. Wimberley, op cit, p. 81
35. NA Kew, WO169/10260, war diary, 1/7 Mx, 1943
36. Kippenberger, *Infantry Brigadier*, p. 267
37. Ibid
38. Wimberley, op cit, p. 86; NA Kew, WO169/8791, war diary, HQ 51 (H) Div (GS), 1943
39. NA Kew, WO169/10260, war diary, 1/7 Mx, 1943
40. Wimberley, op cit, p. 86
41. Ibid
42. Brooke, *War Diaries*, pp. 378–9
43. Quoted in Salmond, op cit, p. 74
44. Playfair, op cit, p. 320
45. NA Kew, WO169/8959, war diary, 153 Bde, 1943
46. Wimberley, op cit, p. 92
47. BBC African Radio-News-Reel, 27 Feb 43, per Mrs Helen J Philip
48. Mrs Helen J Philip to author
49. Montgomery, op cit, p. 158
50. Wimberley, op cit, p. 93
51. NA Kew, WO169/10292, war diary, 5 Seaforth, 1943
52. NA Kew, WO169/9518, war diary, 128 Fd Regt, 1943
53. Salmond, op cit, p. 79

54. Ibid; Playfair, op cit, pp. 325–6; NA Kew, WO169/8963, war diary, 154 Bde, 1943; WO169/10178, war diary, 1 BW, 1943
55. Blaxland, *Plain Cook*, p. 189
56. Playfair, op cit, p. 333. The Italian infantry formations – Young Fascist, Trieste, Spezia and Pistoia – deployed twenty-two battalions and over seventy troops of artillery and presented a redoubtable foe for Eighth Army.
57. Ibid. The total of fit tanks in the armoured divisions was about 142.
58. Wimberley, op cit, p. 103
59. NA Kew, WO169/8791, war diary, HQ 51 (H) Div (GS), 1943
60. Playfair, op cit, p. 333n
61. Ibid, p. 320
62. Salmond, op cit, p. 81
63. Doherty, *A Noble Crusade*, p. 127
64. Playfair, op cit, p. 341
65. Wimberley, op cit, p. 103
66. Borthwick, *Battalion*, p. 81
67. McGregor, *Spirit of Angus*, p. 71
68. Ibid
69. Ibid
70. Quoted in ibid, p. 71
71. Ibid
72. Wimberley, op cit, p. 104
73. Playfair, op cit, p. 362
74. Salmond, op cit, p. 85
75. Wimberley, op cit, p. 104
76. NA Kew, WO169/8791, war diary, HQ 51 (H) Div (GS), 1943
77. Salmond, op cit, p. 86
78. Ibid, p. 87
79. *London Gazette*, VC citation
80. Ibid
81. NA Kew, WO169/10181, war diary, 7 BW, 1943
82. Fergusson, op cit, pp. 166–9
83. Salmond, op cit, pp. 88–9
84. Wimberley, op cit, p. 104
85. Salmond, op cit, p. 89
86. NA Kew, WO169/10292, war diary, 5 Seaforth, 1943
87. Salmond, op cit, p. 89
88. Wimberley, op cit, p. 108
89. Ibid
90. Salmond, op cit, p. 91
91. Ibid
92. Ibid
93. Quoted in Salmond, p. 92
94. NA Kew, WO169/8791, war diary, HQ 51 (H) Div (GS), 1943, IntSum No. 135
95. NA Kew, WO169/8959, war diary, 153 Bde, 1943
96. Ibid
97. Salmond, op cit, p. 94
98. Ibid, pp. 95–6

99. NA Kew, WO169/9516, war diary 126 Fd Regt, 1943

100. Salmond, op cit, p. 96; NA Kew, WO169/8792, war diary, HQ 51 (H) Div (GS), 1943

101. Wimberley, op cit, p. 126

102. NA Kew, WO169/10178 & 10292, war diaries, 1 BW & 5 Seaforth, 1943

103. Wimberley, op cit, pp. 127–9

104. NA Kew, WO169/8793, war diary, HQ 51 (H) Div (GS), 1943

105. Ibid

106. Chesneau, *Conway's All the World's Fighting Ships 1922–1946*, pp. 72–7

107. Delaforce, *Monty's Highlanders*, p. 99

108. Wimberley, op cit, p. 126

109. NA Kew, WO169/10292, war diary, 5 Seaforth, 1943

110. NA Kew, WO169/8955, war diary, 152 Bde, 1943

111. Ibid

112. Wimberley, op cit, p. 126

113. Ibid

114. Salmond, op cit, p. 102n

115. NA Kew, WO169/9518, war diary, 128 Fd Regt, 1943

116. Wimberley, op cit, p. 138

117. Ibid

118. NA Kew, WO169/10245, war diary, 1 Gordons, 1943

119. Ibid

CHAPTER VII

Sicily

The decision to invade Sicily was reached at the Casablanca conference in January 1943 at which Churchill and Roosevelt agreed to continue a Mediterranean strategy following the North African campaign.[1] Although the US chiefs of staff would have preferred a cross-Channel invasion in 1943 they were persuaded that this was not feasible and that further operations in the Mediterranean would make best use of the forces in North Africa. However, American agreement to the invasion of Sicily did not bring automatic consent to continued operations in the region once Sicily had been conquered.

Churchill hoped that wresting Sicily from Axis control would secure the Allied lines of communication through the Mediterranean, divert German pressure from the eastern front and intensify pressure on Italy to quit the Axis partnership.[2] Americans suspected that British motives were underpinned by imperial interests and, since they wished to see the end of the British Empire, they continued to be wary of any strategy that might hint of protecting that Empire. Nonetheless, agreement was given to the plans for Operation HUSKY, which was to be carried out by two armies, Seventh (US) and Eighth British, with Alexander commanding the Army Group, now designated 15 Army Group, George Patton commanding Seventh Army and Montgomery still CinC of Eighth Army.[3]

There were to be twenty-six landing beaches in Sicily, spread over 105 miles, a dispersion of effort that might have proved disastrous had there been elaborate defences. H-Hour for the first landings was 2.45am on 10 July, before which the defenders' communications, airfields and defensive positions were to be plastered by heavy bombers.[4] Although 51st (Highland) Division had been transferred temporarily to X Corps following victory in Tunisia, it had returned to its former home of XXX Corps for HUSKY; Sir Oliver Leese remained as corps commander.[5]

Convoys carrying the invasion force sailed from ports in North Africa, from Malta and from as far away as the Clyde, whence sailed 1st Canadian

Division, to the rendezvous point south of Malta, where they were to meet on 9 July. Unfortunately for the soldiers on board the transports, the Mediterranean summer weather chose that day to break and high seas and gales threatened the landings the following morning. Eisenhower, facing a choice that would recur in June 1944, decided to continue with the plan and the invasion fleet made for Sicily.[6] Such were the conditions that many men – sailors as well as soldiers – suffered from seasickness. One soldier of 1st Black Watch, sailing from Malta, was so stricken by seasickness that he died en route.[7] On board LCI 2, carrying Battalion HQ of 1st Gordons, the port ramp 'was carried away in the swell'. With a certain sense of the ridiculous, the Gordons' war diarist noted that the 'remainder of the journey was not without its ups and downs'.[8] As would be the case with many invading France the following year, soldiers preferred the prospect of action ashore to suffering further aboard ship.

At H-Hour on 10 July, 7th Argylls, now commanded by Lieutenant-Colonel Mathieson, landed unopposed, although a grenade was tossed into a landing craft, wounding fifteen men of D Company. As day dawned the Argylls were able to ascertain that they were on the correct beach, recognising prominent features from photographs studied during training.[9] Following bombardment by warships the Italian soldiers of the coast defence batteries were in no mood for fighting and surrendered with alacrity, allowing the Argylls to form their bridgehead.[10] For the rest of the day, supplies, equipment and vehicles came ashore through that lodgement. The other assaulting battalion of 154 Brigade was 7th Black Watch who did not have quite such a straightforward experience. C Company had no problems getting ashore but the remaining companies were landed on the wrong beaches, the commanders of their LCAs having been driven off course by the sea conditions. Not until 6.15am could the Black Watch advance from the beach to tackle their first objectives. Fortunately, they, too, met no opposition although there were some casualties from anti-personnel mines. Within forty-five minutes the battalion's objectives had been secured.[11]

Elsewhere, Green Force, the Gordons Group, had a slightly different experience. Following a safe landing the Group was to take several objectives, including a tunny factory, a lighthouse, Portopalo village, Capo Passero Island, and a 200-foot-high ridge dominating the approaches to Pachino. The battalion war diary summarises the Gordons' day:

> The Battalion ... landed on the South Eastern tip of Sicily, Cap[o] Passero at 03.45 hrs.
> 04.30 B Coy attacked a medium Breda gun, situated in the buildings above the Tunny factory, inflicting casualties on the enemy and capturing the gun.

07.25 By this time all opposition had been overcome and a firm bridgehead established round the village of Portopalo, the vital ridge 'Colorado', the lighthouse and the Tunny factory.

Up to 20 casualties had been inflicted on the enemy, chiefly Coastguards and Coastal defence units, the majority by B Coy;

The Battalion's casualties were less than six, including the Intelligence Sergeant, who was shot in the shoulder, while transferring from LCI to LCA as the LCI had struck a rock and could not go inshore. Over 100 prisoners were taken.[12]

A Company captured the island with little trouble and all the prisoners were sent there. Advance parties of 1st Gordons entered Pachino shortly after noon and the battalion had also linked up with 5th Black Watch. Thereafter, the Gordons returned to the command of their own brigade. Detailed preparation had played a major part in the success of the operation: 'thanks to wide distribution of the aerial photographs, every man "knew" the ground before he set foot on it and, missing the rear of his section, could get to pre-arranged positions with no loss of time'.[13]

By 6.30am, 153 Brigade was starting to disembark on Red beach. The emphasis in this brigade's training had been on rock-climbing and mountain fighting and it was intended that its battalions should pass through 154 Brigade unless the latter was in need of assistance.[14] So well had the landings gone that 153 was able to move forward soon after landing with 5th/7th Gordons advancing by the left of Pachino and hence northward on the left of the main road. Their CO, Lieutenant-Colonel Hay, was out of action, having been wounded by a round from a Thompson SMG that had been dropped to the ground. Lieutenant-Colonel Thomson's 5th Black Watch, having cleared up the beach area, moved level with 5th/7th Gordons, skirting Pachino to the right and then advancing on the right of the main road. Some opposition was met by the Gordons but two troops of Sherman tanks soon helped overcome the defenders while an enemy strongpoint surrendered to 5th Black Watch without a fight. Thereafter, 5th Black Watch made contact with 231 (Malta) Brigade to their right and with 1st Gordons who reverted to their parent brigade and entered brigade reserve.[15]

Both Tactical Divisional HQ and 152 Brigade landed on Amber beach on D-Day without opposition.[16] Lieutenant-Colonel Rory Horne's 2nd Seaforth moved up on the 11th to a position between Noto and Rosolini while 5th Seaforth moved by the Rosolini–Noto road and then via Palazzolo and Buccheri to reach the Francofonte area by noon on 13 July. The third unit of 152 Brigade, 5th Camerons, suffered some bombing – the RQMS was wounded – but led the brigade advance through Pachino towards Rosolini.[17] C Company met anti-tank fire some five miles beyond Pachino and went to ground for the night. The enemy position was taken next day, with some guns, and some other strongpoints along the road also fell to the

Camerons who entered Noto and, then, on the 13th, moved up behind 5th Seaforth near Francofonte.[18] So far little transport was ashore and the infantry had done some hard marching in very hot conditions. Not for nothing did one veteran describe Sicily as a 'land of heat and smelly socks'.[19]

Meanwhile, 7th Argylls had reached Noto on the evening of the 12th before moving into positions in the hills at Palazzolo where the transport caught up with the marching soldiers and carried them some two miles north-west of Palazzolo.[20] Nearby were 7th Black Watch, who were near the railway station, with 1st Black Watch on their right flank. XIII Corps had also enjoyed success and took Augusta on the night of 12–13 July.[21] To the left of the Highland Division the Canadians had made steady progress while Seventh (US) Army had overcome determined German opposition, destroying forty-three German tanks in a counter-attack, to link up with the Canadians near Raguso.[22] Thus far all had gone well for the invaders but that was about to change.

The first real glitch came near Francofonte on the morning of 13 July as 5th Seaforth advanced towards the village. Since no significant opposition had been met until now, a report of sniping from the provost party, which had gone ahead to signpost the route, was not considered to be a major problem. The Seaforth advance guard included tanks from 23 Armoured Brigade as well as battalion carriers.[23] Francofonte sits on a hill clad with olive and orange groves and the approach road followed a 'nasty hairpin bend' close to the village. It was there that the leading Seaforth carrier ran into a German 37mm anti-tank gun; the carrier was destroyed and its crew killed. Machine guns joined in the carefully-prepared ambush from a nearby cemetery and the battalion debussed from their trucks to seek cover.[24] However, it soon became clear that this was not the main defence of Francofonte as the Germans withdrew with their 37mm. As tanks of 23 Armoured Brigade approached the village they met a hail of fire from the defenders, men of the German 2nd Parachute Regiment, who had but recently been flown in from France. These were Luftwaffe troops and are generally acknowledged as being among the finest fighting soldiers of the Wehrmacht. (The title Wehrmacht included Germany's three fighting services, the army, or Heer, air force, or Luftwaffe, and navy, or Kriegsmarine.) They would demonstrate their skills over the next thirty-six hours in what one Seaforth officer described as 'a text-book example of what can happen to a battalion when it is launched into the blue over ground which has not been adequately reconnoitred'.[25] (This was not country that favoured tanks. As Wimberley noted 'the terrain was such that tracked and wheeled vehicles alike were confined to the twisting narrow roads'.[26])

The German paratroopers numbered only about 300 but had the advantage of choosing the location for this ambush. Groves of oranges and olives hid most of the village, bar a few rooftops, from the view of the

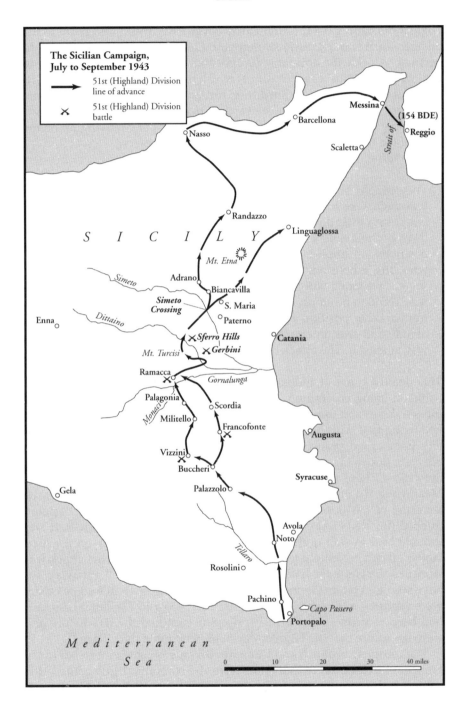

The Sicilian Campaign,
July to September 1943

51st (Highland) Division
line of advance

51st (Highland) Division
battle

S I C I L Y

Messina

(154 BDE)

Barcellona

Reggio

Scaletta

Strait of

Nasso

Randazzo

Linguaglossa

Simeto

Mt. Etna

Adrano

Biancavilla

Simeto
Crossing

S. Maria

Enna

Dittaino

Paterno

Sferro Hills

Catania

Mt. Turcisi

Gerbini

Ramacca

Gornalunga

Palagonia

Scordia

Militello

Francofonte

Augusta

Vizzini

Buccheri

Gela

Palazzolo

Syracuse

Avola

Noto

Tellaro

Rosolini

Pachino

Capo Passero

Portopalo

M e d i t e r r a n e a n
S e a

0   10   20   30   40 miles

127

Highlanders and gave the ambushers cover. They could also retire to the village which was a natural strongpoint. Lieutenant-Colonel J H Walford decided to tackle the anti-tank gun position first, sending C Company to deal with it, but this was the point at which the gunners and their supporting infantry withdrew. Walford then turned his attention to Francofonte itself, sending out a carrier screen with a troop of tanks along the branch road to the village. The battalion followed, A Company moving up on the right of the road, B Company on the left and D in reserve.

Defending their positions the paras proved their quality.

They fought fanatically (of the three hundred in the village, more than half were found dead when it was eventually taken), but did not permit their devotion to their Führer to cloud either their judgement or their skill. They were particularly good at using alternative positions, an unpleasant change from the average run of German who dug a hole and then clung to it: a heavy burst of fire from several weapons would come from a point which, when engaged, was found to be empty. Meanwhile they were blazing happily away from another position a couple of hundred yards off. It was a game of hide-and-seek among the olive trees, and we could make no headway against it. The attack bogged down.[27]

This deadly game of hide-and-seek drew in 2nd Seaforth as well, the battalion being committed by Brigadier MacMillan when the 5th were pinned down and forced to withdraw to a defensive line along the road. Following that withdrawal, and before 2nd Seaforth advanced, the artillery bombarded Francofonte.[28] A Company, 2nd Seaforth were able to advance under the protection of that bombardment and close with the defenders. There followed a bitter close-quarter battle with the paras. Meanwhile, the other companies of 2nd Seaforth had been held up by the terracing of the slopes before the village while one enemy strongpoint, dubbed the 'Red House', proved an especial bulwark to progress. It was thought best to wait until nightfall before making an attack on the 'Red House', using moonlight to show the way. But by the time that attack was launched the Germans had evacuated Francofonte. Not all got away: we have seen that many German paras died in the village while some others were captured in the early morning by 2nd Seaforth. The latter Germans had been escorting some British prisoners captured the day before and were not aware that the Highlanders had penetrated the village.[29]

The complete Seaforth and Cameron Brigade became embroiled in the Francofonte battle as 5th Camerons were also committed, going into battle behind 2nd Seaforth. They too were pinned down, their CO, Lieutenant-Colonel Sorel-Cameron, was wounded and one sergeant, John McLean by name, led a ferocious bayonet charge, shouting out the battle cry of

Clan McLean. Sergeant McLean's charge put to flight a group of Germans whose position, with two anti-tank guns, had been blocking an entire company. McLean was later awarded the DCM.[30] Elsewhere the Camerons were attacking enemy transport on the road to Lentini and, by evening, A Company was astride that road on which the Camerons advanced on the morning of the 15th, making contact with the German rearguard who were making for Scordia. D and B Companies made a pincer movement to the north of Scordia and, as other Camerons entered the village, took a considerable haul of prisoners.[31]

The infantry had been supported not only by the Gunners but by a squadron of tanks from 50th Royal Tanks of 23 Armoured Brigade. (At this time 23 Armoured Brigade was re-equipping with diesel-engined Shermans and only one regiment was in Sicily. A rear HQ had been left in North Africa to supervise the re-equipment of 40th and 46th (Liverpool Welsh) Royal Tanks. Re-equipment of the former was complete by 13 July and the regiment rejoined the Brigade in Sicily.[32]) It was not ideal terrain for tanks and one was knocked out by a German para who stalked it and dropped a mine through the driver's hatch. The German was killed by machine-gun fire from another tank but the damage had already been done. By the end of the day on 14 July there was only a solitary tank of the squadron still in action.[33] It had been an expensive battle for the tank-ies. The Gunners had also performed well with 128th (Highland) Field Regiment providing support for 152 Brigade. Lieutenant-Colonel Jerry Sheil earned a Bar to the DSO he had been awarded at El Alamein when

> with complete disregard of danger [he] went right forward in person to identify the actual centre of resistance which no one else could locate. After a daring reconnaissance he observed the fire of his regiment on to several strong-points and, when this was impossible, himself manhandled 6-pounders and a 17-pounder into action at short range, and then directed their fire. His leadership and inspiring example were a considerable contributory factor to the successful issue of a hard-fought fight.[34]

Sheil commented to Wimberley that he had never encountered a more difficult area in which to obtain artillery observation and provide observed fire. 'I noticed, however, that, despite this, his guns were firing hard.'[35]

The machine gunners of 1/7th Middlesex had also given considerable assistance to the infantry with Private Percy Crowhurst knocking out two troop-carrying vehicles and wounding a machine-gun team. On 14 July he also brought his MMG into action against a German counter-attack, held the attackers off for two hours and allowed the infantry to withdraw to a commanding position. Later that day, Crowhurst brought a seriously wounded soldier to safety.[36]

The Divisional Provost Company had made the first contact with the enemy and Lieutenant James MacKintosh of the Camerons and Corporal N Paterson, of the Military Police, who were marking the route from Cassibile to Francofonte, had taken prisoner some Italian soldiers before they were attacked by two groups of enemy troops. Paterson was wounded but managed to crawl round a bend in the road to warn approaching Highlanders of the danger. MacKintosh held off the enemy to cover their withdrawal. Sergeant Alexander Smith, of 275 Field Company, Royal Engineers, not only penetrated Francofonte village and removed mines behind the German positions but also cleared two tanks that were blocking the road and again entered Francofonte to check a suspicious object in the village street.[37]

Although it could be argued that the Highlanders had blundered into this battle, the result was a fine example of teamwork, indicating just how well the infantry, armour, artillery, engineers, provost staff and machine gunners could work together. It was as good a demonstration of teamwork, of divisional esprit, as Wimberley could have wished for. However, it did demonstrate the value of a reconnaissance regiment, which would have detected the ambush earlier and saved many casualties and much time.

By 16 July the Division was positioned on high ground overlooking the Gornalunga river, which defends the Catania plain from an attack from the west.[38] The river has a series of tributaries with the Monaci flowing north-easterly to join it while both the Dittaino and Simeto flow south-easterly on their path to join the Gornalunga. Highland Division's line now stretched from Scordia to Palagonia with forward elements close to the Monaci and it was decided that 154 Brigade would cross the Monaci to take the village of Ramacca while 152 Brigade would advance on the right; 23 Armoured Brigade was in reserve behind 152. Before this happened, however, 153 Brigade had taken Vizzini, a town whose garrison had defied the efforts of 231 Brigade to evict them.[39] Vizzini sits on a hilltop, some 2,000 feet above sea level, and was a formidable defensive location. A two-pronged attack was made on the 14th with 5th Black Watch advancing from the left and 1st Gordons from the right, south-west of the town. This was an extremely hot day, reckoned the hottest so far experienced, and water was scarce, as was cover for the advancing troops. Nonetheless, the Black Watch fought their way into the edge of the town, with American troops to their left, and the CO then sent a patrol into the south-west of Vizzini. This was followed by two companies in succession. Stiff resistance was met but the garrison used the cover of night to slip away and Vizzini was in British hands the following morning.[40]

Although 1st Gordons had lost touch with Brigade HQ the battalion also played a part in taking Vizzini, pushing two companies into the town's outskirts and occupying a church tower from which they were able to command a significant part of the town. Overnight the artillery bombarded the remaining enemy positions in Vizzini and, although most withdrew, some were still present when the Gordons moved in at daylight, taking many prisoners and much equipment and stores.[41]

> White sheets were much in evidence as tokens of surrender. As was the case in most of the Sicilian towns, the walls were crudely painted with large Italian slogans, urging the people to support Mussolini and the War. Despite these, the populace welcomed the troops enthusiastically, and indeed hysterically.[42]

With 5th/7th Gordons positioned between Buccheri and Vizzini, 1st Canadian Division was able to pass behind 153 Brigade and through Vizzini en route to Caltigirone.

Returning to the advance of 154 Brigade to the Monaci, the battalions were first lorried to Palagonia whence they advanced on foot with 7th Black Watch on the right, 7th Argylls in the centre and 1st Black Watch on the left. The first-named made the last part of the journey in vehicles, reaching the Ramacca area on the night of 17 July and having suffered some casualties from shellfire en route. The Argylls followed and 1st Black Watch were last to reach Ramacca. Out on the left flank the battalion had encountered considerable resistance on the western edge of the Catania plain and were ordered to continue the advance behind the Argylls.[43]

Ordered to take a ridge north of Ramacca, 7th Argylls had to establish a bridgehead across the Gornalunga.[44] This was achieved after a sharp skirmish and allowed both 152 and 153 Brigades to leap-frog forward. By nightfall on the 18th, the Division had put bridgeheads across the Dittaino river.[45] This was not achieved without some loss and considerable bravery from the attacking troops. General Wimberley witnessed the action of one Gordons officer, Captain John Grant. Grant commanded the carriers of 1st Gordons as they moved forward against intense machine-gun fire to secure the crossings of the Dittaino. This advance was made under bright moonlight on 16 July and, next day, Grant's carrier screen covered the brigade advance. Grant then pushed across the bridge over the Dittaino and, in spite of tough opposition, advanced a further mile to place his carriers and anti-tank guns in strong defensive positions and hold the bridgehead while the brigade sent forward reinforcements.[46]

Emboldened by this success, 154 Brigade's commander, Tom Rennie, decided to thrust on quickly to Gerbini, a village with a railway station, military barracks and airfield, and then across the Simeto to the Catania plain. The plan was for 1st Black Watch to take a road junction about a half mile beyond the Dittaino bridgehead and then advance on and seize both the barracks and railway station at Gerbini. Following this, 7th Black Watch would advance via the airfield to the Simeto, seize the road bridge if it was still standing, hold it, and allow 7th Argylls to pass over to form a bridgehead in the Catania plain.[47] But once again the Highlanders were to pay the price of inadequate reconnaissance.

> We found the Germans holding the airfields of Gerbini with wire and concrete belonging to the old aerodrome defences. We had come so fast that we had not been able to get the detailed aeroplane photographs which we obtained for more deliberate attacks, and I made the mistake of attacking the enemy within twenty-four hours of getting over the river.[48]

The attack on Gerbini was a calculated risk that did not work out. That it did not do so was no reflection on the courage, skill and determination of those making the attack. Problems were met before Gerbini was reached with 1st Black Watch, after taking the road junction, finding a strong enemy force in the barracks on the ridge before them. Nor were the defenders in any hurry to leave. Finding an anti-tank ditch across the road some half mile beyond the junction, the CO of 1st Black Watch decided to hold that flank until proper artillery support could be provided.[49] Although this delayed 7th Black Watch, the latter battalion reached the edge of the airfield and dug in without the Germans knowing they were there. However, they soon discovered the Highlanders as day broke on the 19th and hit James Oliver's battalion very hard. At this point, Rennie decided to change his plan and push the Argylls forward between the two Black Watch battalions in an attack on Gerbini; the plan for the Argylls to cross the river was cancelled. In this preliminary stage of the battle, 1st Black Watch had lost forty-five casualties, of whom ten had been killed.[50]

Thus, on the night of 20 July, a frontal attack was launched on Gerbini, with Sherman tanks of 23 Armoured Brigade supporting the Argylls. It was a bloody confrontation for the Argylls and cost the battalion dear: eighteen officers and over 160 men were killed, wounded or missing at the end of the battle and among the dead was the CO, Lieutenant-Colonel Roy Mathieson DSO OBE TD, while the second-in-command, Major John Lindsay-MacDougall DSO MC, was wounded, captured and later died in captivity.[51] Advancing by the line of the railway towards the barracks and station, the Argylls took the full brunt of the German resistance and were met by machine guns, tanks, armoured cars and thick wire. A Company was hit worst and its survivors became prisoners. Meanwhile, 7th Black Watch, flanking to the right, were trying to clear the road as far as the railway station.

B Squadron 46th Royal Tanks supported the Argylls and also took heavy casualties with their squadron leader, Major John S Routledge MC, one of six men killed. Routledge was killed alongside Roy Mathieson as the latter used the wireless in Routledge's tank to issue orders to his forward companies. Another officer and nine soldiers were wounded and twelve men were missing. In the early stages of the squadron's advance a tank ditched while a second bellied on to a 2,000-lb bomb. A Squadron 50th Royal Tanks was also in action and lost six tanks as well as a scout car; twenty-one men perished.[52] The tank crews were not entirely happy with the Sherman and their brigade commander, Brigadier G W 'Rickie' Richards, noted that 'the peculiar construction of the Sherman ... makes it difficult for the tank and infantry soldiers to converse easily on the battlefield without unduly exposing themselves; added to which there is no means of attracting the tank commander's attention (e.g., the bell on the Valentine)'.[53] That Mathieson and Routledge were killed as they were would seem to support Richards' assertion about communication.

The Argylls' attack was called off and the battalion was ordered back to the anti-tank ditch. An attack by 1st Black Watch reached the barracks, only to find that the enemy had slipped away. Lieutenant-Colonel Blair, the Black Watch CO, was wounded in the leg and a determined German counter-attack forced the leading companies of the battalion to pull back since it was impossible to call down defensive fire from the artillery as the exact positions of the Argylls were not known. The Black Watch also withdrew to the anti-tank ditch.[54] Once again there were many displays of outstanding courage in one of which Lieutenant 'Mike' Wingate-Gray charged a machine-gun post in a carrier and put the occupants to flight; five were killed and others wounded.[55]

In the meantime 153 Brigade had also been in action. Brigadier 'Nap' Murray was pushing his formation towards the village of Sferro, on the Dittaino some three miles from Gerbini. With an armoured brigade deployed to clear up any enemy troops left on the west side of that river, 5th Black Watch were to cross the river and take Sferro.[56] The divisional artillery bombarded the hillside on which Sferro stands and all the trees and crops thereon were soon ablaze. The Black Watch took up positions between the river and the hill and there the soldiers passed the day of the 19th, a day that was described as 'really damnable' by the CO and during which the work of Lance-Corporal Low in bringing water forward was much appreciated.[57] After dark 1st Gordons and two companies of 5th/7th Gordons passed through 5th Black Watch to advance on Sferro. As they did so they met the heaviest shelling that 1st Gordons had experienced either in North Africa or in Sicily. Heavy as that shelling was, the Gordons were to meet yet more of the same.[58]

The way to Sferro was obstructed by railway sidings in which sat many wagons, some of them with loads of tar. When the tar wagons were hit their contents flowed down the line to create yet another obstacle for the advancing infantry.[59] Eventually the railway station was cleared of enemy troops and 5th/7th Gordons reached the village. There they met ferocious resistance and it seemed as if the enemy was firing everything in the inventory at them. This fire was supplemented with a number of vicious counter-attacks, but all were beaten off. A defensive line was formed on 21 July and very accurate artillery support was provided. The infantry were extremely grateful to the Gunners and especially to the Forward Observation Officers (FOOs) who accompanied the foot soldiers and called down fire to assist them. In one 'shoot' an anti-tank gun detachment knocked out a German 88 with a couple of rounds.[60]

When 5th Black Watch relieved 5th/7th Gordons the battalion received considerable punishment from the foe and was subjected to a number of aggressive raids. Relief of 1st Gordons was carried out by 5th Camerons on the 24th but the Gordons were back two nights later to relieve the Camerons.[61] The advance had bogged down in the face of such determined resistance and Montgomery, with 50th and 51st Divisions stalled, decided to switch his attack to objectives farther to the west and north. Both divisions – and 5th Division – were now switched to the defensive.[62] The Highland Division was on the left of XIII Corps and was to continue to hold its line, although 154 Brigade was withdrawn over the Dittaino.[63] No further attacks were made on Gerbini but the enemy did not re-occupy the village after the Highlanders' withdrawal. Although 7th Black Watch continued to hold the Dittaino bridgeheads, these were taken over on the night of 25 July by 13 Brigade of 5th Division. The commander of 13 Brigade was Lorne Campbell VC, late of the Argylls. Campbell's former battalion was withdrawn and sent back to Ramacca to re-organise with their place in the Division being taken by 1st Argylls, previously deployed as a Beach Group Battalion. For a few days, 7th Royal Marines were also included in the Division's order of battle.[64]

The Sferro bridgehead was now held by 153 Brigade with 152 in reserve. Since the left flank of the Division was exposed, Montgomery ordered 231 Brigade to fill in between it and the Canadians. He had also brought 78th Division to Sicily from Tunisia and that formation became part of XXX Corps on the extreme left of whose front Eighth Army's advance was now concentrated.[65] Patton's Seventh Army was regrouping to make for Messina while 1st Canadian Division was to push east from Leonforte towards Adrano, via Agira and to the south of Mount Etna – the Americans were moving to the north of the volcano – and 231 Brigade was to join the Canadians beyond Agira. The Canadians were stalled before the mountaintop town of Centuripe and 78th Division took over the battle for the town with the Irish Brigade seizing 'Cherry Ripe', as the soldiers called it, in an almost unbelievable frontal attack, later described by Montgomery as 'impossible'.[66] In this revised strategy the Highland Division was to take the road from Sferro to Catenanuova, thereby allowing the Corps artillery to move up to shell Adrano. However, the securing of that road first demanded that the Sferro hills, which dominated it from the east, be taken. A Divisional set-piece attack was planned.[67]

This was to be a two-brigade assault with 152 Brigade on the right and 154 on the left. In 152 Brigade, 5th Camerons would lead, followed by 5th Seaforth with 2nd Seaforth in reserve. The two Black Watch battalions of 154 Brigade would lead Rennie's attack with the Argylls in reserve. Saturday 31 July was to be D-Day for the attack.[68] Wimberley made a detailed reconnaissance of the ground from Monte Turcisi, the starting-point for the attack. The hills that his soldiers were going to attack run from north-west to south-east with a high point, Point 224, at the north-west end. About 400 yards along the ridge, in a fold in the hills, is Iazzovecchio farm with Angelico farm another 500 yards farther along and also in a fold in the hills. Behind the latter farm a thick olive grove covered the ground up to the ridge. To the left of the attacking infantry of 152 Brigade would be the Fontana Muralato valley, running down from the high ground to the Dittaino and passing under the railway and road en route. Up this valley a Bofors gun would fire tracer rounds to indicate the direction of attack for 5th Camerons. The infantry would have the support of a squadron of Shermans and a platoon from 1/7th Middlesex. It was known that the upper reaches of the valley were sown liberally with mines and that anti-tank guns were also concealed there.[69]

The Camerons' advance moved off across the dried-up bed of the Dittaino on the night of the 31st behind an artillery bombardment that 'lifted', or moved forward, by a hundred yards every three minutes. There was much opposition on top of the ridge and the leading companies took so many casualties that B and D Companies of 2nd Seaforth were sent up to reinforce the Camerons.[70] One NCO, Lance-Sergeant James Graham of the Seaforth, with another soldier, silenced a machine-gun post and took prisoner five German soldiers. One of Sergeant Graham's prisoners could speak English so the Scot made the German guide him to another machine-gun post that was holding up his platoon. With a Thompson SMG, Graham charged this post alone and added more prisoners to his list.[71] Overall, the opposition was as determined as might be expected from German troops and 128th Field Regiment put down a concentration of smoke and shells on Point 224. The Germans then launched a very heavy counter-attack on the Highlanders, deploying both tanks and infantry. The battle for the ridge continued all through Sunday, the first day of August, but on the Monday came signs that the Germans were pulling out and carriers of the Camerons probed down the reverse slopes to the Strada di Palermo and the Simeto river.[72]

Following in the footsteps of the Camerons, 5th Seaforth had been delayed by traffic congestion in a gully but had moved through the right of the Camerons' line to reach Angelico farm, only to find that the olive grove behind the farm was infested with enemy soldiers. In an effort to find a way to dislodge these Germans, C Company made its way over the crest on the edge of the grove but found that the grove not only crested the hill but continued on the reverse slope. Nonetheless, C Company continued to the bottom of the grove and dug in. Two privates of the battalion, James Graham and James McLaughlan, were instrumental in the partial clearing of enemy soldiers from the grove and both men showed much courage, determination and initiative. Each received the Military Medal.[73] By now the brigade had established a line on the ridge top and a determined attack on them by German tanks and lorried infantry was broken up by the attention of the Divisional artillery. In particular the guns of Lieutenant-Colonel Jerry Sheil's 128th Field Regiment were singled out for praise.[74]

The attack by 154 Brigade also received excellent support from the artillery with 126th Field's guns firing over 2,000 rounds per gun on the brigade front before the battle was over.[75] This attack, as already noted, was led by two Black Watch battalions with the 7th to the left of the Camerons although a deep gully lay between the two battalions.

> The first thousand yards were easy going, across sloping cornlands, but beyond rose the steep crest which was the Brigade objective. Its top, five hundred feet high, was strewn with a rocky outcrop. The two leading companies of the 1st Battalion each had separate tasks: one to overrun certain posts which had been pin-pointed by observation, the other to capture a farm.[76]

The regimental history notes that the 'whole operation went like clockwork, until the objectives were taken' and then the 7th Battalion ran into trouble. C Company advanced to the crest and then passed over to the far side and into a German ambush. Heavy machine-gun fire was directed on the company from the top of the hill and it was then that Lance-Corporal Forbes climbed to the rocks where the machine guns were concealed and captured one of the positions, making the gun team prisoners. Forbes then held the position against counter-attacks, showing great coolness and courage. However, the company commander, Captain Scott, had been wounded and captured and most of the company were also in captivity.[77]

D Company, which had slogged its way up the scree, fought a stern battle with the defenders, withdrew from the crest and then took their objectives on the ridge. Major Hutchison, the company commander, was also a casualty and later died of his wounds. The other two companies had similar stories: following C Company, B came under very heavy fire from the crest and were pinned down while A Company carried on down the reverse slope. Just before dawn, carriers brought up ammunition and anti-tank guns, the latter towed behind them. Mortars were brought into play and the Germans suffered heavily. They chose to depart but, throughout that day, continued to counter-attack the position but, largely due to the excellent work of the Gunners, these attacks were broken up.[78]

Meanwhile 1st Black Watch had a much easier time with total casualties of fewer than thirty men and all objectives taken. One officer, Major Patrick Sholto Douglas, led an attack that eliminated two enemy machine-gun posts. This battalion also paid tribute to the work of the Gunners.[79] For this battle the Highland Division had not only had the support of its own Divisional artillery but also a medium regiment from corps. Happily, this unit was 80th Medium Regiment, the Scottish Horse under a temporary retitling.

The Battle of the Sferro Hills was over and the Highland Division could reflect on another success. It was believed that their eviction of the Germans hastened the departure of Hitler's men from Sicily and it is true that Eighth Army's advance now began to gain pace. Although the Division's major fighting on the island was over, there was still some to be done by 154 Brigade with 7th Argylls ordered to advance on Pietraperciata on the afternoon of 1 August. This high ridge to the left of the position held by 1st Black Watch was taken with only one casualty – a soldier wounded. The ridge gave its holders a view as far as Centuripe in the distance. In between, however, was another ridge, the highest point of which was Monte Spezia. Although it had been intended that 153 Brigade should take Monte Spezia, the operation became redundant when an Argylls patrol, with Middlesex support, reached the ridge to find that the garrison consisted of no more than nine Germans, who were all happy to be finished with fighting.[80]

By 3 August Axis forces had withdrawn east of the Simeto river and 154 Brigade was deployed to cover the right flank of 78th Division, which was to attack Adrano on the night of 6–7 August. During the evening of the 3rd Lieutenant-Colonel John Hopwood's 1st Black Watch had patrols out as far as the high ground at Cocola whence, next morning, they moved by the track from Massa Parlata.[81] In the meantime the Argylls held the Cocola foothills while 7th Black Watch was in reserve.[82] The task of securing crossings of the Simeto was assigned to 1st Black Watch and 7th Argylls on the morning of the 5th and this the two battalions achieved with few casualties. In the advance to the river, Corporal Forsyth of the Black Watch made a flanking attack on a machine-gun position at a farmhouse, knocking out the machine-gun team and thus preventing many casualties amongst his comrades. B Company of the Argylls captured fifteen Germans, including an officer, as well as a 75mm SPG, a Mercedes 10-seater carrier and a motorcycle combination. Both battalions crossed the river after which a Black Watch patrol probed close to Biancavilla, which was taken by 152 Brigade the next day. Following this, 154 Brigade was allowed to take a rest near the Simeto.[83]

The other two brigades had also entered the final phase of their operations with 153 Brigade taking high ground at Spezia and Guzzarano to protect the right flank of 78th Division's advance to Adrano. There were few casualties although one carrier of 5th Black Watch was destroyed by a mine. With 78th Division's seizure of Adrano on 7 August, the brigade's task came to an end and it was deployed to relieve 13 Brigade to the south-east of Etna.[84] This turned out to be a garrison task and 5th Black Watch found themselves repairing roads, a job they were performing when the news was received that Messina had fallen on 17 August and enemy forces had evacuated Sicily;[85] 100,000 had been captured. General Wimberley noted that, after the Simeto crossing, the Highland Division was 'squeezed out of the hunt'.[86] In that final period, as the campaign wore to a close, four Seaforth battalions beat Retreat in Catania. These were 2nd and 5th Seaforth from the Highland Division, 6th Seaforth from 5th Division and the Seaforth Highlanders of Canada from 1st Canadian Division.[87]

> For us, now all fighting had ceased, though of course there was plenty of road repairing to be done, and odd batches of straggler prisoners to be rounded up for a few days. At daylight on 15th, the 5th/7th Gordons, who had passed through the 1st and occupied Castiglione, sent patrols forward to a place called Francavilla, and found it already occupied by American troops who had come in from the West.[88]

During the thirty-nine days of the campaign, the Highland Division had suffered a total of 1,436 casualties, of whom 224, including thirty officers, had been killed. The GOC noted that his nine battalions had, on average, lost about a dozen officers and over 100 men with the Argylls having suffered most of all.[89] The Argylls had lost their CO killed on 20 July while 2nd Seaforth's CO, Lieutenant-Colonel Rory Horne, had been captured while on a night recce on 19 July; the Seaforth had also lost their second-in-command, intelligence officer, a company commander and thirty-five soldiers on the same night. The battalion war diary described 19 July as a 'most unfortunate [day], any movement bringing down heavy and accurate artillery and mortar fire'; fifteen casualties, including one fatality, had been incurred by midday. That afternoon, Major Geordie Andrews arrived to take over command of 2nd Seaforth.[90]

Training began as soon as the fighting was over and a battlefield tour of the Gerbini and Sferro battles was conducted. At the end of this tour Wimberley informed his assembled officers that he was to leave the Division. On 8 August Montgomery had told him that, as soon as the campaign was over, he would relieve Alan Cunningham as Commandant of the Staff College at Camberley. 'Plenty of recent battle experience' was required of the new Commandant and Wimberley was an ideal candidate for the post.[91]

Wimberley also passed to his men a message that he had received from Oliver Leese:

> It must be a great source of pride and satisfaction to you to know that you have created a magnificent fighting machine which has carried on in battle all the finest traditions of your Highland Brigade.[92]

Montgomery also wrote to congratulate the Division and told Wimberley that he had 'always been proud to have the Highland Division' in Eighth Army. In his own farewell special order of the day, Wimberley wrote:

> By your deeds, it is not too much to claim that you have added to the pages of military history, pages which may well bear comparison with the stories of our youth, telling us of our kinsmen who fought at Bannockburn, Culloden, Waterloo, the Alma and at Loos. Further, in achieving this, you have earned, as is indeed your due, the grateful acknowledgements of your Country.[93]

Following a round of farewell visits, Wimberley left Sicily by air for his new appointment. For his Highlanders it was a sad parting for Tartan Tam was one of the most highly respected generals in the Army and an inspiration to all who served in the Highland Division. He was succeeded by Major-General Charles Bullen-Smith, a Lowlander (whose own regiment was the King's Own Scottish Borderers), who had commanded 15th (Scottish) Division in the UK and had served on Montgomery's staff with 3rd Division in the BEF. There must have been some who thought that a game of musical chairs was being played by those responsible for senior officer postings as Brigadier MacMillan of 152 Brigade was also sent back to Britain on promotion to command 15th (Scottish) Division. James Oliver, formerly CO of 7th Black Watch, succeeded MacMillan as commander of 152 Brigade.[94]

It was to be some time before the Division quit Sicily and some expected to be involved in the invasion of Italy. This was not to be, although the artillery did play their part, moving to Messina to take part in a XXX Corps bombardment programme across the straits as XIII Corps sailed to the mainland.[95] Also involved in a peripheral role was 154 Brigade. Rennie's brigade had moved to Messina on 17 August and took over from 3rd (US) Division three days later, carrying out a security role. When XIII Corps crossed the Straits of Messina, 154 Brigade followed on 5 September and formed a base around Reggio. After three days at Reggio the brigade was ferried back to Messina.[96]

The Highland Division made itself at home in Sicily over the next few months during which the training routine was maintained, sports and entertainments were organised and there were ceremonial events. The latter included a presentation by General Montgomery of the ribbons of gallantry awards made to members of the Division since El Alamein. This presentation took place on 25 September and, at the conclusion, Montgomery announced that, if he could possibly arrange it, the Division would be going home.[97] It is more than likely that Monty already knew that 51st (Highland) Division would be returning to Britain to prepare for the invasion of north-west Europe. Closer to the time of the Division's departure for home another, and very poignant, event was held when a memorial to those who had died in the Sicilian campaign was dedicated near Gerbini on 4 November. The memorial, in the form of a Celtic cross, recalled the sacrifice of all those Jocks who had died in the short campaign.[98] Interestingly, the Division's historian noted that, although the Division had suffered some 7,000 casualties within a year, it still included a majority of Scotsmen within its ranks: '81 per cent of the officers and 72 per cent other ranks in the Highland Regiments of the Division.'[99]

Sports activities were popular and Highland Games were held on 23 October, the first anniversary of the opening of the Battle of El Alamein, which was declared a Divisional holiday. Concert parties entertained, with 'The Balmorals' continuing to please audiences, while there was an opportunity for personnel to attend an American show given by a concert party that included the comedian Jack Benny and the musician Larry Adler.[100] However, the same welcome might not have been given to the new GOC's comment to the officers of the Division on 17 September: Bullen-Smith declared that an improvement was needed in discipline and saluting.[101] It is hard to credit that such a rejoinder was necessary in a formation that had been commanded by Douglas Wimberley for twenty-six months.

There was almost a touch of farce in an episode during October in which a soldier of B Company 1st Black Watch, who had deserted, was captured. Before the day was out the man had escaped again. He was re-captured on the 27th and handcuffed. This did not discourage the man who seemed determined to be a serial runaway: he escaped another time later that day. However, his ability to escape seemed to be balanced by an inability to remain at large and, next day, he was recaptured. To ensure that no further escape attempts could be made, the man was 'shackled securely and placed in his cell, clothed only in his shirt'.[102]

At last came the time to say farewell to Sicily. The first elements of the Division boarded ships in late-October and set sail across the Mediterranean, passed through the Straits of Gibraltar and turned for home. By mid-November the complete Highland Division had left that island for the green hills of the United Kingdom.[103]

Notes

1. Churchill, *The Second World War, Book VIII; The Hinge of Fate, Africa Redeemed,* pp. 338–9
2. Ibid
3. Molony, *The Mediterranean and the Middle East, Vol V*, pp. 2–4. Initially, the assaulting forces were known as Eastern Task Force (Montgomery) and Western Task Force (Patton).
4. Ibid, pp. 25–9 & map 4, facing p. 25
5. Ibid, p. 26; NA Kew, WO169/8793, war diary, HQ 51 (H) Div (GS), 1943
6. Molony, op cit, p. 52
7. NA Kew, WO169/10178, war diary, 1 BW, 1943
8. NA Kew, WO169/10215, war diary, 1 Gordons, 1943
9. NA Kew, WO169/8963, war diary, 154 Bde, 1943; Salmond, *The History of the 51st Highland Division*, p. 105
10. Ibid
11. NA Kew, WO169/8963, war diary, 154 Bde, 1943; WO169/10181, war diary, 7 BW, 1943; Salmond, op cit, pp. 105–6
12. NA Kew, WO169/10215, war diary, 1 Gordons
13. Ibid
14. NA Kew, WO169/8959, war diary, 153 Bde, 1943
15. Ibid; WO169/10246, war diary 5/7 Gordons, 1943; WO169/10179, war diary, 5 BW, 1943; Salmond, op cit, pp. 106–7; McGregor, *The Spirit of Angus*, p. 87
16. NA Kew, WO169/8955, war diary, 152 Bde, 1943
17. Ibid; WO169/10188, war diary, 5 Camerons, 1943; WO169/10291, war diary, 2 Seaforth, 1943; WO169/10292, war diary, 5 Seaforth, 1943
18. NA Kew, WO169/10188, war diary, 5 Camerons, 1943
19. A comment made to the author by the late Bobby Baxter BEM, who served in Sicily in 2nd London Irish Rifles.
20. NA Kew, WO169/8963, war diary, 154 Bde, 1943
21. Molony, op cit, p. 88
22. Ibid, p. 93; Salmond, op cit, p. 108
23. Borthwick, *Battalion*, p. 106; Salmond, op cit, pp. 108–9
24. Borthwick, op cit, pp. 106–7
25. Ibid, p. 105
26. Wimberley, *Memoirs*, p. 151
27. Borthwick, op cit, p. 107
28. Ibid, p. 112; NA Kew, WO169/8955, war diary, 152 Bde, 1943; Salmond, op cit, p. 109
29. Salmond, op cit, p. 109
30. Ibid, pp. 109–10; NA Kew, WO169/8955, war diary, 152 Bde, 1943; WO169/10188, war diary, 5 Camerons, 1943
31. NA Kew, WO169/10188, war diary, 5 Camerons, 1943; Salmond, op cit, p. 110
32. NA Kew, WO169/8907, war diary, 23 Armd Bde, 1943
33. Salmond, op cit, p. 110
34. *Volunteers from Éire who have won distinction serving with the British Forces*
35. Wimberley, op cit, p. 154
36. Salmond, op cit, pp. 110–11

37. Ibid, p. 111
38. Ibid
39. Ibid, pp. 111–13
40. NA Kew, WO169/8959, war diary, 153 Bde, 1943
41. Wimberley, op cit, p. 175
42. Ibid
43. NA Kew, WO169/8963, war diary, 154 Bde, 1943
44. Ibid
45. Salmond, op cit, p. 113
46. Ibid, pp. 113–15; NA Kew, WO169/8963, war diary, 154 Bde, 1943
47. Wimberley, op cit, p. 189
48. Ibid; NA Kew, WO169/10178, war diary, 1 BW, 1943
49. NA Kew, WO169/10178, war diary, 1 BW, 1943; Fergusson, *The Black Watch and the King's Enemies*, pp. 177–8
50. NA Kew, WO169/8963, war diary, 154 Bde, 1943; Fergusson, op cit, pp. 178–9
51. NA Kew, WO169/8963, war diary, 154 Bde, 1943; WO169/10178, war diary, 1 BW, 1943; Fergusson, op cit, pp. 179–81
52. Quoted in Salmond, op cit, p. 118
53. NA Kew, WO169/10178, war diary, 1 BW, 1943
54. Ibid
55. Salmond, op cit, p. 117
56. NA Kew, WO169/8959, war diary, 153 Bde, 1943; Fergusson, op cit, p. 182
57. Salmond, op cit, p. 118
58. Ibid, p. 119
59. Ibid
60. Ibid
61. Ibid
62. Molony, op cit, pp. 114 & 117
63. Salmond, op cit, p. 121
64. Ibid
65. Molony, op cit, p. 122
66. Doherty, *Clear The Way!*, p. 73
67. Salmond, op cit, p. 122
68. NA Kew, WO169/8793, war diary, HQ 51 (H) Div, 1943
69. NA Kew, WO169/8963, war diary, 154 Bde, 1943
70. Ibid
71. NA Kew, Wo169/8955, war diary, 152 Bde, 1943
72. Salmond, op cit, p. 123
73. Borthwick, op cit, pp. 122–3
74. Ibid, pp. 123–4
75. Wimberley, op cit, p. 192
76. Fergusson, op cit, pp. 184–5
77. Ibid, p. 185
78. Salmond, op cit, p. 124
79. Fergusson, op cit, p. 186; Salmond, op cit, pp. 124–5
80. Salmond, op cit, p. 126
81. Ibid
82. Ibid

83. Ibid, pp. 126–7; NA Kew, WO169/8963, war diary, 154 Bde, 1943
84. Salmond, op cit, p. 127
85. NA Kew, WO169/10179, war diary, 5 BW, 1943; McGregor, op cit, p. 102
86. Wimberley, op cit, p. 197
87. NA Kew, WO169/10291, war diary, 2 Seaforth, 1943; Borthwick, op cit, p. 125
88. Wimberley, op cit, p. 199
89. Ibid
90. NA Kew, WO169/10291, war diary 2 Seaforth, 1943; obit: Brig G L W Andrews CBE DSO, *The Highlander*, Winter 2001, p. 135
91. Wimberley, op cit, p. 197
92. Ibid, p. 201
93. Ibid; NA Kew, WO169/8793, war diary, HQ 51 (H) Div (GS), 1943
94. Ibid; WO169/8955, war diary, 152 Bde, 1943
95. NA Kew, WO169/9516, war diary, 126 Fd Regt, 1943; WO169/9517, war diary, 127 Fd Regt, 1943; WO169/9518, war diary, 128 Fd Regt, 1943
96. NA Kew, WO169/8963, war diary, 154 Bde, 1943
97. NA Kew, WO169/10178, war diary, 1 BW, 1943
98. NA Kew, WO169/10245, war diary, 1 Gordons, 1943
99. Salmond, op cit, p. 133
100. NA Kew, WO169/10188, war diary, 5 Camerons, 1943
101. NA Kew, WO169/9516, war diary, 126 Fd Regt, 1943
102. NA Kew, WO169/10178, war diary, 1 BW, 1943
103. Salmond, op cit, p. 135

CHAPTER VIII

Return to Britain

By the end of November the Highland Division was in its new home, spread throughout the counties of Buckinghamshire and Hertfordshire in rural England.[1] They were home but not quite, although leave arrangements allowed many to return to their own Scottish firesides. Perhaps those who had landed on the Clyde felt the pull of home most strongly for they had come ashore in Scotland only to entrain for England almost immediately.

No one doubted that the Division would soon be in action again, this time in the invasion of Europe. Had not Montgomery promised that it would be so? And it was not long before training for the invasion was underway. At the same time, units of the Division were being restored to full strength and there were new personalities in some of the most senior positions. We have already seen that Major-General Charles Bullen-Smith had succeeded Douglas Wimberley before the departure from Sicily while Brigadiers Gordon MacMillan and Thomas Rennie had been promoted to divisional commands; Douglas Graham had also become commander of 50th (Northumbrian) Division. James Oliver, former CO of 7th Black Watch, had taken command of 152 Brigade when MacMillan left to become GOC of 15th (Scottish) Division but when Tom Rennie left to command 3rd Division in December, Oliver moved to command 154 Brigade.[2] Brigadier D H Haugh succeeded to the command of 152 Brigade, Nap Murray remained at the helm of 153 Brigade and when the Division again went to war, in June 1944, Haugh would be relieved by Brigadier A J H Cassels. Of the triumvirate of Cassels, Murray and Oliver, Colonel Sir Martin Lindsay wrote: 'I should not think that any Division anywhere had three better or more trusted Brigade Commanders.'[3]

During January units issued new battledress to their soldiers and the veterans of North Africa received the ribbon of the Africa Star.[4] These were stitched to battledress tunics and provided an instant identification of the veterans to civilians. The little sand-coloured ribbon with red, dark blue and light blue stripes earned many Highlanders free drinks in the public houses they visited as other customers were keen to show their appreciation of the Desert army's achievements.

The training programme, which began in earnest in February, included co-operation with tanks as well as 'hardening' for the infantry. There were also river-crossing exercises, known as SPLASH,[5] night exercises and training specific to the artillery, engineers, signals and the machine gunners of the Middlesex. And a new weapon was demonstrated in the form of the Wasp, a flamethrower mounted on a carrier. Then they moved on to loading and landing exercises at Lowestoft, which involved the temporary move of units to East Anglia. Also at Lowestoft, the Jocks learned about waterproofing of vehicles and carried out tests to ensure that this process had been carried out properly.[6] Those who had not achieved a complete waterproof state gave their comrades cause for some laughter. In the east end of London training in street fighting was conducted at the Limehouse Street-Fighting Area;[7] this proved both interesting and exciting with the devastated streets of the east end a harbinger of what could be expected in towns on the mainland. Battalion, brigade and divisional exercises honed the readiness of the Division while in Exercise FABIUS, in May, the marshalling and concentration of the Division was tested.[8]

Of course, there was also a stream of VIP visitors. Among the first was Lieutenant-General Sir Kenneth Anderson, commander of Second Army to which the Division now belonged. Anderson visited on 5 January,[9] three days before Douglas Wimberley paid an 'informal' but most welcome visit.[10] (Anderson, who had commanded First Army in Tunisia, was to fall victim to Montgomery, who had earlier described him as a 'plain cook'; he was later relieved of command of Second Army and became GOC Eastern Command.) Then the Duke of Gloucester and Major-General Sir James L Burnett of Lys visited 153 Brigade and 1st Gordons; on the evening of this visit, on 18 January, the combined Pipe Bands of 1st and 5/7th Gordons played Retreat.[11] Montgomery, now commanding 21 Army Group, was another visitor as was General Dwight D Eisenhower, Supreme Allied Commander, with the latter's Deputy, Air Chief Marshal Sir Arthur Tedder and the Moderator of the Church of Scotland.[12] But perhaps the most popular of all visitors were the Royal Family. Queen Elizabeth paid a visit on 23 February while King George VI inspected training on the 28th and the young Princesses Elizabeth and Margaret watched the Massed Pipes and Drums of the Division beat Retreat at Clarence Park, St Albans on the same day.[13] Another visitor marked a change of 'home' for the Division: this was Lieutenant-General Crocker, commander of I Corps to which the Division had been transferred from XXX Corps on 5 April.[14]

In January a new name was added to the Divisional order of battle when, at last, a reconnaissance regiment was restored to that orbat. But this was not a reborn 51 (Highland) Recce. Instead, the recce role was assigned to

2nd Derbyshire Yeomanry, an armoured car regiment, which joined the Division on 6 January.[15] The Reconnaissance Corps had become part of the RAC on the 1st[16] and the Derby Yeomanry were now to be reconfigured as a reconnaissance regiment. No effort appears to have been made by the War Office to have a Scottish regiment assigned to the role even though 9th Gordons, once part of the Division, had been converted to armour, as 116th Regiment, RAC,[17] and might just as easily have been converted yet again to a reconnaissance regiment to maintain the Highland ethos of the Division. (There was a precedent for such further conversion: 12th Green Howards converted to 161st Regiment RAC in July 1942 and became 161st Reconnaissance Regiment in October 1943.[18]) However, as the Yeomen were already armoured-car operators this must have played a part in the decision.

The tempo of training continued and Tactical Exercises Without Troops (TEWTS) tested the abilities of officers while both officers and soldiers pounded the roads on lengthy route marches to reach the standards of fitness laid down by Montgomery. Replacement 25-pounders were issued to the three field regiments which took part in a series of exercises designed to test their skills and effectiveness. New weapons came the way of the anti-tank platoons and they learned to use their 6-pounders in range-firing at Foulness in Essex. The Middlesex also received a new weapon: the 4.2-inch mortar which was to provide extremely effective support in action. With the arrival of the new mortars the battalion adopted a new organisation with five companies: A Company was the Mortar company while the machine guns were assigned to B, C and D Companies, with HQ Company the fifth sub-unit.[19] In April the Division moved to East Anglia where the emphasis was laid on crossing rivers, advancing at night and patrolling. Although there was some training in tactics for fighting in rural areas restricted by woods and small fields there were insufficient areas available for this and, at this time, the peculiar difficulties of the Normandy bocage were not appreciated fully.

On 1 April the Duke of Devonshire KG MBE TD visited 2nd Derbyshire Yeomanry and later expressed his high opinion of the unit's morale.[20] The regiment took part in Exercise SNAFFLE, an assault river crossing with an armoured brigade, on the 24th but was still short of its full complement of vehicles. Although it had Humber MkIV armoured cars and universal carriers, there were no Humber Light Reconnaissance Cars (LRCs); it would take a few more weeks before these arrived. Ten jeeps on the regimental inventory were described as 4 x 4 5-cwt cars.[21] A recce regiment organisation had long been adopted with Regimental HQ, HQ Squadron – including a Mortar Troop with six 3-inch mortars, an Anti-Tank Battery with eight 6-pounders and a Signal Troop – and three recce squadrons.[22] Each of the latter deployed seven troops, of which three were scout troops, three carrier and one assault. The Recce ethos was assisted by drafts of recce soldiers: on 1 February ninety men from 161 Recce arrived, including twelve sergeants, sixteen corporals, sixteen driver/mechanics, twenty-seven anti-tank gunners and nineteen mortarmen; a further draft was received from 38 Recce.[23]

There was some light relief at times. ENSA concert parties visited and, of course, 'The Balmorals' continued entertaining the Division. Sport played its usual part in maintaining morale and sharpening rivalry between units. There were football matches, athletic events and Highland Games with war diaries noting that a battalion or regiment had won this or that event with almost the same pride that the diarist would have shown had a battle been won.[24] Relations with local civilians were generally good, as demonstrated at St Albans in January when the Mayor gave a reception followed by a concert to personnel of 2nd Seaforth. Before the concert began the Mayor presented RSM A Wilson with a portrait of the RSM painted by a local artist.[25]

By mid-May almost all the preparations were complete. Bullen-Smith briefed his senior officers on the Division's role in OVERLORD and the Division began moving into its concentration areas on the 17th.[26] In those areas the troops were sealed up although, until 26 May, short leave passes were available. Thereafter everyone lived behind barbed wire with wet and dry canteens and cinemas to relieve the monotony. All the vehicles moved into the marshalling area and 'waterproofing … was again set in motion … trucks began to assume a Wellsian appearance' according to the war diarist of 152 Brigade.[27] The same officer noted that with all the paper-work for the brigade plan for OVERLORD complete it was 'all quiet at HQ – quiet amidst rural England' on 20 May. Even a visit by Bullen-Smith 'did not destroy this peace'.[28]

Even at this late hour few knew where they were going. Maps used for briefings had had place names changed and all that was known for certain was that the Division was not to be involved in the initial assault. Instead the Highlanders were to provide the immediate 'follow up' to 3rd British and 3rd Canadian Divisions, which would assault Sword and Juno Beaches respectively. In this role the Division's Tactical HQ (Tac HQ) and 153 Brigade Group would land on D + 1, to be followed by 4 Armoured Brigade, 152 and 154 Brigade Groups.[29] (4 Armoured Brigade was commanded by Brigadier John Currie DSO, an Alamein veteran, this formation included The Royal Scots Greys, 3rd County of London Yeomanry (Sharpshooters), 44th Royal Tank Regiment and 2nd King's Royal Rifle Corps.[30])

Finally it was time to board. The ships that would carry the Highlanders to France lay in the Thames near Tilbury and it was from there that the Division once more bade goodbye to Britain. Bullen-Smith and his HQ sailed on HMS *Hilary*, the troopships *Cheshire* and *Lancashire* carried 5th Camerons while 7th Black Watch sailed again to war on *Fort Brunswick*, a liberty ship, and the LSI *Isle of Jersey*. Whatever the vessel that bore them, the Highlanders now struck out into the Channel en route to the coast of Normandy. Ahead lay the battles to liberate Europe, battles that would mean death for many men of 51st Highland Division. Such thoughts must have occupied many minds that June night.

Notes

1. NA Kew, WO171/527, war diary, HQ 51 (H) Div (G), 1944; Fergusson, *The Black Watch and the King's Enemies*, p. 262
2. Salmond, *The History of the 51st Highland Division*, pp. 135–6
3. Quoted in ibid, p. 136
4. Delaforce, *Monty's Highlanders*, p. 122
5. NA Kew, WO171/678, war diary 153 Bde, 1944; WO171/1299, war diary, 1 Gordons, 1944
6. Salmond, op cit, p. 137
7. NA Kew, WO171/1369, war diary, 2 Seaforth, 1944
8. NA Kew, WO171/673, war diary, 152 Bde, 1944; WO171/11640, war diary, 40 LAA Regt, 1944
9. NA Kew, WO171/678, war diary, 153 Bde, 1944
10. NA Kew, WO171/527, war diary, HQ 51 (H) Div (G), 1944
11. NA Kew, WO171/678, war diary, 153 Bde, 1944
12. Ibid; NA Kew, WO171/11640, war diary, 40 LAA Regt, 1944
13. NA Kew, WO171/527, war diary, HQ 51 (H) Div (G), 1944
14. Ibid
15. NA Kew, WO171/527, war diary HQ 51 (H) Div (G), 1944
16. Doherty, *Only The Enemy in Front*, p. 118; NA Kew, WO32/10425: *The amalgamation of the Reconnaissance Corps with the Royal Armoured Corps.*
17. Frederick, *Lineage Book of British Land Forces, Vol I*, p. 12
18. Ibid, pp. 12–13
19. NA Kew, WO171/1344, war diary, 1/7 Mx, 1944
20. NA Kew, WO171/850, war diary, 2 Derby Yeo (2 DY), 1944
21. Ibid
22. Ibid
23. Ibid
24. NA Kew, WO171/673, war diary, 152 Bde, 1944
25. NA Kew, WO171/1369, war diary, 2 Seaforth, 1944
26. NA Kew, WO171/527, HQ 51 (H) Div (G), 1944
27. NA Kew, WO171/673, war diary, 152 Bde, 1944
28. Ibid
29. NA Kew, WO171/527, war diary, HQ 51 (H) Div (G), 1944.
30. Joslen, *Orders of Battle* p. 153

CHAPTER IX

The Invasion of Europe

At dawn on D-Day the vessels carrying the Highland Division were some ten miles off the coast of Normandy with, as far as the eye could see, a huge armada of warships, troop-carrying vessels and assault ships. But it would not be until the afternoon that the first soldiers of the Division, men of 153 Brigade, also referred to as the Black Watch and Gordon Brigade,[1] began disembarking on a section of beach that 'somewhat resembled the West Sands of St Andrews'.[2] Since the Highland Division was a follow-up formation, its initial role was to be deployed not as a complete division but in a 'fire brigade' role to provide support wherever such support was most needed by other elements of I Corps.

Before studying the Highlanders' experience in Normandy a brief look at I Corps' part in the overall invasion plan is desirable. All Allied ground forces, British, Canadian and American, were under command of General Montgomery's 21 Army Group in the initial phase.[3] The first troops to arrive in Normandy were airborne soldiers from 6th (British), 82nd (US) and 101st (US) Airborne Divisions. Dropped at night, the airborne divisions were to secure the flanks of the seaborne invasion which was to take place on a series of beaches from the Cotentin peninsula in the west to the Orne estuary in the east. With US forces landing in the west – on Utah Beach, on the east coast of the Cotentin, and Omaha Beach – the two US divisions dropped on that flank. Meanwhile 6th Airborne was dropped on the Orne flank to guard the landings on Sword Beach; the latter were to be made by 3rd British Division, under Major-General Tom Rennie. Between Omaha Beach and Sword Beach were two further landing areas, Gold and Juno Beaches, where the divisions of XXX Corps would land. With the airborne holding their left flank, Rennie's soldiers were to advance inland towards the city of Caen and, if possible, take that city on D-Day.[4] As 3rd Division advanced, the units of the Highland Division were to begin disembarking.

No plan ever survives first contact with the enemy and this was true of Montgomery's plan for D-Day. German forces reacted to the airborne landings and then to the landing of 3rd Division and its first inland probes. Much of that reaction came from 21st Panzer Division, some of whose tanks almost reached the coast on the evening of D-Day.[5] Thus, as the Highlanders began coming ashore, the picture that was unfolding was one of stout German resistance in many areas which demanded the deployment of reinforcements to the assaulting formations. Lieutenant-Colonel 'Chick' Thomson had temporary command of 153 Brigade and he led the three battalions inland during the afternoon establishing 'them in close proximity to each other in the woods' while he made for the HQ of a brigade of 3rd Canadian Division, which had landed on Juno Beach. However, the Canadians felt that they needed no assistance at that stage and so 153 Brigade did not deploy into action on D-Day.[6] The situation changed on the morning of 7 June when Bullen-Smith came ashore from HMS *Hilary* with an order from I Corps HQ to send a battalion to assist the seizure of the radar station at Douvres la Delivrande, where the small German garrison was still holding out. Thomson took 5th Black Watch and two AVREs of the Royal Engineers and made for Douvres.[7]

The Black Watch were soon in action but their 'foes' were, in fact, Canadian troops. Thomson had been assured that the Canadians were well south of a wood east of Douvres and thus when troops were encountered in that wood these were taken to be German. Fortunately, this misunderstanding, which might have had tragic results, was resolved quickly and Thomson pushed on for Douvres. However, when the battalion debouched from the wood it was to find a wide, open space between them and the radar station; and that space was swept by intense fire from the defenders. It seemed that the Douvres garrison was much stronger than had been appreciated, a fact that was confirmed when the two armoured vehicles were knocked out by an anti-tank gun, situated in or about Douvres village. (This weapon was identified as an 88. Although it was common for Allied soldiers to identify 88s when other anti-tank weapons were involved, the identification in this case is probably accurate due to the range involved.) Movement across the open ground against the radar station would have been suicidal and so Thomson decided to move to the rear of the objective and attack from there. In the meantime he sought reinforcements but was told to leave the radar station to be dealt with by the Royal Navy and move by Hermanville to Pegasus bridge, the crossing of the Orne that had been taken by 6th Airborne Division. In the meantime, 5th Camerons, on temporary attachment to 153 Brigade, were left to mask the radar station which would hold out for many days yet.[8]

On D+1, 152 Brigade landed but the bulk of the brigade's transport was not unloaded until two days later, during which time the brigade remained concentrated near Douvres; it was then ordered to follow 153 Brigade across the Orne to engage the enemy.[9] Finally, 154 Brigade landed on D+4 to be held in I Corps reserve.[10] Not until 13 June – D+7 – was its first battalion committed to action, once again east of the Orne. This was

7th Argylls; the remainder of 154 Brigade followed the Argylls five days later under temporary command of 6th Airborne Division.[11] In such manner began a period of very scrappy fighting that was to prove one of the most testing times in the Division's history. Until almost the end of July the Highlanders would fight a series of engagements at platoon, company battalion and brigade level but rarely as a division. Since the fighting was in this fashion it is appropriate to look at the Highlanders' experiences brigade by brigade beginning with 153 Brigade, the first to see action.

We have already seen that 153 Brigade had been sent to Douvres and then recalled to Pegasus Bridge. Once there, and under temporary command of 6th Airborne Division, the battalions were assigned a number of tasks with 5th Black Watch ordered to march on Breville, 5th/7th Gordons to move south to Touffreville and 1st Gordons to deploy into the area that would become infamous as the 'Triangle'.[12] Advancing along the Ranville–Breville road, the Black Watch had not marched far before meeting opposition. German troops positioned in the ditches alongside the road opened a withering fire on the Highlanders. A Company was all but annihilated and every soldier in the lead platoon was killed; every man in that platoon 'died with his face to the foe'.[13] The CO then ordered his soldiers to occupy the grounds of Breville château, which lay about 800 yards south of the village. However, the Germans were not willing to let the Black Watch take up occupancy of the château grounds and first bombarded both building and grounds heavily before launching a determined frontal attack. The assault was almost suicidal and the attackers were 'killed literally by the hundred'.[14]

Defying all the German efforts, 5th Black Watch, in spite of their weakened state, held out and the enemy eventually withdrew. Before that withdrawal, however, some Black Watch soldiers on the battalion flank had been captured. Instead of sending the captured Jocks back as prisoners, the Germans pushed them against a nearby wall and shot them. One soldier survived by feigning death and thus was able to tell his comrades what had happened. This was a shock to the Highlanders who had assumed that all German soldiers fought with the chivalry and respect for their foes that had been experienced in North Africa, especially from the men of 90th Light Division. Although there was considerable anger within the Battalion at this news, there was no retaliation when a German prisoner was taken by the Black Watch. Instead, the captured man was given a cigarette by a Jock.[15]

The two Gordon battalions had not suffered as did the Black Watch and both occupied their positions without opposition. At Touffreville, 5th/7th Gordons fought off a sharp counter-attack, during which Sergeant Aitkenhead of B Company was captured by the Germans. Taken to a German HQ, Aitkenhead was later to escape by stabbing the single guard left to watch him. His captors had failed to find a knife when searching him. Later that day, Aitkenhead arrived back with the Gordons.[16]

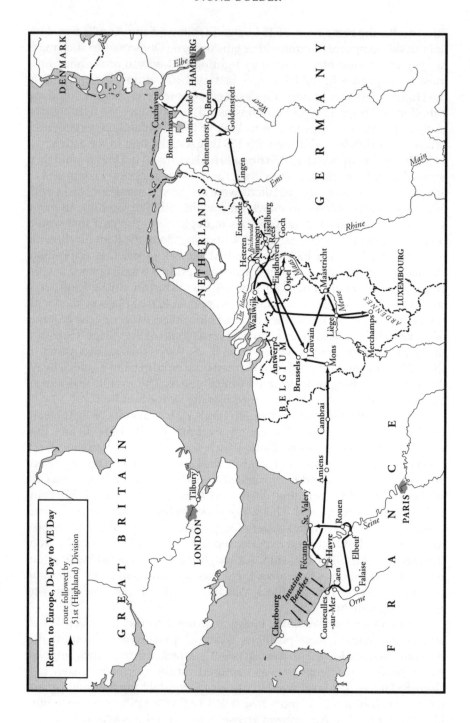

Return to Europe, D-Day to VE Day
route followed by
51st (Highland) Division

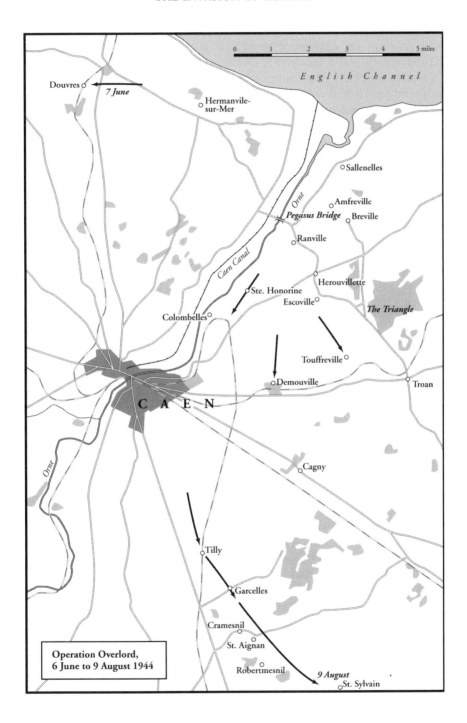

0   1   2   3   4   5 miles

English Channel

Douvres

7 June

Hermanvile-
sur-Mer

Sallenelles

Orne

Amfreville

Pegasus Bridge   Breville

Ranville

Caen Canal

Herouvillette

Ste. Honorine

The Triangle

Escoville

Colombelles

Touffreville

Demouville

Troan

C A E N

Orne

Cagny

Tilly

Garcelles

Cramesnil

St. Aignan

Robertmesnil

9 August

St. Sylvain

Operation Overlord,
6 June to 9 August 1944

Two battalions of 152 Brigade were, meanwhile, assigned the task of capturing the villages of Ste Honorine la Chardonnerette (Spelled 'Chardonnette' on a modern Michelin map) and Demouville as part of Operation SMOCK.[17] The former was assigned to 5th Camerons while 2nd Seaforth was to deal with the latter; the third battalion of the brigade, 5th Seaforth, was attached temporarily to 153 Brigade. Concentrating in the Ranville area, the Camerons launched their attack on the morning of 13 June. Even on the start-line, the Battalion suffered bombardment by enemy artillery while three of the four tanks assigned for support were knocked out before reaching the start-line. An eyewitness to the Camerons' operation was Lieutenant Jack Chapman MC, 1st Royal Ulster Rifles, whose platoon had cleared the start-line.

> We had various attempts at Sainte Honorine and each time we were hammered. … The powers-that-be decided that some of the other battalions would come through us and take Sainte Honorine. We cleared the start-line without any bother, they took over and we got back. I got hit on the way back, and most of my platoon was wiped out. And they [the Camerons] got about halfway across a large open space and got massacred themselves.[18]

The Camerons suffered so heavily that the battalion was ordered to pull back although C Company did not receive the order and held out for some time before withdrawing. When C Company finally came back the remnants of 5th Camerons were re-formed at Longueval.[19]

With the failure of this attack and the heavy German artillery fire it proved impossible for 2nd Seaforth to advance on Demouville and so the battalion was ordered into defensive positions on high ground north of Sainte Honorine while 5th Seaforth, returned from 153 Brigade, deployed to close the gap between the 2nd Battalion and 5th Camerons.

The Camerons were sent back to attack Sainte Honorine for a second time on 22 June. This time the battalion's efforts were crowned with success and the village was in Cameron hands by 10 o'clock. Several determined counter-attacks were made but each was repulsed until, that night, the Camerons were relieved and returned to Herouvillette. The relief was carried out by 2nd Seaforth, detachments of which had reinforced the Camerons' attack. In turn the Seaforth were relieved by their own 5th Battalion 'in that village of evil memory'.[20] And it was in and around that village that the Seaforth and Cameron Brigade first met 'Moaning Minnie' the German multi-barrelled mortar, or *Nebelwerfer*, a weapon that frayed the nerves of even the toughest men. On the night of 1–2 July Sainte Honorine was handed over to 5th Black Watch and 5th Seaforth bade it goodbye.[21]

Other elements of the Highland Division had also been busily engaged during this period. Both 1st and 5th/7th Gordons had seen much action, both in attack and defence, around Escoville and Sainte Honorine[22] where a Middlesex NCO, Sergeant Faiers, found an enemy map that detailed the entire German order of battle from Troarn to Caen. This proved a valuable intelligence asset for which Faiers was commended.[23] The Diehards had been deployed, as usual, in companies and platoons to support the infantry battalions while the Derbyshire Yeomanry had also played their part. The natural role of the reconnaissance regiment was ranging in front of its division but this role was denied those recce units in Normandy. Instead the armoured cars, LRCs, carriers and other elements of the regiment had deployed in a defensive role with many yeomen serving as infantry. However, the regiment continued to provide a reconnaissance role with troops holding observation positions and reporting on enemy movements.

At last light on 15 June, 2 Troop of C Squadron, under Lieutenant C S Richards, withdrew from positions facing south-west from Herouvillette, having been 'in observation during daylight for 48hrs seeing no enemy but reporting 3 apparently derelict tanks in the direction of la Chardonnerette'. Since the latter might have been used as OPs by the Germans they were demolished by 2nd Seaforth during the night of 15–16 June. On the 16th Lieutenant Richards' Troop was engaged in action with enemy infantry and armour. The infantry were spotted on the skyline at 5.40am and kept well down in the corn as they made for Escoville church. Twenty minutes later, enemy infantry, supported by mortar and machine-gun fire, attacked 5 Troop but were in turn engaged by armoured cars of Richards' Troop, using both their 37mm guns and machine guns. Then enemy troops were spotted crossing the road near the church to enter the wood east of the road, thereby threatening 5 Troop's left flank. When 2 Troop reported this movement, 5 Troop was ordered to withdraw under cover of fire from 2 Troop. However, 5 Troop suffered nine casualties, including the troop leader and both sergeants.

At 6.15am a direct hit from an 88 killed the sergeant-commander and injured seriously the wireless operator of the third car of 2 Troop. A car from 1 Troop deployed almost immediately to engage the enemy and the woods into which German infantry had been spotted slipping were sprayed spasmodically with machine-gun fire; mortar fire from the Middlesex was directed on those enemy in the vicinity of the church. Enemy reinforcements arrived at 7.50 in the form of six tanks, including a Tiger, which deployed in a cornfield some 500 yards from 2 Troop. 'These proceeded to fire all guns except the 88mm in general direction of 2 Tp who did not reply. There were no casualties'.[24]

A 6-pounder anti-tank gun of the Yeomanry got a shot at the left flank of a German tank at 8.15, whereupon the tanks turned to their right and made off towards the church. As they did so they came into the field of fire of a concealed 17-pounder which struck the Tiger, breaking a track. Return fire from the Tiger killed two of the 17-pounder's detachment, following which no more shots were fired and three of the Tiger's crew dismounted to repair the track, covered by fire from two SPGs. Apart from occasional figures on the skyline, the German infantry seemed to have abandoned the fight. At 8.45 a platoon of airborne soldiers counter-attacked through the woods and cleared the enemy from there. Thirty prisoners were taken and forty Germans killed for British losses in the engagement of four wounded.[25]

The German SPGs continued to fire sporadically until C Squadron's leader called down fire from the Divisional artillery which forced the Germans to withdraw at about 11 o'clock. As they withdrew the 25-pounders continued to fire and a patrol later found two of the SPGs burned out some 300 yards south-west of Escoville church; this was on the line of withdrawal. Fire from the 25-pounders also put paid to a 50mm SPG that fired many rounds at 2 Troop's positions between 9.00 and 11.00am. The artillery also engaged and demolished the church tower fifteen minutes after first reports of a sniper firing from there. By 11.30am the action was over and 4 Troop reported that Escoville was clear of enemy; the opposition was identified as troops from 24th Panzer Recce and 125th Panzer Grenadiers.[26]

This was the pattern of life in the Triangle. It was an almost claustrophobic existence, especially for men who had served in North Africa and had many echoes of the Great War, not least in the level of patrolling that was carried out. An example of these patrols was a recce patrol commanded by Corporal Murray of A Company 1st Gordons on 2 July. The patrol included Murray and six soldiers who set out from the positions of 8 Platoon to make their way through a strip of woodland south of A Company's positions. Some extracts from Corporal Murray's detailed report provide an insight into the life of an infantryman on Second British Army's left flank in Normandy.

1. ... Crossed open ground and entered NORTH end of wood 083714 and found 3 or 4 coils of dannert wire across top end of wood from r[oa]d to river. No movement seen on river bank.

2. Very thick undergrowth. Made way down wood looking out from time to time over r[oa]d. Very few slit trenches seen in actual wood and ones seen were 2½ ft long by 9 ins deep. One slit trench covered with corrugated iron was seen on EAST side of r[oa]d at top end of wood 084714.

4. About 200 yds from Chateau, wood stopped and low scrub and bushes took its place. Patrol Comd climbed tree and looked towards the factory. Saw only one German, who ran from outhouse to factory. Guns appeared to be firing from area EAST of factory in dead ground at approx 085695. No movement seen in chateau area.

5. Descending tree, patrol continued to within 150 yds of chateau and turned down towards river bank. Coils of dannert wire were seen in SW corner of wood, hedging off possible pl[atoon] pos[itio]n. Wire was booby trapped with trip wire and 2 blocks of substance thought to be flares (or picric block charge?) fitted with pull igniter. Tins hung on wire.

6. On return, climbed tree again but still no movement seen.

…

9. Wood very well 'stonked' by own art[iller]y and 4.2" mortars (in the past). Many craters and body of 6 Airborne Div man found with head and shoulders blown off. No idea of name, rank or number.

11. NORTH of cemetery on EAST side of r[oa]d, several bushes seen in f[iel]d (can be seen in aerial photo) with possible German type bivouac pitched among them.[27]

Such reports illustrate the nature of patrolling which was also a risk-filled undertaking. Even so it provided an often welcome change from the routine of sitting waiting for enemy attack or bombardment and helped develop the leadership skills of NCOs such as Corporal Murray.

Similar stories could be told of 154 Brigade during this time. On 14 June 7th Argylls deployed under command of 6th Airborne Division to the east bank of the Orne with the role of defending the bridges over the river. However, the effectiveness of the artillery, which broke up enemy attacks, made the battalion redundant and it returned to 154 Brigade to take up defensive positions in the Bois de Bavent. Of the two Black Watch battalions in the brigade, the 1st had been helping to watch the Douvres radar station where Lance-Corporal McPhail carried out a one-man recce patrol from which he returned with a German prisoner and two large portraits – one of Hitler and the other of Göring.[28] Following this interlude the battalion rejoined 154 Brigade in the Bois de Bavent where, during heavy shelling by the enemy on 26 June, several men were killed including Captain Ronald Milligan, the Adjutant, and Company Sergeant Major Robert McGarry. (WOII McGarry, who died on 27 June, was only 24 years old. That such a young man had reached the rank of WOII, even in wartime, was an indication of his qualities as a soldier.[29])

All three brigades of the Highland Division were now committed to defensive roles in the Orne bridgehead, leaving no reserves for any attacks that might be ordered. All that commanders could do was re-adjust the tasks assigned to the defending troops. The bridgehead had its southernmost point at Longueval and from the British line ran north-easterly along the road to Ranville before turning south-east to Herouvillette and from there to the brickworks north-east of Touffreville by way of the Triangle, 'the ghastliest hole of all'.[30] From Touffreville the line turned north, through the

Bois de Bavent and thence via Breville and Amfreville to Sallenelles, close to the mouth of the Orne and where was located one of the batteries taken by the airborne in the early hours of D-Day. The Triangle area was so ghastly because the Germans pressed close on two sides and the early failure to take Sainte Honorine left the entire right flank in considerable danger. It was a constricted area, the base of the Triangle being no more than 300 yards and each side some 800 yards long, surrounded by woodland.[31]

The penning in of the Division in this bridgehead led to that sense of claustrophobia. The physical proximity of the enemy, his aggression and the constant attention of his artillery and mortars were all factors that eroded morale. It has already been noted that there was a parallel here to a Great War battlefield but it is also worthy of note that, normally, battalions would not have been kept for so long a period in the front line in such close proximity to the enemy during that conflict. Regular reliefs ensured that battalions could be drawn into reserve within brigades, brigades within divisions and divisions within corps. Such relief was not possible in the Orne bridgehead in the summer of 1944. Even the best of soldiers must have wondered what was being asked of them and how long they would have to endure the purgatory of the bridgehead. The heat of summer, the enervating effects of holding static positions with little change of scenery and the constant danger from enemy fire all conspired to chew at individuals' rations of morale. In such circumstances, all the more credit is due to the Highlanders' display of doughty courage in those savage days.

It seemed as if the Division's period in the bridgehead might be coming to a close when plans were made to attack the village of Colombelles. In 1944 Colombelles was about a mile outside Caen whereas today it is part of the conurbation of that city. The village was marked by the presence of high factory chimneys which were believed to be used as OPs by the Germans. In fact, it would have been incredible had the Germans not been using the factory chimneys for that purpose as they provided a splendid vantage point with a view over the Orne bridgehead and elsewhere in the Allied lines. Had Caen been captured on D-Day, as had been hoped, then Colombelles would not have been a problem but with Caen still in German hands, and much reinforced, Colombelles was a thorn in the Allies' side. And so it was that 153 Brigade was detailed to take the village in a night attack. The plan was simple: 1st Gordons would advance on the right from Longueval and attack the village; 5th Black Watch would make for the factory's north-east corner and capture a crossroads there; 7th Black Watch, detached from 154 Brigade, would then pass through 1st Gordons to occupy the factory area after which the Divisional Sappers were to demolish the chimneys. All this was to be done in twenty-four hours, following which the troops would withdraw.[32]

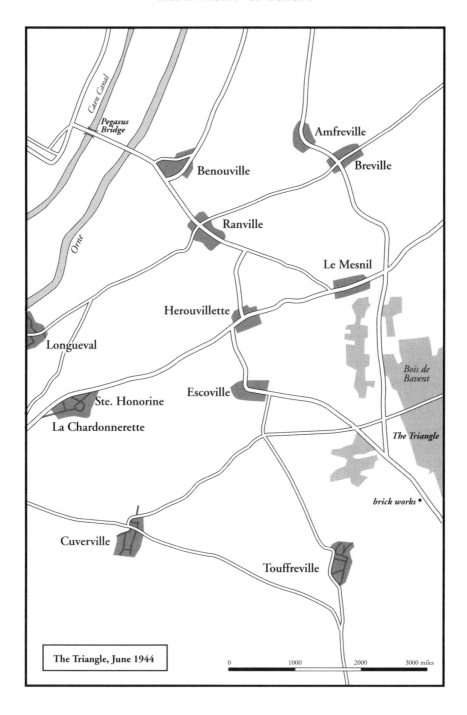

The Triangle, June 1944

0   1000   2000   3000 miles

The attack began at 1 o'clock on the morning of 11 July and the two right-hand companies of 1st Gordons advanced by the Orne towpath into the western corner of Colombelles but the left-hand companies were stalled by heavy shell, mortar, machine-gun and small-arms fire. Elsewhere, 5th Black Watch had reached the crossroads and occupied some houses. Three hours after the operation began, the two left companies of 1st Gordons were ordered to withdraw and re-organise for a fresh attack at dawn. Once again the Gordons suffered severe casualties as the Germans illuminated the retiring troops with flares and brought down considerable fire. The CO, Lieutenant-Colonel Stevenson, was among the casualties; Major the Hon. Cumming-Bruce assumed command.[33]

Nor were the Gordons the only ones to suffer as 5th Black Watch found that the ground in their area resisted all efforts to dig in and the Germans overlooked them from the factory chimneys. Thus the battalion was subjected to accurate mortar and artillery fire while German troops to the right also added enfilading fire. As if this predicament were not enough the distinctive sounds of advancing tanks could be heard at about 6.30am as five enemy tanks advanced from the southern end of the factory. Of the eleven Sherman tanks supporting the Black Watch, ten were knocked out by the panzers which seemed immune to fire from the battalion's anti-tank weapons. The German tanks were identified as being two PzKpfw MkIVs and three PzKpfw MkVIs, the latter being the dreaded Tiger. However, it is likely that the identification of some of these tanks as Tigers was mistaken.[34]

Irrespective of the exact type of tanks facing them, the Black Watch were now in a horrendous position. The entire plan had gone awry, having been much too ambitious in the first instance. It was to take the power of two divisions finally to wrest Colombelles from German hands. At 8.30am orders for a withdrawal were issued and the forward battalions began pulling back. During this manoeuvre they suffered further losses as they withdrew to their positions in Sainte Honorine and Longueval. For 7th Black Watch, their role had been made redundant but, although the battalion was not sent forward, there were still casualties from shellfire in their forming-up positions.[35]

As the plan for the attack on Colombelles was being drawn up, 5th Seaforth, under Lieutenant-Colonel Jack Walford, relieved 7th Black Watch on the edge of the Triangle on 9 July. The Triangle was now in German hands and the Seaforth were to have a most unpleasant time in these positions as the Germans were keen to escape from it. Both the south and east apices of the Triangle, which were made by crossroads, were in enemy hands. Some enemy soldiers made their way surreptitiously out of the Triangle to surrender to Highlanders or other British troops. In the main these deserters were east Europeans, Poles or Russians, who had been forced to fight for the Germans, and many brought useful intelligence information on units and dispositions.[36] Nine days after moving into these positions, 5th Seaforth took part in the infantry attacks of Operation GOODWOOD, the largest armoured battle to date in the west. Although the overall operation met with less than complete success, the Seaforth had a successful battle, supported for the first time by Churchill Crocodiles of 79th Armoured Division. This was the flamethrower version of the Churchill and its flame gun struck terror into the enemy; 'Spandaus just faded out before it'.[37]

Passing through 5th Seaforth, the 2nd Battalion and 5th Camerons advanced down the road to Troarn, moving through the Triangle as they did so. Both battalions took their objectives but suffered many casualties. The Camerons were then ordered to hold the area taken and this they did for the next ten days, during which 'they were shelled literally every hour'.[38] But the battalion endured until relieved by 7th Black Watch, who had advanced as far as Demouville, just east of Caen. During their time in those positions the Camerons had two acting COs – Majors H W Cairns and C A Noble – wounded. When the battalion was relieved Lieutenant-Colonel D B Lang assumed command.[39] The Seaforth and Cameron Brigade was now relieved by 153 Brigade and crossed to the west bank of the Orne and a 'rest' area round Gazelle. For 5th Camerons there was an unwelcome start to their 'rest': for the first few hours the battalion was shelled by a German long-range gun.[40]

In the course of Operation GOODWOOD the Highland battalions had done much good work in clearing mines – these were British minefields in the Orne bridgehead – for the passage of the armour of VIII Corps and their work brought a letter of appreciation from Lieutenant-General Sir Richard O'Connor, commanding VIII Corps to Crocker in which he asked the latter to convey

> my thanks to the 51st Highland Division for the wonderful work they
> have done in removing the minefields and so enabling our armour to
> pass through. It is greatly appreciated by everyone in this Corps.[41]

With GOODWOOD at a standstill, and British tanks bogged down in the mud, the Germans had enjoyed their last success in Normandy. But it had been a Pyrrhic victory and their strength continued to ebb while that of the Allied armies was growing. On the right flank the Americans had secured the entire Cotentin peninsula including the port of Cherbourg and were expanding their muscle in readiness for the breakout from Normandy. By the end of July the Americans had launched Operation COBRA, the prelude to the planned breakout, and Second British Army was driving south from Caumont. New Allied armies had been formed in Normandy; these included First Canadian Army which was to thrust towards Falaise with its axis of advance on the Lisieux–Rouen road while Second British

Army drove for Argentan. A crucial strategic blunder by Hitler, in launching German armour into a counter-attack towards Mortain, assisted in the wearing down of that armour and in destroying it as a strategic asset.[42]

First Canadian Army was to provide a new home for the Highland Division as the Allies made their final efforts to break out of Normandy and drive for the Seine. The Highlanders would say goodbye to I Corps, in which the Division had never been happy, and come under command of II Canadian Corps and its energetic commander Lieutenant-General Guy Simonds, a capable and respected leader who was prepared to use his imagination to develop new tactical practices for use by his troops. With Simonds' Corps, the Highland Division would return to manoeuvre warfare in the breakout from Normandy.

Notes

1. NA Kew, WO171/678, war diary 153 Black Watch & Gordon Bde, 1944
2. Salmond, *The History of the 51st Highland Division*, p. 139
3. Ellis, *Victory in the West Vol I*, p. 31
4. Ibid, pp. 183–95. The airborne assaults are outlined in pp. 149–58
5. Ibid, pp. 203–5
6. Salmond, op cit, p. 139
7. Ibid, pp. 139–40
8. Ibid, p. 140
9. NA Kew, WO171/673, war diary, 152 Bde, 1944
10. NA Kew, WO171/680, war diary, 154 Bde, 1944
11. NA Kew, WO171/1263, war diary, 7 A & SH, 1944
12. NA Kew, WO171/678, war diary, 153 Bde; WO171/1266, war diary, 5 BW; WO171/1299, war diary, 1 Gordons; WO171/1301, war diary, 5/7 Gordons, 1944
13. NA Kew, WO171/1266, war diary, 5 BW; Salmond, op cit, p. 142
14. Ibid
15. Fergusson, op cit, p. 267
16. NA Kew, WO171/1301, war diary, 5/7 Gordons; Salmond, op cit, p. 142
17. NA Kew, WO171/673, war diary, 152 Bde, 1944
18. Chapman, interview with author
19. NA Kew, WO171/1270, war diary, 5 Camerons, 1944
20. Salmond, op cit, p. 143
21. Ibid
22. NA Kew, WO171/1299, war diary, 1 Gordons; WO171/1301, war diary, 5/7 Gordons, 1944; Salmond, op cit, p. 143
23. NA Kew, WO171/1345, war diary, 1/7 Mx, 1944; Salmond, op cit, p. 143n
24. NA Kew, WO171/850, war diary, 2 DY, 1944
25. Ibid
26. Ibid
27. NA Kew, WO171/678, war diary, 1 Gordons, 1944
28. NA Kew, WO171/1265, war diary, 1 BW, 1944; Fergusson, op cit, p. 268

29. Commonwealth War Graves Commission website, www.cwgc.org
30. Salmond, op cit, p. 144
31. Ibid
32. Ibid, p. 145; Fergusson, op cit, p. 271; NA Kew, WO171/78, war diary, 153 Bde, 1944
33. NA Kew, WO171/1266, war diary, 5 BW; WO171/1299, war diary, 1 Gordons; Salmond, op cit, pp. 145–7; Fergusson, op cit, pp. 271–2
34. NA Kew, WO171/1266, war diary, 5 BW; Fergusson, op cit, pp. 271–2
35. Ibid
36. NA Kew, WO171/1370, war diary, 5 Seaforth, 1944; Salmond, op cit, p. 147
37. Salmond, op cit, pp. 147–8
38. Ibid, p. 148
39. NA Kew, WO171/1271, war diary, 5 Camerons, 1944
40. Ibid; Salmond, op cit, p. 148
41. Quoted in Salmond, op cit, p. 148
42. Ellis, op cit, pp. 406–16

CHAPTER X

Breakout from Normandy

Montgomery had not been impressed by the performances of many British officers in Normandy. Among these were some very senior men, including a corps commander, Bucknall of XXX Corps, and the unfortunate Bullen-Smith of 51st (Highland) Division. In Monty's eyes the Highland Division had not fought with determination and had 'failed in every operation it has been given to do'. The blame for this he laid squarely with Bullen-Smith who, he opined, had 'failed to lead Highland Division and I cannot – repeat, cannot – therefore recommend him to command any other division'. On 26 July Montgomery had an interview with Bullen-Smith and relieved the latter of his command, telling him that the men would not fight for him and that he must go to prevent unnecessary casualties.[1]

To succeed Bullen-Smith, Montgomery recommended Tom Rennie, now recovered from the wound he had received while commanding 3rd Division on D-Day + 6. Rennie was an inspired and popular choice and no one in the Division could have suggested a better candidate for the post.[2] One officer of 5th Black Watch, Rennie's old battalion wrote of his appointment:

> To the Battalion it was especially welcome; he was their CO who had taught them so much; had led them into their first battle at Alamein; had then commanded 154 Brigade with distinction and, more recently, had taken the 3rd Division into the D-Day landings and secured his final objectives. He was 'one of their own' and a real successor to General Wimberley. The effect on Divisional morale was immediate and lasting and the Battalion noted with pride that they were one of the first units to receive a visit from General Rennie.[3]

Rennie's record spoke for itself. If anyone now epitomised the spirit of the Highland soldier and of the Highland Division it was Thomas Rennie.

With the Division based at Gazelle, drafts of reinforcements were received for the infantry battalions to make up their losses. Hundreds of newcomers, most of them freshly-trained soldiers straight from training centres, were absorbed and the majority were Scots. There were other reinforcements, including men from a disbanded battalion of the Duke of Wellington's Regiment, who went to 5th/7th Gordons,[4] while 1st Black Watch received 100 men from the Oxfordshire and Buckinghamshire Light Infantry, to whom joining a Highland battalion must have been an extreme culture shock.[5] However, there were not enough reinforcements to bring every battalion up to strength and 7th Black Watch was forced to reduce to a three-company basis[6] while 5th Camerons disbanded their Carrier Platoon and distributed its soldiers through the rifle companies.[7] Such were the effects on the Highland Division of the increasing man-power shortage affecting the British forces, especially the Army, which had already seen Eighth Army in Italy denied any reinforcements from the United Kingdom.[8]

On 26 June a Divisional rest camp was established on the coast which allowed groups of soldiers to enjoy leave with the opportunity to swim, relax, watch film shows or visit Bayeux.[9] The padre of 5th Seaforth 'had liberated a cheese factory' and so the Battalion's rations now included 'camembert cheese, rich and creamy, and ... plenty of fresh butter to go with it'.[10] It was a time of recuperation for those who had endured the Orne bridgehead but it could be only a brief respite as everyone knew that the call to battle would come again soon.

First Canadian Army was due to launch its attack, Operation TOTALIZE (referred to as Operation TOTALISATOR in the war diary of 153 Brigade[11]), down the road from Caen to Falaise on 7 August. As already noted, the attack was to be made by Guy Simonds' II Corps and Simonds had been busy planning for the offensive. His preparations included a number of innovations, among them 'artificial moonlight' and 'Kangaroos'. The former, sometimes called 'Monty's moonlight', involved deploying search-lights close to the start-lines with their beams directed on low clouds. By the light thus reflected from the clouds, advancing troops, both infantry and armoured, could see the enemy but the way in which the light was reflected was no aid to the enemy. Crucially, this innovation allowed tanks to operate at night. Conventional wisdom decreed that tanks could not operate during darkness as they would be easy prey for enemy infantry – and German anti-tank tactics had become much more sophisticated. The 'Kangaroos' were Priest SPGs with the 105mm howitzers removed and a section of infantry carried in the vehicle instead, in the manner in which the eponymous marsupial carries its young. This was not an entirely new idea. It had been suggested by Sir Richard O'Connor in an earlier operation but had been rejected by Dempsey, Second Army's commander, and Montgomery. Dempsey could not influence a Canadian commander and Montgomery did not usually interfere in Canadian planning and so

Simonds was free to make the first use of such armoured personnel carriers, thereby allowing his infantry to advance at the same speed as the armour.[12]

Although Montgomery gives no credit to the Canadian generals for their work in planning TOTALIZE, Crerar, the commander of First Canadian Army, had told Simonds to begin planning for such an operation several days before Montgomery issued a directive.[13] Those extra days allowed Simonds to refine his plans and build up a strong force for the offensive: II Canadian Corps included 2nd and 3rd Canadian Divisions, the latter a D-Day assault division, 4th Canadian Armoured Division, which had landed in Normandy during the previous week, 1st Polish Armoured Division, another newly-arrived formation, as well as the Highland Division with its supporting armour.[14] One of Montgomery's biographers, and admirers, Ronald Lewin, wrote of Simonds' plans as providing something that

> Patton might well have studied ... for in daring and ingenuity they surpassed anything so far attempted by the British army – or the Americans. Simonds' difficulty was this: he had to thrust down the Caen–Falaise road amid open country which, as several preliminary probes had revealed, gave ample scope to the 88s, the mortars and the machine-guns in the strong enemy line. This hard crust he had to crack with his armour: but until his armour had reached the crust he must keep the heads of the enemy down without providing the conventional means of an artillery preparation. He therefore adopted the wholly unconventional plan of using heavy bombers, *in a tactical role at night*, to carpet the flanks of his line of advance; meanwhile his assault troops moved in the centre, the forward infantry being transported in armoured troop carriers ... Ingenious devices were also evolved for the maintenance of direction in this unprecedented attack: radio-directional beams for the tanks, target-indicator shells with coloured bursts, tracer from Bofors firing on fixed lines, and searchlights to illuminate the sky as the moon failed.[15]

Simonds decided to advance on a two-brigade front with the Caen–Falaise road as the axis of advance. The Highland Division was to be in the van of his attack with 154 Brigade deployed left of the road and a Canadian brigade to the right. Each would be supported by armour. In the case of 154 Brigade that armour was to be provided by 33 Armoured Brigade, which included 1st Northamptonshire Yeomanry and 144th and 148th Regiments, RAC; 2 Canadian Armoured Brigade was assigned to the Canadian infantry.[16] The 'marriage' of 154 Brigade and 33 Armoured Brigade proved so successful that the latter was assigned to the Highland Division as its affiliated armoured formation thereafter. [17] (The orbat of 33 Armoured Brigade changed on 16 August when 1st East Riding Yeomanry replaced 148 RAC. Thereafter the brigade/regimental affiliations were: 152 Brigade with 1st East Riding Yeomanry; 153 Brigade with 144 RAC; 154 Brigade with 1st Northamptonshire Yeomanry.[18]) An additional benefit of this new affiliation was that the Northamptons were equipped with, and trained to use, amphibious AFVs, which would prove a major asset in the Rhine crossing in March 1945.

The task of 154 Brigade, under Brigadier James Oliver, was to smash through the German line to a depth of just over three miles to occupy and hold the area of Cramesnil–St Aignan–Garcelles–Secqueville. With that achieved 153 Brigade would follow, and then 152, to expand the salient and allow the Canadian and Polish armoured divisions to pass through and strike out to the south and south-east.[19]

In a special order of the day on 7 August, Rennie wrote

The Highland Division is about to take part in a battle under command of the 2nd Canadian Corps. This may well prove to be the decisive battle in France. The Division has an enterprising part to play, well suited to its particular characteristics. The battle also plays a strong resemblance to some of those great battles in North Africa in which the Division added laurels to its reputation of the last war. In Africa we fought side by side with Australians and New Zealanders. Now we are with Canadians and it is a coincidence that during the closing stages of the Great War we were also fighting beside a Canadian Corps. The Highland Division fought at El Alamein, which great victory was the turning-point in our fortunes. Now we are to take part in what may be the decisive battle of France. The success of the battle depends on the determination and offensive spirit of every Commander and Soldier in the Division and in the 33rd Armoured Brigade and other units with the Division. Good luck to every one of you.[20]

The attacking force was to deploy in separate columns, each of which had a four-tank front, with vehicles 'packed nose to tail'.[21] Specialist tanks, or 'Funnies', from 79th Armoured Division would precede each column to flail paths through minefields and give immediate engineer support. More than 1,000 aircraft would provide the bombing programme and some 360 guns were to fire a bombardment in the path of the assaulting formations. (A total of 1,019 aircraft, including 614 Lancasters, 392 Halifaxes and thirteen Mosquitoes, took part.)[22] Facing Simonds' assault force was I SS Panzer Corps with 89th Infantry Division under command – the latter had been formed in Norway in the spring of 1944 – and the front was held in strength; an SS battlegroup, Kampfgruppe Meyer, was deployed immediately behind 89th Division and, on 7 August, moved to the area south-east of Bretteville-sur-Laize with forty-seven tanks, including eight Tigers of

101st Heavy Tank Battalion, commanded by the Panzer 'ace' Michael Wittman, and twenty-seven Jagdpanzer IVs.[23]

Operation TOTALIZE opened an hour before midnight on 7 August when RAF bombers began dropping their cargoes on aiming points in front of the Allied ground forces. There had been concern about casualties to Allied soldiers from their own aircraft in previous operations and this attack was planned and controlled carefully to prevent such casualties. Because of this, only 660 aircraft dropped their bombs; the remainder could not identify clearly their targets. Ten aircraft were lost. Bombs fell on Fontenay le Marmion and May sur Orne on the right flank and from la Hogue to Marc de Magne on the left but none hit Allied troops.[24]

At 11.30pm the assault columns crossed their start-lines, led by the Flail tanks and AVREs of 79th Armoured Division. They moved off into a huge cloud of dust, raised by the bombing – and the reason why a third of the aircraft could not bomb – and the armoured vehicles soon added their own contribution to the dust storm. Although the poor visibility led to crashes and collisions amongst the advancing vehicles, the columns pressed on. Brigadier Oliver's brigade deployed in two columns: 7th Argylls with 144 RAC were to make for Cramesnil on the right, followed by 7th Black Watch with 148 RAC, making for Garcelles-Secqueville while, on the left, 1st Black Watch with the Northamptonshire Yeomanry had St Aignan as their objective. In this most mobile attack thus far in the Division's history, 154 Brigade was using 350 armoured tracked vehicles.[25] Preparation for the attack had included a full-scale rehearsal with all the AFVs that were to take part in 154 Brigade's attack.[26] In the tradition of the Division nothing was left to chance, especially as a successful outcome was critical to the Allied breakout from Normandy and to restore the confidence of the powers-that-be in the fighting ability of 51st (Highland) Division.

Led by the Flails, the Kangaroos and tanks raced across a landscape that was quite flat. Fields were divided by strips of wooded land and there were sunken roads with high embankments topped by thick poplar hedges. But it was not the close deadly country of the bocage where the advantage lay always with the defender and tank crews dreaded the embankments and deep, narrow lanes. Round about were typical Norman villages, small groups of houses clustered around a church, and many apple orchards – for this is calvados country as well as dairy farming land – surrounded by hedges or walls. The column had also to cross a railway line, which provided a further obstacle.[27]

Lieutenant-Colonel Meiklejohn's Argylls lost the tanks carrying the column navigators when these fell into a crater about midway to their objectives. The Argylls also met some opposition from German infantry, some of whom hurled grenades at the AFVs. These did not present a problem for the tanks, unless a lucky grenade damaged a track, but they were much more deadly for the occupants of the Kangaroos, which had no overhead cover. Private Jarvis of HQ Company reacted very quickly when a grenade dropped into his Kangaroo. Picking the device up immediately, Jarvis hurled it back at the defenders before it could explode. By 4.00am the battalion was debussing and the companies were making for their objectives.[28] These were reached in spite of the heavy ground mist that is a feature of harvest time in the area, with A Company having the most difficult fight. However, Major T R Lorrbond of 144 RAC was killed as he led his tanks 'in a most fearless manner'.[29] A member of his regiment wrote that Lorrbond's 'superb leadership during this operation had a direct bearing on the success of the operation'.[30]

On the other flank 1st Black Watch had suffered some delays through having to cross sunken roads and from a German SPG that had knocked out two Kangaroos.

> But the Black Watch, having advanced in their carriers right through the cornfields up to St Aignan, debussed at exactly the place that had been arranged on the map, formed up, and launched their attack, all according to plan and as had been rehearsed and practised beforehand.[31]

All battalion objectives had been taken by 6 o'clock and 1st Black Watch began digging in, mindful of the ever-present threat of counter-attack. One soldier of the anti-tank platoon charged into a house where a German machine-gun team had taken cover and from which they were firing on the Black Watch. The gunner wiped out the German team.[32] The battalion later suffered the brunt of the enemy counter-attack, which came in with infantry and tanks but the Northamptonshire Yeomanry played a spectacular role, advancing to meet the German armour and knocking out eleven tanks, of which four were identified as Tigers and the remainder as Mk IVs.[33] Michael Wittman was one of the casualties, killed when his Tiger was knocked out by a Northamptonshires' Sherman Firefly, which also accounted for a further two Tigers.[34] Defensive fire was put down by the Divisional artillery, now under the command of Brigadier Jerry Sheil, former CO of 128th Field Regiment.[35] A bombing mission by American aircraft went awry when bombs were dropped in the Battalion area, killing two signallers of B Company.[36]

Seventh Black Watch, meanwhile, had also reached their debussing area on schedule, in spite of the attentions of a German anti-tank gun en route, and, against strong opposition, the battalion took all its objectives. Lieutenant John McAllister, who had knocked out several German machine-gun posts, was killed in the course of the fighting. The battalion was still digging in as daylight broke and there were some casualties from enemy mortar fire before everyone was safely dug in.[37]

The role of 152 Brigade was to follow in the tracks of 154 and mop up any lingering opposition. Since the leading units would have penetrated the German line and taken up positions behind that line, it had been assumed that the task of mopping up would be relatively straightforward, as the Germans would have been anxious to withdraw from a situation in which they had Allied troops both before and behind them. That had been to underestimate the tenacity of the defenders who appeared determined to hold on as long as possible. Resistance was especially tough at the village of Tilly la Campagne on which 2nd Seaforth were to make the first attack. Such was the ferocity of the defence that the Seaforth had to be reinforced by D Company of their 5th Battalion.[38] The commander of that company, Captain Grant Murray, was one of the casualties of the action for Tilly; he was killed with ten of his men in what had clearly been a hand-to-hand struggle in the German line; several of the Scottish dead were found in that line with dead Germans alongside them.[39] Reinforcements in the form of tanks from 33 Armoured Brigade came back from 154 Brigade's positions to assist in the capture of Tilly by attacking the village from the rear. Twice the tanks drove through the village until finally the battle was over.[40] While the Seaforth were battling it out for Tilly, 5th Camerons advanced through standing wheat towards Lorquichon. Although they met sniper fire in the course of their advance – the wheat provided good cover for the snipers – the Camerons took Lorquichon without difficulty and pressed on through a wood to Poussy la Campagne, about two miles to the south, where defensive positions were dug.[41]

During the assault 152 Brigade had provided the firm base for the Highland Division but, on 8 August, 1st Gordons were lifted in Kangaroos to the Garcelles–Secqueville area from where the battalion attacked Secqueville la Campagne, taking the village with over ninety prisoners, including two German officers. Casualties in the Gordons were slight.[42] As they set off for their objective, the village of Soliers, 5th Black Watch were fortunate not to lose the CO, Adjutant and the RAP personnel. All were travelling in two jeeps when a heavy bomber dropped its load around the vehicles, blowing the men out of them but, miraculously, without wounding anyone. Soliers was taken and occupied by the battalion.[43]

During TOTALIZE 1/7th Middlesex had played an enthusiastic part, discharging 250 bombs from each of their mortars and loosing off forty-four belts of ammunition from each Vickers gun.[44] Perhaps no one had been more grateful to quit the Orne bridgehead than the Diehards who, while there, had been able to engage only close-range targets. In the breakout attack they had been presented with a multitude of excellent targets.

Simonds' plan had deserved to meet complete success but had not done so. Much had been achieved but the final outcome fell short of the original plan. Neither armoured division had exploited as intended and stubborn German defence plus a determined counter-attack by SS troops stopped the armour short of Falaise, thus depriving the Canadian Corps of the full fruits of their efforts. As the fighting rumbled on the Canadians began planning a fresh offensive, Operation TRACTABLE, to renew the advance on Falaise.[45]

On 9 August the Highland Division was able to report the successful conclusion of its part in TOTALIZE.[46] But the Division had more fighting to do before II Canadian Corps finally declared the operation over. The Polish Armoured Division had taken St Sylvain but the woods around that village provided cover for many Germans. While 5th Black Watch and 1st Gordons held the village and the perimeter of the woods, 154 Brigade was ordered to clear the enemy from them. To achieve this, 1st Black Watch and 7th Argylls passed through 7th Black Watch close to Robertmesnil with the Argylls carrying out a night attack without artillery support. Passing through St Sylvain the battalion was met with machine-gun fire from three sides but continued the advance. The following day the Argylls fought off several determined counter-attacks. A similar experience befell 1st Black Watch.[47]

Although both battalions achieved their objectives their new positions were not comfortable. The situation was exacerbated by the failure of the Polish armour to advance through the Division's positions and push out to the east. Then a German counter-attack struck the Poles, destroying a number of their tanks and forcing the remainder to withdraw. Two days later, on 12 August, the Polish Armoured Division was relieved by a Canadian armoured regiment while 2nd Derbyshire Yeomanry also deployed to support the Highlanders.[48] On the night of the 12th, the Argylls were relieved by 7th Black Watch while 5th/7th Gordons attacked a ridge to the left front, from which the Germans had been engaging the Highlanders' positions. The Gordons' attack was successful, the ridge was cleared and the situation on the lower ground much improved.[49]

On the left of the line 153 Brigade continued the advance eastward with 1st Gordons taking the villages of Doux Marais and Ste Marie aux Anglais, with its château and a tower dating from the 16th century which had once been held by the English, thus accounting for the village's name.[50] On the left of 1st Gordons the regiment's 5th/7th Battalion came up, having engaged in some brisk fighting in the St Sylvain woods. During that fighting Sergeant Briley, D Company, played a significant role. With his company commander wounded and *hors de combat* together with about half the company, Briley took charge of the remnants of D Company, re-organised them and led them forward on to their objective. Then the battalion, with 5th Black Watch, crossed the Dives river before 1st Gordons attacked the village of St Maclou.[51]

The latter attack was on the night of 16–17 August and followed a fifteen-mile march in darkness. With no preliminary artillery bombardment the attack was a complete surprise to the German garrison of the village, many of whom were killed in the initial assault or made prisoner by the Gordons. One Gordon officer, Captain Jamieson, discovered an enemy observation post with a telephone connected to the garrison's HQ. Jamieson dialled up the HQ and, in German, invited those on the other end of the line to 'come out with their hands up' as the 'English swine' had arrived. This was greeted with hilarity by the Germans but when Jamieson made the demand again he heard what he took to be the sounds of a rushed evacuation before the line went dead. Some Highlanders were not amused at Jamieson's use of the term 'English swine' and thought that he ought to have described the Battalion correctly as Scottish. It was even suggested that he might have received a severe reprimand had Douglas Wimberley still been in command. As St Maclou's civilian population had not been evacuated, this was the first town or village since the breakout in which any unit of the Highland Division received a welcome from the French people. Since the village had not been bombarded prior to the attack that welcome was all the warmer.[52]

On the night of 18 August, 5th/7th Gordons attacked the village of Grandchamp on the Vie river, took their objective, crossed the Vie and established a bridgehead. The battalion then had two tasks: to cover the reconstruction of the bridge at Grandchamp by 276 Field Company RE, and provide a firm base for 5th Black Watch's attack on the horseshoe-shaped feature less than a mile north of the Vie. Although under fire, from which casualties were sustained, the Gordons achieved the first task and, at about midnight, the first two companies of 5th Black Watch crossed to attack the high ground. As these companies advanced, very heavy enemy shellfire came down on the Black Watch Battalion HQ, still on the south side of the river. The CO, Lieutenant-Colonel Bradford, was wounded, the Signals Officer, Captain Arthur Forfar, Carrier Officer, Captain Home, the commander of the supporting battery of 127th (Highland) Field Regiment, Major Ken Aitken MC, and almost all the battalion signallers were killed. Those who survived were out of contact both with the leading companies and with brigade HQ as all the wireless sets had been destroyed and the A Echelon transport, which had begun to arrive, also suffered from the shellfire. Major Dunn decided to continue with the operation lest the two companies already moving up be cut off. It was at this stage that the Gordons also lost their CO, killed by shellfire. Lieutenant-Colonel Hew Blair Imrie DSO MC was a Black Watch officer who had come to command the Gordons from 5th Black Watch.[53] A courageous and inspiring soldier, his loss was felt greatly both in the Gordons and in the Black Watch.

With Blair Imrie dead and his second-in-command not fully aware of what was happening across the river, the situation looked dire. However, work continued on reconstructing the bridge and the Gordons, although in difficult straits, considered that the structure could now take transport. The remaining Black Watch companies were brought forward and rushed across the Vie to follow their comrades. As day broke the leading companies were fighting their way onto the horseshoe feature and were eventually able to reach the top, in spite of many casualties. By now Colonel Bradford had recovered sufficiently from his wounds and, although in much pain, took command of the battle, calling forward a troop of tanks to support his infantry. Sitting on top of one of the tanks, Bradford drove right up to the forward positions where his presence, and that of the tank, proved a fillip to morale. By noon 5th Black Watch were established firmly on the horseshoe and 1st Gordons then came up and, covered by fire from the Black Watch, established themselves on the left flank of the feature. In spite of many enemy counter-attacks the two battalions held firm and the ridge was well and truly in Scottish hands by nightfall. By then, also, communications had been restored and gunner liaison re-established. This had been a difficult battle but its outcome had proved the quality of leadership in the battalions involved. Not for nothing did General Rennie send a message reading 'Well done, 5th Black Watch!'.[54]

This brought the Division closer to the cathedral city of Lisieux and on 22 August 5th/7th Gordons entered that city. Enemy troops, including SS personnel, contested the Gordons' advance and the opposing forces fought street by street. D Company in particular fought with considerable panache; this company was composed, almost completely, of men of the East Lancashires, drafted into the Gordons. A platoon-strength patrol of C Company found that the railway line was held by SS who allowed the Gordons to reach their objective before opening fire at point-blank range. Half the patrol reached the cover of the ruins of a house but such was the intensity of enemy fire that movement seemed impossible. One man did not think so, however: Private Redican rushed out of the ruins into the hail of enemy fire. Shooting from the hip he matched the SS burst for burst and even when hit in both legs and lying on the ground continued to fire. Redican's action distracted the Germans and allowed the survivors of his platoon to quit the ruins and move to a flank position from where they were able to engage the enemy and bring the action to a conclusion. Fighting continued in Lisieux until the city fell to the Highlanders. This brought to an end the work of 5th/7th Gordons in the breakout during which the battalion had sustained 155 casualties and taken some 500 prisoners.[55]

We have already noted that 5th Black Watch co-operated with 5th/7th Gordons to create the bridgehead over the Vie on 18 August. Before this the Black Watch, under temporary command of 154 Brigade, had taken la Bû sur Rouvres with the assistance of Canadian tanks and infantry. The Canadians had lost their bearings but were more than willing to throw in their lot with the Scots in this action before re-establishing contact with their own formations. From la Bû the Black Watch moved to Percy on the 16th and, next day, to St Pierre, crossing the Dives before advancing north to contact 1st Gordons at Ecajeul and then joining 5th/7th Gordons for the Vie crossing and the battle that we have already noted. The battalion later relieved 5th/7th Gordons in Lisieux and, on 26 August, the CO received a note from Lieutenant-Colonel Cumming-Bruce, who had been acting brigade commander, congratulating the Black Watch. Cumming-Bruce commented that

> The two major attacks at Bretteville [Ecajeul] and Grandchamp when you 'achieved the impossible,' are to my mind the two finest feats that a Battalion has ever accomplished in my own experience.[56]

On 21 August 1st Gordons occupied the village of la Forge Vallée, where they found a stud farm that belonged to an Englishman, Sam Ambler, who had hidden his racehorses on small neighbouring farms. The battalion then moved to Lisieux, which was reached on the 23rd, and were ordered to advance beyond the town to some high ground. One company sustained forty casualties but support from tanks of 7th Armoured Division helped clear the ridge and the Gordons moved south-east of Lisieux.[57]

On 14 August 152 Brigade had begun an advance towards Lisieux with 5th Seaforth in the van. At Favières the battalion was held up by enemy troops on high ground. However, the Seaforth had established their positions by 9.00pm on the 15th and, next day, moved off through St Pierre sur Dives, held by 5th Camerons, and then along the main road to Lisieux to about a mile short of the Vie. At this stage of the advance the Brigade suffered considerably from strafing by aircraft. However, these were not Luftwaffe machines, relatively rare sights in the skies over Normandy, but Allied aircraft: 5th Camerons had to come to a halt because RAF Spitfires had knocked out every one of the battalion's wireless vehicles while 5th Seaforth came under regular attention from USAAF P-38 Lightnings.[58] Attacks such as these may be ascribed to one or both of two factors: the speed of the ground forces' advance and the difficulty in positively identifying vehicles from the air. Nonetheless, such incidents left a bad taste in the mouths of the soldiers and many found it hard to forgive their own air arms for attacking them. A common reaction was to blame all such incidents on the Americans but, as has been shown, the RAF was equally capable of committing these errors.

Following the crossing of the Vie at St Julien le Fauçon, 5th Seaforth endured many days of hard fighting with small but determined German rearguards. As ever when the Germans had been pushed out of a position a counter-attack could be expected.[59] On one occasion, however, a counter-attack came in as the Seaforth were preparing breakfast and the water for the tea was about to boil.[60] However, tanks of the East Riding Yeomanry, which replaced 148 RAC in 33 Armoured Brigade on 16 August, assisted in repulsing the attackers and attention returned to matters domestic.[61] Advancing into St Pierre des Ifs, the Seaforth were guided by the local butcher, a venerable septuagenarian, and then the battalion set off for Lisieux which was reached on 22 August.[62]

In their advance, 5th Camerons were also supported by East Riding Yeomanry tanks. The battalion crossed the Vie on 20 August, advanced southwards, parallel to the road to Lisieux, dug in for the night at St Fressard le Chère and moved to St Pierre des Ifs the following day. The Camerons remained at St Pierre until the 26th, while 2nd Seaforth, who had fought alongside the Camerons from the crossing of the Vie, established positions on high ground overlooking Lisieux on the 28th.[63]

How had 154 Brigade fared in this advance? Moving forward from la Bû sur Rouvres the brigade adopted a system used in Sicily of advancing on a battalion front with the other battalions carried in transport. Once the leading battalion had accomplished its task, it was relieved by another thus ensuring that the leading battalion was always fresh when deploying for action. In the case of the leading battalion being held up by the enemy, the next battalion would seek an alternative line of march so that the enemy strongpoint might be outflanked. On 17 August the brigade advance on St Pierre sur Dives was led by 7th Black Watch. Crossing the river the Black Watch, supported by tanks of 1st Northamptonshire Yeomanry, launched an attack on high ground at le Godet. Accurate fire from German tanks knocked out ten of the Northamptonshires' tanks as they crossed open ground in front of the objective and a subsequent infantry attack, under cover of darkness, hit strong opposition.[64]

Next morning 7th Black Watch launched a fresh attack and took their objectives, following which 7th Argylls passed through to make for a crossroads short of St Julien. Before long the Argylls came under fire from mortars, and bombs exploding in trees caused much damage. Getting out into the open road exposed the battalion to observed fire and the CO, Lieutenant-Colonel Meiklejohn, and two company commanders were wounded. The Argylls finally took their objective, having lost twenty dead and almost sixty wounded. With their objective being St Julien, 1st Black Watch took over the advance the next day and, believing that the village might have been evacuated by the enemy, sent a small patrol to reconnoitre. That patrol, led by Sergeant Stevenson, entered the village, had a clash with some enemy troops, who were overcome, found that, otherwise, St Julien was free of Germans and returned to report that all was clear. The battalion occupied St Julien and remained there until 23 August before passing through their 7th Battalion, who had advanced beyond la Corne cross-roads, and occupied their objective without casualties. On 25 August 154 Brigade Group moved east of Lisieux, to a concentration area at Marolles.[65]

When mopping up in Lisieux was completed on 23 August there ended what was 'undoubtedly one of the most strenuous periods of continuous fighting which the Highland Division had experienced in the course of both World Wars'.[66] Rennie's men had fought without a break from the beginning of TOTALIZE on 7 August until the 23rd. During that period the Highlanders had been engaged with a determined and highly professional enemy who fought doughty rearguard actions over thirty miles of country and seemed never to be prepared to quit. Each battalion had fought 'at least four main actions' with the invaluable support of the regiments of 33 Armoured Brigade, the Divisional artillery, Corps artillery and by all the other arms and services that came under Rennie's command. In seventeen days' fighting the Highland Division took 1,600 prisoners.[67]

By now the Canadians had reached Falaise in Operation TRACTABLE and the Germans were withdrawing from Normandy.[68] Such had been their losses that there was no major stand along the Seine as the Allies had expected and Allied troops over the next few weeks were able to advance rapidly across France and into Belgium, with Brussels being liberated on 3 September, the fifth anniversary of the outbreak of war. The Highland Division was now able to have a few days' well-earned rest at Lisieux where they received a message of congratulations from the commander of First Canadian Army, General Crerar.

> Please congratulate Highland Division on fine aggressive work. The 51st of this War is showing the same unbeatable spirit which the Canadians got to know and admire in 1918.[69]

The Highlanders could now reflect on their recent achievements as they waited for the call to return to action. For the Catholic soldiers of 153 Brigade, part of that reflection took the form of a church parade in the Basilica of Sainte Thérèse at Lisieux on 25 August, a day that the brigade war diary described as 'peaceful'.[70]

Notes

1. Hamilton, *Monty: Master of the Battlefield*, p. 715; Salmond, *The History of the 51st Highland Division*, pp. 150–2
2. Salmond, op cit, p. 150
3. McGregor, *Spirit of Angus*, p. 132
4. NA Kew, WO171/1301, war diary, 5/7 Gordons, 1944
5. NA Kew, WO171/1265, war diary, 1 BW, 1944
6. NA Kew, WO171/1267, war diary, 7 BW, 1944
7. NA Kew, WO171/1271, war diary, 5 Camerons, 1944
8. Doherty, *A Noble Crusade*, p. 226
9. NA Kew, WO171/528, war diary, HQ 51 (H) Div (G), 1944
10. Borthwick, *Battalion*, p. 161
11. NA Kew, WO171/678, war diary, 153 Bde, 1944

12. Ellis, *Victory in the West, vol I*, pp. 419–20; Doherty, *Ireland's Generals in the Second World War*, p. 86; Salmond, op cit, p. 156; Jarymowycz, *Tank Tactics from Normandy to Lorraine*, p. 166. Jarymowycz is critical of the planning of the operation, noting that the armour was packed too tightly to allow manoeuvre.
13. Doherty, *Normandy 1944*, p. 251
14. Ibid, pp. 251–2
15. Lewin, *Montgomery as Military Commander*, pp. 227–8
16. NA Kew, WO171/680, war diary, 154 Bde, 1944
17. Salmond, op cit, p. 154
18. Joslen, *Orders of Battle*, p. 183; Salmond, op cit, p. 154
19. Ellis, op cit, p. 420
20. NA Kew, WO171/528, war diary, HQ 51 (H) Div (G), 1944
21. Lewin, op cit, p. 228
22. Ellis, op cit, p. 421
23. Ibid, p. 423; Reynolds, *Steel Inferno*, p. 234
24. Ellis, op cit, p. 422
25. Salmond, op cit, p. 154
26. Ibid, p. 155
27. Ibid, pp. 154–5
28. Ibid, pp. 156–7; NA Kew, WO171/1263, war diary, 7 A & SH, 1944
29. Salmond, op cit, p. 157; Lorrbond's name does not appear on the CWGC Register (CWGC to author)
30. Ibid
31. Ibid
32. Ibid
33. Ibid; NA Kew, WO171/1265, war diary, 1 BW; Tout, *Roads to Falaise*, p. 187
34. Tout, op cit, pp. 187 & 202. Tpr Ekins accounted for three Tigers with three rounds from the 17-pounder of his Sherman Firefly.
35. NA Kew, WO171/1265, war diary, 1 BW
36. Salmond, op cit, p. 157
37. Fergusson, *The Black Watch and the King's Enemies*, pp. 274–5
38. Salmond, op cit, p. 158; NA Kew, WO171/1369, war diary, 2 Seaforth; Borthwick, op cit, p. 163
39. Salmond, op cit, p. 158; CWGC website: www.cwgc.org
40. Salmond, op cit, p. 158
41. Ibid; NA Kew, WO171/1271, war diary, 5 Camerons, 1944
42. Salmond, op cit, pp. 158–9; Lindsay, *So Few Got Through*, pp. 29–31; NA Kew, WO171/1299, war diary, 1 Gordons, 1944
43. Salmond, op cit, p. 159
44. Ibid; WO171/1345, war diary, 1/7 Mx, 1944
45. Doherty, *Normandy 1944*, pp. 257 & 259
46. Salmond, op cit, p. 159
47. Ibid
48. Ibid, p. 160; WO171/851, war diary, 2 DY, 1944
49. Salmond, op cit, p. 160; NA Kew, WO171/1301, war diary, 5/7 Gordons, 1944
50. NA Kew, WO171/1299, war diary, 1 Gordons; Lindsay, op cit, pp. 41–3
51. Salmond, op cit, p. 161

52. Ibid; Lindsay, op cit, p. 44
53. NA Kew, WO171/1301, war diary, 5/7 Gordons, 1944; WO171/1266, war diary, 5 BW, 1944; Salmond, op cit, p. 161; Lindsay, op cit, p. 44; CWGC website: www.cwgc.org
54. NA Kew, WO171/1266, war diary, 5 BW, 1944; Fergusson, op cit, p. 276; Lindsay, op cit, pp. 44–8
55. NA Kew, WO171/1301, war diary, 5/7 Gordons, 1944; Salmond, op cit, 162
56. Salmond, op cit, p. 164
57. NA Kew, WO171/1299, war diary, 1 Gordons, 1944; Lindsay, op cit, pp. 49–56
58. NA Kew, WO171/675, war diary, 152 Bde, 1944; WO171/1271, war diary, 5 Camerons; WO171/1371, war diary, 5 Seaforth; Salmond, pp. 165–6
59. NA Kew, WO171/1371, war diary, 5 Seaforth; Borthwick, op cit, pp. 173–4
60. Borthwick, op cit, p. 173
61. Ibid, pp. 173–4; Joslen, op cit, p. 183
62. Borthwick, op cit, p. 174
63. NA Kew, WO171/1271, war diary, 5 Camerons, 1944
64. NA Kew, WO171/680, war diary, 154 Bde, 1944; Salmond, op cit, pp. 166–8
65. NA Kew, WO171/680, war diary, 154 Bde, 1944; WO171/1265, war diary, 1 BW, 1944; WO171/1267, war diary, 7 BW, 1944; WO171/1263, war diary, 7 A & SH, 1944; Salmond, op cit, p. 168
66. Salmond, op cit, p. 168
67. Ibid, pp. 168–9
68. Ellis, op cit, pp. 429–32
69. NA Kew, WO171/528, war diary HQ 51 (H) Div (G), 1944
70. NA Kew, WO171/678, war diary, 153 Bde, 1944

CHAPTER XI

The 'Great Swan'

As the German forces drew back like a rapidly receding tide, the Allies launched a pursuit that saw the Seine crossed on 19 August and Paris liberated by troops of General Leclerc's armoured division on 25 August.[1] This was the period that became known to veterans of those heady summer weeks as the 'great swan' when it seemed as if the war might be over by Christmas. However, while the German tide receded there were still islands of resistance and not all the Allied armies took part in the main element of the pursuit. Some were deployed to deal with those islands of resistance, German garrisons that remained in the larger Channel ports from le Havre eastwards. This was to be the task of the Highland Division, still under Canadian command: to cross the Seine, cut off the le Havre peninsula and move against and capture le Havre. En route there was some outstanding business to be transacted: the Division would also liberate St Valéry en Caux, thereby repaying a debt from 1940.[2]

On 25 August, as Leclerc's men entered Paris, 154 Brigade left Lisieux to continue the Division's eastward advance.[3] Passing through Marolles the Division concentrated at St Georges du Vièvre on the 26th from where 152 Brigade advanced to the Seine.[4] As day broke on the 28th the Brigade reached that great river where Middlesex machine gunners engaged barges evacuating enemy troops from the Falaise pocket. The reconnoitrers of the Derbyshire Yeomanry were in their element as they probed ahead of the infantry.[5] From St Georges the division struck north-east towards Bourg Achard, crossing the Seine at Duclair and Mauny. Progress was not simple as enemy rearguards held high ground commanding the approaches to the Seine and four battalions were involved in action against these. At the loop in the river at Mauny, 5th/7th Gordons put in five attacks before cracking the resistance and clearing the way for the armour to move on. Some hundred prisoners were taken by the battalion while barges ferrying German troops across the river were fired on by artillery and machine gunners.[6]

Once across the Seine the Highlanders' route was eastward to Elbœuf and Rouen where the Jocks were greeted with great enthusiasm. From

Rouen the Division then set course for St Valéry, which Montgomery had decreed should be liberated by the Highlanders. As the Division made for St Valéry, their Canadian comrades struck across country towards Dieppe, to repay another debt.[7] These moves also had the effect of cutting off le Havre, the garrison of which could be reduced in due course. As 152 Brigade led the way towards St Valéry, armoured cars of the Derbyshire Yeomanry reconnoitred the route and soon learned from local people that the Germans had gone completely. So swift had been the withdrawal that no mines were encountered.[8] And so

> On went 152 Brigade some eighty miles north-west across country, kissed and garlanded, cheered and wined, handing out the 'cigarette pour papa' in the beflagged villages, until the leading battalion, the 5th Seaforth, found themselves in Veules les Roses, a little seaport just north of St Valéry, whence a few of the Highland Division had got away in 1940, but where many of them had found a last resting-place.[9]

Who were first to enter St Valéry? Certainly the first troops of the Highland Division to move into the town on 2 September were men of the Derbyshire Yeomanry. However, honorary Jocks though they were, the Derbyshires had no connection with St Valéry in 1940 and so we seek the first Highland battalion to enter. It is claimed by the Seaforth that the honour fell to a patrol from 5th Seaforth led by Captain Dawson. But 5th Camerons also sent a patrol into the town and when the Seaforth and Cameron COs met in the station square it was agreed that there had been a dead heat. Honours were even in the Seaforth and Cameron Brigade but it was the Camerons who had their pipers with them and thus Cameron pipers playing 'Blue Bonnets over the Border' heralded the return of the Highland Division to St Valéry and five of the original 4th Camerons were chosen to play a set in the square. The men who made this particular piece of history were: Sergeant A MacRae, Lance-Corporal A McDonald and Pipers J Chisholm, R McNeil and J MacLean. When the pipers had finished playing the mayor of St Valéry presented bouquets to the COs of 5th Seaforth and 5th Camerons, Lieutenant-Colonels Walford and Lang.[10]

In 1940 Jack Walford, then commanding a Seaforth company, had been one of those to escape from St Valéry. On this return to the town, he found his company shield and sign in a local farmhouse. Other discoveries were four cemeteries in which lay the remains of men of the Highland Division of 1940. Each cemetery, although created by the Germans, had been cared for by French civilians and each grave was marked by a cross bearing the name and number of the dead soldier. Inevitably there had been cases when it was impossible to identify the dead man, in which case the grave bore the inscription 'Anglais Inconnu'. Had the Division of 1940 been wearing the kilt the graves would almost certainly have been marked 'Ecossais Inconnu'. Elsewhere, the Camerons met two elderly ladies who had sheltered men of 4th Camerons in 1940 and recalled the work of the Medical Officer, Captain MacKay, and still had MacKay's sheepskin coat with his name on it. Soldiers of the Black Watch found a memorial to their regiment – 'Honour The Black Watch Regiment who fought with courage in 1940' – that had not been removed or damaged by the Germans. Vehicles that had belonged to 152 Brigade in 1940 were found on the St Valéry–Veules les Roses road. Abandoned at that time and now in various states of decrepitude, the erstwhile staghead vehicular emblem of the Division in 152 Brigade colours could still be seen.[11]

Divisional HQ was established in the château de Cailleville which had also housed General Fortune's last HQ in 1940 while 152 and 153 Brigades, the originals of which had been lost here in 1940, were deployed in much the same areas as their predecessor formations four years earlier. These dispositions were the choice of General Rennie.[12] And it was at Cailleville on 3 September, the fifth anniversary of Britain's declaration of war and the very day on which Brussels was being liberated, that the Massed Bands of the Highland Division beat Retreat. Rennie spoke to the soldiers of the Division.

> Officers and men of the Highland Division. This is a very great occasion in the history of our famous Division.
>
> Here, at ST VALÉRY on the 12th June 1940, a portion of the Highland Division, including its Headquarters, 152 and 153 Brigades, was captured by a large German force.
>
> That magnificent Division was sacrificed in a last effort to keep the French in the war. True to Highland tradition the Division remained to the last with the remnants of our French Allies, although it was within its capacity to withdraw on LE HAVRE.
>
> The Division drew on ST VALÉRY the German 4th Corps, a Panzer and a Motor Division – in all six Divisions – and thereby diverted this force from harassing the withdrawal of other British troops on LE HAVRE and CHERBOURG.
>
> General Victor Fortune ordered the surrender of the Division at ST VALÉRY when it had run out of ammunition and food and when all prospects of evacuation, which had been carefully planned by him, had failed.
>
> That Highland Division was Scotland's pride; and its loss, and with it the magnificent men drawn from practically every town, village and croft in Scotland, was a great blow. But this Division, then the 9th Highland Division, took its place and became the new 51st Highland Division. It had been our task to avenge the fate of our less fortunate comrades and that we have nearly accomplished. We have

played a major part in both the great decisive battles of this war – the Battle of EGYPT and the Battle of FRANCE – and have also borne our share of the skirmishes and those costly periods of defensive fighting which made those great victories possible. We have lived up to the great traditions of the 51st and of Scotland.

I have disposed the Division, as far as is possible, in the areas where it fought at ST VALÉRY. General Victor Fortune had his HQ here, 152 Brigade held the sector to the WEST and 153 Brigade to the EAST. The Lothians and Border Horse held the sector to the SOUTH. The 154 Brigade and A Brigade embarked at LE HAVRE.

I hoped by disposing the Division in that way to make it easier for some of you to find the graves of your relatives or friends who lost their lives with the ST VALÉRY 51st. you will find at ST VALÉRY and in the village cemeteries around, that the graves of your comrades have been beautifully cared for.

We have today playing with the Pipe and Drums of the Highland Division those of the Scottish Horse. There are also officers and men of the Lothians and Border Horse at this meeting.[13]

The ceremony had a moving and very fitting conclusion: the pipe majors of the Division played 'The Flowers of the Forest' to commemorate all those soldiers of the Highland Division who lost their lives at St Valéry in 1940. One officer who was present described 'the GOC's address on this occasion [as] one of the most moving he has ever heard in his life'.[14]

As Allied formations pushed into Belgium and towards the Siegfried Line, an altogether different task awaited the men of 51st (Highland) Division. Reverting to command of I Corps, and alongside 49th (West Riding) Division, the Highlanders were to attack le Havre. Although cut off from reinforcement and supply, the German garrison was determined to hold out; its commander had lost his wife and children in an Allied air raid on Berlin and had decided that he would fight to the last.[15] Le Havre was a tough proposition for any attacker. The port lies on the north shore of the Seine estuary with the waters of the Channel on its north-west side. Any attack by land would have to come from east or north and overcome a series of defensive obstacles before getting to grips with the garrison. A defensive line from the estuary shore to the Channel coast was as much as a mile in depth in places and was typical of German engineering. The defenders had had four years in which to create defences for le Havre and although these would not all have been aimed to deal with an attack from the landward side, those defences were still formidable. Concrete dugouts had been provided for troop accommodation and artillery was also deployed behind and under concrete. A minefield perimeter had been sown and any stretch of ground that might allow tanks to approach had been cut by anti-tank ditches.[16] This was the objective assigned to 49th and 51st Divisions.

I Corps HQ proposed that 49th Division should attack le Havre from the east with the Highland Division attacking from the north.[17] Rennie suggested an alternative. Since the Germans had obviously considered that the most likely approach by an attacker would be from the sea, the defences were at their strongest close to the coast and Rennie proposed a diversionary attack from the north but that 51st Division's main effort be made from about Montevilliers, today almost a suburb of le Havre, on the Lézarde river. This plan was accepted and the roles of the brigades were assigned: 154 Brigade would provide the firm base from which 152 Brigade, followed by 153, would overcome defences in the Montgeon forest, and clear that forest up to the outskirts of le Havre. Thereafter, 154 Brigade would lead the advance into the town. Once again the armour of 33 Armoured Brigade would support the infantry as well as 'Funnies' from 79th Armoured Division. The latter included Flails to clear paths through the minefields and bridge-laying AVREs to deal with the anti-tank ditches. Much vital information on the defences had been provided by local civilians; this included the German artillery fireplan which had been stolen by a Frenchman and handed over to the Allies.[18]

And so the Division's brief sojourn in St Valéry came to an end on 4 September when 152 Brigade drove away from the town. The Brigade now had much more transport than its official allocation with many captured enemy vehicles being pressed into service. As the column wound its way from St Valéry it presented a surreal vision with 'Grotesquely shaped and painted wagons from practically every country in Europe [breaking up] the uniformity of WD vehicles, and it seemed as though the more grotesque a vehicle was, the more fun the driver got out of driving it'. Some soldiers even travelled in the luxury of a Mercedes saloon car.[19] Attached to 152 Brigade for this operation – codenamed ASTONIA – was a Royal Navy officer from HMS *Erebus* as it would be possible to employ ship-to-shore bombardment of enemy coastal defences. The ship (a monitor mounting two 15-inch guns) would play a vital part in the operation, until it was put out of action by German coastal guns and had to return to Britain for repairs.[20] RAF bombers also made two raids on le Havre before the operation began. Unfortunately these caused heavy loss of civilian life and did little to disrupt the defences.[21]

D-Day for Operation ASTONIA was 10 September, postponed for a day because of heavy rain.[22] This was also the day on which Luxembourg was liberated by First (US) Army and on which the new provisional government of France abolished officially the Vichy regime. The leading battalion was 5th Seaforth, who set off from a start-line about a mile east of Fontaine la Mallet under cover of darkness; H-Hour was 11.00pm. Artificial moonlight was in use, but to little effect, as the Seaforth advanced on their objective,

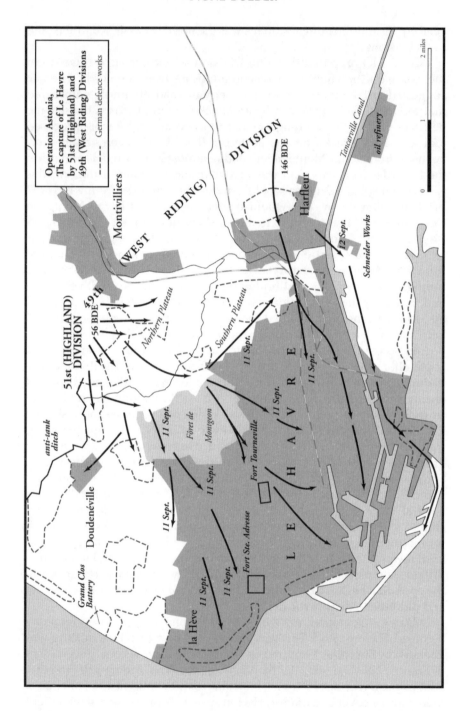

an enemy strongpoint on high ground just to the north-east of Fontaine. Heavy shelling assailed them as they made their way forward and the anti-tank ditch that they met as the first obstacle in their path proved a real impediment. Since there was no AVRE to bridge the ditch, the Jocks had to heft all their impedimenta down the near side and then up the far side. Naturally, casualties had to be taken back on stretchers in like fashion. However, there was one consolation for the Seaforth as they advanced: the German infantry seemed not to be as determined as their artillerymen and opposition was not as strong as expected with many Germans surrendering. The terrain proved to be the biggest problem but the Seaforth pressed on and daylight found them dug in on or close to their objectives. Fontaine la Mallet lay in ruins following the bombing attack.[23]

The Seaforth were followed by 5th Camerons who also endured heavy shelling from the enemy guns which inflicted a number of casualties. These included the Intelligence Officer, Captain Douglas Milne, and Major Angus MacNab who were killed. However, the Camerons overran a strongpoint in the German outer defences where Major Alfred Parker, later killed in action, used the telephone to contact the German commander in le Havre and asked him to surrender or risk annihilation. There was 'no satisfactory answer' and the Camerons continued their advance to Fontaine where they, too, dug in.[24] With white flags popping up here, there and everywhere, 2nd Seaforth remained in brigade reserve. Rather than make a last man-last round stand, the German garrison of le Havre surrendered next day, the 12th.[25]

The Camerons had been accompanied in their advance by a company of 1st Gordons from 153 Brigade while the other Gordon companies were employed mostly in collecting prisoners. Le Havre presented the unusual sight of Germans surrendering with enthusiasm. Many enemy soldiers approached the Highlanders with printed notices, dropped by Allied planes, advising them that the Allies would treat prisoners well and concluding 'This man is to be well treated and sent back from the front as soon as possible'. The notices were signed by Eisenhower and Montgomery. Meanwhile 5th/7th Gordons had not only taken many prisoners but had come across copious quantities of food and drink in the German fort that they occupied. As their CO, Lieutenant-Colonel Douglas Rennie, commented, the Jocks were able to have champagne with their evening meal but the battalion also had to establish firm control to keep looters away. This prompted 153 Brigade's Brigade Major to comment that it had been easier to get into the fort when the Germans held it than when 5th/7th Gordons took control.[26]

What might have been an especially bloody battle proved not to be the case and 154 Brigade had a comparatively easy time with only 7th Black Watch and the Northamptonshire Yeomanry committed to action. The Black Watch and Northamptons had moved to Cap de la Héve, at the north end of the town, and collected about 1,400 prisoners. Le Havre's commander and his staff surrendered to the Black Watch and seemed to expect a formal surrender ceremony as they were decked out in their best uniforms complete with medals. They had a rude awakening, noted by the second-in-command of 7th Black Watch, Major David Russell, who was wounded seriously in the attack: 'Their hopes were soon dispelled, however, when they were hustled off by a diminutive Jock, who looked keen to use his bayonet.'[27]

During the battle for le Havre the Highland Division had suffered only 138 casualties and had taken over 4,600 prisoners. Enemy casualty figures were not known but must have been high and the number of weapons captured was, initially, impossible to calculate. On 13 September General Rennie issued a special order of the day:

> The capture of le Havre is another important task successfully accomplished by the Highland Division, this time in close co-operation with the 49th Division. ... The capture of the port ... should make a great difference to the future course of operations and will speed up the final destruction of the German army.[28]

The Division remained on garrison duties in le Havre for the next ten days. There were few complaints about this since the German garrison of the town had been well provided for and had anticipated a long siege. Once again the pipes and drums played Retreat in the town square and wreaths were laid on le Havre's war memorial. Field Marshal Montgomery (who had been promoted at the beginning of September) issued a special personal message to all troops in 21 Army Group, which included Second (British) and First (Canadian) Armies, on 17 September in which he reviewed the great progress made by the Allies since 21 August, and his last message to the troops.

> Such a historic march of events can seldom have taken place in history in such a short space of time. You have every reason to be very proud of what you have done. Let us say to each other:
> 'This was the Lord's doing, and it is marvellous in our eyes.'[29]

Montgomery went on to note that the battle was now being taken to Germany and that 'Our American Allies are fighting on German soil in many places'. Germany's fate was certain and its defeat would be absolute. His message ended with the exhortation: 'The triumphant cry now is "Forward into Germany".'[30]

As the Division's time in le Havre drew to a close, 154 Brigade was deployed on a special task of its own. Brigadier Oliver's brigade was to come under Canadian command in the siege of Dunkirk, that port where so many Allied servicemen had escaped from the advancing German armies in 1940. Dunkirk had been by-passed by the advancing Allies but the port's garrison was especially strong, numbering some 15,000 men, and there were concerns that it might become aggressive and raid 21 Army Group's lines of communications. To prevent this, Dunkirk was masked by 4 Special Service Brigade which formation 154 Brigade was to relieve, allowing the commandos to be deployed for operations in the Walcheren area. (The designation 'Special Service Brigade' was later changed to 'Commando Brigade' as the abbreviation SS Brigade had unfortunate connotations.) That relief took place on 26 September with 7th Argylls in positions north-east of Dunkirk at Bray-Dunes Plage, while 7th Black Watch were three miles south of them at Ghyvelde and 1st Black Watch were west of the town. A composite group of all the brigade carrier platoons with some tanks commanded the road to Bergues; this group was commanded by Major Campbell of 7th Argylls. In all, the brigade held a perimeter of twenty-five miles but the task was not quite as difficult as might be thought since extensive flooding had restricted the possible routes from Dunkirk.[31]

Inside Dunkirk the garrison was aware of the handover and seemed keen to identify their new besiegers. During the night of 26–27 September B Company 7th Black Watch in Ghyvelde were set upon by a strong enemy fighting patrol. The Germans penetrated to the main street, demolished the windmill, used as an observation post, set ablaze several houses and departed with five prisoners. Some time later, 7th Argylls had a similar experience with Germans fighting their way into Battalion HQ where two Argylls and two Germans were killed; the Argylls' Adjutant, Captain W O Williamson, was wounded. In addition to the dead left at 7th Argylls HQ, both German patrols lost several men captured by the Highlanders. Such commando-style operations were not normally expected from German soldiers.[32]

Shortly afterwards Brigadier Oliver received a deputation from the French Red Cross who asked him to arrange a truce during which the civilian population of Dunkirk would be evacuated. A period of thirty-six hours was suggested and when First Army HQ approved of the proposal a letter was sent to the German commander in Dunkirk asking for his coop-eration. This letter was sent through the French Red Cross on 2 October. When the Germans indicated their approval, Captain Wingate-Gray, 154 Brigade's Intelligence Officer, who spoke both French and German flu-ently, approached Dunkirk under a flag of truce. On the outskirts of the town he was met, blindfolded and escorted to the German HQ where the garrison commander agreed to the terms of the truce with the proviso that no changes in military dispositions were made while the truce was in effect.[33]

Both Brigadier Oliver and his German counterpart gave written guarantees that the truce would be honoured and so, at 6.00am on 4 October, the truce began. Nearly 20,000 French civilians were evacuated from Dunkirk as well as a number of seriously wounded German soldiers; one wounded Allied soldier was evacuated for each German. An extension of the truce by twelve hours was later agreed to allow the defenders of Dunkirk to demolish bridges and replace mines. This had been a most unusual experience for the Highlanders but they had been impressed by the way in which the Germans observed scrupulously the terms of the truce.[34]

In turn 154 Brigade was relieved by the Czech Brigade on 8 and 9 October and departed the Dunkirk perimeter to rejoin the Division which was now in The Netherlands, between Eindhoven and Nijmegen, in the area of St Oedenrode. By now the names of Eindhoven and Nijmegen had become familiar to many, following the ill-fated attempt to bounce the Rhine that was Operation MARKET GARDEN and which had come to grief at Arnhem. En route to St Oedenrode, Brigadier Oliver received a message instructing him to report to Corps HQ at Turnhout, just south of the Belgian border. There he was ordered to concentrate 154 Brigade at Zeelst, an airfield about three miles west of Eindhoven. The reason for this deployment was highly secret, to be known only to Oliver and his Brigade Major: His Majesty King George VI was to fly into Zeelst to visit his troops in the area.[35]

The airfield at Zeelst served Eindhoven and lay close to the Wilhelmina canal, on the north bank of which the Germans were dug in. Defence of the airfield was in the hands of the RAF Regiment, raised earlier in the war for such purposes, but the RAF soldiers at Zeelst had no experience of close combat and had not been prepared fully when German troops raided across the canal, inflicting several casualties. With the King about to visit it was considered that Zeelst should be protected by a force of brigade strength at least and that the defenders should be combat hardened troops. Hence the order deploying Brigadier Oliver's command to Zeelst.[36]

Since the only people who knew of the proposed Royal visit were Brigadier Oliver and his Brigade Major, his surprise may be imagined when, during a conference of his senior officers, all of whom were ignorant of the imminent arrival of the King, a local teenage girl, the schoolmaster's daughter, knocked on the door of the room in which the meeting was being held and enquired 'very politely' the time at which His Majesty would arrive at Zeelst the following day for his visit to Nijmegen and Montgomery. Security can never be complete but the ways in which it may be breached are often quite simple and, occasionally, laughable – although the implications can be dramatic. On this occasion the Dutch girl, 'a charming *meishe*, caused at least two red faces but no threat to the security of the King whose visit went ahead without interruption from the enemy'.[37] Such visits to front-line troops, with the personal risks involved, did much to endear George VI to his service personnel.

The Royal visit over and the Brigade's task complete, the Royal Netherlands Brigade relieved 154 allowing the Highlanders to rejoin their Division which was now in the Nijmegen corridor. On 18 October 154 Brigade left Zeelst to move into the line and relieve 158 Brigade of 53rd (Welsh) Division. The latter had, temporarily, taken the place of the Black Watch and Argylls in the Highland Division.

While 154 Brigade was engaged on its peregrinations, the remainder of the Division had, at first, stayed at le Havre where training had been organised with sufficient free time for soldiers to enjoy bathing in the sea and making friends with the local community. For the infantry that training involved much marching while the Gunners found suitable areas in which to carry out live-firing practice. The latter also found themselves involved in firing on the besieged ports of Boulogne and Calais. However, the Divisional transport had little opportunity to rest; the RASC men were kept busy throughout this period.[38]

Orders to leave le Havre came on 26 September. The Highland Division was to move to Belgium and 153 Brigade led the way, cheered along their route by enthusiastic French men, women and children, delighted to see these British soldiers whose presence meant an end to the four long years of occupation. Through Amiens, Cambrai, Valenciennes and Mons 153 Brigade wove its way, along a route that evoked thoughts of the Great War and of the Highland Division of that era, the fathers, uncles and neighbours of many of the men now making their way to Belgium. On 30 September 153 Brigade arrived in Brussels to be assigned a sector of the line previously held by a brigade of 15th (Scottish) Division.[39] The latter formation was commanded by Major-General Colin Barber, a Cameron Highlander, who had been a staff officer of 51st (Highland) Division in 1940.[40]

When 152 Brigade arrived in Belgium it, too, relieved a brigade – 46 (Highland) – of 15th (Scottish) Division with 2nd Seaforth relieving 7th Seaforth and 9th Cameronians; 5th Seaforth relieved 2nd Glasgow Highlanders, 5th Camerons took over from 2nd Gordons and 2nd Derbyshire Yeomanry went into the line in place of 2nd Argylls. (The Glasgow Highlanders were a TA battalion of The Highland Light Infantry, which, in spite of its Highland title, was a Lowland regiment.) This relief had all the characteristics of a family reunion writ large. Gunners of 243 Anti-Tank Battery as well as two platoons from H Company 1/7th Middlesex were also deployed as infantry.[41] We have already noted that 158 Brigade of 53rd (Welsh) Division came under Highland Division command as a temporary replacement for 154 Brigade.

By now the war had taken a new complexion. The 'great swan' was over, the attempt to bounce the Rhine in Operation MARKET GARDEN had failed and German resistance was stiffening. Crerar's First Canadian Army was operating around the Scheldt estuary and the approaches to Antwerp with the aim of getting that port into operation as early as possible so as to shorten the Allied logistical tail, thereby easing the task of re-supplying the armies in north-west Europe. Canadian forces were also in action at Walcheren with the objective of capturing Beveland and clearing enemy forces from the area south of the Maas river to Geertruidenberg. Second British Army held the line from the southern outskirts of Tilburg with the Highland Division on the left flank, deployed from Tilburg to just north of St Oedenrode, whence the line swung towards Nijmegen and then back to Helmond. This latter 'finger' included the Nijmegen 'corridor'. Not surprisingly, someone now had the idea that Second Army should widen that corridor, as part of the effort to get Antwerp open to Allied shipping. Widening the Nijmegen corridor meant pushing the Germans across the Maas on the entire line as far west as Geertruidenberg, where a junction could be made with First Canadian Army.[42] Overall responsibility for this task lay with XII Corps, commanded by Lieutenant-General Neil Ritchie, one-time commander of 51st (Highland) Division, who had gone on to command Eighth Army before being relieved during the 1942 retreat to El Alamein. Ritchie's command now included 7th Armoured Division and 33 Armoured Brigade as well as 15th (Scottish), 51st (Highland) and 53rd (Welsh) Divisions.[43] As a Black Watch soldier, Ritchie might have chosen to style his command XII (Celtic) Corps.

Initially the Highlanders had a relatively quiet time in the line as XII Corps prepared for Operation COLIN, which was to become known as the Battle of the Maas. There was some sniping, an activity in which 5th Seaforth specialised, and raiding of the enemy lines.[44] The dismounted yeomen of Derby carried out one very successful raid when, with the support of four Churchill tanks, they hit a German position and took prisoner every man therein. This raid had an interesting sequel. One German soldier, from the party in the position, had been away from his post when the Derbyshires made their visit. On his return, discovering that all his comrades had been captured, this soldier packed his kit and walked into the British lines so that he might rejoin his friends.[45] In another raid, 5th Camerons found a German sound asleep in his trench. The somnambulist awoke only when he was lifted from the trench and dropped unceremoniously on the ground. However, he did not seem to object to his rest having been disturbed, nor to being conveyed to the Camerons' lines.[46]

The Germans also made raids and the hours immediately after a relief were the most dangerous for such activity as 1st Black Watch discovered on relieving 1/5th Welch (this spelling was adopted in 1921 in preference to 'Welsh'). During the Watch's first morning stand-to in the line there arrived a group of uninvited and unwanted visitors. An enemy fighting patrol, including an officer and twenty men, penetrated the line and made it as far as C Company HQ before being spotted by the Company Sergeant-Major who challenged two men whom he did not recognise. The challenge was answered with a burst of automatic fire to which the CSM responded by throwing two grenades. A brief firefight ensued before the raiders made off with three prisoners, two officers' batmen and the driver of a jeep. However, the three men did not remain captive for long. The German patrol ran into No. 14 Platoon who opened fire whereupon the prisoners seized the opportunity to make their escape. The German officer was killed during this fracas and only five Germans returned to their own lines.[47]

D-Day for Operation COLIN was 23 October – El Alamein day – and the Highland Division's role was to attack north from St Oedenrode to seize the town of Schijndel before swinging north-west and taking crossings over the Dommel and Halsche rivers, to the south of s'Hertogenbosch. In this operation, the Division was to have its usual support from 33 Armoured Brigade. The day before the Highlanders' attack, 7th Armoured and 53rd (Welsh) Divisions were to clear the ground between the Zuidwilhelms canal and s'Hertogenbosch while, the day after, 15th (Scottish) Division was to take Tilburg and advance north. Within the Highland Division the task of taking Schijndel was assigned to 153 Brigade with 152 clearing the wooded area east of the Dommel river while 154, mounted in Kangaroos, was to act as an exploitation force.[48]

At midnight, 22–23 October, 153 Brigade began advancing with 5th/7th Gordons, making a silent attack on Wijbosch, a village close to Schijndel. Although the attackers suffered many casualties, Wijbosch was taken and 5th Black Watch passed through on their way to the south-east end of Schijndel. Their particular objective was a large factory that appeared to dominate the entire town. At 8.00am 1st Gordons began their advance. This was largely unopposed and the Gordons captured the south-west end of Schijndel, taking prisoner over twenty paratroopers in the process. The leading battalion of 152 Brigade, 5th Camerons, had moved off an hour before 153. No sooner were the Camerons in open country than they came under intense fire from enemy machine guns but, in spite of this, B Company reached its objective. However, A Company's opposition was much stiffer and the company's casualties included its commander, Major Nigel Parker, who was wounded severely and later died. A Company's advance was brought to a halt. D Company, which attempted to make a flanking attack, was also held up but the situation was relieved somewhat when C Company, by dint of a wide detour, came in on A Company's original objective and wrested it from the enemy. By evening the battalion had taken its objectives in the woods at Schijndel. The brigade objective was to clear the land between the Schijndel dyke, opposite Boxtel, up to Schijndel itself and south to Olland.[49]

Both Seaforth battalions achieved their objectives without difficulty, with the 5th Battalion walking into theirs without any opposition, as the Germans had abandoned Olland some nine hours before the attack began. Considerable valuable information about that withdrawal came from three men who walked into 5th Seaforth's lines. One was the pilot of a crashed Dakota who had been hidden by Resistance members, and the other two were local priests. Such was the quality of their information that 5th Seaforth were able to move north towards s'Hertogenbosch and had almost reached the Zuidwilhelms canal when their progress was stopped by a demolished bridge.[50]

The APC-borne 154 Brigade were led off by 7th Argylls, supported by a half squadron of tanks, at 8.00am on the 23rd. Their role was to protect the Division's right flank and, in spite of many mines, the Argylls were on their objective by 1.00pm. Next to move off was the 7th Black Watch group which left the start-line at 11.15am and headed through Schijndel towards St Michielsgestel. The tanks of the group cleared roadblocks, allowing A and D Companies of the Black Watch to enter the town, but the infantry were only about a hundred yards away when the town's bridge across the river was blown. However, a platoon of A Company crossed the river in small boats at about 4.00pm and the Pioneer Platoon set about erecting a Class 9 bridge which allowed the remainder of the battalion to cross by 9 o'clock that evening, followed by 1st Black Watch. Both Black Watch battalions then formed a strong bridgehead which drew particular praise from General Rennie. By this stage in the operation, 5th/7th Gordons had come under command of 154 Brigade while 7th Argylls came under that of 153 Brigade.[51]

The next obstacle in 154 Brigade's progress was the Halsche river at Halder. Once again the bridge had been demolished but a company of 1st Black Watch, concealed by a smokescreen, crossed the wreckage to establish a bridgehead. A new bridge was built by the Pioneers but Sappers then constructed a heavier bridge to take armour. Black Watch carriers also crossed over the bridge and a platoon of these, en route to s'Hertogenbosch, had the misfortune to meet a German counter-attack that included SPGs. The carrier platoon was hit heavily by the Germans but, fortunately, the Argylls, passing through 1st Black Watch and making for Vught, came on the scene and engaged in a pitched battle with the Germans. This encounter ended with 'honours ... fairly even' but the Argylls held the ground they had reached. The battalion consolidated there and 7th Black Watch, with a troop of tanks in support, passed through next morning. Before long the Black Watch encountered stiff opposition, some of which included Green Police, 'unmentionable guards from the equally unmentionable concentration camp in the vicinity of Vught'. In spite of this opposition, however, Vught fell to the Black Watch that afternoon.[52] The regimental historian, Fergusson, describes the fight between Vught and Halder as 'an elegant little action'.[53]

Vught had also been in the sights of 152 Brigade which had been pushing towards the town with 5th Camerons advancing from Groenendal to the line of the Vught–Tilburg road. South of the same road, 5th Seaforth were positioned in woods with 2nd Seaforth to their left. With a heavy artillery programme supporting them, all three battalions advanced on their objectives where they halted to consolidate while news was sought of the situation of 7th Armoured Division. The Desert Rats were held up before the village of Loon op Zand as a result of which the Highland Division deployed to support them and it was 153 Brigade which captured the village. On 27 October Holeind, Haaren and Oisterwijk were taken by 5th/7th Gordons, 5th Black Watch and 1st Gordons respectively. And it was 1st Gordons who attacked Loon op Zand on the 28th. Advancing against stern opposition, the Gordons took the northern half of the village, allowing 5th Black Watch to pass through and push northwards up the road to reach Horst next morning.[54] Meanwhile, 5th/7th Gordons advanced on Kaatschevez and both Gordon battalions took Sprang on 30 October. The mobile 154 Brigade was now redeployed westwards to try to cut off Germans seeking to cross to the north side of the Maas, and to link up with the Canadians at Geertruidenberg. As 154 Brigade made its sweep, 152 and 153 Brigades were to push northwards to s'Hertogenbosch.[55]

At noon on 29 October, 1st Black Watch led 154 Brigade's westward advance, moving up to Hooge bridge where a strong enemy position was located. During this advance, Lieutenant Viney, who commanded the leading platoon of A Company, was cut off when a tree, felled by artillery fire, blocked his way. Viney fought his way out of this predicament, killing five Germans in the process. Advancing on Waspik, where the bridge looked intact, the Black Watch had a tough fight to secure the village and suffered a number of casualties, including Lieutenant Donald Cox, who later died, and Major Anderson who was wounded badly.[56] When 7th Argylls came up they were ordered to strike immediately towards Geertruidenberg. Setting off in their Kangaroos, the Argylls met strong opposition en route which forced them to dismount and take up defensive positions for the night. They were midway to their objective. In the morning the advance was resumed and, following a sharp battle with an advancing German column, the Argylls reached Raamsdonk, just a few miles from Geertruidenberg, where they were ordered to stop.[57]

The baton was now taken up by 7th Black Watch. A platoon of A Company, commanded by Lieutenant I Donaldson, was in the van of the battalion's advance. Donaldson's platoon was disposed with two tanks in front, two Kangaroos carrying the infantry, and a second pair of tanks. About halfway to their objective they met machine-gun fire but this was dealt with quickly and the advance continued. Then, farther along the road, came a more serious enemy intervention. The leading tanks had passed the junction with a side road that was little more than a track, when a German self-propelled gun emerged on to the road. However, Donaldson assessed the situation quickly and ordered the driver of his Kangaroo to accelerate and ram the SPG. This tactic proved eminently successful and the SPG was disabled. Although the Kangaroo overturned into the ditch, the occupants were able to get out and deal with the SPG crew. Donaldson's platoon then withdrew to Raamsdonk. Another platoon made a wide sweeping attack that cut the enemy's escape route at Geertruidenberg and, next day, mopping-up operations were carried out in the area. That same day a carrier patrol of 7th Black Watch pushed through Geertruidenberg as far as the bridge over the Maas. No one was surprised to find that the bridge had been blown. General Rennie complimented 7th Black Watch on its achievement and, next day, the battalion was withdrawn to Vught.[58]

Waalwijk on the Maas was assigned to 5th Camerons but the battalion met no opposition at all, being greeted in the town by cheering residents. After two days in Waalwijk, the Camerons were relieved by troops from 7th Armoured Division.[59] There now remained but two pockets of enemy troops south of the Maas. One of these was the 'Island', a piece of land some six miles long by four wide, which lies in a bend of the river and is defined by the Maas and the Afwaterings canal. Taking the 'Island' demanded an attack across water and XII Corps had originally assigned this task to 53rd (Welsh) Division. However, a German counter-attack on 7th US Armored Division, temporarily under Second Army command, had punched through the Allied line some twelve miles west of Roermond and the Germans were now only twenty miles from Eindhoven. XII Corps was ordered to deploy a division to the Weert sector to reinforce the Americans and the Welsh Division was chosen. Ritchie was also ordered to use another division to eliminate the 'Island' as quickly as possible and then organise a corps attack to clear the enemy from the area between Venlo and Roermond, west of the Meuse (Maas). With the Welshmen assigned to Weert, the task of clearing the 'Island' was allocated to the Highland Division.[60] On 2 November 154 Brigade deployed to relieve 152 Brigade at s'Hertogenbosch; the latter, with 152 Brigade, was to make the attack on the 'Island'.[61]

Within 152 Brigade 2nd Seaforth were to take the crossroads at Drunen, a town on the road that ran through the 'Island', 5th Seaforth were to seize Groenwoud, a town about three-quarters of a mile from Drunen and on the same road, while 5th Camerons were to advance on Drunen itself. On the right flank 153 Brigade's objectives were Nieuwkuijk, Vlijmen and Haarsteg. Diversionary attacks were to be staged by 154 and 131 (Queen's) Brigades, the latter from 7th Armoured Division.[62] Since it was but a day to 5 November, the attack on the 'Island' was codenamed Operation GUY FAWKES which, although rather obvious, broke the rule of assigning only a single word to the names of operations. (Although, at first glance, Operation MARKET GARDEN might also appear to break this rule, that is not the case since this is a combination of the names of two separate operations, MARKET and GARDEN.)

The operation was a complete success and little opposition was met. Collapsible canvas boats were used for the canal crossing and a heavy artillery concentration was laid down on the enemy positions. There were few casualties in the crossing of the dyke and canal and even the Drunesche dyke, believed to be the main enemy defensive line, was no obstacle. At Groenwoud, 5th Seaforth found no Germans at all while 2nd Seaforth and 5th Camerons were also completely successful. One story from the Camerons' experience adds some levity to the story. CSM Gordon, C Company, found a German soldier who was trying, without success, to get his machine gun into action. Grabbing the unfortunate German by the scruff of the neck, Gordon took the weapon from him and explained what was wrong with it before stripping the machine gun and sending its owner back as a prisoner. One imagines that the German appreciated being taken prisoner more than the lesson in weapon handling. The Camerons continued across the 'Island' to the line of the Maas where the battalion also captured the town of Helsden.[63]

Equal success crowned the efforts of 153 Brigade with 1st Gordons and 5th Black Watch taking their first objectives before 5th/7th Gordons passed through for Nieuwkuijk and 5th Black Watch made for Haarsteg. All brigade objectives had been taken by 6.00pm on 5 November. When 5th/7th Gordons reached Nieuwkuijk, the village was in flames and its church lay in ruins.[64] The entire brigade area up to the Maas was now clear of Germans.

The other pocket of resistance south of the Maas was at Empel, north of s'Hertogenbosch, where there was an enemy bridgehead. This bridgehead was attacked on the night of the 6th by 7th Argylls who met little opposition, most Germans encountered being pleased to become prisoners.[65] For this attack the Argylls had a new CO, Lieutenant-Colonel McKinnon MC. McKinnon had earned his MC with the Highland Division in France in 1940, had rejoined the Division shortly before D-Day and had been second-in-command of the Argylls before taking command of the battalion.[66]

The Highland Division emerged from this two-week period of fighting with 674 casualties, of whom 122 had been killed. Thirty German officers and 2,378 other ranks had been captured and 'enemy casualties must have been heavy'. General Dempsey, of Second Army, wrote to congratulate the Highland Division.

Now that you have entirely cleared the country south of the River MAAS, I want to tell you how greatly I appreciate the splendid way in which your Division has fought during the recent operations. You had a great many difficulties to contend with; you overcame them all in the best possible way. Please give the Division my very sincere congratulations.[67]

In passing on Dempsey's message to his soldiers, Rennie added his own comment.

We will undoubtedly have some heavy fighting to contend with before the war is won, and we shall encounter better troops than those we have seen lately. It is the duty of every one of us to ensure that the fighting spirit of the Highland Division remains 'second to none'.[68]

Notes

1. Ellis, *Victory in the West*, pp. 457–8
2. Ibid, pp. 470–1; Salmond, *The History of The 51st Highland Division*, pp. 172–3; NA Kew, WO171/528, war diary, HQ 51 (H) Div (G), 1944
3. NA Kew, WO171/680, war diary, 154 Bde, 1944
4. NA Kew, WO171/528, war diary, HQ 51 (H) Div (G), 1944; WO171/675, war diary, 152 Bde, 1944
5. NA Kew, WO171/1345, war diary, 1/7 Mx, 1944; WO171/851, war diary, 2 DY, 1944
6. NA Kew, WO171/528, war diary, HQ 51 (H) Div (G), 1944; WO171/1301, war diary, 5/7 Gordons, 1944; Salmond, op cit, pp. 172–3
7. NA Kew, WO171/528, war diary, 51 (H) Div (G), 1944; Salmond, op cit, p. 173
8. Salmond, op cit, p. 173; Borthwick, *Battalion*, p. 179
9. Borthwick, op cit, p. 179
10. Ibid; NA Kew, WO171/1271, war diary, 5 Camerons; WO171/1370, war diary, 5 Seaforth
11. Salmond, op cit, pp. 173–4
12. NA Kew, WO171/529, HQ 51 (H) Div (G), 1944
13. Ibid
14. Ibid; Salmond, op cit, p. 175; Young, *The Highland Division Transport and Supply Column* (The officer was Maj Roy Munford)
15. Salmond, op cit, pp. 175–6
16. Ibid; NA Kew, WO171/529, war diary, HQ 51 (H) Div (G), 1944
17. NA Kew, WO171/529, war diary, HQ 51 (H) Div (G), 1944
18. Ibid
19. Salmond, op cit, pp. 176–7
20. Ibid, p. 177
21. NA Kew, WO171/1370, war diary, 5 Seaforth, 1944; Salmond, op cit, p. 177;

Borthwick, op cit, p. 183

22. Borthwick, op cit, pp. 183–7
23. Salmond, op cit, p. 177
24. NA Kew, WO171/529, war diary 51 (H) Div (G), 1944; Salmond, op cit, p. 177
25. Salmond, op cit, pp. 177–8
26. Ibid
27. Ibid; Fergusson, *The Black Watch and the King's Enemies*, p. 279
28. NA Kew, WO171/529, war diary, 51 (H) Div (G), 1944
29. Ibid
30. Ibid
31. NA Kew, WO171/680, war diary, 154 Bde, 1944
32. NA Kew, WO171/1267, war diary, 7 BW, 1944; Fergusson, op cit, pp. 279–80; Salmond, op cit, pp. 180–1
33. NA Kew, WO171/680, war diary, 154 Bde, 1944; Salmond, op cit, pp. 180–1
34. Salmond, op cit, pp. 180–1
35. NA Kew, WO171/680, war diary, 154 Bde, 1944
36. Ibid; Salmond, op cit, p. 183
37. Salmond, op cit, p. 183
38. NA Kew, WO 171/529, war diary, 51 (H) Div (G), 1944
39. Salmond, op cit, pp. 183–4; NA Kew, WO171/529, war diary HQ 51 (H) Div (G), 1944; WO171/678, war diary, 153 Bde, 1944
40. Joslen, *Orders of Battle*, p. 58
41. Salmond, op cit, p. 184
42. Ellis, *Victory in the West, Vol II*, pp. 99–100 & 123–5
43. Ibid, pp. 123–4
44. NA Kew, WO171/1370, war diary 5 Seaforth; Borthwick, op cit, pp. 192–4
45. NA Kew, WO171/851, war diary 2 DY, 1944; Salmond, op cit, p. 186
46. NA Kew, WO171/1271, war diary, 5 Camerons, 1944; Salmond, op cit, p. 187
47. NA Kew, WO171/1266, war diary, 5 BW, 1944; Fergusson op cit, p. 283; Salmond, op cit, pp. 186–7
48. NA Kew, WO171/529, war diary, HQ 51 (H) Div (G), 1944
49. Ibid; Salmond, op cit, p. 187
50. NA Kew, WO171/1370, war diary, 5 Seaforth, 1944; Borthwick, op cit, pp. 195–6
51. NA Kew, WO171/680, war diary, 154 Bde, 1944; Fergusson, op cit, pp. 283–6
52. Fergusson, op cit, pp. 283–6; Salmond, op cit, p. 189 (quotes from Salmond)
53. Fergusson, op cit, p. 286
54. Fergusson, op cit, p. 287; NA Kew, WO171/678, war diary, 153 Bde, 1944; Salmond, op cit, p. 189
55. Salmond, op cit, p. 189
56. Fergusson, op cit, pp. 286–7; Salmond, op cit, pp. 189–90; NA Kew, WO171/1265, war diary, 1 BW, 1944
57. NA Kew, WO171/1263, war diary, 7 A & SH, 1944; Salmond, op cit, p. 190
58. NA Kew, WO171/1267, war diary, 7 BW, 1944; Salmond, op cit, p. 190
59. NA Kew, WO171/1271, war diary, 5 Camerons, 1944
60. Ellis, op cit, p. 237
61. NA Kew, WO171/676, war diary, 152 Bde, 1944; WO171/680, war diary, 154 Bde, 1944

62. Salmond, op cit, p. 191
63. Ibid
64. NA Kew, WO171/678, war diary, 153 Bde, 1944
65. NA Kew, WO171/680, war diary, 154 Bde, 1944; WO171/1263, war diary, 7 A & SH, 1944
66. Salmond, op cit, p. 192
67. NA Kew, WO171/529, war diary, HQ 51 (H) Div (G), 1944
68. Ibid

CHAPTER XII

The Final Winter

Winter was approaching and it was to be one of the worst in living memory in northern Europe. In centuries past it had been the practice for fighting to cease while armies went into winter quarters. But this was no longer the case and, in spite of the difficulties that vehicles, including tracked vehicles, would have in moving on ice-bound or snow-covered roads, or across sodden or snow-covered countryside, neither the Germans nor the Allies intended there to be any respite at all for the fighting men. At the beginning of November, the full fury of winter had not appeared, but in the Low Countries

> It was an unhappy time of year in an unhappy countryside. Rain poured down on a chilly world of drenched fields and miserable villages, which had been battered to pieces by both sides, and especially during the latest German attack.[1]

That 'latest German attack' was the offensive that drew 53rd (Welsh) Division to the assistance of the Americans. Although not a spectacular success in the manner of the later attack on US forces in the Ardennes in December, the Germans had increased their bridgehead across the Maas, with troops disposed between Roermond and Venlo, thereby threatening Eindhoven. It was now imperative that the Germans be prised out of their bridgehead and pushed back across the Maas. The plan to execute this, Operation ASCOT, was to include the Highland Division.[2]

The Division's role in ASCOT was to force the enemy out to the south of the road from Weert to Roermond, then wheel and continue the push across the Maas up to Venlo. Once again it was a Celtic operation with both 15th (Scottish) and 53rd (Welsh) Divisions also involved.[3] D-Day for ASCOT was 14 November with 51st (Highland) Division attacking on a two-brigade front: 152 Brigade would cross the Noorder canal and 153 Brigade the Wessem. These canals joined at right angles near the village of Nederweert, where the enemy was especially well emplaced. Controlling the lock gates near the Maas the Germans could flood or empty both canals as they chose and the Highlanders could not get to grips with their foes until they had crossed the waterways.[4] Once 153 Brigade reported success, 154 Brigade was to enter the fray by advancing to and seizing Heythuijen, a small town about half-way to the Maas. But first, the Division had to move to its operational area. That move began on 6 November when 152 and 153 Brigades moved south to Nederweert where 152 Brigade relieved elements of Seventh (US) Armored Division.[5] The relief was completed by the 7th and the American tankmen, doubtless doubly relieved at no longer being deployed as infantry, departed the area.

As an armoured formation the Americans had little appreciation of the typically infantry task of holding ground and the Highlanders took over a very poor defensive layout. In fact, it was virtually porous and German patrols had been crossing the canal on a regular basis, sowing mines wherever they chose. Since the frontage taken over from the Americans was so long, 152 Brigade was reinforced by 2nd Argylls from 15th (Scottish) Division, who moved into the line on the left of 2nd Seaforth. In turn 154 Brigade moved into the line on 9 November to relieve 152 and 2nd Argylls returned to their parent division three days later.[6]

In the days before the attack, 152 and 153 Brigades trained in a new method of going into battle: by Buffalo.[7] These were not the beasts of that name but American-built tracked amphibious vehicles, first developed for use in the Pacific but which also proved invaluable in north-west Europe and Italy. The Buffalo was really an amphibious assault landing craft, able to traverse water obstacles and travel over land while carrying troops, vehicles or equipment.[8] For the canal crossings both Buffaloes and assault boats were to be used with East Riding Yeomanry tanks towing the assault boats on sledges to the canal banks. This procedure had also to be rehearsed as was the loading of the Buffaloes.[9]

On D-Day the Buffaloes were loaded with jeeps, anti-tank guns and men. Assault boats were lifted from their sledges and launched and the attacking brigades set off across the two waterways. In spite of heavy mortar fire, 1st Gordons crossed with little difficulty but the Buffaloes demonstrated a major shortcoming in being unable to negotiate the steep banks of the Wessem. The other Gordons battalion, 5th/7th, also crossed successfully and quickly achieved all their objectives. During the first thirty minutes of 5th/7th Gordons' attack, the war correspondent Chester Wilmot gave a commentary from a BBC recording van. Such an occurrence was unusual enough at that time to merit mention. Meanwhile 5th Black Watch also made a successful crossing but, although Sappers blew gaps in the far bank, this still proved too steep an obstacle for the Buffaloes.[10]

In 152 Brigade the Buffaloes proved much more successful and 5th Seaforth and 5th Camerons crossed the Noorder without major mishap although the Germans opened the lock gates to drain the canal of water, causing the Seaforth to create a bridge of boats to cross the glutinous black mud that was left when the waters disappeared. The Seaforth then went on to take their objectives some thousand yards away. Piper McLean played C Company of the Camerons across the canal and the battalion crossed without difficulty to take their objectives 'in less than the ambitious time allotted'.[11] One participant described the progress of the Cameron men as 'an extraordinary sight, reminiscent of mobile columns in the desert: infantry on tanks, infantry on Buffaloes, infantry on their feet, all rolling southwards, spread out on a front of half a mile with a tremendous barrage screaming overhead'.[12] With the assault battalions safely on their objectives, 5th Seaforth completed 152 Brigade's operation.[13]

It was now the turn of 154 Brigade to go for the lock gates and their assault was led by 7th Argylls. The brigade group included an engineer bridging team complete with a Churchill AVRE carrying a readymade bridge that could span the canal at the gates. The Argylls had also to deal with a small island at the canal bifurcation; this was assaulted by a platoon at the same time as the leading Argylls reached the lock gates. German mines, especially the deadly Schu-mines, many camouflaged as bricks, proved the most serious opposition. Nonetheless, the bridge was soon in place and the Argylls overcame some slight opposition to gain mastery of the village of Hulsen. Some Germans retreating from the Argylls at Hulsen ran into men of 5th/7th Gordons who were moving up from their bridgehead.[14]

Before the crossing 1st Black Watch had a scrap with several Germans from a patrol that penetrated the battalion's lines and made off with a number of prisoners, machine gunners from the Middlesex and some Seaforth. The raiders then had the misfortune to clash with a Black Watch standing patrol and in the ensuing mêlée the prisoners made good their escape. The Black Watch then crossed by Bailey bridge in 153 Brigade's bridgehead, on the morning of 15 November, to advance in their Kangaroos as far as Leveroi where houses, destroyed by Allied aircraft and artillery, blocked the road. At this point, 7th Black Watch passed through the 1st Battalion and, with a tank squadron in support, made for Heythuijzen.[15]

En route the Black Watch group lost two tanks to mines but the infantry debussed and occupied Heythuijzen. The town had already been abandoned by the enemy and Black Watch patrols pushed out towards Reggel. D Company occupied Neer the next day and the battalion concentrated in Onder two days later. As 1st Black Watch continued the advance towards Baarlo, many SPGs appeared in their path but these were dealt with quickly. However, enemy heavy shelling continued and was considered the worst experienced since those unpleasant days in the Bois de Bavent in Normandy. This was especially marked as the battalion debussed again to advance on foot through the village of Bong to Baarlo. Brigadier Oliver paid a visit to the Black Watch CO at this time and, on his return to Brigade

HQ, summed up the ferocity of the enemy shellfire by commenting that Lieutenant-Colonel John Hopwood was wearing his steel helmet. It was the custom in the Division to wear the Tam O'Shanter whenever possible, a practice abandoned only when heavy shellfire made it an act of folly. Hopwood's battalion remained in Baarlo until relieved by a battalion of the Welch Regiment on 26 November.[16]

While 154 Brigade had been pushing ahead so, too, had the Seaforth and Cameron Brigade with 5th Camerons taking yet another canal crossing on the morning of the 17th. The night before the battalion deployed patrols to ascertain the enemy's positions along the Uitwaterings canal, known locally as the Zig canal. German activity was noted at the junction of this and the Nederweert canal and, at first light on the 17th, C Company dashed across a broken bridge to dig in on the far side of the canal. There they were subjected to intense mortar and shellfire which increased as A Company came across at the sluice gates. Smoke was also put down by the Germans in an effort to blind the tanks supporting the Highlanders with covering fire from the opposite bank. Then came the customary counter-attack on the Camerons who resisted fiercely. C Company had Captain Douglas Tilly, the FOO of 492 Highland Field Battery, with them and he brought down the full power of the divisional artillery as well as medium fire. In spite of this, and the added weight of both mortar and small-arms fire, the Germans persisted in their attack. The battle lasted until after noon when the enemy finally withdrew and the Camerons had all but run out of ammunition. While this battle was underway both 1st Gordons and 5th Black Watch crossed the canal in an effort to ease some of the pressure that 5th Camerons were suffering. The two battalions crossed safely and 5th/7th Gordons followed them next day to occupy the Keup-Egehel area.[17]

This battle brought a special message from General Ritchie commending the Camerons.

> Had not the 5th Camerons held on to their foothold on the east bank of the Zig Canal, the advance of the whole [XII] Corps might well have been delayed for an appreciable time.[18]

The canal was spanned by the Sappers with a Class 40 bridge that was immediately dubbed 'Cameron Bridge'. Both company commanders were decorated for their leadership, as were several other Camerons.[19]

From the Cameron bridgehead, 5th Seaforth set out for Zelen with 2nd Seaforth on their left flank. Both battalions were lashed by heavy rain and had to make their way through thick mud but still managed to reach their objectives and dig in. That they should have made such good progress and arrived exactly where they intended was a remarkable feat in very unpleasant conditions.[20] With 5th Black Watch and the two Gordon battalions almost on the banks of the Maas by the 18th, this phase of the battle was drawing to a close. On 24 November both Highland Brigades were relieved by elements of the Welsh Division. This marked the end of the Division's part in Operation ASCOT as 15th (Scottish) Division deployed to attack from farther north to roll up the remnants of the German bridgehead on what was now the British side of the Maas.[21]

However, there was to be no opportunity for rest for the Highland Division as Rennie's command was deployed to the Nijmegen bridgehead to relieve 101st (US) Airborne Division.[22] This relief was effected on 28 November and at much the same time the CO of 1st Gordons, Lieutenant-Colonel Cumming-Bruce, was promoted to command 44 Brigade in 15th (Scottish) Division and was succeeded as CO of the Gordons by Lieutenant-Colonel J A Grant-Peterkin.[23]

By now there were no Germans south or west of the Maas in 21 Army Group's area of operations and that Group had a bridgehead across the river, from Cuyjx to Driel. The former is about ten miles south of Nijmegen and the latter about six miles north-east of s'Hertogenbosch in the Nijmegen corridor. Not far from Nijmegen the Rhine makes a sharp westward turn on its seaward journey and close to Nijmegen the great river branches into two: the southern of those branches, on which Nijmegen is to be found, is called the Waal while the northern is the Neder Rijn (Lower Rhine) or Lek. Between the two rivers lay an advanced Allied bridgehead in the area where, in September, the ground forces had tried so desperately to reach the men of 1st (British) Airborne Division in the Arnhem bridgehead. This area was the 'Island' and it was here that the Highland Division was now to deploy, to share the defence of that area with 49th (West Riding) Division which had two brigades on the 'Island'; the third brigade of 49th Division was in Nijmegen.[24]

The 'Island' was an unpleasant location but this was due more to the weather than to enemy activity. The Highlanders had expected to come under regular fire from the enemy but this proved not to be the case. In fact, Dutch civilians were going about their everyday lives in villages and farms on the 'Island' and the troops were billeted in buildings, which gave a degree of unaccustomed comfort. Local people were friendly and generous while food was plentiful with much unclaimed livestock, including a considerable amount of poultry, wandering about. There was occasional shelling by the Germans and the odd appearance by a Luftwaffe aircraft but the bridge across the Waal at Nijmegen, although in clear view of the opposition, received only a little attention from the German artillery; but that attention tended to be very accurate. The forward positions were in the villages of Randwijk, Heteren and Opheusden with reserve positions at Zetter, Andelst and Valburg. Now and again the Germans would carry out a mortar bombardment of one of the villages while the battalions

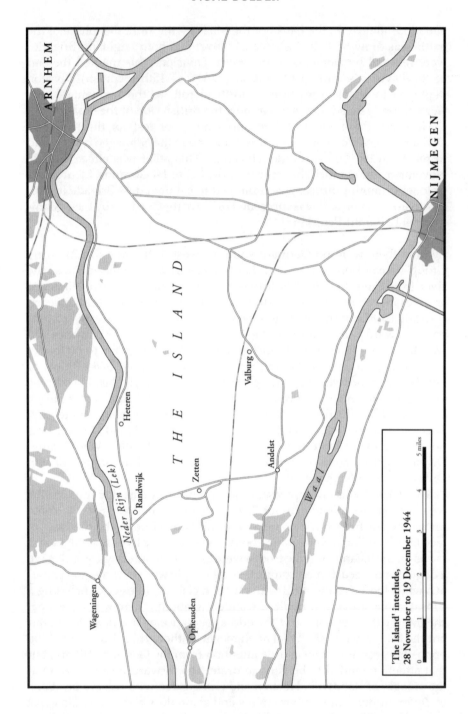

'The Island' interlude,
28 November to 19 December 1944

on the 'Island' were asked infrequently to create tracks in open fields under cover of darkness to make the Germans think that preparations for an offensive were underway. The only other danger came from Schu-mines and the ever-present danger that accompanied patrolling; one Black Watch officer was captured when out on a reconnaissance patrol. And it was in such low country that the Highlanders celebrated the feast-day of Scotland's national saint, the last St Andrew's Day of the war, on 30 November.[25]

But there was another danger that was always in the minds of the Allied command: the Germans might destroy the dykes and flood the 'Island'. To cope with this eventuality an evacuation plan was devised: Operation NOAH.[26] On 2 December, NOAH had to be put into practice. The sound of a loud explosion heralded the bursting of the Lek dyke and the beginning of the inundation of the 'Island'. The West Riding Division pulled back to higher ground on the 'Island' while 152 Brigade sent its transport back across the river by the Nijmegen bridge to be followed by the two Seaforth battalions. Two days later 5th Camerons were also withdrawn from the 'Island' as were 5th Black Watch and 1st Gordons. The waters continued to rise until even more of the 'Island' was flooded and only two Black Watch battalions – 1st and 7th – remained north of the Maas. By now all civilians had been evacuated as most homes had been destroyed in the flooding. However, patrolling activity continued, usually by boat, and led to occasional clashes including one in which a 7th Black Watch patrol took prisoner five members of 13th Fallschirmjäger Regiment. On 19 December 152 Brigade returned to the 'Island' to relieve the two battalions of 154 Brigade.[27]

With the bulk of the Division withdrawn from the 'Island' the bat-talions were located in villages in the Nijmegen–s'Hertogenbosch area where a training programme began as well as preparations for Christmas. Against a relatively peaceful background, there was a return to that prac-tice initiated by General Wimberley of emphasising 'spit and polish'. Guards paraded in kilts whenever possible, battalion flags were flown and uniforms were smartened up. But there was also an opportunity for rest and recreation with 'The Balmorals' presenting shows, football matches being organised and cinema shows laid on. Dutch civilians, who had established an enthusiastic rapport with British troops generally, threw parties for soldiers and virtually adopted battalions, companies, batter-ies and squadrons. Pipers played and Highland dancing displays enter-tained both civilians and soldiers. Field Marshal Montgomery visited the Division – 7th Argylls provided the Guard of Honour – to present decora-tions and medals, while another visitor was the Moderator of the Church of Scotland. The Massed Pipes and Drums of 5th Camerons, The Queen's Own Cameron Highlanders of Canada and The Cameron Highlanders of Ottawa beat Retreat in both Nijmegen and s'Hertogenbosch.[28]

This proved a pleasant interlude amidst the clamour of war but no one believed that they had seen the end of fighting. On 19 December General Rennie took his brigade commanders on a reconnaissance trip to show them the ground over which the Division would be fighting when it returned to action. This was in the most easterly part of the Nijmegen corridor close to Cuyjx where the line was held by Canadians. First Canadian Army's attention was turned to the Reichswald, on the German–Dutch border where, in the first week of January, a new offensive would be launched to clear the land between the Maas and the Rhine of German troops. Canadian troops would attack on the left with XXX Corps on the right, the latter including 51st (Highland) Division, whose attack was to be led by 154 Brigade, followed by 153. The news that the Division was to return to XXX Corps was received well since it had fought in that Corps, now commanded by Lieutenant-General Brian Horrocks, throughout most of the North African and Sicilian campaigns. In the meantime, battalion COs and senior officers would be allowed to return to the UK for home leave over Christmas, a welcome thought. However, on the other side of the hill, Adolf Hitler had other plans.[29]

Three days earlier, German forces had launched a surprise attack on US positions in the Ardennes. Commanded by Field Marshal Gerd von Rundstedt, three German armies of 250,000 men, deployed in twenty-four divisions with 950 tanks, struck the American line, which was held by First Army with 83,000 men in six divisions, supported by 420 tanks. (These were Sixth Panzer Army in the north, Fifth Panzer Army in the centre and Seventh Army in the south.) The German aim was to reach Antwerp and wrest control of the port from the Allies, thereby lengthening the Allied logistical support line, as well as the Allied supply bases at Liège and Brussels.[30] Thus began what became known as the Battle of the Bulge.

The German attack punched through the thin American line and, by the 19th, had thrust as far east as Hotton, Marche and Bastogne. And it was on that day, when Rennie briefed his brigadiers on the forthcoming offensive, that Eisenhower ordered Montgomery to take Ninth (US) Army under his command as well as those elements of First (US) Army holding the line north of the German penetration.[31] All plans for offensive action by 21 Army Group were stopped and XXX Corps was ordered to move south into the Maastricht–Louvain area, to prevent a German crossing of the Maas.[32] It was said that at least two COs of the Highland Division had already boarded planes for home at Brussels when they received orders to return to their units.[33] However, the enemy offensive was stopped and no crossing of the Maas was made. Although enemy troops reached Celles, near Dinant, they were unable to push any farther westward. Weather conditions had helped the Germans, with thick fog shrouding the battleground and keeping Allied tactical aircraft grounded. When the fog lifted on 22 December Allied aircraft were able to lend support to the ground troops and hasten the end of the German offensive.[34]

On moving south the Highland Division came under command of Ninth (US) Army and there followed a period, from 20 to 23 December, 'when they were pushed from pillar to post all over Belgium and elsewhere'.[35] At Maastricht on Christmas Day the Division received orders to move to Liège, which move put an end to any planned festivities.[36] Rennie had sent a special Christmas message to all his troops in which he noted that he had intended to visit all company or equivalent units in the Division to wish them a Happy Christmas and New Year and thank them for all they had done for the Division but that this plan had been thwarted by events.

> I am afraid Christmas will not be as well organised as it might have been, but I hope the food and drink turn up, and that you will all have as happy a Christmas as can be under the circumstances.[37]

Since the order to move was not received until late-morning, most units had some form of Christmas routine underway. The padre of 5th Seaforth had organised a church service which took place at 10.30am, two hours before the scheduled hour for Christmas dinner to be served.

> At 1145 the advance party was ordered to move immediately. They gulped their roast pork, roast potatoes, and Christmas pudding in ten minutes flat, grabbed their bottles of beer, and fled to the trucks. By noon they were on their way again, and at 1500 hours the rest of the Battalion followed. By evening we were in les Cours, south of Liège.[38]

In 5th Black Watch there was a similar experience. An invitation had been accepted to a voluntary church service in a local Calvinist church, which was reminiscent of a Scottish kirk, where the congregation gave the Black Watch soldiers a warm welcome. Then

> At noon the CO, the Adjutant and the RSM started their tour of the Companies to wish everyone a Happy Christmas and they had reached the half-way point when a message was received for the Battalion to cross a Start Point at 1400 hours. As this was quite impossible to comply with, Colonel Bradford insisted that Dinners should go on as arranged and the move would be commenced on completion.[39]

John McGregor noted that food had rarely disappeared faster. By 3.00pm the battalion was ready to move and it travelled through Liège to Plaineveux, which was reached by early evening. Incidentally, in common with the other Black Watch battalions, 5th Black Watch had received a consignment of Christmas puddings from Her Majesty The Queen, Colonel-in-Chief of the Regiment. Queen Elizabeth can hardly have imagined that her gift would have been consumed in such circumstances.[40]

Martin Lindsay of 1st Gordons recalled that 'we put forward the men's dinners from 5 p.m. to 2 p.m., though without any great degree of confidence'.[41] Sure enough, the order to move was received at 12.30pm; the battalion was to be on the road at 2.15pm. Meals were rushed and Lindsay went ahead to allot accommodation in the new area. He describes a scene that summarises the Division's move and the Highlanders' attitude to being moved at such short notice.

> Perhaps Christmas had a little to do with it. Yet few formations have done anything so creditable as that move at short notice on Christmas Day. The sappers said that every one of their drivers was drunk, but never before had they completed a move without a single vehicle breaking down. There were certainly a few comic sights, such as a sergeant of 5-7th Gordons riding in the front of a carrier, wearing neither hat nor coat, in fact scarcely anything except a very happy smile, and frantically waving a small red flag. Liege was said to be one of the most communist towns in Europe. At any rate, this spectacle drove the population almost into a frenzy and largely accounted for the warmth of our welcome.[42]

Following the urgency with which the move was ordered and carried out, the Division's time at Liège proved an anti-climax, although there was much German activity in the form of V1 flying-bombs falling in the area: this averaged about fifty to sixty 'doodlebugs' per day.[43] (Major Joe Wright, a company commander in 5th Black Watch, was killed by a V1 in Antwerp as he was on his way home to become second-in-command of a training battalion.[44]) On the last day of 1944 the Highlanders were assigned to guard crossings along the Maas between Liège and Namur and remained in these positions for a week. Hogmanay was celebrated, however, and most soldiers managed to enjoy the occasion.[45]

On 7 January the Highland Division quit its positions along the Maas and moved forward to Houffalize and thence to a concentration area near the little town of Marche which 'was under occasional shellfire'.[46] Weather conditions exacerbated the normal difficulties of such a move. Ice gripped the road surfaces and tracked vehicles could not be used. Those who tried to use carriers found them sliding off roads and units had to rely on jeeps and 15cwts in four-wheel drive.[47] The front line was not far from Marche, running along high ground beyond the town, and was held by 53rd (Welsh) Division. The Highland, Welsh and 6th Airborne Divisions were the only British formations in the area. An Allied counter-offensive was underway and the Highland Division was to relieve the Welsh Division in the line prior to attacking down the valley of the Ourthe river. The area in which the Division now found itself was

> An extension of that plateau, the Eifel of West Germany, and is made a kind of country of fairyland romance by the beautiful valleys (those of the Maas, the Ourthe, and other rivers) on the bluffs surrounding which stand many castles old in story, and between which torrents foam.[48]

This offensive was to give the Highlanders a new fighting experience. Having fought in North Africa in desert conditions, in the heat of Sicily and the varied weather thus far of north-west Europe, they were now to enter battle in snow and ice on land where the few roads were blocked by drifting snow. An attack down the Ourthe valley presented many problems. The river flows through a deep gorge and the countryside was easy to defend but difficult to attack. Rennie proposed a novel form of advance. Since the main southbound road through the valley was intersected by side roads to east and west, Rennie decided to push a brigade through the open country to the right until it reached one of those side roads onto which it would turn and follow it down to the main road through the valley. Once this brigade was engaging the enemy, a second brigade would advance down the main road to link up with it and both would hold their positions until their transport could reach them. Conditions meant that the artillery, which could travel only by road, would also have to come into action on the roads, but the Gunners had done likewise in Sicily; up to twelve half-tracks of 2nd Derbyshire Yeomanry were to be available to tow anti-tank guns up snow-covered hill roads. Armour support would be provided by 33 Armoured Brigade whose tanks would be fitted with snow studs on their tracks. Sledges, such as those used in the canal attacks, would also be pressed into service to replenish supplies of ammunition for the infantry.[49]

Rennie chose 153 Brigade to lead the advance. In turn, 153 was led by 1st Gordons, whose acting CO, Major Martin Lindsay, had considerable experience of such conditions. The operation began at 8.00am – before daylight – on 9 January when the Gordons moved from the village of Verdenne under artificial moonlight. As the Gordons trudged uphill through a forest that resembled a Scottish hillside, the sun lifted slowly over the eastern horizon to make the searchlights redundant.

> Gradually its rays gained strength until they were reflected on the crystals of frost, so that the forest was soon shot with a million twinkling gems. It was a lovely unforgettable sight, and there were we

going to war: Frank Philip the Battery Commander, and I, walking together up that slope as if it were leading us to a ski hut.[50]

Two hours after setting out the Gordons were on the plateau from where they crossed a valley and climbed the far side. With A Company holding a firm base at la ferme du Chauvaimont, where Captain Albert Brown, the Medical Officer, established an Aid Post, C Company crossed the valley, with their supporting tanks. When C Company was seen to move without opposition into the scrub at the top of the slope, D and B Companies, together with Major Lindsay's HQ, set off in their tracks. But C Company had run into the first opposition in the form of mines in the woods which imposed a two-hour delay. A section of Sappers from 276 Field Company did sterling work in clearing mines which were laid at various points along the Gordons' path.[51] With the advancing companies thus engaged, the enemy began a bombardment of la ferme du Chauvaimont, during which Bert Brown was wounded fatally.[52]

In spite of this shelling, which was also targeted on the track forward from the farm, the Gordons were able to continue their advance and secure their objective, which gave the companies excellent defensive positions and good fields of fire and allowed the supporting tanks to adopt good hull-down positions. In fact the positions were so good that Martin Lindsay 'fervently wished we would be counter-attacked' when a report was received of twelve enemy tanks about a mile away. With the Gordons firmly in position, 5th Black Watch and 5th/7th Gordons passed through to advance to Hodister. A bulldozer cleared the way for 5th/7th Gordons who occupied Hodister in the early evening. There was no opposition.[53]

Little opposition was faced by 154 Brigade, which had been advancing down the 'defile road of the Ourthe' towards Laroche, the road into which is 'cut out of solid rock'.[54] On the morning of the 11th, at 8.00am, a troop of Derbyshire Yeomanry armoured cars led 1st Black Watch as the battalion advanced on foot to the town. The crew of the first armoured car must have thought their days were finished as their car rounded a bend in the road close to Laroche for there the yeomen found themselves looking down the menacing barrel of a Tiger tank's 88mm gun (the Regiment had lost a soldier, Trooper Gallagher, killed the previous day). Fortunately for the Derbyshires, the tank had been abandoned earlier by the enemy; the advance continued. Only when the Black Watch had reached the far side of the town did they meet opposition, from a ridge beyond the built-up area. With the 1st Battalion held up by a group of determined Germans, 7th Black Watch flanked through a wooded hill to the right and advanced towards the village of Hives. There they, too, were held up, this time by a tank that was firing down the sole track into Hives. However, under cover of darkness, 7th Black Watch pushed into the village and engaged the defenders in some confused scrapping that ended with the Jocks in command of the village and with about forty German prisoners. Although mortared heavily and shelled by an SPG, the battalion held its positions until the 18th.[55]

The senior Black Watch battalion had also made progress, launching a successful attack on the ridge beyond Laroche and clearing it of enemy before advancing to Emeuville from where, next morning, contact was made with the Americans moving up from the south. This, the last action for the Division in the Ardennes, cost 1st Black Watch four platoon commanders. Armoured bulldozers had assisted both Black Watch battalions and had also cleared a way through the rubble of Laroche, allowing tanks to move up to support the infantry. 'Weasels', light but very versatile carriers, were also in use and proved invaluable.[56]

Elsewhere the Argylls had been greeted with much more opposition and a Northamptonshire Yeomanry tank supporting the battalion had been knocked out. Opposition included mortars, machine guns and tanks and A Company's commander, Major Peter Samwell MC, was one of the fatal casualties of the advance. But the Argylls fought through to the Lavaux ridge and, next day, 13 January, took their final objective, Beaulieu. They had knocked out a Panther en route, although three of their supporting Shermans had been knocked out. On that same day 5th/7th Gordons advanced from Laroche to seize Roupage and Ortho. There was no opposition in either case.[57]

Also on 13 January, 5th Black Watch and 1st Gordons linked up in Hubermont from where the Gordons advanced on Nisramont. However,

> The country between Hubermont and Nisramont was open and devoid of cover – 'Quite like the desert,' Hastings, my signaller, remarked. I did not like the look of it one bit.[58]

In fact, Nisramont overlooks Hubermont and the Gordons were subjected to some shellfire as they made their way into the village, although a thick haze reduced visibility. But, as the supporting tanks and SPGs began to arrive, the enemy fire fell on them and three Shermans and an SPG were hit with several men killed or wounded. Martin Lindsay recorded that his driver, Private Ackers, 'showed the greatest gallantry pulling wounded up through the turret of one of these tanks while they were still under fire'.[59] Heavy fire continued throughout the day and the Gordons had to make best use of whatever cover was available since snow precluded the use of smoke to obscure the village; the chemicals in artillery smoke are extinguished by snow. When the Gordons finally went in, at 8.00pm, they found that the Germans had used the onset of darkness to evacuate Nisramont.[60]

For 152 Brigade recent days had seen the battalions engaged principally on mopping-up and patrolling. Nonetheless, they had been busy with

5th Camerons crossing the Laroche–Marche road on the 10th to clear the woods towards the Champlon crossroads. The Camerons also took the village of Ronchamps and the battalion Scout Platoon and another platoon from A Company met patrols from Third (US) Army as they pushed up from the south; the war diary notes this as having occurred on the 14th, 'a day of tremendous patrolling activity' and that Captain MacDonald, A Company's commander, was leading the patrol that met the Americans. Genes was captured by 5th Seaforth on 9 January while 2nd Seaforth occupied Halleux before moving to relieve the Camerons at Ronchamps. Two days later, 5th Seaforth advanced on the village of Mierchamps which fell with virtually no fight at all. Of some seventy Germans in the village, only six offered any resistance. Over the next two days, more Germans surrendered and the final toll of prisoners was 180 men. And yet the defenders could have inflicted serious loss on the Seaforth as they advanced across the open valley from Vecmont. German soldiers lacking in morale to such an extent was an unusual enough phenomenon, even at this stage of the war, that the Seaforth historian commented further on the incident and suggested that the Germans had been taken by surprise by the attack and had not spotted the Seaforth as they advanced. Local residents also confirmed the crumbling of German morale as the offensive ground to a standstill and Allied aircraft returned to the skies as the weather cleared.[61]

Over the past weeks, the Highlanders had fought in exceptionally cold conditions with snow beginning to fall on 28 December and continuing to do so at intervals until 2 February. Temperatures dropped, falling at times to 0° F and there were many cases of frostbite while some weapons also froze; a new 'Low Cold Test' oil was introduced for weapons. Conditions were made tolerable only by the efforts of the cooks in providing hot food and by the availability of buildings in which to shelter from the worst of the elements. The Battle of the Bulge had been one of the most trying episodes in the Division's history but its soldiers had once again maintained the reputation of the Highland Division and triumphed not only over the enemy but also over the conditions in which the battle was fought.[62]

On 14 January the Highland Division met the US 84th Division. The Ardennes salient was cut and the Highlanders' immediate task was accomplished. Now the Division could move north again, ready for its part in the next offensive. The Germans had lost heavily in the Ardennes, Hitler's gamble had failed and his armies had lost some 120,000 men and 600 tanks, losses that the German army could not afford.[63] However, the Allies had been caught off guard and had now to regain the initiative and ensure that they did not lose it again. Ahead lay the battle for Germany, the last great battle in the war for Europe.

Notes

1. Salmond, *The History of The 51st Highland Division*, p. 195
2. Ellis, *Victory in the West Vol II*, pp. 158–60
3. Ibid, p. 160n; Salmond, op cit, p. 194
4. Salmond, op cit, p. 194; NA Kew, WO171/529, war diary, HQ 51 (H) Div (G), 1944
5. NA Kew, WO171/529, war diary, HQ 51 (H) Div (G), 1944
6. Salmond, op cit, p. 195
7. NA Kew, WO171/676, war diary, 152 Bde, 1944; WO171/678, war diary, 153 Bde, 1944
8. Hogg & Weeks, *Illus. Encyclopedia of Military Vehicle*, pp. 311–12; Salmond, op cit, p. 195
9. Salmond, op cit, pp. 195–6
10. Ibid; NA Kew, WO171/678, war diary, 153 Bde; WO171/1299, war diary, 1 Gordons, 1944; WO171/1301, war diary, 5/7 Gordons, 1944; WO171/1266, war diary, 5 BW, 1944; McGregor, *The Spirit of Angus*, p. 153
11. Salmond, op cit, p. 196
12. Ibid
13. NA Kew, WO171/676, war diary, 152 Bde, 1944; WO171/1370, war diary, 5 Seaforth, 1944
14. NA Kew, WO171/680, war diary, 154 Bde, 1944; Salmond, op cit, pp. 196–7
15. Salmond, op cit, p. 197
16. NA Kew, WO171/1265, war diary, 1 BW, 1944; WO/171/1267, war diary, 7 BW, 1944; WO171/680, war diary, 154 Bde, 1944; Fergusson, *The Black Watch and the King's Enemies*, p. 288
17. NA Kew, WO171/676, war diary, 152 Bde, 1944; WO171/1271, war diary, 5 Camerons, 1944
18. Ibid
19. Salmond, op cit, pp. 199–200
20. NA Kew, WO171/676, war diary, 152 Bde, 1944; Salmond, op cit, p. 200; Borthwick, *Battalion*, pp. 213–14
21. Salmond, op cit, p. 200
22. NA Kew, WO171/529, war diary, HQ 51 (H) Div (G), 1944
23. Salmond, op cit, p. 200
24. NA Kew, WO171, 529, war diary, HQ 51 (H) Div (G), 1944
25. Ibid; Salmond, op cit, pp. 200–1
26. Salmond, op cit, p. 201
27. Ibid, pp. 201–2; Fergusson, op cit, p. 289
28. Salmond, op cit, p. 202; NA Kew, WO171/1263, war diary, 7 A&SH, 1944; WO171/1271, war diary, 5 Camerons, 1944
29. NA Kew, WO171/529, war diary, HQ 51 (H) Div (G), 1944; Salmond, op cit, pp. 202–4
30. Ellis, op cit, pp. 178–9
31. Ibid, pp. 182–3
32. Ibid, pp. 183–4; Gill and Groves, *Club Route in Europe*, p. 115
33. Salmond, op cit, p. 204
34. Ellis, op cit, p. 186

35. Salmond, op cit, p. 206
36. NA Kew, WO171/529, war diary, HQ 51 (H) Div (G), 1944
37. Ibid
38. Borthwick, op cit, p. 222
39. McGregor, op cit, p. 161
40. Ibid; Fergusson, op cit, p. 290
41. Lindsay, *So Few Got Through*, p. 141
42. Ibid, p. 142
43. Salmond, op cit, p. 206n
44. Fergusson, op cit, p. 290; McGregor, op cit, p. 159. McGregor notes that two officers – the second was Major Charles Monro – had been killed in Antwerp on 27 November, although he describes the missile as a V2.
45. NA Kew, WO171/529, war diary, HQ 51 (H) Div (G), 1944; Salmond, op cit, p. 207
46. Lindsay, op cit, p. 148
47. NA Kew, WO171/5158, war diary, 1 BW, 1945
48. Salmond, op cit, p. 207
49. Ibid; NA Kew, WO1714696, war diary, 2 DY, 1945
50. Lindsay, op cit, p. 152
51. Ibid, p. 153; NA Kew, WO171/5196, war diary, 1 Gordons, 1945; WO171/4250, war diary, CRE, 51 (H) Div, 1945
52. Lindsay, op cit, p. 154; NA Kew, WO171/5196, war diary, 1 Gordons, 1945
53. NA Kew, WO171/4409, war diary, 153 Bde, 1944
54. Salmond, op cit, p. 208
55. NA Kew, WO171/4696, war diary, 2 DY, 1945; WO171/5158, 1 BW, 1945; WO171/5160, 7 BW, 1945; Salmond, op cit, p. 208
56. Fergusson, op cit, p. 292; Salmond, op cit, p. 209; NA Kew, WO171/5158, war diary, 1 BW, 1945
57. NA Kew, WO171/5154, war diary, 7 A & SH, 1945; WO171/5198, war diary, 5/7 Gordons, 1945
58. Lindsay, op cit, p. 156
59. Ibid, p. 157
60. Ibid; NA Kew, WO171/5196, war diary, 1 Gordons, 1945
61. NA Kew, W171/4406, war diary, 152 Bde, 1945; WO171/5164, war diary, 5 Camerons, 1945; WO171/5268, war diary, 5 Seaforth, 1945.
62. NA Kew, WO171/4245, war diary, HQ 51 (H) Div (G), 1945; Ellis, op cit, pp. 191–7
63. Salmond, op cit, p. 212; NA Kew, WO171/4245, war diary, HQ 51 (H) Div (G), 1945; Ellis, op cit, p. 185. Ellis notes the German manpower losses as being 81,834 casualties, including 12,652 dead, according to a contemporary German estimate, or 92,234 casualties according to another estimate. Allied forces took over 50,000 prisoners.

CHAPTER XIII

Into Germany

With the Ardennes offensive concluded, Allied planners returned to the operations projected before Hitler's attack had taken them off guard. For 21 Army Group those plans had centred on clearing the area between the Maas and Rhine rivers and, to this task, thoughts now turned. Operation VERITABLE was the codename assigned to the outworking of those plans, the preparation for the stepping-off platform for the invasion of the heart of Hitler's Third Reich.[1]

VERITABLE was to include British, Canadian and American forces in an assault that was intended to crumble German strength so much that they would 'not be able to put up much of a show later on the east bank of the Rhine'.[2] First Canadian and elements of Second British Armies would push forward from the Nijmegen bridgehead to create such pressure on the enemy defences that the Germans would be forced to pull in reserves to reinforce their positions. The American Ninth Army, temporarily part of 21 Army Group, would then cross the Maas south of the British/Canadian assault to push north and link up with the latter. Planning for the operation had to take account of two possible sets of weather conditions: frost and snow or thaw, with consequent mud and flooding. Neither would make for ease of operations for the attackers. Since both major rivers had overflowed their banks during the December rains, the land between was very wet and almost swampy. While freezing conditions might make the ground more solid, it would not provide much alleviation for the infantry who would have to try to dig into frozen ground.[3]

Of course, there were factors other than the weather. Facing the Canadians were three lines of defences, the first over a mile in depth and consisting of an anti-tank ditch backed up by fortified farms and villages. Once through this line the attackers would have to cross about two miles of fairly open country before meeting the next line, which was the northern stretch of the Siegfried Line. This ran southward from a point on the Nijmegen–Cleve road to the town of Goch, which had been turned into a strongly-fortified defensive position. En route the line passed through the Reichswald (State Forest), the closely-planted trees of which would provide another obstacle for the attackers and would make infantry even more vulnerable to shell and mortar fire from the defenders. In this sector the Siegfried line included a forward trench system, with tactically-located strongpoints, as well as a secondary defensive line from Cleve to Goch. As if these two lines were not sufficient, the attackers would then have to crack a third line, six miles farther to the east. This line had been dubbed the Hochwald 'lay-back' by Montgomery.[4]

Since the Canadian front was narrow the attack would have to be launched on a corps front and Brian Horrocks' XXX Corps was selected to lead, widening their front as they advanced so that II Canadian Corps could then come in on the left flank to make a two-corps front. D-Day for XXX Corps' attack was to be 8 February with H-Hour at 10.30am.[5] Two armoured divisions, three armoured brigades and six infantry divisions were to make the assault, supported by 'Funnies' of 79th Armoured Division, including Flails and Crocodile flamethrowers, and by some 1,000 artillery pieces as well as the Allied tactical air forces. The initial move would include five infantry divisions: 3rd Canadian was to be on the left flank and the Highland Division on the right; in between, from right to left, would be 53rd (Welsh), 15th (Scottish) and 2nd Canadian Divisions.[6]

The wisdom of being prepared for conditions of either soggy or hard-frozen ground was made clear when the frost that gripped the land gave way to a thaw about a week before D-Day which led to the creation of soft, almost boggy, terrain.[7] Within the Highland Division, General Rennie had decided to attack on a single-brigade front, the Division's frontage precluding any other plan. The chosen brigade was James Oliver's 154, reinforced to four-battalion strength for the occasion by 5th/7th Gordons. Final preparations included study of large-scale maps and a sand-table model of the ground over which the brigade would advance. All were ready when, at 5.00am on the 8th, Allied artillery opened up on the enemy positions, beginning a bombardment the like of which the Highlanders had not experienced since El Alamein. The guns roared for over three hours before 7th Black Watch left their assembly area for the start-line, from which the battalion's advance began at 10.46am, the leading companies following close behind the curtain of shells. Since a heavily wooded ridge lay between 154 Brigade's start-line and the enemy positions, the Black Watch were initially out of the enemy line of sight.[8]

The village of Breedeweg, the first objective, fell without real difficulty to A Company but D Company lost three officers to snipers as they advanced. Among the dead was Major Kenneth Lowe MC, who had served in North Africa, where he had twice been wounded severely, but rejoined the battalion in Sicily and had been with it ever since.[9] The snipers who had accounted for Lowe and his comrades were themselves accounted for by the tanks supporting 154 Brigade before 5th/7th Gordons passed through 7th Black Watch to continue the advance.[10] Minutes before 11.00am the senior Black Watch battalion moved off from their start-line for their objective, which lay just inside the Reichswald. By 1.20pm the Black Watch were able to report 'Positions taken', a report that brought a special note of congratulations from Horrocks to 1st Black Watch for being the first British troops to set foot on German soil. Commanding the battalion that day was Major Peter Taylor who had begun the war as Private Taylor of 6th Black Watch.[11]

Thus far all had gone well with the Division's part in VERITABLE, although congestion had developed on the track to the front. While the anti-tank ditch had presented no real difficulties for the infantry it had to be bridged for vehicles and there was some confusion while this was carried out. Nonetheless, bridging was completed in time for 5th/7th Gordons to push into the edge of the forest as darkness began to fall. The Gordons met stiff opposition in the forest where there was fierce fighting. However, C Company, advancing towards a cross-roads among the trees, came on a German unit handing over to its relief. The Gordons did not fail to take advantage of the opportunity thus offered and attacked the surprised enemy. No relief took place and the Gordons netted 148 prisoners. In the meantime, 7th Argylls had passed through 1st Black Watch to continue the battle among the trees.[12]

Brigadier James Cassels' 152 Brigade was scheduled to follow 154, and 5th Camerons followed through 5th/7th Gordons to fight their way to their initial objective in the forest. The Camerons met stout opposition but continued to make steady progress, in spite of losses, that saw them on their objective by mid-afternoon. Next morning, at 7.00am, 5th Seaforth joined the battle, passing through Breedeweg and then, in the afternoon, pushing into the forest some 800 yards north of the Camerons. The Seaforth advance was met by a determined German counter-attack which the Jocks fought off at close quarters before bayonet-charging the enemy, forcing them back. Eventually the Seaforth dug in some 1,000 yards deeper into the forest than any other unit of the Division. On 5th Seaforth's flank, 2nd Seaforth had advanced through 5th Camerons before being held up by the garrison of a German strongpoint. The battalion took cover and waited for the dawn of 10 February when Crocodile flame-throwers arrived to assist overrunning the enemy positions.[13] At about 4.30pm some thirty-five soldiers of 7th Parachute Regiment were captured by 2nd Seaforth. As these men were being marched back to captivity they refused to walk along a path leading to a cross-roads but ran instead. This alerted their captors to the presence of a 'booby trap consisting of a large bomb … at the cross-roads 826494'; the device was removed by Sappers.[14]

The Division's other brigade, 153, under temporary command of Lieutenant-Colonel Grant-Peterkin of 1st Gordons (the brigade

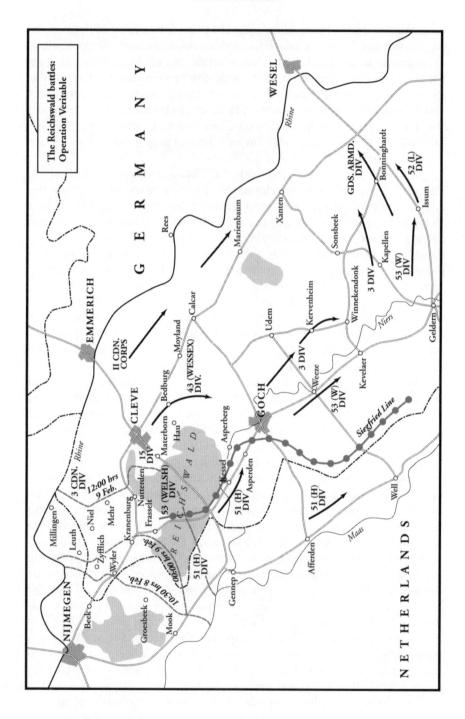

The Reichswald battles:
Operation Veritable

commander, Brigadier Roddy Sinclair, was in hospital), had been assigned the triple tasks of forming a firm base on the elevated ground in the south-west corner of the forest, dislodging Germans from their positions on a wooded plateau, the Kieksberg woods, west of that point, and cutting the Mook–Gennep road. Since 153 Brigade was to use the same axis of advance as 154 Brigade, it was not to leave its start-line until the latter had seized its first objectives.[15] It will be remembered that 153 Brigade was reduced to two battalions, having 'lent' 5th/7th Gordons to 154 Brigade. These were 5th Black Watch, under Major George Dunn, and 1st Gordons, under Major Martin Lindsay, and it fell to the Black Watch to lead off, at 4.00pm on the 8th; the Gordons moved off at 5.20pm. The Black Watch took their objectives in the forest and, on the morning of the 9th, wheeled right to attack southwards. Under cover of thick smoke several defended houses were taken and the battalion was soon making ready for an attack on Gennep, on the Niers river, to the east of the Maas.[16] Recce'ing forward for the Division, No. 2 Troop, C Squadron of the Derbyshire Yeomanry had driven into an ambush in Zelderheide; most were killed except the troop leader, Lieutenant Partridge, who was wounded, and Sergeant Brown, who managed to bale out with two other soldiers. Although Partridge was captured, the others reached cover and, under cover of darkness, returned to their own lines. Partridge was subsequently rescued when Black Watch soldiers captured the German medical station in which he was being treated.[17]

The tanks supporting 1st Gordons bogged down in the mud leaving the infantry to move forward alone, although one vehicle did manage to reach the battalion; this was a Weasel carrying rations – 500 tins of self-heating soup.[18] That evening the Gordons occupied their night positions and on the morrow mopped up what German resistance remained in St Martensberg and Grafwegen, as well as the country between those vil-lages and a valley to the south. The valley proved the most difficult obsta-cle but tanks had at last reached the Gordons and with their support the advance continued. A well-fortified defensive system lay on the valley's far side but this was subjected to a heavy artillery stonk, after which C Company took the positions and went on to seize the nearby village of Del Hel. Although 5th Black Watch had cut the road from Mook to Gennep, A Company 1st Gordons were held up by a strongpoint that denied XXX Corps the use of the road as an artery of advance.[19]

Since it was vital that the road be cleared to allow XXX Corps to con-tinue, Major Martin Lindsay took command of his leading company and led them against the strongpoint.

Just as we got there we were ambushed. There was a burst of Schmeisser in front, and the sharp explosions of one or two German grenades. Immediately five or six Germans came to life in trenches on either side of the path. They must have been asleep, for one-third of us had already passed them. There was an instantaneous crash of automatic fire from the column and every one of them fell, riddled with bullets. It was all over in about two seconds, and our only casualty was Macpherson, slightly wounded in the leg. Actually it was a most efficient performance on our part, but all I thought at the time was: 'God, how bloody! Ambushed before we've even started, this is going to be the bloodiest show that's ever been.'[20]

The advance continued and the Gordons successfully assaulted the German strongpoint, taking seventy-one prisoners. It was soon clear that there were no more enemy troops; the Gordons had cleared the road. For his role in this action Martin Lindsay received the DSO.[21]

By the morning of 12 February most of the defenders of Gennep were dead, captured or had withdrawn and 5th/7th Gordons had crossed the river. Both Gordon battalions took the ridge overlooking the town and dug in ready to meet the expected counter-attack. This came next day when German infantry, with fire support from three SPGs, attacked. However, the enemy advance was stopped by accurate mortar fire; the Germans later withdrew. Strangely, this was the first counter-attack launched on 1st Gordons since Escoville in June 1944.[22]

Thus far the attack on the Reichswald had been successful with the attackers making good and steady progress despite the lack of roads and the boggy ground. To the Highlanders' right, 15th (Scottish) Division was advancing on Kranenburg while, on the other flank, 53rd (Welsh) Division was also well forward.[23] Beyond the Reichswald the country changes as land that is more open slopes down to a plain intersected by several tributaries of the Maas. For the Highland Division, the most important of these rivers were the Niers and Kendel. Across the Niers lay Kessel, a town that had been turned into a strongpoint by the Germans with the flooded river providing an anti-tank ditch as good as, if not better than, any engineers could have created. Another major impediment to XXX Corps' advance was provided by the little town of Hekkens, through which the Siegfried Line ran; at Hekkens the line was defended by reinforced concrete fortifications. Since Hekkens occupied a strategic location on the junction of the Gennep–Cleve and Kessel–Goch roads at the southern border of the Reichswald, it was vital that the village should be taken. This objective had been assigned to 152 Brigade, which 'had come up against a very difficult obstacle, the southern portion of the German anti-tank ditch, which was lined by a determined enemy armed with all sorts of automatic weapons'.[24]

Some fifty yards from the German lines 5th Seaforth had been forced to take cover at the roadside where they remained throughout a night and a day until, supported by fire from tanks, they could withdraw into the forest. On their right flank, 2nd Seaforth also withdrew into the forest. In their advance 5th Camerons had met stout resistance and the battalion had launched several bayonet charges on the enemy. One NCO, Sergeant McClew, took command of his platoon when his platoon commander was wounded, and led its remnants across a hundred yards of open ground to attack five machine-gun positions. All the positions were over-run, some twenty Germans were killed, and McClew was awarded the DCM. Elsewhere, Lieutenant J R le Mesurier, a Canloan officer with the Camerons, made another cold-steel charge on a German machine-gun post. In this case, however, the cold steel was not a bayonet but a shovel. (A Canadian Loan officer; this was a scheme whereby Canadian officers could be attached to British units, usually those with affiliations to Canadian regiments. Most Canloan officers served in north-west Europe although there were also some in Italy.) Having used all his ammunition, le Mesurier grabbed the shovel, charged the machine-gun post and knocked out what must have been a very surprised gun team.[25]

When the Camerons reached their final objective there occurred an incident that illustrates the nature of what is often called the fog of war. A Cameron corporal went back to the cooks' lorry to collect breakfasts for his section and was returning to his platoon position with full mess-tins when, in the dim light, he saw three men approaching, each carrying a mess-tin and obviously eager for breakfast. They were, he assumed, members of another section of his platoon. Then he realised that the trio were wearing German uniforms and helmets. The Cameron corporal reacted much faster than the Germans and was able to make all three prisoners. Although the Germans had a hearty breakfast, it was not in the circumstances they had expected.[26]

With 152 Brigade stalled before Hekkens, General Rennie ordered 154 Brigade to seize the village. Rennie also arranged for all XXX Corps' artillery to bombard Hekkens. Brigadier Oliver decided on a daylight assault, as night fighting in the Reichswald amidst standing and fallen trees, with the latter blocking the paths, was not a sensible option, and so H-Hour was set for 3.30pm on 11 February. This would leave one and a half hours of daylight and thus the leading battalions, 1st and 7th Black Watch, left the start-line, a mile and a quarter north-east of Hekkens, at that time. By 7 o'clock that evening both Black Watch battalions had taken the village with over 300 prisoners and virtually no casualties in either unit. The attack had been a master class in cooperation between Gunners and infantry with the Jocks following close behind the bombardment and falling on the defenders of Hekkens before they realised what was happening. Bernard Fergusson noted that the 'devastating fire' was provided by fourteen field regiments, four medium regiments, four heavy batteries and the brigade mortars. Following the capture of Hekkens, Major Peter Taylor was appointed to command the Divisional Battle School while Colonel John Hopwood, sometimes known as 'The Colonel-General', returned to command 1st Black Watch.[27]

The third Black Watch battalion, 5th under Major George Dunn, had seized the village of Gennep on the third day of VERITABLE, having ferried his men across the Niers in assault boats. Gennep was taken without any real difficulty but, beyond the village, there was considerable heavy fighting for both 5th Black Watch and 1st Gordons, who had also crossed the river. It was at this stage that Major Alex Brodie, 'the most perforated officer in the Regiment', was seen walking down the street carrying an unfurled umbrella.[28] Asked why he was doing so, Brodie replied that it was raining. It was, but no one else had noticed, being too concerned about the showers of bullets that also swept the area. And it was here that Major Donald Beales, commanding his battalion's leading company, died. Beales had established his company HQ in a large house and had sent his runner, Private Gipsy Smith, on an errand. As Smith made off down the road he called back to Beales 'I'll see you in twenty minutes'. No sooner had Smith gone than Beales was killed. Twenty minutes later, Smith was also killed.[29] The two deaths, and the significance of Smith's last words, were much remarked upon by the Jocks, many of whom must have asked if Smith was fey.

With Hekkens in British hands, the next task facing the Division was the crossing of the Niers by the remaining battalions. Although 153 and 154 Brigades had linked up and the main road was clear, that road was still under direct observation from high ground across the Niers, making the capture of that high ground essential. Normally, the Niers was only about ninety feet wide but the floods after the thaw had increased its width to some 200 feet while the approaches were waterlogged. The task of crossing the river and establishing a bridgehead that included Kessel village, on the main road to Goch, the Division's final objective had now to be undertaken. Goch was also the objective of 43rd (Wessex) Division, which was advancing towards the town via Cleve; the Highlanders were to approach Goch from the west.[30]

Early on 12 February 7th Argylls took up positions in the woods where the Reichswald slopes down to the Niers, north-east of Kessel. The crossing was to be made in Buffaloes by the two Black Watch battalions with the Argylls following them across the river; this was the first occasion on which 154 Brigade had used Buffaloes. On the night of 13–14 February the Black Watch crossed the Niers with the 7th Battalion moving first and crossing at a loop in the river south-west of the Hekkens crossroads. This operation was completed without difficulty and the battalion then moved to take the villages of Kapelle and Villers, the Buffaloes re-crossing the river to lift the 7th Battalion. While Kapelle presented little resistance – fifty prisoners were taken – Villers was somewhat more difficult with a strongpoint, based on a house in the middle of the village, offering considerable opposition to the Jocks. However, this opposition was soon overcome and a hundred prisoners were taken, although five Highlanders were killed.[31]

It was a different story with 1st Black Watch. The Buffaloes had come under heavy enemy shellfire and only three were serviceable when it was time to cross. Nonetheless, the battalion made its crossing and passed through the bridgehead established by the 7th Battalion. Then came more trouble as the Black Watch met resistance from the defenders of isolated buildings. One of these buildings was taken in an attack led by the Gunner FOO, Captain Hogg, but the battalion had a pressing problem with its ammunition supply. The loss of so many Buffaloes had restricted the replenishment of ammunition and thus Germans were able to infiltrate the company positions. Colonel Hopwood was forced to draw in his perimeter although some help did arrive in the form of a company of Camerons with anti-tank guns while the RAF did sterling work in strafing the German positions.[32]

> For three days the two battalions stayed where they were, despite heavy shelling; the cellar which John Hopwood was using as a command post had eighteen direct hits during that time. The Niers was so flooded that for a time it baffled every effort of the sappers to bridge it, and it was not until the following day that the tanks were able to get across.[33]

The Argylls crossed into the Black Watch bridgehead on St Valentine's Day and moved on Kessel, capturing the village with seventy prisoners that night. On the 15th they consolidated their positions in Kessel, ready to meet an enemy counter-attack. The Germans did not come but British tanks did with Churchills passing through 7th Argylls on the 16th, advancing some 300 yards and overrunning a German defensive line, thereby adding about another seventy prisoners to the Argylls' total.[34]

It was on the same day that tanks reached 1st Black Watch's positions, to the great relief of the infantrymen. These were Churchill Crocodiles of 1st Fife and Forfar Yeomanry, now serving in 31 Armoured Brigade of 79th Armoured Division (this had been 31 Tank Brigade until 2 February although it had been serving as part of 79th Armoured Division since 4 September 1944).[35] Not only did the Yeomanry also hail from the Highlands, but the squadron leader who arrived at 1st Black Watch's positions was Major Harry Walker, whose uncle, also Harry Walker, had commanded 4th Black Watch during the Great War and had been killed commanding that battalion.[36] Together the Fife and Forfar and 1st Black Watch were to attack southward from the latter's positions towards Hassum railway station. As the Black Watch historian noted this attack 'went in with all the bite that comes from a couple of days' uncomfortable sitting still'.[37] It was a complete success, the railway was taken as well as a hundred prisoners, many of whom were probably inspired to surrender by the presence of the flame-throwing Crocodiles. There were casualties among the attackers but, as on previous occasions, the Germans then laid down a heavy artillery bombardment on their previous positions, during which the Black Watch suffered some twenty dead or wounded; it had not been possible to dig in quickly enough to avoid the worst of the shelling. Included in the dead was a remarkable officer who had only rejoined the battalion thirty-six hours earlier. This was Major Donald Ian Molteno who had been wounded badly in North Africa where he had suffered severe head injuries and lost an eye. He ought not to have returned to active service and, indeed, his requests to do so were opposed strenuously, but Ian Molteno at last had his way, only to die less than two days after rejoining his comrades.[38]

It was now the turn of 152 Brigade to take the van of the advance. Following their difficult advance, during which they had suffered many casualties, the two Seaforth battalions had been out of action for four days whilst the Camerons, less one company, were holding Hekkens. The other Cameron company had been sent to support the Black Watch bridgehead and it would not now be called upon to join 152 Brigade's advance. This was to be made down the main road to Goch; the brigade was to clear four villages en route: 2nd Seaforth were to take Grafenthal, 5th Seaforth Hervost and Asperden and 5th Camerons Asper; the villages lay roughly in a triangle. Once again there would be support from the Crocodiles of the Fife and Forfar Yeomanry.[39]

At 7.00pm on 16 February 2nd Seaforth left Kessel for Grafenthal, reaching the fork in the road that leads to the village about ninety minutes later. Thirty minutes before midnight they were on their final objective, a large hospital building in Grafenthal. Now the 5th Battalion passed the road fork and made for Asperden, which had been attacked by rocket-firing Typhoons of the RAF that afternoon and then subjected to artillery bombardment. As the Seaforth approached the village it was also struck by a new Allied weapon. This was a multi-barrelled rocket launcher mounted on a carrier, with each tube firing a canister containing ten pounds of explosives. Ten carriers were concentrated to fire their weaponry with the result that a 'Mattress' of some 300 rounds fell on the target. With artificial moonlight over the area, Asperden was subjected to three such 'Mattresses' and, by midnight, the village was in Seaforth hands. Needless to say, the Germans reacted by shelling Asperden. By now the Camerons had moved through 2nd Seaforth at Grafenthal and made for Hervost. In spite of losses from mines, the Camerons took Hervost. The following day the battalion carried out mopping-up operations against some German pillboxes in the area. One of these proved to be a particularly tough objective as a number of SPGs helped defend it. A smokescreen was laid down and the area around the pillbox was shelled before the Camerons moved in. During this attack, members of the Pioneer Platoon climbed on to the roof of the pillbox and dropped several No. 36 grenades down the ventilation shafts. The achievements of 152 Brigade in this advance received the personal congratulations of General Horrocks.[40]

Goch now beckoned and 153 Brigade was to take up the running. (Both 43rd (Wessex) and 53rd (Welsh) Divisions were also converging on Goch.) The town, whose peacetime population was about 10,000, was fortified strongly with the Niers on one side and the other three covered by an anti-tank ditch as well as many strongpoints; about a mile to the north an escarpment overlooked the town.[41] Orders to attack Goch were issued to 153 Brigade on the 18th. With 5th Black Watch as the vanguard, 153 Brigade was to attack early on the 19th. The Black Watch were to do their best to break into the town and, having done so, clear that part of Goch south of the river; this included the main square. Following through the Black Watch, 5th/7th Gordons would then clear the area from the square to the railway while 1st Gordons would deal with the main road leading south-west and clear a number of cross-roads as well as several prominent buildings.[42] The latter included a school and a factory. Rennie had also ordered 152 Brigade to cross the anti-tank ditch and this was accomplished by 2nd Seaforth on the 18th.[43] An ARK bridge was in place by midnight, over which 5th Black Watch entered Goch. Amazingly, 'they found the defenders mostly peacefully asleep in cellars' but 5th/7th Gordons were not so fortunate and found their Germans wide awake and ready for them.[44]

The street fighting that followed lasted throughout that day and the following night. With the streets covered in rubble it was impossible for tanks to advance until tracks had been cleared through the debris. In the struggle in the streets and buildings the Gordons had a difficult task and Martin Lindsay decided to clear the main street running south from the square. A Company set to on this task and within minutes the company commander, Major Arthur Thomson, was killed, shot through the head by a sniper as he stood in a doorway with Bill Kyle, his second-in-command. Arthur Thomson, a London Scottish officer – and a Londoner of Scots extraction – had joined the battalion only three days earlier and was in his first action. Captain Kyle took over but it soon became clear that it would be very difficult to make progress down the main street. Lindsay therefore decided to recast his plans. A troop of tanks that was trying to find an alternative route to support the infantry came under fire and the leading vehicle was hit by a *panzerfaust* round that knocked out the tank.[45]

The new plan called for an attack through a housing estate to the west which was to be carried out by B and C Companies, both of which were close to the road junction that was to be their start-line. Mounting the attack was delayed by ninety minutes to permit reconnaissance and allow a troop of gun tanks and one of Crocodiles to provide support. A smoke screen was also to be laid to defilade the attackers' right flank. Such careful planning deserved to be rewarded by success and this was the case; C Company occupied the housing estate, allowing B to pass through to the school and factory at the main road junctions. C Company then took the lead again to advance to the buildings beyond. All the while the tanks and Crocodiles gave unstinting support – a Crocodile was blown up on a mine at the road junction in B Company's objective – and the smoke proved a valuable protector of the flank. However, just after B Company left the housing estate and while C Company were still there, the Germans made 'a very heavy mortar stonk' on the area. Company Sergeant Major Morrice considered this the heaviest single concentration of mortar fire the battalion had experienced since El Alamein.[46]

The mortaring caused few casualties and this was also the case with the subsequent shelling. On this and the next day the Gordons endured considerable mortaring and shelling but were able to sit it out in the cellars of the houses. Martin Lindsay considered that the shelling was 'certainly the heaviest … the battalion had had since D-Day' and that only 'the excellent cellars, which seemed to be a feature of all those German houses, saved us from having very heavy casualties'.[47] There is more than a little irony in the quality of German workmanship saving British troops from the wrath of German gunners and mortarmen.

While the action in the housing estate was underway, Brigadier Sinclair resumed command of the brigade and told Major Lindsay that he wanted 1st Gordons to deploy a company to the crossroads south-west of the housing estate and another to Thomashof, a large farm with several outbuildings. Lindsay agreed that he would effect this deployment before first light next day as the heavy mortaring made it essential to cross the open ground under cover of darkness. D Company, under Major Casey Petrie, was assigned to the crossroads; the Derbyshire Yeomanry had reconnoitred almost as far as there that afternoon, reporting that they believed the area to be clear. For the advance to Thomashof, Lindsay decided to use A Company but to command it himself as Bill Kyle was 'not very experienced' and the only other officer in the company was in his first action.[48]

Nothing was known about Thomashof except what I could learn from the air-photos. From these I saw that our objective consisted of one very large building with five biggish outhouses round it. In addition there were two smaller houses detached from and about a hundred yards our side of the main group. Several enemy trenches could be seen.[49]

Major Lindsay's plan was simple: following an overnight bombardment of Thomashof by medium artillery, with sixteen guns each firing eighty rounds, A Company would move off at 4.45am. The start-line would be secured by B Company and the Intelligence Officer would lay out white tape for the first hundred yards of the advance, after which the company would cross about 1,100 yards of open country on a compass bearing. H-Hour was later delayed by an hour so that the attackers might cross the open ground in darkness but have the benefit of the first light of day for the actual assault.[50]

A Company crossed the open ground and engaged the enemy in the buildings. There was sporadic fighting and it became clear that more men would be needed to clear all the buildings. Major Lindsay then returned to bring up B Company but it took about two hours to get some tanks to support the company in its attack. Just as B Company was about to move off some men from A Company returned with the unwelcome news that the company had been overwhelmed and that, other than themselves, there were no survivors; Captain Kyle and some fifty men had been made prisoners. However, B Company's attack met with success, although they had a tough battle and lost ten men killed. Only one Crocodile had been able to cross the open ground before the objective. Some eighty prisoners were taken and the company commander, George Morrison, was subsequently awarded the DSO. With Thomashof in Gordon hands, 5th Black Watch passed through to attack positions about 400 yards to the east. Next day the Black Watch mopped up some other positions near Thomashof.[51]

With 153 Brigade's strength much reduced due to the fighting for Goch, 7th Black Watch was placed under its command and attacked through 1st Gordons on 20 February.[52] Enemy resistance was strong and determined with infantry and SPGs in a large barrack building. This was dealt with by a troop of Crocodiles from the Fife and Forfar Yeomanry who 'brewed up the barracks most efficiently'. On the 21st 7th Argylls moved into positions on the outskirts of Goch and 1st Black Watch relieved 5th Black Watch south of the town; 7th Black Watch returned to 154 Brigade and 53rd (Welsh) Division passed through the latter en route to attack Weeze.[53]

German resistance continued with constant shelling and mortaring of the Highlanders' positions. This steady pounding not only frayed nerves but also caused many casualties. In 1st Gordons Lieutenant Ian Edgar, a 21-year-old Glaswegian, and three men of his platoon HQ were killed by a shell that struck a cellar window ledge – two others were wounded – while Sergeant Archibald Coutts, 39 and from Aberdeenshire, who had been with the Carrier Platoon since El Alamein, was killed while standing in a doorway that same day.[54] In the fighting since VERITABLE began, this battalion alone had lost nearly half its fighting strength with 203 officers and men killed, wounded or missing.[55] The battles had taken place in horrific conditions with weather too bad for some days to allow close support from aircraft

> except for one brief interlude when the Cleve Forest, and defended localities along the Niers, were bombed and 'winkled' by Typhoons and Spitfires, a marked feature of the operations being the effective and pre-arranged anti-flak work of the Royal Artillery.[56]

However, on 14 February, a day with clear blue skies, Allied strategic and tactical aircraft flew some 9,000 sorties against enemy targets along or behind the battle line and even deeper into Germany. This was an effort unmatched since the early days in Normandy. Ground conditions continued to militate against deployment of the armoured divisions since the ground was heavily waterlogged and even roads were sometimes deep in water. On the 15th Lieutenant-General Simonds was ordered to take over the left of XXX Corps' sector with his II Canadian Corps, operating on the axis Cleve–Üdem, while XXX Corps concentrated on a Goch–Weeze–Kevelaer line. By the 22nd Allied casualties in VERITABLE totalled over 6,000. Of these some 80 per cent were British. Over 11,000 German prisoners had been taken and it was believed that total German losses were about 20,000.[57]

The Highland Division's role in VERITABLE was not yet over although a follow-up operation, codenamed BLOCKBUSTER, was about to get underway. II Canadian Corps was to clear what the Germans called the Schlieffen Position, the Hochwald-Balbergerwald, with three Canadian divisions and two British on loan from XXX Corps. (The Canadian divisions were 2nd and 3rd Infantry and 4th Armoured while the two from XXX Corps were 11th Armoured and 43rd (Wessex).) The latter corps would be responsible for the southern half of the front, striking eastwards, on the Canadian right, and southwards to clear the ground along the Maas and allow Ninth US Army to attack north-eastwards to the Rhine above Wesel; this was Operation GRENADE. Before BLOCKBUSTER began – D-Day was 26 February – the Highland Division was given the task of clearing an area south-west of Goch to the line of the lateral road beyond the Kendel river, a tributary of the Niers.[58]

The opening phase of 51st (Highland) Division's task was undertaken by 152 Brigade which moved on and captured the village of Boeckelt. This advance was led by 5th Camerons who attacked Boeckelt on the 26th and took over 200 prisoners for one casualty, a soldier injured on a Schu-mine; the German garrison was eager to surrender. On the previous night Guards Armoured Division had put a bridge across the Kendel south of Boeckelt and over this crossed 2nd Seaforth to capture farmhouses at Terpoten and Blumenthalsop, which lay in a loop of the river. In contrast to the Camerons' attack, this met determined opposition from Germans who defied all efforts to evict them. C Company of 5th Seaforth then

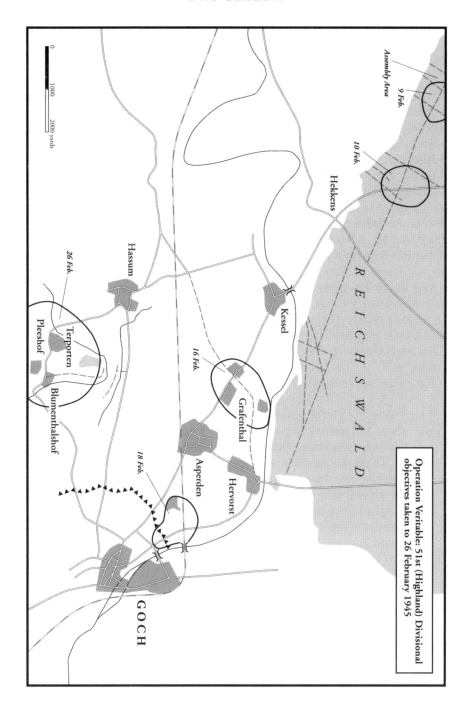

Operation Veritable: 51st (Highland) Divisional
objectives taken to 26 February 1945

moved forward and while artillery plastered Terpoten farm, the Seaforth moved past it and occupied Jenkenhof farm which had been unoccupied. This caused the Germans at Terpoten to see the situation in a different light and when, in the morning, they realised that the Jocks were also behind them they surrendered quickly. The defenders of Blumenthalhof followed suit. Thus 5th Seaforth, who had been waiting to advance on Siebengewald, the brigade's final objective, were able to move forward to their objective with no opposition at all. Next evening, the 27th, 156 Brigade of 52nd (Lowland) Division relieved the Seaforth and Cameron Brigade which left for Nijmegen on 28 February.[59]

On the 25th the Argylls of 154 Brigade crossed the Kendel to the west of 152 Brigade to capture Hulm. Shortly after midnight 1st Black Watch also made the crossing and captured Winkel before linking up with their 5th Battalion in Robbenhof. Next night 7th Black Watch waded the river to attack Boyenhof, fighting a brief skirmish with some Germans on the riverbank before advancing on and taking the village. Sadly, two members of 154 Brigade HQ, Lieutenant Duncan Colquhoun, Argylls, and Sergeant Hewan, Corps of Military Police (which became the Corps of Royal Military Police after the war as a tribute to its service), were killed by mortarfire after completing their task. Following relief by 52nd (Lowland) Division, 154 Brigade withdrew to Goch.[60]

The end of the Division's part in VERITABLE brought a slew of congratulatory messages including one from Horrocks:

I have seen the 51st Highland Division fight many battles since I first met them just before ALAMEIN. But I am certain that the Division has never fought better than in the recent offensive into Germany. You breached the enemy's defences in the initial attack, fought your way through the southern part of the Reichswald, overcame in succession several strong-points of the Siegfried Line such as Hekkens, etc, and then finally cleared the southern half of Goch – a key centre in the German defences. You have accomplished everything that you have been asked to do in spite of the number of additional German reserves that have been thrown in on your front. No Division has ever been asked to do more and no Division has ever accomplished more. Well done, the Highland Division.[61]

In passing this message to the units of the Division, General Rennie added his own thanks and congratulations, noting that the operations culminating in the capture of Goch would go down as one of the finest achievements of the Fifty-First. He added:

Although the brunt of the fighting has necessarily been borne by the infantry, who were magnificent, success was only made possible by the great co-operation of all the arms and by the determined effort of every single man in the Division to give of his best. I thank every one of you for what you have done towards the destruction of the German Army. There may be tough times ahead but the end is at last clearly in sight. Good luck to you all.[62]

In addition to the units of the Highland Division, these messages were also passed on to 107th Regiment RAC, The Scottish Horse, A Squadron 1st Fife and Forfar Yeomanry, D Squadron 1st Lothians and Border Horse and 222 Assault Squadron Royal Engineers, all of whom formed part of the Divisional Group during Operation VERITABLE.[63] Further words of congratulations came from the Prime Minister when he visited the Division at Grafenthal on 4 March. Accompanied by Sir Alan Brooke, the CIGS, Montgomery and General Crerar, Churchill watched the Massed Pipes and Drums of the Division and the Scottish Horse beat Retreat. In 'a short, but encouraging, speech on the progress of the war', he told the parade that the Division's achievements equalled those of any other formation in the Army and that, despite the sufferings of St Valéry, the spirit of Scotland had never wavered.[64]

Before the German counter-offensive in the Ardennes Montgomery had planned that the Rhine would be crossed in mid-March and attention now focused on crossing that mighty river.[65] At the beginning of March, Montgomery issued a message to 21 Army Group in which he noted that

> Events are moving rapidly. The complete and decisive defeat of the Germans is certain; there is no possibility of doubt on this matter.
> 21ST ARMY GROUP WILL NOW CROSS THE RHINE.
> The enemy possibly thinks that he is safe behind this great river obstacle. We all agree that it is a great obstacle; but we will show the enemy that he is far from safe behind it.[66]

On 9 March General Rennie held a conference for all officers of the Highland Division down to company commanders. This conference, in the model room of Main HQ XII Corps at Eysden, was to acquaint those attending with the basic scheme for crossing the Rhine and a model of the river was laid out to illustrate the proposed layout for marshalling, loading and waiting areas, traffic control, and dispersal control on the opposite bank. The assault brigades would cross in Buffaloes while those following would do so in boats. Thereafter, bridges would be erected to facilitate the crossing of further units and maintenance convoys. Two days later a second conference was held, this time at the Division's own HQ, for the staff officers of the brigades at which the outline plan for the crossing was outlined. The Rhine crossing was codenamed Operation PLUNDER and was to be preceded by a full-scale exercise, SPLOSH, on 14 March in which the Maas would serve as the Rhine.[67]

SPLOSH proved not to be the most successful exercise ever held. Crossing the Rhine was practised by day and night but the Maas was not a suitable substitute. Its banks were very steep which caused the Buffaloes problems in launching and the area available for the exercise was restricted by the presence of many mines on the far bank. The Buffaloes also had steering problems and although

> some of the troops in the night exercise [marvelled] at the short time
> it had taken them to get across … [t]hey were somewhat disgruntled
> when they discovered that they had merely turned back and landed
> at their embarking point.[68]

Operation PLUNDER was to be carried out on a two-corps front with Horrocks' XXX Corps on the left and Neil Ritchie's XII Corps on the right. (Ritchie had been GOC of the Highland Division in 1940–1 prior to Douglas Wimberley.[69]). In each Corps the initial assaults were to be made by Scottish divisions, with 15th (Scottish) leading XII Corps and the Highland Division leading XXX Corps.[70] The Division was to cross with two brigades up, 154 on the left flank, which was also the extreme left of the overall assault, near Honnepel and 153 on either side of Rees; 152 Brigade would follow 153 while 9 Canadian Brigade would follow 154 to provide a flank guard. The task allotted to 154 Brigade was to hold the east bank of the river to Wardmannshof in the north, capture the villages of Klein Esserden, Speldrop and Bienen and then advance northwards using the lead battalion of 9 Canadian Brigade, the Highland Light Infantry of Canada. The HLI of Canada would advance on Millingen and Grietherbosch. Meanwhile, 153 Brigade's role was to take Esserden, block the northern, north-eastern and eastern approaches to Rees, capture Rees and then advance northwards on the road to Isselburg. For this operation 2nd Seaforth of 152 Brigade would be under command of 153; the other two battalions of 152 – 5th Seaforth and 5th Camerons – were also to move north towards Isselburg after capturing Mittelburg, Groin and Haldern.[71]

While preparing for Operation PLUNDER, the Division was quartered in the Roermond–Nijmegen area. This proved a relaxing time for most and the Highlanders enjoyed the hospitality of local people, had a range of entertainments laid on, including film shows and dances, and were not short of food, rations being supplemented by local produce and livestock 'liberated' from the Reichswald area. Needless to say, there was the inevitable touch of ceremonial and the pipe bands played on many occasions. The Massed Pipes and Drums of 1st, 2nd and 5th/7th Gordons played Retreat together. On this occasion 5th/7th Gordons produced white sporrans for their bandsmen as well as white spats and diced hose, but the Camerons beat this display by 'turning out each man in a kilt'.[72] During this period, Major George Dunn, of 5th Black Watch, was promoted to command 2nd Seaforth while the Northamptonshire Yeomanry returned to the Division, having been away to train on Buffaloes in which they would carry the attacking Highland brigades over the Rhine.[73] (There was now only one regiment of Northamptonshire Yeomanry; 2nd Northamptonshire Yeomanry had been disbanded in August 1944, following heavy losses.)

D-Day for Operation PLUNDER was 24 March, less than ten days after Montgomery's original schedule in spite of the Ardennes offensive, and H-Hour for the Highland Division's first units was 9.00pm on 23 March, D – 1. At that time the assaulting units would begin crossing the river under cover of a heavy smokescreen on the west bank and with artillery support that would begin at 5.00pm on D – 1. So that the infantry would have immediate armoured support as they landed on the east bank, Sherman DD tanks of the Staffordshire Yeomanry would 'swim' across the river at the same time. (These were the amphibious Duplex Drive Shermans developed prior to the invasion of Europe and which had already proved invaluable on many occasions.) Close air support would also be provided with fighter-bombers on immediate call. With a bridgehead secured, Sappers would begin building bridges across the river for the follow-up units, tanks and maintenance convoys.[74] The Divisional Intelligence Summary for 12 March noted that the first recorded crossing of the Rhine by an army had been made by Julius Caesar who, in about 55 BC, crossed from Gaul into Germany at a spot somewhere between Andermach and Coblenz. Since Caesar 'did not deem it worthy of either himself or the Roman people to make the crossing by boat', Roman engineers had worked for ten days to construct a bridge over which Caesar's legions could march.[75] When they saw the legionnaires cross the river, the local inhabitants, the Sicambri, fled for the safety of the forests. Montgomery did not expect Hitler's troops to do likewise.

The assault brigades moved into their marshalling areas on 21 March under cover of the smokescreen which was laid down from that day until the crossing was complete. In the immediate area of the west bank there were no civilians although the land was good farmland and there were many farmhouses; the German population had crossed the river with their retreating armies and left their livestock to wander the fields of the Rhine plain. Many of those animals and fowl supplemented the diet of Allied troops. While final briefings were being conducted, many soldiers were amazed to see a VIP party driving around the area. This party included the CIGS, Sir Alan Brooke, and the Prime Minister, Winston Churchill, whose trademark cigar was much in evidence. Churchill had been determined to be present at the Rhine crossing.[76]

At 5.00pm on the 23rd the artillery fireplan began and German artillery and infantry positions on the far bank were subjected to a severe pounding

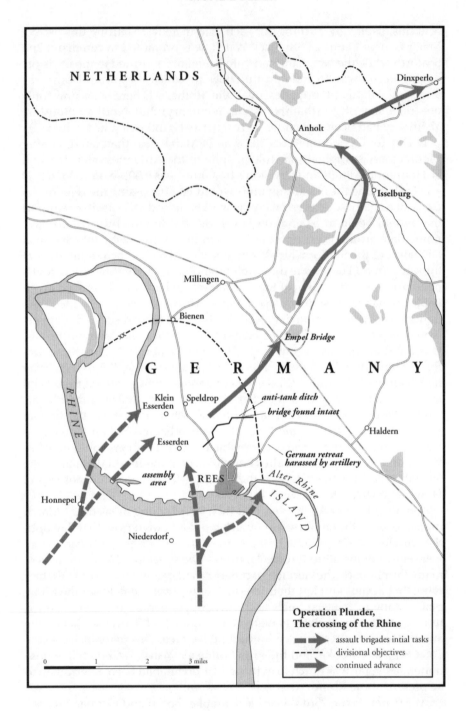

NETHERLANDS

Dinxperlo

Anholt

Isselburg

Millingen

Bienen

Empel Bridge

G E R M A N Y

Klein
Esserden   Speldrop

anti-tank ditch
bridge found intact

Haldern

RHINE

Esserden

German retreat
harassed by artillery

assembly
area   REES   *Alter Rhine*

ISLAND

Honnepel

Niederdorf

Operation Plunder,
The crossing of the Rhine

assault brigades intial tasks

divisional objectives

continued advance

0   1   2   3 miles

from the Allied guns.[77] Three hours later the assaulting battalions began boarding Buffaloes for the short journey across the Rhine. On the extreme left flank of the Allied assault, 7th Black Watch took to the water at H-Hour and two and a half minutes later were on the east bank. They were followed by 7th Argylls and by 9.06pm both battalions had reported to 154 Brigade HQ that they were ashore. Subsequently, 154 Brigade HQ received a message from Horrocks congratulating 7th Black Watch on being 'the first Allied troops from whom word had been received that they had landed on the far bank'.[78] The Black Watch had lost one Buffalo to a Teller-mine and suffered some casualties from Schu-mines; two members of the Unit Landing Officer's (ULO) party, Captain Duncan Kermack and Lance Corporal James Wright, were killed and the ULO, Major Rollo, had a narrow escape when bullets lodged in his pack and haversack.[79]

B Company of the Black Watch took Pottdeckel where battalion HQ was soon established and A Company captured Scholtenhof. Two Wasp flame-throwers (the smaller cousins of the Crocodile, mounted in carriers) assisted D Company's successful assault on Wardmannshof and, by dawn, the Black Watch had achieved all their objectives. The battalion moved into positions ready for its next advance with a platoon of 1/7th Middlesex under command.[80] Success had also greeted the Argylls who had captured Ratshoff and the nearby crossroads. They, too, stood ready for the next phase. For the Argylls that was to hold a firm base while 1st Black Watch, who crossed the river about ninety minutes after the first two battalions, passed through to attack a creamery outside Klein Esserden.[81] This was a stubbornly held strongpoint and the Black Watch came under heavy mortar fire as they attacked. Their Gunner FOO lost his carrier to a mine and the radio set was destroyed which, temporarily, left him out of touch with his battery. Major Richard Boyle of B Company was killed but A Company took the creamery and B Company moved on to attack the village. With only one officer left in B Company, the CO, John Hopwood, sent all of A Company up to support B. C Company attacked Speldrop and, by 6.00am on the 24th, both Klein Esserden and Speldrop were clear of enemy troops.[82]

The enemy on 1st Black Watch's front proved particularly resilient and within thirty minutes of battalion HQ moving up to the creamery came news that a German counter-attack had infiltrated Speldrop. Since this was an especially heavy attack, Hopwood decided to withdraw both B and C Companies to the creamery area. One of C Company's platoons was unable to extricate itself from its positions and Second-Lieutenant Robert Henderson, a 19-year-old, led a patrol to try to contact the platoon. Henderson's patrol came under machine-gun fire and the young officer decided to press ahead with only a Bren gunner for company. The two men crawled along a ditch close to the embankment along which ran the main road and from that embankment a German machine gunner fired

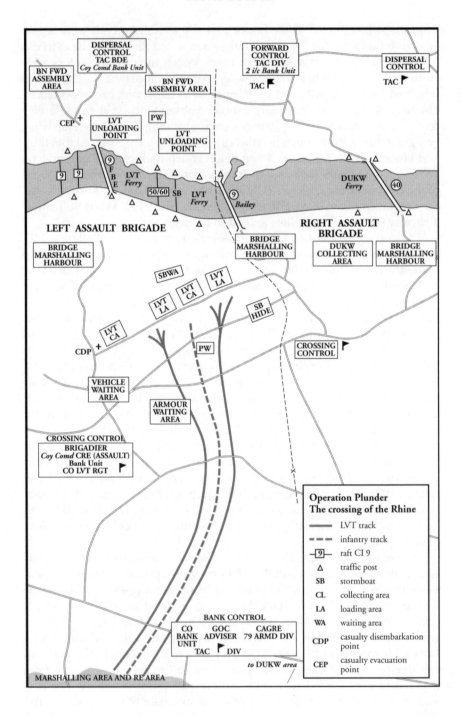

on them, killing the Bren gunner and knocking Henderson's revolver from his grip. Undaunted, Henderson grabbed his entrenching tool and charged the machine gunner, knocking him about the head with the shovel, with fatal results. He then signalled his patrol to join him and led them to the cover of a house before returning some sixty yards to retrieve his dead comrade's Bren. When the Germans set the house on fire the patrol was forced to evacuate the building but sought cover in another house from which the enemy were unable to dislodge them. For his gallantry and leadership Robert Henderson received an immediate award of the DSO, to become one of the youngest recipients of that award.[83]

With daylight the battalion, supported by a troop of tanks, a Middlesex platoon, some anti-tank guns and two Wasps, advanced on and recaptured Klein Esserden. Speldrop continued to hold out, however, and the battalion was again forced to withdraw to the creamery. That evening, the HLI of Canada, under brigade command, attacked the village behind a heavy bombardment. Much fierce fighting ensued but the Canadians cleared the village and relieved three besieged platoons of 1st Black Watch who had been isolated throughout the day but had defied all German efforts to overcome them.

> All three had every reason to be pleased with themselves, not only for their courage, but also for their battle discipline. Their only ammunition was what they had brought over with them the night before, and of this every round had to count. They had been attacked by tanks, by SP guns and with explosives; at times they had been driven into a single room or cellar; but they had held out, and when relieved were found to have retained twenty-five prisoners.[84]

A determined counter-attack was also launched on 7th Black Watch at Kivitt and throughout the day the battalion endured shelling and mortaring. That evening the Black Watch were relieved by Canadians of 9 Canadian Brigade and went into reserve at Pottdeckel. Although 7th Argylls took Rosau they failed in their attack on Bienen which was later captured by two Canadian battalions, the Nova Scotia Highlanders and the HLI of Canada.[85]

The other assaulting brigade was Brigadier Sinclair's 153 which was led across the Rhine by 5th Black Watch and 5th/7th Gordons; 1st Gordons followed the Black Watch as soon as the latter's Buffaloes returned to the east bank to lift them. For the Black Watch there were few difficulties as the battalion crossed just west of Rees.

> The troops holding the river bank, through whom the attack was to pass, had compiled excellent reports, showing, for instance, across what fields the enemy had been moving freely, thus declaring them

free of mines. With these reports, panoramic sketches and air photo-graphs, junior commanders were briefed.[86]

By morning 5th Black Watch had taken all their objectives. Along the way they had found the enemy to be dazed by the murderously heavy shelling and rocketing to which they had been subjected. The leading companies secured a farm and the following two companies passed through to the main objective, the outskirts of Esserden – not to be confused with Klein Esserden – where the few remaining inhabitants were found to be in abject terror. They had been told by German paratroopers, the recent defenders of the area, that the British would slaughter any civilians they found. In spite of the fact that no one was murdered, the inhabitants of Esserden continued to cry in terror all night. After fighting house-to-house during the night, 5th Black Watch secured the entire village in the morning but with dawn also came enemy retaliation in the form of mortaring on the Jocks' positions.[87]

The crossing had also been straightforward for 5th/7th Gordons whose first objective had been an 'island' created by the river and a strip of water, the Alter Rhine, to the right of Rees. The Gordons secured the farmhouses on the island and took some prisoners but the bridge over the Alter Rhine had been demolished and the Gordons' positions were overlooked from the east bank. Because of the work of snipers the battalion had to lie low throughout the day but, that night, the Carrier Platoon brought assault boats across the island ready for a crossing of the Alter Rhine. However, opposition was so fierce that this operation was called off and the Gordons had to endure another day on the island. Their purgatory was brought to an end when 5th Black Watch were ordered to capture the east bank of the Alter Rhine and did so, thus allowing the Gordons to cross by a bridge that was found to be still intact.[88]

The town of Rees had been completely devastated by Allied bombers. Streets were filled with rubble and pocked with craters. Ruined buildings were the principal feature of the landscape.

> The Germans' main funk-holes were a series of tunnels, of which the attacking forces had no knowledge. The result was that the enemy could appear in a most disconcerting way from openings in the ground after the clearing troops had passed forward. Broken-down trees, mines, and trenches were further obstacles in the path of 153 Brigade.[89]

Following 5th Black Watch, 1st Gordons had an uneventful crossing and lost not a single man. Ashore on the far bank, D Company took their first objectives but had to evacuate some of them when buildings were set alight by an incendiary. Under cover of a smokescreen both B and C

Companies advanced over 300 yards and took their objectives after some sharp fighting around isolated buildings. B Company then made a further advance, reaching the Rees–Speldrop road where they turned right towards Rees, fighting their way towards the cemetery and clearing the way for C Company to advance on the town.

The fighting in Rees involved all four rifle companies of the Gordons. C Company was first to enter the town, making a slow advance through the streets. A Company joined them at 10.00am, having entered Rees via the river bank while D Company fought its way through to the main square. B Company cleared the northern end of the town and by noon the companies had linked up. There remained much mopping-up to be done which took the remainder of that day and the following night. Throughout these operations the battalion was supported by a section of 454 Mountain Battery, Royal Artillery, with three 3.7-inch howitzers. The mountain guns were a welcome addition to the armoury of the battalion for the task before them was difficult.

> It all sounds very easy when one writes it down, but this was far from being so. The clearing of every single house was a separate little military operation requiring a special reconnaissance, plan and execution. And the enemy were resisting fiercely all the time with Spandaus, bazookas and snipers, and only withdrawing a little further back at the last moment when their position became untenable.[90]

The officer commanding the mountain guns, Captain McNair, was in his first action but behaved like a veteran and was to be seen hauling his guns over rubble, stripping a gun down to take it upstairs in a building and asking which window a sniper happened to be behind. The accuracy of the mountain gun was such that it could put one of its 21lb shells through a specific window or opening. McNair's gunners set buildings alight and put many enemy troops to flight. Martin Lindsay notes that the Gunner officer had become 'an almost legendary character' in only a few hours.[91]

With 5th Black Watch clearing the station and its surrounding area, the Gordons concentrated on the final hot spot of enemy resistance, an area of about 10,000 square yards in a corner of the town, which was taken shortly after darkness. This brought to an end 'forty-eight hours of continuous fighting against the most determined enemy we had seen since D-Day'. Both the Corps commander and the GOC of the Highland Division made special visits to the Gordons, again under command of Martin Lindsay as the CO had been wounded, to congratulate them on capturing Rees, an achievement that the brigade commander considered the 'best thing the Battalion had ever done'.[92]

But the GOC who came to congratulate 1st Gordons was not Thomas Rennie. To the dismay of all his soldiers General Rennie had joined the ranks of the Division's dead. On the morning of the 24th he had driven to visit 154 Brigade's Tactical HQ and left James Oliver to drive back to his HQ across the Rhine. As his jeep passed the Adjutant of 7th Argylls, Captain Angus Stewart, who was travelling in a carrier, Rennie bade the latter 'Good luck'. Stewart had been Rennie's ADC in 3rd Division. Then a concentration of German mortar bombs fell, the jeep took a direct hit and Rennie fell out onto the grass. His wireless operator, Lance-Corporal Craig of the Royal Signals, was wounded but his ADC, Lieutenant Tweedie, was unhurt. The latter asked Rennie if he was all right and, receiving no reply, had the GOC carried to Casualty Clearing Post of the nearby 176 Field Ambulance where he was pronounced dead. His death was a tremendous blow to the Highland Division for Rennie had appeared almost indestructible: had he not escaped from captivity after St Valéry to rejoin his beloved Black Watch and survived wounds in North Africa and Normandy? This was the man who had so often inspired his soldiers simply by his presence, his tall figure – he was one of the tallest men in the Highland Division – obvious to all as he stood by a roadside clad in his trademark blue naval duffle coat and his Tam O'Shanter with the proud red hackle of the Black Watch.[93]

Thomas Rennie, superlative leader and soldier par excellence, was laid to rest at Appeldorn to the sound of the pipes and with Brian Horrocks, his corps commander, present alongside the GOCs of 3rd British and Canadian Divisions as well as his own staff. The Senior Chaplain to the Forces conducted the service and four Black Watch soldiers acted as pall bearers. Rennie had been snatched from life by a splinter in the hour of victory and Brian Horrocks wondered if he had been fey, since he had appeared to be unusually most apprehensive about the operation beforehand.[94]

The new GOC of the Highland Division was another familiar face: Major-General G H MacMillan of the Argylls, known as 'Babe', was to succeed Rennie. MacMillan had commanded 152 Brigade in Sicily and, latterly, 49th (West Riding) Division; he had also taken 15th (Scottish) Division to France in June 1944. Babe MacMillan crossed the Rhine to take up his new command on the morning after Tom Rennie's death. James Oliver had commanded in the meantime.[95]

So far we have not looked at the experience of Brigadier Cassels' 152 Brigade in PLUNDER. George Dunn's 2nd Seaforth had crossed with 153 Brigade on the night of the 23rd and were thus the first battalion of the Seaforth and Cameron Brigade in action. By 5.00am next day they had taken all their objectives, the toughest having been a pipe factory in the northern outskirts of Rees. Next to cross, also under cover of darkness, were 5th Camerons who were due to attack Mittelburg before first light. However, on reaching 5th Black Watch's positions, the Camerons discovered that they could not reach their objective by first light and so the attack was delayed until a squadron of tanks could provide support.

The assault on Mittelburg went in at 7 o'clock with the tanks having to overcome an anti-tank ditch. Then three of the four leading tanks were hit by fire from SPGs concealed in buildings on the edge of Mittelburg. In the circumstances it was decided to wait until darkness fell before attacking again. This time A and B Companies put in the assault and phosphorous grenades were used to clear snipers from the upper floors of houses. Major A W Lee led his company in a determined attack on a brickworks where the defenders were well ensconced and stubborn, but the assault succeeded, Mittelburg fell to the Camerons and the battalion garrisoned the village for forty-eight hours.[96]

The last battalion of 152 Brigade to cross was 5th Seaforth who crossed in dribs and drabs from dawn on the morning of the 24th. Many of the boats used by the infantry had been knocked out thus forcing the Seaforth to cross in small groups. Having concentrated on the far bank, the battalion moved to positions south of Esserden where they endured an extremely heavy bombardment from German artillery. Orders were then received to move to the industrial area north of Rees where the Seaforth crossed the path of 5th Camerons, intent on the reduction of Mittelburg. The resulting confusion was soon settled and when the Camerons took Mittelburg the Seaforth were directed on Groin, a village covering a main road into Rees. Their task was to prevent German reinforcements moving to Rees along that road. However, before they could prevent any German movement, the Seaforth had first to capture Groin which proved one of the toughest assignments the battalion had ever had.

> [Groin] was a small village of no peacetime importance set in flat, featureless country; but covered a main exit from Rees, and it was essential that no enemy reinforcements should reach Rees. Also, our bridgehead had to be expanded. We had to have it. Snugly tucked away in the village were our old playmates the Para-boys, prepared, as usual, to be bloody-minded.[97]

Those buildings in the village that were not ablaze were defended heavily by the German paras and, as Alastair Borthwick commented, this battle 'was the hardest village fight the Battalion ever fought';[98] the Seaforth had to tackle their objective on a house-by-house basis. Such fighting is always nerve-racking and extremely dangerous and the attack on Groin had to be planned with considerable thought. The Seaforth attack began at 1.00am with A and C Companies leading. Initially it appeared as if the defenders had the upper hand but several vigorous assaults saw the village in Seaforth hands by 7.30am. However, an outlying farm, Hollands Hof, 'a solid building', remained in German hands. D Company, supported by tanks, attacked in broad daylight and suffered heavily at the hands of the paras. The Seaforth were met with mortar fire, machine-gun fire and artillery and only two officers of D Company escaped injury. Captain Gardiner continued the attack with the two remaining tanks and, as these plastered the area with shells, Lieutenant Evans led part of the company into the house, where they fought 'room by room, outbuilding by outbuilding'. But Evans was then ordered to withdraw his men to Groin, leaving Hollands Hof in enemy hands. Later that day the Germans decided that the buildings had no further use and withdrew so that when A Company attacked that night they met no opposition and found the buildings empty.[99]

A patrol from 1st Gordons – the battalion had been clearing houses along the river east of Rees – discovered that the town of Isselburg had also been abandoned by the Germans which saved 152 Brigade the problem of attacking it. The Seaforth and Camerons had been relieved by 9 Brigade and assigned to take Isselburg and create a bridgehead over the Issel river. Thus 5th Camerons were able to enter the town unopposed while 2nd Seaforth crossed the river on a bridge that German engineers had failed to demolish properly. As ever the German artillery came into play and Isselburg was subjected to very heavy shelling while 2nd Seaforth ran up against a strong-point facing their bridgehead. This German position, located in a wood north-west of the Seaforth, was given the attention of RAF Typhoons which attacked it with rockets and ended opposition from there.[100]

Next day, 29 March, a bridge that could carry tanks was constructed across the Issel and 5th Seaforth, with a company of Camerons, were ordered to advance to the Astrang river and seize crossings. The villages of Anholt and Astrang were still in enemy hands and when the Seaforth seized the surviving of the two Astrang bridges their new positions formed a salient with enemy to the front and both sides. Although the Germans opted to evacuate Anholt rather than defend it, this aggravated the situation as the German garrison was making for Dinxperlo along a route that would take them to the crossing held by the Camerons. The latter were hard pressed and the enemy overran battalion HQ of 5th Seaforth. The CO, Colonel Sym, was taken prisoner but his incarceration did not last long. Across the river his C and D Companies created a strongpoint that prevented a German advance over the river. This was held until tanks arrived and the Germans chose to surrender; some 206 went into captivity and Sym and the other Seaforth prisoners were liberated. Allied armour then advanced over the bridges.[101]

While 152 Brigade had been engaged in these battles, 154 Brigade had also been busy. On 25 March 7th Black Watch had captured the intact Empel bridge with ease although the first platoon to cross came under heavy fire from Empel village. Despite this pressure, Lance-Corporal MacBride, with five unwounded and a number of wounded men of the platoon, occupied a nearby house from which they thwarted the intentions of a German patrol that was crawling towards the bridge to demolish it. That night, two hours before midnight, Northants' Buffaloes conveyed 1st Black Watch and then 7th Argylls across the river. The Black Watch took Empel after a skirmish with German SPGs. Following up, the Argylls knocked out several of those SPGs. Next morning, 27 Brigade of 43rd (Wessex) Division passed though the Highlanders and Brigadier Oliver's brigade had two days of comparative rest before receiving orders, on 29 March, to capture Dinxperlo. Oliver deployed all three of his battalions on this task which was successful. Guards Armoured Division then passed through 154 Brigade.[102]

Thus ended the Highland Division's part in what General Sir Miles Dempsey, commander of Second Army, called the Battle of the Rhine in a message to Major-General MacMillan on 31 March, congratulating the Division on its achievement.

> Now that the Battle of the Rhine had been won, and the break-out from the bridge-head is well under way, I would like to give you and your magnificent Division my very sincere congratulations. Yours was one of the two Divisions which carried out the assault crossing of the river, defeated the enemy on the other side, and paved the way for all that followed. A great achievement – and I am sure you are all very proud of it.[103]

The Rhine crossing had been made possible by all those who had contributed to the execution of Montgomery's plan. As well as the infantry of the two Scottish divisions – the other was 15th Division – there were the men who manned the Buffaloes, those who controlled traffic on either bank, the Sappers who had lifted mines, built bridges and manned many of the 'Funnies' of 79th Armoured Division, the Gunners, the signallers, the tankies, the medics of the RAMC and the men of the RASC. As J B Salmond summed up: 'Never, perhaps, since Alamein had there been such an interlocked unity of purpose and achievement.'[104]

And, of course, there were others, chief among them those who flew the tactical aircraft – RAF Typhoons and Spitfires, USAAF P47s and P51s – that supported the ground forces and whose intervention often helped eliminate dangerous enemy strongpoints. As the campaign in north-west Europe developed the cooperation between air and ground forces had improved so that, by this stage, it was as good as it had been in the desert. (Cooperation between US ground and tactical air forces had been much better than that of their British counterparts from the beginning of the campaign.) Many veterans would speak movingly of the courage of the Typhoon pilots as they flew in to engage their targets, often through a cloud of enemy fire. One Gunner told this author that he considered the Typhoon pilots the bravest men he had ever seen as they would 'fly right into the muzzle of an eighty-eight'.[105]

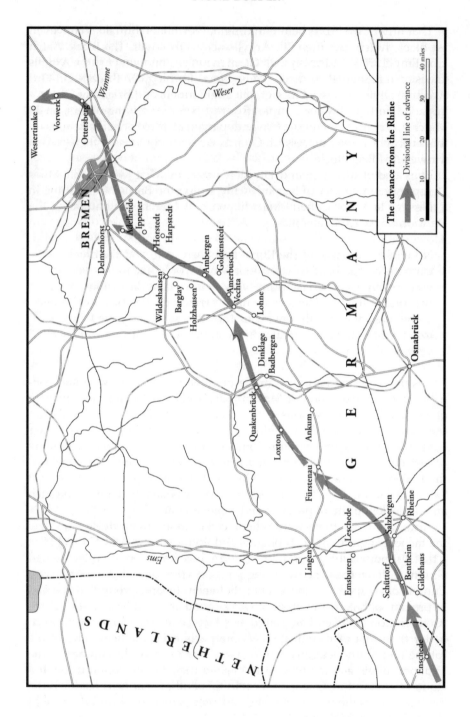

One arm of the Army that often goes unsung is the Royal Signals. The work of the signallers, however, is indispensable and the level of risk that they took led to many casualties amongst the men of the Highland Divisional Signals Regiment. Commanded by Lieutenant-Colonel James Cochrane the signallers had excelled themselves in PLUNDER. Laying cable by hand to the bank of the Rhine as the first Buffaloes took to the water, Cochrane's men then broke down a section of riverbank to create a launch point for the DUKW that would carry the line across the river. However, that vehicle was struck by a shell splinter when only some thirty yards out and began to sink, forcing the signals team to swim back to the shore. A spare DUKW was pressed into service and the underwater cable was laid across the river. A network of cables was then laid to the various brigade tactical HQs, a task that had been completed by 3.30am. However, the work of the signals team was not ended: since the cables were liable to be cut by shell or mortar fire and by the tracks of tanks and other tracked AFVs, the lines had to be patrolled regularly to ensure their integrity. No one begrudged the gallantry awards made to Highland signallers for the Rhine crossing: Major Henderson received the DSO and Signalmen Clark and Reilly, 'who were the leading hands of the cable crews on that crossing', were each awarded the Military Medal. Nor was enemy action the only danger faced by personnel: on 18 March a lorry carrying nine soldiers of 51st Divisional Signals back from leave in the UK was involved in a collision with a tank transporter. All nine men were injured and one, Driver Jeffreys, died of head injuries in 79th General Hospital.[106]

The Allies were now on the last lap of the war in Europe. But although Adolf Hitler's thousand-year Reich lay in ruins, his soldiers continued to fight with courage, skill and tenacity. However, the cohesion that had so long marked the German army was dying as the Reich died and there was the feeling that although the German soldier would still fight hard his capacity to counter-attack was all but gone. Even when staring defeat in the eyes, those soldiers were still dangerous foes and could not be underestimated.

One certain reminder that the Germans could not be written off was the Memorial Parade Service held for General Rennie at Isselburg on the afternoon of 1 April. The service was conducted by the Senior Chaplain to the Forces and General MacMillan read the lesson. Nine pipe-majors, one from each of the Highland battalions, played the lament 'The Flowers of the Forest' and the parade was also attended by General Crerar, commander of First Canadian Army, General Simonds, commander of II Canadian Corps, General Barber, GOC of 15th (Scottish) Division, the brigade commanders of that Division and the commander of 33 Armoured Brigade, Brigadier H B Scott.[107]

The Division remained at Isselburg until the 3rd when orders were received to concentrate near the Dutch town of Enschede, some forty miles to the north.[108] Two days later 153 Brigade led the move to Enschede, a pleasant town that had not suffered much bombing and where civic pride was symbolised in window boxes bright with flowers on every windowsill.[109] For a couple of days there was an opportunity to catch up on maintenance, and to reflect. The war was almost over and the Allied armies were squeezing the Germans into a diminishing perimeter. To the east, the Red Army was thrusting for Berlin, while the great industrial area of the Ruhr was now a besieged and battered island as First and Ninth US Armies had met up at Lippstadt on 1 April, cutting off some 325,000 Germans. American and British formations were swarming over the north German plain and Montgomery reckoned that the Allies in the west had taken over 300,000 prisoners during March, a loss that the Reich could not make good. But, in spite of the devastation being visited on the Fatherland, German troops still occupied the northern Netherlands and First Canadian Army was now directed to liberate that region. Horrocks' XXX Corps was placed under Canadian command and thus the Highland Division was, once again, to fight alongside Canadians.[110]

The task assigned to the Canadian Army was to advance through Arnhem to clear the Germans from north-east Holland and the coastal area to the mouth of the Elbe river.[111] Within that overall advance the Highlanders were to move off from Enschede to Salzbergen, about twenty miles to the east on the main Lingen–Rheine road before turning north to Lingen. Later the Division would travel the further thirty miles to Quakenbrück, thence to Vechta and on to Wildeshausen and Delmenhorst, to the outskirts of Bremen, to Bremervörde, on the Weser–Elbe peninsula and, finally, to Bremerhaven. The total distance of this advance was almost 190 miles and it was

> to be somewhat different to anything so far undertaken by the Division. It was obvious to everyone that Hitler had shot his bolt, and that the war was more or less over. But such knowledge leads to an unhappy frame of mind in most people – the idea that it would really be too bad to be hit now. Fighting was to be spasmodic; advances were all to have about them a kind of question mark.[112]

And so it proved. The advancing troops passed long columns of German soldiers being marched in the opposite direction to prisoner-of-war camps but there were still pockets of Germans determined to resist. Brigadier Sinclair's 153 Brigade was the first to move from Enschede which they left on 5 April to relieve 5 Guards Brigade; 5th Black Watch moved to Schüttorf, 1st Gordons to Gildehaus and 5th/7th Gordons to Bentheim. Black Watch patrols met some opposition from German infantry as they patrolled in front of Schüttorf but this was nothing compared to that encountered by 5th/7th Gordons when they passed the Black Watch to cross the Ems at Schüttorf en route to Emsburen. The Gordons met considerable spirited opposition both to their front and from both flanks but, by the morning of the 7th, had occupied Emsburen. This proved to be another brief respite as the battalion remained in Emsburen for the next three days. Brigade soccer matches were arranged and 5th/7th Gordons beat their 1st Battalion but lost to 5th Black Watch; the scores were 7:2 and 6:3 respectively. On 12 April 5th/7th Gordons left Emsburen and reached Amerbusch on the 13th, turning north for Wildeshausen where they relieved a battalion from 3rd (British) Division. Having rested in Leschede for four days 1st Gordons crossed the Ems to move to Goldenstedt.[113]

James Oliver's 154 Brigade relieved 9 Brigade near Lingen on 8 April and then took over from 5 Guards Brigade near Fürstenau on the 10th. From there the Argylls moved on Ankum and captured the village without difficulty next day, allowing both Black Watch battalions to pass through. The Argylls then relieved 2nd Royal Ulster Rifles, of 3rd (British) Division. Meanwhile 7th Black Watch, who had been on the Dortmund canal near Albergen on the 8th, moved to Mundersum and then, on the 11th, occupied Quakenbrück; there was no opposition. Although there was some difficulty during a recce of the bridge spanning the Lager-Hase river, the Black Watch moved on to Vechta and remained there until the 16th. Meanwhile 1st Black Watch had passed through Guards Armoured Division at Loxton on 10 April in an operation to take Badbergen. The battalion moved in Kangaroos manned by 2nd Staffordshire Yeomanry 'through woods and villages and over small streams' meeting no real opposition although there were many felled chestnut trees that were intended to camouflage mines. Once the Black Watch had occupied Badbergen they had the novel experience of a visit from the burgomeister of Dinklage, a nearby village. This worthy explained that his citizens were weary of the shelling and that he wished to surrender Dinklage. The offer was accepted and the village was occupied. During this advance, 154 Brigade discovered that the local telephone system was still working and decided to press it into service. Where it was considered that a village or town might be a focus of opposition a German-speaking officer would telephone and demand to talk to the burgomeister who would be told that failure to surrender immediately would have dire consequences with the town being shelled and attacked by Crocodile flamethrowers; similarly, any resistance following an agreement to surrender would bring similar retribution. Surrender could be indicated by displaying white sheets on prominent local buildings. This psychological warfare proved most effective and must have saved many lives, both German and British.[114]

The Seaforth and Cameron Brigade had relieved 8 Brigade at Lingen on 10 April before joining in the advance with 2nd Seaforth relieving 7th

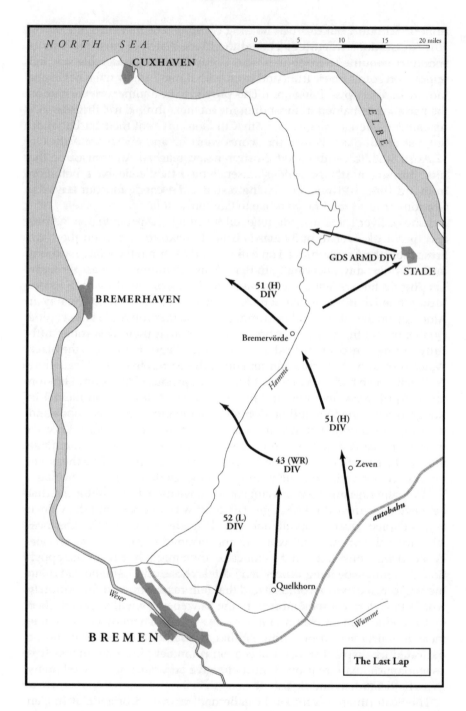

The Last Lap

Black Watch at Quakenbrück on the 12th after which the brigade moved via Vechta to Goldenstedt.[115] At the latter location 2nd Seaforth took prisoner about a hundred Germans who were still abed when the battalion arrived.[116] Thereafter 152 Brigade continued leading the Divisional advance, following patrols of the Derbyshire Yeomanry who carried out sterling work. The latter's war diary notes that, on 13 April, the Regiment 'swanned out' on all roads from Goldenstedt and Amerbusch as 5th Seaforth and 5th Camerons began their northward move.[117] That advance took 5th Seaforth, embussed in Kangaroos, through Azbergen, Holzhausen and Barglay, all villages which were taken with little trouble on the 13th, although boggy ground before Holzhausen and Barglay forced the infantry to take to their feet. At the same time 5th Camerons had taken Visbek and Varnhorn. The Camerons were followed by 2nd Seaforth. On the 14th, 2nd Seaforth contacted elements of Guards Armoured Division about two miles to the west of Visbek while the Camerons made contact with 43rd (Wessex) Reconnaissance Regiment.[118] This latter junction was celebrated by the Camerons with a pipe band practice. However, some German gunners, who seemed not to appreciate the skirl of pipes, objected to the music with a salvo of four 105mm shells, a reaction that 'failed to put the drum-major out of step'.[119] Following the capture of Varnhorn, 152 Brigade went into Divisional reserve. Over two days the Brigade Group had taken prisoner eleven German officers and 650 soldiers.[120]

The Division still had miles to cover on its advance to Bremerhaven and, on 14 April 5th/7th Gordons relieved a battalion from 3rd Division in Wildeshausen. While filling craters on the road out of the town, the Gordons came under heavy fire from SPGs but completed their task and moved on to capture Dotlingen where the garrison tried to escape on bicycles. That same day 1st Gordons cleared the villages of Hockensburg and Brettorf, overcoming determined resistance in doing so.[121]

Delmenhorst was the Division's next major objective and the advance thereon was led by 154 Brigade which cleared the main road as far as Ippener and Annen, about halfway to Delmenhorst. From there 153 Brigade moved into the lead and 5th Camerons came up against the stiffest opposition of this phase of the campaign as they launched a night attack on the Adelheide area; their objective included Adelheide village, an airfield and two bridges. One defender was destined to be imprinted on the memories of the Camerons as he blazed away with a *panzerfaust* to a shouted refrain of 'Heil Hitler'. This was obviously one German soldier who still believed in his Führer, although many others were fighting to defend their country and homes against what they had been led to believe were barbarians intent on destruction and plunder. One bridge was so heavily defended that artillery fire had to be brought down on its garrison before the Camerons could seize it. Before long the second bridge, the airfield and much of the village were also in Cameron hands. The north end of Adelheide remained in German hands until an attack by D Company, supported by Crocodiles and Flail tanks, finally cleared it. This left the way clear for the Derbyshire Yeomanry to probe ahead to Delmenhorst where stiff opposition had been expected. However, the reconnoitrers found Delmenhorst clear of enemy troops; the defence of Delmenhorst had been conducted around Adelheide.[122]

During the latter part of April the Division saw little major fighting. On the 21st Brigadier Oliver's brigade relieved a brigade of 3rd (British) Division; four days later 153 Brigade relieved 154. The next major corps objective was Bremen but 43rd (Wessex) and 52nd (Lowland) Divisions were assigned to this task and the Highlanders were restricted to providing right-flank protection for the Wessexmen with the deployment of 154 Brigade. Once it was clear that the advance on Bremen was going smoothly, the Highland Division was deployed north-westwards to link up with Guards Armoured Division while 154 Brigade was left to clear the enemy from the far bank of the Wümme river. This was achieved by leaving 7th Black Watch along the near bank to screen the enemy while the other two battalions of 154 moved through Robertburg to take the Germans in the flank. Thus, on 27 April, the Argylls took Stuckenborstel while 1st Black Watch captured Ottersberg, Otterstedt and Vorwerk. That evening 7th Black Watch moved up to make contact with the Guards at Westertimke.[123]

Meanwhile the Seaforth and Cameron Brigade had advanced on Ganderkese on the night of 20–21 April to find the village defended by a strong body of quite determined enemy troops. These were paratroopers, whose opposition was always doughty. It took the strength of 2nd Seaforth, supported by a thunderous artillery programme and a half-squadron of Crocodiles to overcome the defenders and it was only when the flames spewing from the Crocodiles had set the entire village alight that the paras decided that enough was enough. On the 27th a brigade move was completed 'despite the efforts of the Corps Military Police to strip the brigade of all its captured enemy vehicles'. By the end of the month the brigade was at Selsingen, making ready to attack Bremervörde, while 153 Brigade, having held the line near Delmenhorst until the 28th, moved to Horstedt and Stafel.[124]

Thus ended the last April of the Second World War. But the month finished on a bitterly sad note for all in the Division, especially those in the Gunner regiments. Brigadier Sheil CBE DSO*, the popular and very effective Irish commander of the Divisional Artillery, was killed on 29 April when his jeep drove over a mine. Typically, Sheil was driving the vehicle, having relieved his driver at the wheel because the latter was exhausted; the driver survived the explosion. From Clonsilla, County Dublin, William Anthony Sheil, known as Jerry, was one of the most respected officers in the Highland Division. He was popular with the infantry who knew that they could always rely on his guns and with the Gunners who knew and appreciated his professionalism. And his Irish background had always allowed him to be at home with Scottish Highlanders, whom he understood and who understood him. Sheil had left the Army before the war to take over the management of one of the most famous racing studs in his native Ireland but had returned to the Royal Artillery when war broke out. He had served with distinction as an instructor at 125 OCTU in Britain before obtaining a posting to the Highland Division. That he should die so close to the end of the war made his death an even greater tragedy for those who knew him.[125]

As May dawned the Highland Division was disposed along the east bank of the Oste river, facing the town of Bremervörde, their next objective. Bremerhaven and Wesermünde were the ultimate objectives of the Division but Bremervörde had first to be taken.[126] To this task General MacMillan assigned 152 Brigade as the van of the Division; the attack was to be launched under cover of darkness on 1 May. But it was a strange assault, when compared with the many that had gone before, from El Alamein to the Rhine. At Bremervörde the Oste runs in two channels, spanned by two bridges, neither of which had been demolished fully and so Colonel Dunn of 2nd Seaforth sent forth a recce patrol the members of which crossed the bridge over the Oste's eastern channel, had a good look at the other side and returned with the pleasing news that they had not even been challenged. This led to a revision of the plan of attack. Originally the Seaforth had been due to embark in Buffaloes to cross the Oste but it was now decided to deploy Sappers to repair the nearer bridge that very night.[127]

The Sappers were able to complete their task without interference from the enemy and, in the early hours of the morning, an AVRE drove to the second channel to drop a bridge across the gap. Two companies of Seaforth advanced over the bridge and found the German infantry facing them to be happy to surrender, although the enemy artillery continued firing. Following the initial crossing by 2nd Seaforth, 5th Seaforth passed into Bremervörde and through to the far end of the town whence 5th Camerons took the lead. The latter were embussed in Kangaroos and made considerable progress that day. However, the German artillery remained active and an SPG shelled the temporary bridge over the Oste causing a number of casualties in 152 Brigade's battalions. Fifth Seaforth's last fatal casualty 'and so nearly a survivor' was Lance-Corporal A J Woodley.[128]

The Camerons were able to drive as far as Orel where they met strong opposition from units of 15th Panzer Grenadier Division, a formation whose morale and fighting spirit remained high; this was a reborn formation of the old Afrika Korps which, as 15th Panzer Division, had opposed the Highlanders in North Africa.[129] An assault on Orel by 1st Gordons, supported by Crocodiles, was planned but the tanks were held up in traffic congestion and the Gordons attacked unsupported. Although the battalion took Orel, B Company, advancing towards the nearby village of Barchel, suffered heavy counter-attacks not only from the front but also from both flanks. It was clear the Panzer Grenadiers were determined to hold out for as long as possible. From some prisoners it was learned that the garrison of Barchel comprised two battalions of 15th Panzer Grenadier Division, which gave a new complexion to the situation. The Gordons were ordered to pull back to Orel and a new plan of attack was laid; this was for a full-scale assault with both artillery and armour support and was to be launched next day. However, when the following day dawned it was found that the Germans had abandoned Barchel and no attack was necessary.[130]

Elsewhere, 5th/7th Gordons had moved through Bremervörde to Ebersdorf, meeting considerable opposition en route. In fact it was said the battalion had to 'fight for every building along the road'.[131] This continued right up to Ebersdorf where a determined German garrison was met. Mortar bombs, SPG and machine-gun fire met the Gordons who launched an attack to envelop the village. By morning, only two SPGs with some infantry were still in action. Unable to advance or retreat but determined to continue the fight, these were shelled by the Gordons' supporting artillery and both guns were destroyed, bringing to an end the battle for Ebersdorf. The Gordons resumed their advance, moving on to Waterbeck. The third battalion of 153 Brigade, 5th Black Watch, had taken the village of Hipstedt against little more than token opposition.[132]

It was the turn of 154 Brigade to take the lead and, early on 3 May, the brigade received orders to pass through 153. This advance was led by 7th Argylls, mounted in Kangaroos, as far as Meckelstedt where the battalion took to their feet for the advance on their objective, Lintig. During the afternoon of 4 May, two German Red Cross representatives arrived in the Argylls' positions to ask that the British should cease shelling the village of Bederkesa, in which was located a large hospital with many wounded patients. However, German artillery continued firing in the area for some time after this. Meanwhile 7th Black Watch, having passed through Abersdorf, had captured Grossenham without opposition, taking prisoner a complete company of the Regiment Lubeck, and had moved on to Meckelstedt; 1st Black Watch then moved into Grossenham.[133]

That morning a patrol of Derbyshire Yeomanry, under Lieutenant T R Compton-Bishop, had been probing down the road to Ringstedt when they met a dozen Germans who immediately surrendered. Among the Germans was a major, 'thought at that time to be the Comd of Regt Lubeck'. This officer, who had his hands up, was asked to surrender Ringstedt itself. He demurred, stating that such a surrender would have to be carried out at divisional level.[134] Taking the major at his word, he was despatched to his own divisional HQ to achieve the surrender but the response from the German HQ was that a British officer should come to them to negotiate, a request that was ignored. Another German major, from the divisional artillery, then arrived to deliver a similar proposal which was also rejected. Brigadier Oliver, presumably tiring of this game, then arranged that if a German staff officer came to his HQ a staff officer from 154 Brigade would cross to the German HQ to explain the terms, which were for unconditional surrender. While such negotiations were underway, Oliver arranged for a local truce. The German divisional HQ was that of 15th Panzer Grenadier Division, whence came a staff captain who was escorted to the battalion HQ of the Argylls where Oliver told him that only terms of unconditional surrender were available. However, the German officer stated that such terms would be unacceptable to his divisional commander who considered that, since 15th Panzer Grenadier Division 'was still a reasonably equipped and well-disciplined fighting formation', although much weakened, it continued to constitute a force to be reckoned with and, should it continue to oppose the Highlanders' advance, would put up such a fight that there would be considerable losses on both sides. The German commander asked that his division be allowed to surrender as a formation, that it be given an area in British-controlled territory in which to assemble for disarmament and demobilisation and that, after the war, the division be employed on police duties within Germany, for which purpose its officers be allowed to retain their sidearms. He also drew attention to the 'long and honourable association' between his division and the Highlanders.[135]

Oliver's response was that the terms of surrender had been laid down by the Supreme Allied Commander and were not negotiable. The request for a specified area to complete disarmament might be countenanced but only if the German general agreed to accept the Allies' unconditional surrender terms. The request that the division be deployed on police duties after the war was not one that could be considered. Following discussions with Major-General MacMillan, Brigadier Oliver told the German representative that a specified area might be assigned to 15th Panzer Grenadier Division for its disarmament but that, once that process was complete, no further responsibility for the division's future could be taken. While negotiations continued the village of Ringstedt was declared a neutral area with representative officers from both sides stationed there. Meanwhile the Germans were given until 10.00pm to answer Oliver's message.[136]

While that response was being considered came the first news that all German forces facing Montgomery's 21 Army Group were preparing to surrender. At much the same time 15th Panzer Grenadier Division's representative returned to say that the divisional commander could not accept the unconditional surrender terms but that he would like the current truce to be extended until the results of the overall negotiations were known. Those negotiations ended with the unconditional surrender of

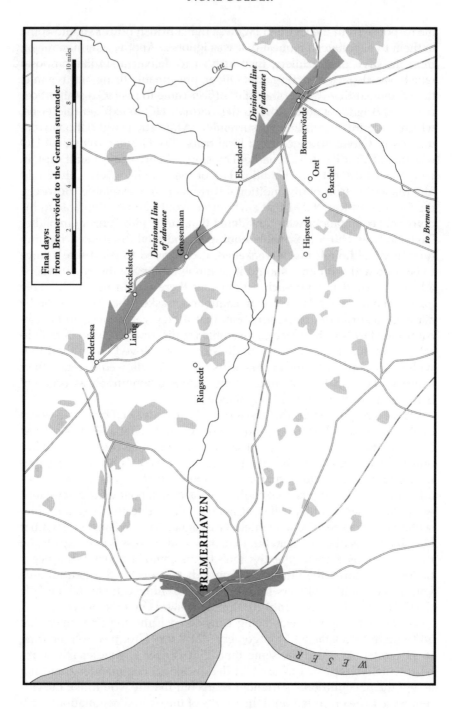

the German forces facing 21 Army Group. The local truce was extended to 8.00am on 5 May when a general ceasefire would begin. In the circumstances the Germans facing the Highland Division decided to comply with the general surrender and, at 10.35am on the 5th, Lieutenant-General Raspe, corps commander, and Major-General Roth, commander of 15th Panzer Grenadier Division, with a Kriegsmarine representative and a party of staff officers and clerks, arrived at HQ 51st (Highland) Division to make the formal surrender.[137]

Notes

1. Ellis, *Victory in the West, Vol II*, pp. 250–1
2. Salmond, *The History of the 51st Highland Division*, p. 213
3. Ellis, op cit, pp. 255–6. Ninth US Army's part in the assault was known as Operation GRENADE; Ninth Army was reinforced by elements of Seventh US Army.
4. Ibid
5. Ibid
6. Ibid; Salmond, op cit, p. 214; NA Kew, WO171/4245, war diary, HQ 51 (H) Div (G), 1945
7. Salmond, op cit, p. 214; NA Kew, WO171/4245, war diary, 51 (H) Div (G), 1945
8. NA Kew, WO171/4411, war diary, 154 Bde, 1945; WO171/5198, war diary, 5/7 Gordons, 1945
9. NA Kew, WO171/1265, war diary, 1 BW, 1945; Salmond, op cit, p.
10. NA Kew, WO171/ 1265, war diary, 1 BW, 1945; WO171/5198, war diary, 5/7 Gordons, 1945; Salmond, op cit, p. 215
11. NA Kew, WO171/1265, war diary, 1 BW, 1945; Fergusson, *The Black Watch and the King's Enemies*, p. 295; Salmond, op cit, p. 215
12. NA Kew, WO171/,4411 war diary, 154 Bde, 1945; WO171/4250, war diary, CRE, 51 (H) Div, 1945; WO171/, war diary, 5/7 Gordons, 1945; Salmond, op cit, p. 215
13. NA Kew, WO171/4406, war diary, 152 Bde, 1945; WO171/5164, war diary, 5 Camerons, 1945; WO171/5268, war diary, 5 Seaforth, 1945; WO171/5267, war diary, 2 Seaforth, 1945
14. NA Kew, WO171/5267, war diary, 2 Seaforth, 1945
15. NA Kew, WO171/4409, war diary, 153 Bde, 1945
16. NA Kew, WO171/1265, war diary, 1 BW, 1945; Fergusson, op cit, p. 296
17. Gill and Groves, *Club Route in Europe*, p. 137; NA Kew, WO171/4696, war diary, 2 DY, 1945 (C Sqn report on operations)
18. Lindsay, *So Few Got Through*, p. 170; Salmond, op cit, p. 217
19. NA Kew, WO171/5196, war diary, 1 Gordons, 1945
20. Lindsay, op cit, pp. 174–5
21. Salmond, op cit, p. 217
22. NA Kew, WO171/5196, war diary, 1 Gordons, 1945; WO171/5198, war diary, 5/7 Gordons, 1945

23. Salmond, op cit, p. 217
24. Ibid, p. 218
25. NA Kew, WO171/4406, war diary, 152 Bde, 1945; WO171/5164, war diary, 5 Camerons, 1945
26. Salmond, op cit, p. 218
27. NA Kew, WO171/4411, war diary, 154 Bde, 1945; WO171/1265, war diary, 1 BW, 1945; WO171/1267, war diary, 7 BW, 1945; Fergusson, op cit, pp. 297–8
28. Fergusson, op cit, p. 297
29. Ibid. Only Beales' death is recorded in the Commonwealth War Graves Commission's records but this does not detract from the authenticity of the story as the CWGC records, especially those on-line at www.cwgc.org, include many errors and omissions.
30. Salmond, op cit, pp. 219–20
31. NA Kew, WO171/4411, war diary, 154 Bde, 1945; Fergusson, op cit, p. 298
32. NA Kew, WO171/1265, war diary, 1 BW, 1945; Fergusson, op cit, pp. 298–9
33. Fergusson, op cit, p. 299
34. NA Kew, WO171/1263, war diary, 7 A&SH, 1945; Salmond, op cit, p. 220
35. Joslen, *Orders of Battle*, pp. 182 & 204
36. Fergusson, op cit, p. 299
37. Ibid
38. Ibid, pp. 299–300
39. NA Kew, WO171/673, war diary, 152 Bde, 1945
40. Ibid; Salmond, op cit, pp. 221; Borthwick, *Battalion*, p. 249
41. Salmond, op cit, p. 223
42. NA Kew, WO171/4409, war diary, 153 Bde, 1945
43. NA Kew, WO171/4406, war diary, 152 Bde, 1945
44. Salmond, op cit, p. 224; Fergusson, op cit, p. 300
45. Lindsay, op cit, p. 192; CWGC website www.cwgc.org
46. Ibid, pp. 192–3
47. Ibid, p. 193
48. Ibid, pp. 193–4
49. Ibid, p. 194
50. Ibid, pp. 194–5
51. Ibid, pp. 195–200
52. NA Kew, WO171/4409, war diary, 153 Bde, 1945; Salmond, op cit, p. 224
53. Fergusson, op cit, pp. 301–2
54. Lindsay, op cit, p. 200; CWGC website www.cwgc.org
55. Lindsay, op cit, p. 202
56. Ellis, op cit, p. 266
57. Ibid, p. 271
58. Ibid; Salmond, op cit, pp. 224–5
59. Salmond, op cit, pp. 225–7; NA Kew, WO171/4245, HQ 51 (H) Div (G), 1945; WO171/4406, war diary, 152 Bde, 1945; WO171/5164, war diary, 5 Camerons, 1945; Borthwick, op cit, pp. 251–3
60. Salmond, op cit, pp. 226–7
61. NA Kew, WO171/5245, war diary, HQ 51 (H) Div (G), 1945
62. Ibid
63. Ibid

64. Ibid; NA Kew, WO171/5198, war diary, 5/7 Gordons; Salmond, op cit, p. 228. The quotation describing Churchill's speech is taken from the Gordons' war diary.

65. Ellis, op cit, p. 196n

66. NA Kew, WO171/4245, war diary, HQ 51 (H) Div (G), 1945

67. Ibid; Salmond, op cit, pp. 230–1. Salmond refers to the exercise as SLOSH.

68. Salmond, op cit, p. 231

69. Joslen, op cit, p. 83

70. Ellis, op cit, pp. 288–9

71. NA Kew, WO171/4245, war diary, HQ 51 (H) Div (G), 1945; Salmond op cit, p. 231

72. NA Kew, WO171/5196, war diary, 1 Gordons, 1945; WO171/5198, war diary, 5/7 Gordons; Salmond, op cit, p. 230

73. Salmond, op cit, p. 230

74. NA Kew, WO171/5245, war diary, HQ 51 (H) Div (G), 1945; Salmond, op cit, p. 232

75. NA Kew, WO171/4245, war diary, HQ 51 (H) Div (G), 1945. IntSum No. 330, dated 12 March 1945, includes the information on Caesar's Rhine crossing with a translation from the original Latin by an American officer.

76. Ellis, op cit, p. 292; Salmond, op cit, p. 232

77. NA Kew, WO171/4245, war diary, HQ 51 (H) Div (G), 1945

78. NA Kew, WO171/4411, war diary, 154 Bde, 1945

79. Salmond, op cit, p. 233; NA Kew, Wo171/5158, war diary, 1 BW, 1945

80. NA Kew, WO171/5158, war diary, 1 BW, 1945; WO171/5242, war diary, 1/7 Mx, 1945

81. NA Kew, WO171/4411, war diary, 154 Bde, 1945; WO171/5154, war diary, 7 A & SH, 1945

82. Fergusson, op cit, p. 306; NA Kew, WO171/5158, war diary, 1 BW, 1945

83. Fergusson, op cit, pp. 306–7; NA Kew, WO171/5158, war diary, 1 BW, 1945; Salmond, op cit, p. 235

84. Fergusson, op cit, p. 307; NA Kew, WO171/4411, war diary, 154 Bde, 1945; Salmond, op cit, pp. 235–6

85. Salmond, op cit, p. 236

86. Fergusson, op cit, p. 307; NA Kew, WO171/4409, war diary, 153 Bde, 1945; WO171/5159, war diary, 5 BW, 1945

87. Fergusson, op cit, pp. 307–8

88. Salmond, op cit, pp. 236–7; NA Kew, WO171/5198, war diary, 5/7 Gordons, 1945

89. Salmond, op cit, p. 237

90. Lindsay, op cit, pp. 220–2

91. Ibid, pp. 222–3

92. Ibid, pp. 222–5; NA Kew, WO171/5196, war diary, 1 Gordons, 1945

93. NA Kew, WO171/4245, war diary, HQ 51 (H) Div (G), 1945; Salmond, op cit, p. 239; Fergusson, op cit, pp. 308–9. Fergusson comments that Rennie was 'found to be dead' at the CCP while Salmond suggests that he died 'almost immediately' after admission. The Divisional war diary notes that he 'died immediately after admission'. It is likely that he was killed outright by the mortar and pronounced dead at the CCP by an RAMC doctor.

94. Salmond, op cit, p. 239

95. Ibid, p. 240; McGregor, *The Spirit of Angus*, pp. 183–4

96. NA Kew, WO171/4406, war diary, 152 Bde, 1945; WO171/5267, war diary, 2 Seaforth, 1945; WO171/5164, war diary, 5 Camerons, 1945

97. Borthwick, op cit, p. 260; NA Kew, WO171/5268, war diary, 5 Seaforth

98. Borthwick, op cit, p. 260

99. Ibid, pp. 260–8

100. Salmond, op cit, p. 241

101. NA Kew, WO171/4406, war diary, 152 Bde, 1945; WO171/5268, war diary, 5 Seaforth, 1945; Borthwick, op cit, pp. 268–73

102. NA Kew, WO171/4411, war diary, 154 Bde, 1945; WO171/5160, war diary, 7 BW, 1945; Salmond, op cit, p. 241

103. NA Kew, WO171/4245, war diary, HQ 51 (H) Div (G), 1945

104. Salmond, op cit, p. 243

105. Bob Balmer, ext-Sgt, 6 LAA Bty, to author

106. Salmond, op cit, p. 243; NA Kew, WO171/252, war diary, 51 Div Sigs, 1945

107. NA Kew, WO171/4245, HQ 51 (H) Div (G), 1945; Salmond, op cit, p. 245

108. NA Kew, WO171/4245, war diary, HQ 51 (H) Div (G), 1945

109. NA Kew, WO171/4409, war diary, 153 Bde, 1945; Salmond, op cit, p. 245

110. Ellis, op cit, pp. 306–7; Salmond, op cit, pp. 245–6

111. Ellis, op cit, p. 297

112. Salmond, op cit, p. 246

113. NA Kew, WO171/4409, war diary, 153 Bde, 1945

114. NA Kew, WO171/4411, war diary, 154 Bde, 1945; WO171/5158, war diary, 1 BW, 1945; WO171/5160, war diary, 7 BW, 1945; WO171/5154, war diary, 7 A&SH, 1945

115. NA Kew, WO171/4406, war diary, 152 Bde, 1945

116. NA Kew, WO171/5267, war diary, 2 Seaforth, 1945

117. NA Kew, WO171/4696, war diary, 2 DY, 1945

118. NA Kew, WO171/4406, war diary, 152 Bde, 1945

119. Salmond, op cit, p. 248

120. NA Kew, WO171/4406, war diary, 2 DY, 1945

121. NA Kew, WO171/4246, war diary, HQ 51 (H) Div (G), 1945

122. NA Kew, WO171/4411, war diary, 154 Bde, 1945; WO171/4409, war diary, 153 Bde, 1945; WO171/5164, war diary, 5 Camerons, 1945; WO171/4696, war diary, 2 DY, 1945; Salmond, op cit, p. 249

123. NA Kew, WO171/4411, war diary, 154 Bde, 1945; WO171/5160, war diary, 7 BW, 1945; WO171/5154, war diary, 7 A & SH, 1945

124. NA Kew, WO171/4406, war diary, 152 Bde, 1945; WO171/5267, war diary, 2 Seaforth, 1945; WO171/4696, war diary, 2 DY, 1945; WO171/4409, war diary, 153 Bde, 1945

125. Salmond, op cit, p. 251; *The Royal Artillery Commemoration Book 1939–1945*, p. 392

126. Salmond, op cit, p. 253

127. NA Kew, WO171/4406, war diary, 152 Bde, 1945; WO171/5267, war diary, 2 Seaforth, 1945

128. NA Kew, WO171/4250, war diary, CRE, 51 (H) Div, 1945; WO171/4406, war diary, 152 Bde, 1945; WO171/5267, war diary, 2 Seaforth, 1945; WO171/5268,

war diary, 5 Seaforth, 1945; WO71/5164, war diary, 5 Camerons, 1945; Borthwick, op cit. pp. 284–5

129. Salmond, op cit, pp. 254 & 256

130. Ibid, p. 254; NA Kew, WO171/5196, war diary, 1 Gordons, 1945

131. Salmond, op cit, p. 254

132. NA Kew, WO171/5198, war diary, 5/7 Gordons, 1945; WO171/4409, war diary, 153 Bde, 1945; McGregor, op cit, p. 188

133. NA Kew, WO171/4411, war diary, 154 Bde, 1945

134. NA Kew, WO171/4696, war diary, 2 DY, 1945

135. NA Kew, WO171/4411, war diary, 154 Bde, 1945; WO171/4246, war diary, HQ 51 (H) Div (G), 1945

136. NA Kew, WO171/4411, war diary, 154 Bde, 1945; WO171/4246, war diary, HQ 51 (H) Div (G), 1945; Salmond, op cit, pp. 255–8

137. Salmond, op cit, pp. 255–8; NA Kew, WO171/4246, war diary, HQ 51 (H) Div (G), 1945

CHAPTER XIV

Epilogue

And so the long years of fighting had come to an end. On 8 May 1945 the Allied nations celebrated VE – Victory in Europe – Day while Allied soldiers, including those of the Highland Division, felt relief that the war was over and that they would soon be returning to their homes and families. Although the history books record that the European war ended on that day, no war ever ends cleanly and the effects of conflict linger long after the fighting men have gone home. Those effects are felt by those who lost loved ones, those who lost homes, and those who were wounded in war. The physical effects of the war on Germany were obvious to all: shattered towns and cities, razed by Allied bombers; displaced people, many fleeing the Red Army; refugees, many also seeking safety from the Soviets; groups of former enemy soldiers anxious to surrender; all were clear to the soldiers of the Highland Division. Many had also heard of the death camps and wondered how a nation could treat fellow human beings in such barbaric fashion; some felt any shred of sympathy they might have had for German civilians drain away as the enormity of the Nazis' crimes sank in. But Germany could not be left to its desolation and the Allied strategic plan had already made provision for what was described as the second phase of the war: the occupation of post-war Germany. This would demand many soldiers and the creation of a British Army of Occupation, eventually to become the British Army of the Rhine (BAOR). In the meantime, however, there were many tasks for the Highland Division to perform.

Among the tasks that soldiers were called on to discharge was the policing of Germany, the guarding of important civilian establishments, and supervising the movement of refugees. It was whilst engaged on this last task that soldiers of 5th Black Watch played a part in the arrest of Heinrich Himmler, one of the leading Nazis and head of the SS. With two bodyguards, Himmler attempted to cross a bridge over the Weser at Bremervörde on 21 May. Using the name Hizinger, the SS chief had shaved off his moustache and wore a black patch over one eye as a disguise. But his bodyguards were in such fine physical condition that they drew the attention of the Black Watch soldiers on duty and were stopped, together with their chief. They were taken away for questioning by field security police and, while being interrogated by Captain Tom Selvester, of the Reconnaissance Corps, Himmler's arrogance led him to pull off his patch, place his spectacles on his nose and demand of Selvester: 'Don't you know who I am? I am Heinrich Himmler.' Later that day the Nazi leader, the man who had masterminded the Holocaust and overseen both the SS and the Gestapo, committed suicide by biting on a cyanide pill concealed in his mouth.[1]

More than a week before Himmler's apprehension, 51st (Highland) Division held a Victory Parade in Bremerhaven at which the salute was taken by Lieutenant-General Brian Horrocks. Guards of Honour for the Parade, on 12 May, were provided by US forces, both Army and Navy, as well as the Black Watch and on parade were the Massed Pipes and Drums of the Division, plus those of the Scottish Horse and the Royal Corps of Signals. All elements of the Division were represented and 130 Brigade, which included 7th Hampshires, 4th and 5th Dorsets, was also on parade. The Middlesex, who had so often provided such effective support with their Vickers MMGs and 4.2-inch mortars, representative groups of the RASC, RAMC, RAOC and REME, the last-named formed during the war years, marched past to the tune of 'Nut Brown Maiden'. The Divisional artillery, with 79th (Scottish Horse) Medium Regiment, marched to 'Bonnie Dundee' while the Divisional anti-tank and LAA Regiments stepped out to 'Loch Duich'. For the infantry, carriers, ambulances and bulldozers, the march-past tune was the haunting 'Over the Sea to Skye'. The guards of honour marched off to the strains of 'The Muckin' o' Geordie's Byre' and 'Queen Elizabeth'. Her Majesty was, of course, Colonel-in-Chief of the Black Watch.[2] (In the parade programme, 2nd Derbyshire Yeomanry are described as 2nd Derbyshire Yeomanry, 51st Highland Divisional Reconnaissance Regiment.)

Many must have felt that ghosts marched at their shoulders as they remembered those who had not survived to see this day. There were few present who had been with the Division all the way from El Alamein, fewer still who had fought with the original Division in France five years before and even those who had survived the long, bloody road from Normandy did not represent a majority of the marching units, especially in the infantry battalions. Overall, the victory parade was both a spectacular and emotional occasion for everyone in the Division and it was also the last major occasion on which Major-General MacMillan commanded the Highlanders. By the end of the month, MacMillan was in London as Assistant Chief of the Imperial General Staff and had been succeeded in command by Brigadier Cassels of 152 Brigade.[3] The latter would later become CIGS.

In August the Highland Division became part of the Army of the Rhine but, as a Territorial formation, it could not expect to remain in such a front-line role for long. The War Office announced in December 1946 that the Division would cease to have a separate identity and would amalgamate with 52nd (Lowland) Division to form the sole Scottish TA infantry formation, 51st/52nd (Scottish) Division. This decision had been made against the advice of two former Divisional commanders, Sir Neil Ritchie, now GOC, Scottish Command, and Douglas Wimberley, now Director of Infantry at the War Office, both of whom had argued that 51st (Highland) should remain as an infantry formation and 52nd (Lowland) as an armoured formation. But the Army Council's view prevailed and the amalgamation went ahead, although it was short-lived: in 1948 the Highland Division regained its distinct identity once again.[4]

The post-war Army had many responsibilities, including the policing of what was left of the Empire, although independence for India and Pakistan in 1947 removed much of that task almost overnight. But there were still wars to be fought and actions in support of the civil power as countries that had been part of the Empire moved, sometimes violently, towards independence. And there was the Cold War, the confrontation between the western powers and the Soviet Union that began with the dropping of the Iron Curtain across Europe and did not end until the collapse of the Soviet Union in 1989. At times the Cold War became warm and it flared into small hot wars on a number of occasions, including the Korean War from 1950 to 1953. From 1947 the *raison d'être* of the Territorial Army was to provide reinforcements for the Regular Army should war break out between east and west. Thus the TA was organised along the same lines as the Regular Army with ten infantry divisions and an air defence brigade. In October 1964 Major-General Michael Carver became Director of Army Staff Duties. Carver, later Field Marshal Lord Carver, thought that the structure of the TA was out of keeping with the nuclear age and that a force of such size could not be recruited, equipped or trained adequately. He therefore proposed the replacement of the TA by an Army Volunteer Reserve, which, as with the existing Army Emergency Reserve (AER), could provide reinforcements for the Regular Army at individual or sub-unit level. Although Carver's proposals met with much opposition, they were accepted, especially as government saw them as a way of saving money on the defence budget, and, with the Army Board's approval, the TA and AER were combined to create a new force, the Territorial and Army Volunteer Reserve (TAVR). The TAVR was to be organised along the lines that Carver had envisaged and its establishment meant the end of many of the TA's infantry battalions while its armoured and artillery units were reduced to one armoured and six Gunner regiments.[5]

Naturally, this reduction meant the end of the TA divisions, including 51st (Highland) Division and it fell to Major-General E Maitland Makgill

Crichton OBE, the last GOC of the Division, to oversee the disbandment of one of Britain's most distinguished fighting formations.[6] Some of the Division's spirit was allowed to live on in TAVR units in Scotland. The TA infantry battalions were reduced progressively to become 51st Highland and 52nd Lowland Volunteers with companies in each representative of their antecedent battalions. However, the Highland tradition is also carried on by 51 Highland Brigade, which, with 15 Brigade and 52 Lowland Brigade, form 2nd Division, with headquarters in Edinburgh. The headquarters of 51 Highland Brigade is located in Perth. Second Division is a 'regenerative' formation that could be brought up to war establishment if necessary.[7] (Although 15 Brigade bears no territorial designation, it will be noted that its numerical title recalls that of 15th (Scottish) Division.) In addition, the Scottish Transport Regiment of the Royal Logistic Corps carries on the tradition of those units that kept the Highland Division supplied in two world wars and has itself contributed to operations in Iraq since the current TA now provides reinforcements for the Regular Army wherever it may be deployed.[8]

At the time of writing the Army is undergoing yet another review and there are proposals to reduce the Scottish infantry to a single multi-battalion regiment. Already, of course, Seaforth, Gordon and Cameron Highlanders are combined in a single regiment, The Highlanders, so that there now remain only three Highland regiments; there are also three Lowland regiments. Current proposals, if implemented, will combine all six battalions into a five-battalion Royal Regiment of Scotland in which each battalion will maintain the title of the regiment it had earlier been: in the case of the 1st Battalion this will be an amalgamation of The Royal Scots, the oldest regiment in the Army, and The King's Own Scottish Borderers. The 3rd Battalion will be The Black Watch, The Highlanders will form the 4th Battalion and The Argylls the 5th. It is not difficult to predict where future cuts may be made.

Irrespective of the future actions of politicians, Scotland will retain a rich heritage of military history and as long as Scots retain pride in their past the achievements of 51st (Highland) Division in the two world wars of the 20th century will remain a significant part in that pride. The Highlanders of the Second World War deserve to be remembered. Men such as George Morrison of 7th Black Watch, the young company navigating officer who foresaw his own death and who perished on the first night of the Battle of El Alamein, were the cream of their generation. The same may also be said of Corporal Piper Duncan McIntyre of 5th Black Watch who also died that October night but played his pipes until he expired and who deserved a posthumous Victoria Cross but did not receive one. And there were many others: men such as Lorne Campbell VC DSO who had already distinguished himself in the ill-fated campaign in France in 1940 and who went on to earn the VC in Tunisia by an outstanding display of courage and leadership. Such leadership was shown at all levels from divisional command down to section commanders and few divisions could look back on a trio of commanders of the calibre of Victor Fortune, Douglas Wimberley and Tom Rennie.

Many of the Division's officers and men were TA members before the war and the original Division was a TA formation with the result that discontent was felt at the War Office policy of strengthening the Division by replacing a battalion in each brigade with a Regular battalion. Similar resentment was felt at the removal of TA commanding officers in favour of Regular officers. But the TA men were vindicated before the war ended with Peter Taylor, a peacetime private soldier in 6th Black Watch commanding the senior battalion of his regiment and James Oliver, a TA officer with 5th Black Watch before the war, one of the most outstanding brigade commanders in North-West Europe.

It is, however, important not to eulogise since there were faults and problems and not everyone met the standards expected of a Highland Division soldier. There were those who deserted, some of them men who were not fitted to be soldiers, others men who had already given all that they could and whose stock of courage had expired. Some deserters were men who could not fit in with the social grouping that was an Army unit in wartime. Even among those who endured there were times when some of their officers wondered what type of men they commanded. Lieutenant-Colonel J A Grant-Peterkin, commanding 1st Gordon Highlanders, was so worried about the scenes of organised looting that he witnessed in Goch that he felt

> that the discipline in the British Army will disintegrate rapidly unless something is done ... The scenes in Goch had to be seen to be believed. It is a depressing sight seeing the British Army 'occupying' a German town.[9]

Fortunately this problem was resolved with firm control from unit officers, NCOs and the Corps of Military Police. Most Germans found the British soldier to be a different person from the 'monster' that had been created by Nazi propaganda which led them to believe that the Allies would rampage through Germany murdering men, women and children as well as raping and thieving. That was not the experience but some individuals had a different story to tell. One German lady, a young girl and a virgin in 1945, informed the author that but for the intervention of his batman she would have been raped by a British officer and she believed that the officer was a member of the Highland Division.[10] Sadly, it has to be said that such men were to be found in the ranks of all armies.

In spite of such deviations from the path of common decency and good military discipline the overall story of the Highland Division remains a positive one, of which those who served and their families may be proud. Supported by their Gunners, often preceded by their Sappers and with their reconnoitrers, whether 51st (Highland) Recce or 2nd Derbyshire Yeomanry, scouting ahead, the infantrymen of the Highland Division, the Jocks, burdened down by weapons and kit, plodded onward through desert sand, across steep mountainous countryside on either side of the Mediterranean, through the claustrophobia of Normandy, the breakout to Falaise, the liberation of St Valéry, the dismal wet of the Low Countries, through the Reichswald and across the Rhine and, finally, along the road to Bremerhaven and victory in Europe. It was men such as these who won the war, whose dogged determination saw them through and whose belief in the justice of the Allied cause led to victory.

There were none bolder.

Notes

1. *Sunday Mail*, 3 April 2005: 'The Day We Captured Himmler' by Julia Hunt. Copy provided by Peter McDonald. Taylor, *This Band of Brothers*, p. 216
2. NA Kew, WO171/5267, war diary, 2 Seaforth 1945. This file contains a copy of the original programme.
3. NA Kew, WO171/4696, war diary, 2 DY, 1945
4. Salmond, *The History of the 51st Highland Division*, p. 260
5. Heathcote, *Dictionary of the Field Marshals of the British Army*, pp. 81–2
6. Salmond, op cit, p. xxxi
7. Bennett, *Fighting Forces*, p. 40
8. Major Donald Urquhart, The Scottish Transport Regt, to author
9. NA Kew, WO171/4409, war diary, 1 Gordons, 1945
10. Personal correspondence to author

Appendices

Appendices

APPENDIX I

The Highland Regiments

The Childers Reforms of 1881 left the Army with five regiments from the Highlands and Islands of Scotland. These had been created from nine regiments, the antecedents of which are shown below.

The Black Watch (Royal Highland Regiment)

1st Battalion	2nd Battalion
Independent Companies, known as the Black Watch, raised in 1725	Between 1758 and 1762 and 1779 and 1786 a 2nd Battalion of the 42nd existed.
The Highland Regt of Foot from 1739	2nd/42nd (retitled 73rd Highland Regt of Foot in 1786)
The 42nd Foot from 1751	73rd Foot from 1809
42nd (Royal Highland) Foot from 1758	73rd (Perthshire) Foot from 1862
42nd (The Royal Highland) Foot (The Black Watch) from 1861	

In 1881 the 42nd and 73rd amalgamated to form The Black Watch (Royal Highlanders). The regiment was restyled The Black Watch (Royal Highland Regiment) in 1934.

The Seaforth Highlanders (Ross-shire Buffs, The Duke of Albany's)

1st Battalion	2nd Battalion
78th Highland Regt (Seaforth's Hldrs) raised 1778	78th (Highland) Regt, or The Ross-shire Buffs raised in 1793
72nd (Highland) Regt from 1786	
72nd, or The Duke of Albany's Own Hldrs from 1823	

In 1881 the 72nd and 78th amalgamated to form The Seaforth Highlanders (Ross-shire Buffs, The Duke of Albany's).

The Gordon Highlanders

1st Battalion	2nd Battalion
75th Foot raised 1758 and disbanded 1763	100th (Gordon Highlanders) Foot raised 1794
75th (Invalids) Foot raised in 1764 and disbanded 1765	92nd (Highland) Regiment from1798
75th (Prince of Wales's) Foot raised 1778 and disbanded 1783	92nd (Gordon Highlanders) Foot from1861
75th (Highland) Regiment raised 1787	
75th Foot from 1809	
75th (Stirlingshire) Foot from1862	

In 1881 the 75th and 92nd amalgamated to form The Gordon Highlanders.

The Cameron Highlanders

1st Battalion	2nd Battalion
79th Foot (Cameronian Volunteers) formed 1793	
79th Foot (Cameronian Hldrs) from 1804	
79th Foot, or Cameron Hldrs, from 1806	
79th Regiment, The Queen's Own Cameron Hldrs, from 1873	

The regiment was restyled The Queen's Own Cameron Highlanders in 1881 but was not amalgamated with any other regiment. In 1897 a Second Battalion was formed.

The Argyll and Sutherland Highlanders (Princess Louise's)

1st Battalion	2nd Battalion
98th (Argyllshire Hldrs) Foot, raised 1794	93rd Highlanders, raised in 1799
91st (Argyllshire Hldrs) Foot from 1796	93rd (Sutherland Hldrs) Foot from 1861
91st Foot from 1809	
91st (Argyllshire) Foot from 1821	
91st (Argyllshire) Highlanders from 1864	
91st (Princess Louise's) Argyllshire Hldrs from 1872	

In May 1881 the 91st and 93rd amalgamated to form The Princess Louise's (Sutherland and Argyll) Highlanders but the title was modified two months later to The Princess Louise's (Argyll and Sutherland) Highlanders. The modern title of The Argyll and Sutherland Highlanders (Princess Louise's) was adopted in 1920.

The post-war reduction in Army strength followed by Indian independence saw the disbandment of most second battalions of line infantry regiments by the end of the 1940s although a few were re-formed at the time of the Korean War. In the wake of the Sandys defence review a further reduction began in the late 1950s and this took the form of amalgamations to create 'large' regiments, most of which were based on the brigade system that had been introduced in 1948. Scotland did not escape the effects of this reduction. In the Lowland Brigade the Royal Scots Fusiliers and Highland Light Infantry amalgamated to form the Royal Highland Fusiliers while the Cameronians chose disbandment in preference to amalgamation. The Seaforth and Camerons were also amalgamated to form The Queen's Own Highlanders (Seaforth and Cameron) in 1961 while towards the end of the decade a decision to disband the Argylls was announced by the Ministry of Defence. This led to a 'Save the Argylls' campaign which achieved success; although the regiment was reduced to company strength it was restored to full strength in 1972. Following the end of the Cold War another defence review forced amalgamation on The Queen's Own Highlanders and Gordons to produce The Highlanders.

At the time of writing further reductions are threatened and it seems likely that even the Black Watch may not survive this round of cutting and amalgamations. The Ministry of Defence proposes to create a Royal Regiment of Scotland with five battalions, formed from the existing six Scottish line infantry battalions. In this move The Royal Scots and The King's Own Scottish Borderers will merge to form the First Battalion, The Royal Highland Fusiliers will be the Second Battalion, The Black Watch the Third Battalion, the Highlanders the Fourth and the Argylls the Fifth. It is further proposed that a common cap badge, base dress and tartan will be adopted. However, the battalions will be styled by their old names, e.g. The Black Watch (3rd Bn, The Royal Regiment of Scotland).

A massive Save the Scottish Regiments Campaign has been launched but it seems that not even the pressure of public opinion will change the mind of the MoD. Of course, the rationale for this move, which will see the new regiment formed by the end of March 2006, is said to be efficiency. With an Army that has been stretched often beyond reason in recent years – deployments such as Operation TELIC in Iraq require significant elements of the Territorial Army – it is difficult to see how efficiency can be achieved by reducing numbers. The greatest strength that the British Army has had in its history is the regimental system but governments of various political persuasions have tried to destroy this system over the past fifty years since Sandys first began 'rationalising' the Army.

Sadly it appears that many of those who ought to have supported the survival of the Scottish regiments have been complicit in what is seen as a betrayal of the history and traditions of those regiments. That the MoD will in future seek to impose a common corps of infantry on the British Army becomes even more likely with the creation of units such as the Royal Regiment of Scotland, the Yorkshire Regiment and the other 'new' units due to form in the near future.

APPENDIX II

Outline Order of Battle, BEF, 1939–1940

Divisional Troops
1st Fife & Forfar Yeomanry, RAC; replaced by 1st Lothians and Border Yeomanry

Royal Artillery
75th (Highland), 76th (Highland) and 77th (Highland) Field Regiments, RA, TA. The latter two left the Division on 5 March 1940 and 19 February 1940, respectively, and were replaced by 17th and 23rd Field Regiments, both of which were Regular regiments.
51st (West Highland) Anti-Tank Regiment, RA, TA.

Royal Engineers
236th, 237th and 238th Field Companies, RE, TA. The latter left the Division on 29 February 1940 and was replaced by 26th Field Company, a Regular sub-unit.
239th Field Park Company, RE, TA.

Royal Corps of Signals
51st (Highland) Division Signals Regiment.

Infantry
152 (Highland) Brigade
4th Seaforth Hldrs
6th Seaforth Hldrs
4th Queen's Own Cameron Hldrs
152 Infantry Brigade Anti-Tank Company
(On 30 March 1940 the regular 2nd Seaforth replaced 6th Seaforth.)

153 (Highland) Brigade
4th Black Watch
5th Gordon Hldrs
6th Gordon Hldrs
153 Infantry Brigade Anti-Tank Company
(On 7 March 1940 the regular 1st Gordons replaced 4th Gordons while, on 5

June 1940, the regular 1st Black Watch replaced 4th Black Watch.)

154 (Highland) Brigade
6th Black Watch
7th Argyll & Sutherland Hldrs
8th Argyll & Sutherland Hldrs
154 Infantry Brigade Anti-Tank Company
(1st Black Watch replaced 6th Black Watch on 4 March 1940 but, in turn, was
replaced by 4th Black Watch on 5 June 1940.)

This brigade formed the core of Arkforce from 9 to 15 June 1940 with the following
under command: 15th & 17th Field Regiments, 204 Anti-Tank Battery of 15th Anti-
Tank Regiment and 51st Medium Regiment, RA – however, the latter had no guns
– 236th, 237th & 239th Field Companies and 213th Field Park Company, RE; A
Infantry Brigade (an ad-hoc formation made up of personnel from base depots
on the BEF's lines of communication) and two companies of 1st Kensington
Regiment, a machine-gun unit.

Royal Army Service Corps
Div Amm Coy; Div Petrol Coy and Div Supply Column

Royal Army Medical Corps
152, 153 & 154 Field Ambulances

Attached Troops (Saar Force)
51st Medium Regt, RA; 1st Regt, RHA (less one Bty); 97th Fd Regt, RA (one Bty);
213 Fd Coy, RE; 1st Bn Princess Louise's Kensington Regt (MGs); 7th Bn Royal
N'land Fus (MGs); 6th Bn Norfolk Regt (Pioneers); additional elements of RAOC
and RASC.

Order of Battle, 23 October 1942
(El Alamein)

Royal Artillery

126th, 127th & 128th Field Regiments, RA (Highland), TA; 61st Anti-Tank Regiment, RA (West Highland), TA; 40th Light Anti-Aircraft Regiment, RA, TA [formed at Inverness on 27 September 1939].

Royal Engineers

274th, 275th & 276th Field Companies; 239th Field Park Company.

Royal Corps of Signals

51st (Highland) Division Signals Regiment

Reconnaissance Corps

51st (Highland) Reconnaissance Regiment

Machine Guns

1/7th Bn The Middlesex Regiment

Infantry

152 (Seaforth & Camerons) Brigade
2nd Seaforth Hldrs
5th Seaforth Hldrs
5th Queen's Own Cameron Hldrs

153 (Highland) Brigade
5th Black Watch
1st Gordon Hldrs
5/7th Gordon Hldrs

154 (Highland) Brigade
1st Black Watch
7th Black Watch
7th Argyll & Sutherland Hldrs

Royal Army Service Corps

152, 153 & 154 Bde and 51 Div Troops Coys, RASC

Royal Army Medical Corps

174, 175 & 176 Field Ambulances, RAMC

Royal Army Ordnance Corps

152, 153 & 154 Bde Gp Workshops & 51 Div Ord Field Park

Attached from 23 Armoured Brigade

50th Royal Tank Regiment (North Somerset & Bristol Yeomanry), RAC, TA with, under command, 3 Troop, 295th Field Company, RE.

APPENDIX IV

Order of Battle, June 1944, Normandy

Royal Armoured Corps

Reconnaissance: 2nd Derbyshire Yeomanry (as divisional reconnaissance regiment)

Royal Artillery

126th, 127th & 128th Field Regiments, RA (Highland), TA; 61st Anti-Tank Regiment, RA (West Highland), TA; 40th Light Anti-Aircraft Regiment, RA, TA.

Royal Engineers

274th, 275th & 276th Field Companies; 239th Field Park Company, 16 Bridging Pln.

Royal Corps of Signals

51st (Highland) Division Signals Regiment

Machine Guns

1/7th Bn The Middlesex Regiment

Infantry

152 (Seaforth & Camerons) Brigade
2nd Seaforth Hldrs
5th Seaforth Hldrs
5th Queen's Own Cameron Hldrs

153 (Highland) Brigade
5th Black Watch
1st Gordon Hldrs
5/7th Gordon Hldrs

154 (Highland) Brigade
1st Black Watch
7th Black Watch
7th Argyll & Sutherland Hldrs

Royal Army Service Corps

525, 526, 527 & 458 Coys RASC

Royal Army Medical Corps

174, 175 & 176 Field Ambulances and 6 FDS

Royal Army Ordnance Corps

152, 153 & 154 Bde Workshops

Bibliography

Anderson, R C B, *History of the Argyll and Sutherland Highlanders, 1939–1954* (London 1956)

Arthur, Max, *Symbol of Courage: A History of the Victoria Cross* (London 2004)

Ascoli, David, *A Companion to the British Army1660–1983* (London 1983)

Atkin, *Pillar of Fire: Dunkirk 1940* (London 1990)

Barker, Felix, *Gordon Highlanders in North Africa and Sicily, August 1942 to October 1943* (Aberdeen 1944)

Barr, Niall, *Pendulum of War: The Three Battles of El Alamein* (London 2004)

Bellis, Malcolm A, *Brigades of the British Army 1939–45* (Crewe 1986)

Bennett, Richard, *Fighting Forces: An Illustrated Anatomy of the World's Great Armies* (London 2001)

Bewsher, Major F W, *History of the 51st (Highland) Division 1914–1918* (1922)

Blaxland, G, *The Middlesex Regiment* (London 1977)

Borthwick, Alastair, *Sans Peur, 5th Seaforth in WWII* (Stirling 1946); republished as *Battalion* (London 1994)

Buzzell, Nora, *The Register of the Victoria Cross* (Cheltenham 1988)

Carver, Michael, *Alamein* (London 1962)

_____ *Out of Step. The Memoirs of Field Marshal Lord Carver* (London 1989)

_____ *The Imperial War Museum book of the War in Italy 1943–1945* (London 2001)

Chesneau, Roger (ed), *Conway's All The World's Fighting Ships 1922–1946* (London 1980)

Clyde, Robert, *From Rebel to Hero: the image of the Highlander 1745–1830* (East Linton 1995)

Copp, Terry, *Fields of Fire: The Canadians in Normandy* (Toronto 2003)

David, Saul, *Churchill's Sacrifice of the Highland Division, France 1940* (London 1994)

Davis, Brian L, *British Army Uniforms and Insignia of World War Two* (London 1992)

Delaforce, Patrick, *Monty's Highlanders: 51st Highland Division in World War Two* (Brighton 1997)

D'Este, Carlo, *Decision in Normandy* (London 1983)

Doherty, Richard, *Wall of Steel. The history of the 9th (Londonderry) Heavy Anti-Aircraft Regiment, Royal Artillery (SR)* (Limavady 1988)

_____ *Only the Enemy in Front. The Recce Corps at War 1941–1946* (Staplehurst 1994)

_____ *A Noble Crusade: The History of Eighth Army 1941–45* (Staplehurst 1999)

_____ *Irish Volunteers in the Second World War* (Dublin 2002)

_____ *The Sound of History: El Alamein 1942* (Staplehurst 2002)

_____ *Normandy 1944: The Road to Victory* (Staplehurst 2004)

_____ *Ireland's Generals in the Second World War* (Dublin 2004)

Ellis, John, *The World War II Databook* (London 1993)

Ellis, Major L F, *The War in France and Flanders, 1939–1940 (Official History of the Second World War)* (London 1953)

_____ *Victory in the West, Vol I: The Battle of Normandy (Official History of the Second World War)* (London 1962)

_____ *Victory in the West, Vol II: The Defeat of Germany (Official History of the Second World War)* (London 1968)

Fairrie, Angus, *Queen's Own Highlanders: Seaforth and Camerons* (Fort George 1998)

Farndale, Sir Martin, *The Years of Defeat 1939–41 (History of The Royal Regiment of Artillery)* (London 1996)

Fergusson, Bernard, *The Black Watch and the King's Enemies* (London 1950)

Forty, George, *British Army Handbook 1939–1945* (Stroud 1998)

_____ *Fortress Europe: Hitler's Atlantic Wall* (Hersham 2002)

Fraser, David, *And We Shall Shock Them: The British Army in the Second World War* (London 1983)

_____ *Knight's Cross – A Life of Field Marshal Erwin Rommel* (London 1993)

Frederick, J B M, *Lineage Book of British Land Forces 1660–1978* (Two volumes) (Wakefield 1984)

French, David, *Raising Churchill's Army: The British Army and the War against Germany 1919–1945* (London 2000)

Freyberg, Paul, *Bernard Freyberg VC: Soldier of Two Nations* (London 1991)

Gibbs, N H, *Grand Strategy, Vol I* (Official History of the Second World War) (London 1976)

Gilbert, Adrian (ed), *The Imperial War Museum Book of the Desert War 1940–1942* (London 1992)

Gill, Ronald & Groves, John, *Club Route in Europe: The Story of 30 Corps in the European Campaign* (Hanover 1946)

Hastings, Max, *Overlord. D-Day and the Battle for Normandy 1944* (London 1984)

_____ *Armageddon. The Battle for Germany 1944–45* (London 2004)

Heathcote, T A, *Dictionary of the Field Marshals of the British Army* (Barnsley 1999)

Hinsley, F H, *British Intelligence in the Second World War* (London 1993)

Hogg, Ian V, *British & American Artillery of World War 2* (London 1978)

_____ *Allied Artillery of World War Two* (Marlborough 1998)

& Weeks, John, *The Illustrated Encyclopedia of Military Vehicles* (London 1980)

Holmes, Richard, *Battlefields of the Second World War* (London 2001)

Hook, Alex, *World War II Day by Day* (Rochester 2004)

Horrocks, Brian, *A Full Life* (London 1960)

Howard, P, *The Black Watch* (London 1968)

Isby, David C (ed), *Fighting in Normandy: the German army from D-Day to Villers-Bocage* (London 2001)

Jarymowycz, Roman Johann, *Tank Tactics from Normandy to Lorraine* (Boulder, Co 2001)

Joslen, Lieut-Col H F, *Orders of Battle Second World War 1939–1945* (London 1960)

Keegan, John (ed), *Churchill's Generals* (London 1991)

_____ *Who's Who in World War II* (London 1995)

Kemp, P K, *The Middlesex Regiment (Duke of Cambridge's Own) 1919–1952* (Aldershot 1956)

Kippenberger, Major-General Sir Howard KBE CB DSO, *Infantry Brigadier* (London 1949)

Lewin, Ronald, *Montgomery as Military Commander* (London 1971)

Liddell Hart, Basil H, *The Other Side of the Hill* (London 1948)

_____ (ed), *The Rommel Papers* (London 1953)

Lindsay, Martin, *So Few Got Through* (London 1946 & Barnsley 2000)

Linklater, Eric, *The Highland Division* (London 1942)

Lucas, James & Barker, James, *The Killing Ground: The Battle of the Falaise Gap, August 1944* (London 1978)

Lucas Phillips, C E, *Alamein* (London 1962)

McGregor, John, *Spirit of Angus* (Chicester 1983)

Meek, Leslie, *A Brief History of the 51st (H) Reconnaissance Regiment (1941 – 1943) and its involvement in the Desert Campaign* (London 1991)

Mellenthin, Major-General F W von, *Panzer Battles* (London 1955)

Molony, Brigadier C J C, *The Mediterranean and the Middle East, Vol V: The Campaign in Sicily 1943 and the Campaign in Italy – 3rd September 1943 to 31st March 1944 (Official History of the Second World War)* (London 1973)

Montgomery, Viscount of Alamein, *El Alamein to the River Sangro* (London 1948)

_____ *Memoirs* (London 1958)

Moorehead, Alan, *The Desert War – the North African Campaign 1940–1943* (London 1965)

Pitt, Barrie (ed), *The Military History of World War II* (London 1986)

Playfair, Major-General I S O, *The Mediterranean and the Middle East, Vol I: The Early Successes against Italy (Official History of the Second World War)* (London 1954)

_____ *The Mediterranean and the Middle East, Vol II: The Germans Come to the Help of their Ally (Official History of the Second World War)* (London 1956)

_____ *The Mediterranean and the Middle East, Vol III: British Fortunes reach their Lowest Ebb (Official History of the Second World War)* (London 1960)

_____ *The Mediterranean and the Middle East, Vol IV: The Destruction of Axis Forces in Africa (Official History of the Second World War)* (London 1966)

Reynolds, Michael, *Steel Inferno: I SS Panzer Corps in Normandy* (Staplehurst 1997)

Richardson, General Sir Charles, *Send for Freddie: The story of Montgomery's Chief of Staff, Major-General Sir Francis de Guingand KBE CB DSO* (London 1987)

Roberts, G P B, *From the Desert to the Baltic* (London 1987)

Routledge, Brigadier N W, *Anti-Aircraft Artillery, 1914–55* (London 1994)

Salmond, J B, *History of the 51st Highland Division 1939–45* (Edinburgh 1953)

Shepperd, Alan, *France 1940: Bltzkrieg in the West* (London 1990)

Sinclair-Stevenson, C, *The Gordon Highlanders* (London 1968)

Taylor, Jeremy, *This Band of Brothers: A history of the Reconnaissance Corps of the British Army* (Bristol 1947)

Thompson, Julian, *The Imperial War Museum book of Victory in Europe: The North-West European Campaign 1944–1945* (London 1994)

Tout, Ken, *Roads to Falaise. 'Cobra' and 'Goodwood' Reassessed* (Stroud 2002)

Trevor-Roper, H R (ed), *Hitler's War Directives 1939–1945* (London 1948)

Volunteers from Éire who have won distinction serving with the British Forces (np 1944)

Westlake, Ray, *The Territorial Battalions: A Pictorial History 1859–1985* (Tunbridge Wells 1986)

Whitehouse, Stanley, *Fear is the Foe: A Footslogger from Normandy to the Rhine* (London 1995)

Young, M H G, *The Highland Division Transport and Supply Column Army Service Corps (Territorial Force) and its Successors 1908–1980* (np, nd)

Unpublished

Imperial War Museum, London
Department of Documents

Morrison, Lieutenant George F, 7th Black Watch, letters to his mother and grandmother, 1942

Wimberley, Major-General Douglas, *Memoirs, Vol II*

National Archives, Kew
1939–1940

WO167/314	War Diary HQ 51st (Highland) Division (GS), Jan–Jun 1940
315	War Diary HQ 51st (Highland) Division (A&Q), Jan–Jun 1940
316	Commander Royal Artillery (CRA)
317	Commander Royal Engineers (CRE)
318	Signals
319	Commander Royal Army Service Corps (CRASC)
320	Div Ammunition Coy
321	Div Petrol Coy
322	Div Supply Column 406
406	HQ 152 Bde
407	HQ 153 Bde
408	HQ 154 Bde
455	1st Lothians & Border Yeomanry
456	1st Fife & Forfar Yeomanry
473	17th Field Regt
477	23rd Field Regt
495	75th (H) Field Regt
496	76th (H) Field Regt
497	77th (H) Field Regt
579	51st (H) Anti-Tank Regt
710	1 Black Watch
711	6 Black Watch
720	4 Camerons

744	1 Gordons
747	6 Gordons
1412	HQ Beauman Division
WO197/34	Unit establishments of BEF – proposed amendments
35	Deployment of British troops in France
36	BEF Situation Reports
37–39	Composition & build-up of BEF
40–41	Saar Force: operations, training, troop movements and visits, Mar–May 1940
59	Formation of First & Second Armies
68	Move to Saar
124	Movement of 51 (H) Div and attached troops, 16 Apr–12 Jun 1940
135	Le Havre

1941

WO166/619	War Diary HQ 51st (Highland) Division (GS)
620	(A & Q)
621	CRA
622	CRE
623	Signals
624	CRASC
625	Supply Col
626	Petrol Coy
627	Ammunition Coy
634	51st (Highland) Reconnaissance Bn

1942

WO169/4164	HQ 51st (H) Division (GS)	– Sep
4165	– Oct	
4166	– Nov	
4171	51 (H) Recce Regt	
4292	HQ 152 Bde	
4295	HQ 153 Bde	
4298	HQ 154 Bde	
4606	126 (H) Fd Regt	
4607	127 (H) Fd Regt	
4608	128 (H) Fd Regt	
4986	7 Argyll & Sutherland Hldrs (A&SH)	
4988	1 Black Watch	
4990	5 Black Watch	
4991	7 Black Watch	
4997	5 Camerons	
5017	1 Gordons	
5018	5/7 Gordons	
5038	1/7 Middlesex Regt (Mx)	
5059	2 Seaforth	
5060	5 Seaforth	

1943

WO169/8791 HQ 51st (H) Division (GS), Jan–Mar
8792	Apr–Jun
8793	Jul–Aug
8907	HQ 23 Armd Bde, Jul–Sep
8955	HQ 152 Bde
8959	HQ 153 Bde
8963	HQ 154 Bde
9379	50th Royal Tank Regt
9516	126 Fd Regt
9517	127 Fd Regt
9518	128 Fd Regt
10176	7 A&SH
10178	1 Black Watch
10179	5 Black Watch
10181	7 Black Watch
10188	5 Camerons
10245	1 Gordons
10246	5/7 Gordons
10260	1/7 Mx
10291	2 Seaforth
10292	5 Seaforth
10667	293 Fd Pk Coy RE

1944

WO171/527–9 HQ 51st (H) Division (G)
673–6	HQ 152 Bde
678	HQ 153 Bde
680	HQ 154 Bde
850–1	2nd Derbyshire Yeomanry (2 DY)
918	61 A/T Regt
988	126 Fd Regt
989	127 Fd Regt
990	128 Fd Regt
1116	40 LAA Regt
1263	7 A&SH
1265	1 Black Watch
1266	5 Black Watch
1267	7 Black Watch
1270–1	5 Camerons
1299	1 Gordons
1301	5/7 Gordons
1344–6	1/7 Mx
1369	2 Seaforth
1370	5 Seaforth

BIBLIOGRAPHY

1945

WO171/4245–7 HQ 51st (H) Division (G)

4249	HQ RA
4250	CRE
4252	Signals
4257	51 (H) Div Battle School
4406–7	HQ 152 Bde
4409	HQ 153 Bde
4411	HQ 154 Bde
4696	2 DY
5154	7 A&SH
5158	1 Black Watch
5159	5 Black Watch
5160	7 Black Watch
5164	5 Camerons
5196	1 Gordons
5198	5/7 Gordons
5242–3	1/7 Mx
5267	2 Seaforth
5268	5 Seaforth
5347	16 Bridging Pln RE
5516	239 Fd Pk Coy RE
5536	275 Fd Coy RE

Websites

www.1914-1918.net/51div.htm *The Long, Long Trail: The story of the British Army in the Great War of 1914–1918.*

www.warpath.orbat.com/divs/51_div.htm *51st (Highland) Division*

www.army.mod.uk/2div/Organisation/51_Scottish_Brigade.htm *Ministry of Defence website which includes a brief background to the present 51 (Highland) Brigade*

www.lib.byu.edu/~rdh/wwi/memoir/docs/51st/51st1.htm *51st (Highland) Division*

www.houterman.hymlplanet.com/51InfDiv.html *51st (Highland) Infantry Division 1939–1945*

www.geocities.com/Paris/LeftBank/6039/elat.html *The 51st Highland Division at El Alamein*

www.cabarfeidh.com/Womble%farewell.htm *Major-General Wimberley's farewell to 51st (Highland) Division*

www.home.clara.net/clinchy/nneb1.htm *The Cameron Highlanders*

www.iwm.org.uk/upload/package/21creteegypt/standegypt14.htm *Lightfoot start line: 51st Highland Division*

www.spearhead1944.com/brpg/br1.htm *51st Highland Division D-Day to Victory*

www.btinternet.com/~james.mckay/terrdivs.htm *Saturday Night Soldiers - The Territorials to 1973*

www.dickalba.demon.co.uk/songs/texts/sicily.html *51st (Highland) Division's Farewell to Sicily*

Index